Celebrating
Elie Wiesel

Celebrating Elie Wiesel

STORIES, ESSAYS, REFLECTIONS

Edited by

ALAN ROSEN

University of Notre Dame Press

Notre Dame, Indiana

Library of Congress Cataloging-in-Publication Data

Celebrating Elie Wiesel : stories, essays, reflections /
edited by Alan Rosen.
p.   cm.
Festschrift.
Includes bibliographical references.
ISBN 0-268-00835-3 (alk. paper)
1. Holocaust, Jewish (1939–1945), in literature.   2. Holocaust,
Jewish (1939–1945)—Moral and ethical aspects.   3. Holocaust, Jewish
(1939–1945)—Influence.   4. Human rights.   5. Wiesel, Elie, 1928–
I. Wiesel, Elie, 1928–   II. Rosen, Alan Charles.
PN56.H55C45   1998
809'.93358—dc21   98-30612

CONTENTS

Contents

Commentary

Ethical and Religious Reflections

Human and Civil Rights

Contents

Concluding Meditations

Elie Wiesel

A BIBLICAL LIFE

ELIE WIESEL is one of the most important people to have lived in the twentieth century. And yet, the fact that he lived at all beyond his teenage years was purely a matter of luck. He, like millions of other European Jews, was slated for genocide. Most other European Jews, including nearly all of Wiesel's family, were murdered by the Nazis. Elie Wiesel survived. Why he survived, how he survived, and how he could turn his survival into a mission of peace occupied the mind of the young survivor in the years following his liberation. The resulting life work—work that is still incomplete and that will, one hopes, continue for many more years—is among the most remarkable accomplishments in history.

In assessing the life of this great and humble man, what is often unappreciated is what Elie Wiesel did not do. Here was a young man whose father lay dying in his arms, and most of whose family and nearly all of his friends were murdered. Consider what others, who experienced lesser tragedies, have done in response to such evil. They have sought revenge. They have continued the cycles of violence and recrimination. They have become terrorists. They have refused to make peace. They have become cynics.

Elie Wiesel rejected that negative path. He showed the way from brutal victimization to gentle kindness. His very life became a shining example of an alternative to the cycle of violence and retaliation which has characterized history for millennia. In this respect, Elie Wiesel has taken more seriously the teachings of Jesus than have most Christians. He has understood the teaching of the Jewish prophets better than most other Jews. And he has lived the kind of life to which many other religious leaders have urged their followers to aspire.

The Jewish tradition has always tried to strike an appropriate balance between memory and forgiveness, between undue emphasis on one's own victimization and undue concern only for the victimization of others. The argument between God and Abraham over the sinners of Sodom, the argument between God and Moses over the sinner in the desert, the argument between God and Jonah over the sinners of Nineveh—all reflect attempts to resolve this eternal conflict. The great sage Hillel tried to summarize Jewish attitudes toward this issue when he said, "if I am not for myself, who will be for me, but if I am for myself alone, what am I?" Elie Wiesel has succeeded in striking this balance for the post-Holocaust world. He will not forget or forgive. But he will also not allow the evils of the past to justify contemporary recrimination. He has lived Santayana's dictum: by not forgetting history, he has helped us to avoid its repetition.

Indeed, Elie Wiesel's memoirs are almost biblical in nature. Subjected to the satanic testing of a Job, he responded not with the cynicism of Ecclesiastes (though he paradoxically takes the title of his memoir, *All Rivers Run to the Sea,* from this book), but with the passion of an Isaiah. His examined life is an example to all who have experienced pain, victimization, injustice, and survival. Without forgiving the unforgivable, excusing the inexcusable, or forgetting the unforgettable, he has looked to the future. He has placed himself in harm's way repeatedly in the quest for peace, whether in war-torn former Yugoslavia, the rocket-ravaged Israel during the Gulf War, or other places from which even God has seemingly stayed away. There is a wonderful story about a great Chasidic master who was asked whether it is ever proper to act as if God did not exist. He surprised his students by answering "yes": it is not only proper, but mandatory, to act as if there were no God when one is asked to help. Do not say "God will help." You must help. Though Elie Wiesel is a deeply religious man—even when he argues with God or refuses to forgive him—Wiesel acts as if there were no God when he is asked to help. I think I understand why. He saw that God did not help his family and friends. He also saw that human beings did not help, perhaps because they believed that God would help. Wiesel knows that we cannot control God's actions, but we can control our own actions.

I was with Elie Wiesel on the night that Iraq sent rockets into Israel. It was feared that they might contain poison gas or other deadly material. Although he had just returned from Israel, Wiesel decided he had to go back in order to be with his endangered brothers and sisters, even if—especially if—they were confronting the kind of poison gas which killed so many who were so close to him. He understood what it meant to face death alone, and he would not permit embattled Jews to experience that feeling as long as he had strength to join them.

In 1986, I was among the academics qualified by my position as a teacher of public law to propose nominees to the Nobel Prize Committee. I proposed Elie Wiesel. This is part of what I wrote:

> There are many excellent reasons for recognizing Professor Wiesel. But none is more important than his role in teaching survivors and their children how to respond in constructive peace and justice to a worldwide conspiracy of genocide, the components of which included mass killing, mass silence and mass indifference. Professor Wiesel has devoted his life to teaching the survivors of a conspiracy which excluded so few to re-enter and adjust in peace to an alien world that deserved little forgiveness. Wiesel's life works merit the highest degree of recognition, especially from representatives of the world that stood silently by.

Few Nobel Prizes have ever produced as many dividends for the world. May Elie Wiesel continue to challenge us to do more to promote peace. May Elie Wiesel continue to challenge God, who makes peace in his own heavenly domain, to do a better job of bringing peace to our earthly one.

Alan M. Dershowitz
© 1997

ACKNOWLEDGMENTS

MANY PEOPLE HAVE helped in diverse ways over the years that this project grew to fruition. Martha Hauptman, assistant to Elie Wiesel at Boston University for some twenty years, has been an indispensable partner in this enterprise; I have constantly benefited from her resourcefulness, intelligence, and generosity. Barry Walfish provided invaluable counsel on how to proceed with and organize such a volume. Alisa Rivkin and Cicily Wilson of the Wiesel Foundation for the Humanities promptly shared all the resources at their disposal. Alon and Tamara Goshen-Gottstein and Moshe and Libby Werthan and Yossi Chajes graciously gave technical support. Jeff Shapiro read willingly and commented, as always, perceptively. As chair of the English Department at Bar-Ilan University in 1994–95, Kinereth Meyer helped make possible a sabbatical that enabled me to be in useful proximity to many potential contributors. For their kind assistance I thank the office staff of the English Department at Bar-Ilan University as well as the staff at the Center for the Study of World Religions, Harvard University. Jim Langford, director at the University of Notre Dame Press, has from the outset offered unreserved enthusiasm for this volume. Carole Roos, copyeditor for the press, has shown admirable patience and conscientiousness.

I thank the contributors for their substantial time and labors. In particular, Aaron Appelfeld not only gave unqualified encouragement but also made time, again and again, to confer. I regret that for technical reasons Joe Friedman's fine contribution could not be included. It must also be said that, given various restrictions, a number of other remarkable students and colleagues of Elie Wiesel could not here be represented.

My wife, Ruth Clements, herself a meticulous scholar, took time away from her own important work to give untold hours of counsel and attention to every facet of this project. Her knowledge, wisdom, and skill have in countless ways made it better. My children, Shoshana Leah, Tzvia Rachel, and Noam Dov, lighten all burdens.

The inestimable kindness and care of my teacher, Elie Wiesel, came through in this project as in all others. I hope that this volume somehow proves worthy of him.

INTRODUCTION

By DEFINITION, a writer of fiction inhabits many roles. So it is with our teacher, mentor, colleague, and friend, Elie Wiesel: consummate storyteller, commentator on classic Jewish texts, human rights activist, and, probably most acknowledged and central, survivor and witness of the Holocaust. To be sure, this last is crucial for him as well as for us. Yet I place it last with the hope that this volume will not only celebrate and honor Wiesel's contributions, but will lobby for a certain balance in the perception of them, allowing us to know better his breadth of interest and range of commitment, a breadth and range that might otherwise be eclipsed or overlooked.

This task is made easier in that profiles of Elie Wiesel by distinguished colleagues, Alan Dershowitz and Cynthia Ozick, begin and end this volume. Brief though they are, these tributes say what is necessary, addressing in distinctive voices the activities for which Wiesel is more generally known. It remains to speak briefly about his less widely perceived but nonetheless central vocation as a university professor. For those of us fortunate enough to study in Wiesel's Boston University classroom, his abundant itinerary of interest is always in evidence. Indeed, Wiesel's classroom, intimate yet vast, offers a bounty of texts and topics: *Hamlet* and *Oedipus*, Rabbi Nachman of Breslov's "The Lost Princess" and *The Brothers Karamozov*, Toni Morrison's *Song of Solomon* and Kohelet;

xv

hope and madness, suffering and passion, anguish and laughter. The list is surprising, boldly large, wryly unpredictable. One comes (as his students surely come) to Elie Wiesel expecting a single event and a handful of themes to set the agenda. Quickly, however, entering students are brought up short, forced to re-evaluate; eventually, one recovers, and begins to enjoy the expanse of literatures, the respect for a multiplicity of religions, the animation of history and biography through story and personal encounter. This limitless search for a tolerant truth, this adventure in spacious reading, is what Elie Wiesel brings to academia—and, of course, to the world beyond it.

Fittingly, then, this volume both celebrates one of the most celebrated members of the world academic community and also, if perhaps obliquely, poses a challenge to the conventions of that community. On the one hand, Elie Wiesel is a solid member of academia: for over twenty years he has taught at Boston University, and the significant number of Boston University faculty and former students who contribute to this volume registers the kind of intellectual rapport and respect that his presence generates. And yet, on the other hand, Wiesel's teaching is unusual in higher education, emphasizing as it does the worth of the individual student and the virtue of friendship between students. Known for his oratorical eloquence, Wiesel as a classroom teacher chooses to listen. By taking such a stance, he transforms the student's own self-perception from that of passive receptacle to active partner in the quest for knowledge and the secrets that learning can divulge.

I have grouped these contributions into four sections, aligned with four major areas of Elie Wiesel's life and work. Penned by philosophers and theologians, psychologists and sociologists, lawyers and halachists, literary scholars and authors of fiction, the contributions are inspired sometimes directly, sometimes indirectly, by Wiesel's work. All are contiguous to it, shaped by similar issues, motivated by a shared purpose. Through their diversity, the individual pieces serve as an index to the searching diversity of Wiesel's work; through their intensity, they mark and register that of his own.

FICTION: STORIES AND CRITICAL WRITING

The truth of fiction is something that matters greatly to Elie Wiesel; his own remarkable oeuvre centers on the situation of the victim, on the perils and possibilities of solitude, friendship, testimony, and madness. The stories and essays in this first section pay tribute to this domain, whether through stories of loss and the urgency it entails, or through essays that address the capacity of fiction to help us internally register the central dilemmas of our time.

The novels and stories of Aaron Appelfeld, child survivor of the Holocaust, virtually always focus on the Shoah. But by coming at, or toward, this event only by way of indirection, Appelfeld has set a standard for writing about the Holocaust. Included below is the opening section of his previously untranslated novel, "As an Apple of the Eye," which narrates the death of a family matriarch and the momentous loss—physical and metaphysical—it entails. We are made to feel the enormity of a single death, the subtle yet profound disappearance of secrets that can never be reclaimed.

If Appelfeld narrates the disappearance of precious secrets, Ariel Dorfman's story, "What I Always Knew," depicts a world in which everything—words, gestures, events—are secret. Secrecy here, however, is the oppressive, almost hermetically tortuous secrecy that defines daily life under authoritarian regimes. Nevertheless, Dorfman's breathless narrative lets the reader share (and thus perhaps reclaim?) the intimate moments of a victim on the border—the border between familiarity and its destruction, between freedom and its violent abrogation.

Often, many crucial aspects of a survivor's life remain obscured by the largeness of the event they have endured. Nancy Harrowitz's essay, "From Mt. Sinai to the Holocaust," gently peels back a layer of Primo Levi's life and work—his vocation as a scientist—and suggests its consequences for him and for us. Indeed,

Introduction

Levi's celebrity is usually associated with his literary eloquence and his status as a survivor of Auschwitz; his vocation as a scientist (a chemist) is usually viewed as a pragmatic aspect of his life, the way he earned a living. But Harrowitz alters this alignment, viewing his vocation as an essential dimension of his life and writing. Once science is shifted to the foreground, Harrowitz, an Italianist whose expertise is approaching the history of science through cultural studies, provides a dazzling reading—appreciative yet nuanced—of Levi's great book, *The Periodic Table*, and its complex interweaving of ethics and science.

Levi wrote soon after the war, and kept writing. Yet the common assumption about survivors is that testimony came only later, climaxing in the video and oral testimony projects of the 1980s and 1990s. Indeed, certain developments have seemingly established oral testimony as the most authoritative medium through which the voice of the survivor may be heard. My essay, "The Specter of Eloquence: Reading the Survivor's Voice," questions several of these assumptions. Guided by narratives of Art Spiegelman and Cynthia Ozick, I suggest that the special resonances of a survivor's voice inhere not only, or even primarily, in video recording but are lodged deviously in texts. It is in these "speakerly texts" that the survivor's story, often told or penned in the immediate aftermath of the war, finds its powerful, and necessarily oblique, expression—a voicing which is able to circumvent our resistance (in the words of Ozick's novella, our "deafness") to the rigors of testimony.

Known for his prescient philosophical readings of literary texts, Maurice Friedman here juxtaposes two writers whose novels clarify their—and our—position in relation to the absurd. Usually we think of the absurd as equivalent to meaninglessness, but Friedman suggests that, in Franz Kafka's "last and greatest novel," *The Castle*, we see the relation to the absurd as meaningful. Kafka's capacity to elicit meaning from the absurd can be seen even more distinctly when viewed in contrast to a recent novel by Milan Kundera. In *Immortality*, claims Friedman, Kundera's narrative world is clearly steeped in the absurd. But that is the problem: the absurd has become so taken-for-granted that it no longer yields meaning. In a certain sense, Friedman reads Kundera as a foil to Kafka; by doing so he suggests that, in the convulsive twentieth century, the trajectory of the absurd is not so much one of evolution as of devolution.

Jeffrey Mehlman's end point is the oblique representation of the Holocaust in a recent play of British dramatist Tony Harrison; but Mehlman arrives at this point by means of an oblique strategy of his own, an approach which begins by reviewing some important mistranslations and misreadings of Walter Benjamin's writings on the messianic and catastrophe. Mehlman's probing essay itself solicits a range of readings. On one level, he continues a critique of deconstruction that he has undertaken elsewhere; on another level, he suggests that Harrison's drama provokes a re-reading of Benjamin and a more benevolent, if controversial, assessment of Benjamin's postmodern interpreters.

COMMENTARY

The backbone of Jewish tradition and creativity is the rich interplay between sacred text and commentary. The role and necessity of commentary implies the recognition that, facing sacred texts, readers are in need of a guide, someone who, equipped with extraordinary learning, can illuminate what is opaque, who can cull from the vast web of opinion certain ideas or methods which enable the text to be understood meaningfully, engagingly, vitally. In addition, a commentator asks questions of the text, and, by doing so, gives voice to what disturbs, provokes, unsettles; to what is in the text that demands attention, focus, resolution, response.

In his essays on the Bible, the Talmud, and Hasidic masters and disciples—essays which themselves form a distinctive form of commentary on classical and modern religious texts and personages—Wiesel shows how the most urgent questions of our time echo questions asked by predecessors. Yet for Wiesel this echo, this capacity of hearing our perplexity already registered by others, does not diminish the force of our query. Conversely, joining our voice to theirs enlarges the questions, deepens them, and allows the idiom of authority and tradition to ennoble and energize our own distress.

Similarly, the essays of Joseph Polak, Hillel Levine, and Nehemia Polen make manifest the rich traditions of textual commentary. Moreover, each of the essays shows how commentary is stretched and tested—and how, I think it is fair to say, it rises to the occasion—when confronted with the most grievous of human situations.

Prague looms as one of the great cities of European Jewish life. It is against this background of greatness that one reads, I believe, Joseph Polak's extraordinary case study of the fire of Prague in 1689. Polak—himself a child survivor of Bergen-Belsen—bases his comments on the testimony of a survivor of the fire, a testimony that comes, however, by way of a Rabbinic responsum to a question asked (by another survivor, no doubt) about tearing *qri'ah* (rending one's garment) for a burnt Torah scroll. Guiding his reader through an intricate, rich survey of the literature on this question, Polak teases out of this wrenching yet eloquent gesture of mourning a complex and evolving theology of catastrophe.

Collective catastrophe also forms the background for Hillel Levine's elegant study of an enigmatic Rabbinic text concerned with adjudicating the allocation of scarce resources. Trying to account for the ungenerous words of one of the most generous of the sages, Levine delicately moves catastrophe—the Hadrianic persecutions of the second century—from background to foreground, allowing for a certain therapeutic resonance to be heard in Rabbi Yose's perplexing ruling. Moreover, Levine's discussion has implications not only for a generation of survivors but also for thinking about the categories we bring to think about "rescue," an issue that Levine has recently explored at greater length in his important study, *In Search of Sugihara*.

For Jews, the event and experience of catastrophe is often linked to the violation of holy space. In "Coming of Age in Kozienice," Nehemia Polen chronicles Malkah Shapiro's post-holocaust attempt to lovingly reconstitute through the written word the sacred space of her hasidic Polish home. Shapiro's project is extraordinary on several levels. In itself her novel/memoir is an extremely rare commodity emerging from the hasidic world. Moreover, Polen shows that Shapiro's reclamation of sacred space can be read (perhaps *needs* to be read) in relation to the Bible's own configuring of sacred space and place. Finally, Polen suggests that the redemptive space of postwar Israel—the physical locale in which Shapiro composed her novel/memoir—both inspires the project of reclamation and also defines the limits of that project in the face of the destruction the Jewish community of Kozienice in the Second World War.

ETHICAL AND RELIGIOUS REFLECTIONS

If fiction and commentary have served Wiesel as preferred genres, ethics has been the fulcrum around which his thought has turned. Not, to be sure, in the form of a systematic ethics. Like many great contributors to modern moral thought—one thinks of Kierkegaard and Camus, for instance—Wiesel's formulations are poetic rather than systematic. Moreover, Wiesel's reflections are always tethered to the Holocaust—the event, or series of events, that, defined by moral collapse, makes thinking or rethinking about ethics profoundly necessary.

The four essays in this section move ethics into ordinarily resistant domains: into popular culture and the realm of mysticism as well as toward considering the role of "fate" and "experience" in shaping moral philosophy. Inspired by Wiesel's challenge to ethics (indeed, several of the pieces feature or consult Wiesel's work), each of the essays has an iconoclastic bent, and displays a revisionary impatience with analytic categories that remain aloof from the gritty truth of "factual complexities," as John Silber calls them.

One of the preeminent American Christian commentators on the Holocaust, John Roth in this essay argues that Elie Wiesel's presence has changed America's public religious discourse. Moving deftly between popular and elite phenomena and texts, Roth's analysis suggests that Wiesel, as witness yet also as celebrated international figure, has altered both the substance and mode of speaking about God. As Roth outlines in the second part of the essay, Wiesel's work, focusing on questions and contention, can be read as a kind of ethical manual for learning to conduct civil yet passionately religious dialogue.

Like Roth, Dorothee Sölle is known as a preeminent postholocaust Christian commentator and theologian. Again like Roth, her contribution interrogates the relation between religion and language. Whereas Roth begins with the popular and concludes, via Wiesel's Hasidic masters, with the mystical elite, Sölle moves in the reverse direction, first exploring through Martin Buber and Meister Eckhardt the idiom of mystical speech and silence and then turning to the meaning of the mystical to non-elites. For instance, her inquiry into mysticism's rhetorical dimensions—negation, paradox, silence—also enables a view of the way mystical language speaks to women (represented here by Teresa of Avila) or the participants in the more contemporary domains of popular protest.

John Silber's essay poses a set of philosophical questions regarding the nature of collective responsibility and collective guilt. His analysis, however, is not based on the conventional philosophic tradition but on the work of two literary masters, one ancient—Sophocles—and one modern—Elie Wiesel. Silber shows how Wiesel's provocative "inconsistencies" regarding collective responsibility can both challenge systematic philosophy and also direct our reading of Sophocles' masterpiece, *Oedipus Tyrannus*. It is, above all, the notion of fate as spun out in Oedipus's tragedy that, as Silber powerfully argues, can revise our notions of guilt and responsibility, even in relation to the Holocaust.

Writing from the point of view of a Christian theologian born and residing in postwar Germany, Reinhold Boschki argues that, after the Holocaust, one in search of ethical guidelines must take several bold steps: first, listen to and read the testimony of Holocaust victims; second, guided by the notions of experience and memory culled from testimony, interrogate the classics of philosophy and theology; and third, turn to the few sources of the Western philosophic tradition that foreground experience and memory. As he makes vitally clear in the essay, Boschki's German roots and Christian belief have animated his quest for an ethics of memory.

Concern for human rights is the pragmatic, and necessary, complement to a speculative ethics—especially an ethics generated by, and responsive to, cataclysmic events causing vast suffering.

A victim of the Nazi attempt to destroy European Jewry, Wiesel has attempted to bring succor to all victims. As Steven Katz writes, Wiesel's efforts have taken him to "all corners of the world": the former Yugoslavia, various parts of the former Soviet Union, the Middle East, Cambodia, South Africa, and among the Mosquito Indians in Central America. Significantly, Wiesel has paired this global activism with writing, memorializing those lost and protesting on behalf of those who could be saved or helped. Each effort could stand on its own. But the ongoing, eloquent association of act and word has distinguished Wiesel's endeavor.

The authors of the essays in this section have often pursued a similar course, lobbying in courtrooms, hospitals, parliaments on behalf of victims; hence, proximity to the plight of the victim informs these reflections, grounding the abstract and theoretical in the urgent desire to mitigate suffering. Importantly, the human rights cases under investigation in these essays cover a broad expanse of the globe, implying that every persecutor must be held accountable, that every victim is equally crucial. Just as important, however, are those essays that refuse to overlook the familiar, that see the rights of victims at the forefront, for example, in the local hospital room. Moreover, several essays address issues of terminology and principles, solidifying the link between act and word. The tone and style of the essays also testify to what is at stake in the arena of human rights; the authors frequently push their analysis toward manifesto, seeking from the reader an unreserved engagement and urging us toward a passionate response.

Indeed, Marguerite Lederberg's essay is a kind of manifesto on behalf of victims. Yet, unlike several essays in this section, her concern is not primarily victims of direct assault; Lederberg's arena is the more subtle ways in which victims are demeaned when they are made culpable for their own suffering. Exploring and exposing the social and clinical reasons for blame, she locates the syndrome of blaming victims in the more rarefied region of the mind/body dichotomy. She argues, moreover, that the consequences of maintaining this dichotomy, philosophical as well as clinical, heap senseless suffering upon those already too familiar with it.

Whereas Lederberg deals with the individual victim, Steven Katz attends to the plight of the collective. While chronicling and lamenting the disastrous series of crimes committed against the Aché of Peru, Katz's essay is also a quest for accuracy, for bringing a kind of clinical rigor as the most responsible way to assess the crime committed. Those who forego such rigor are led to use the term 'genocide' inappropriately—as in the case of the Aché. We will know better, Katz implies, who are the victims and what they (and their community) have suffered when we endorse accuracy over indignation.

Compassion for victims of state persecution also motivates Per Ahlmark's essay, "Is Democracy for Everybody?" Ahlmark comes at this issue through a case study of Swedish liberals' astonishing acceptance of and support for totalitarian regimes. Ahlmark provocatively suggests that this "toleration" issues from a patronizing stance toward Third World peoples, a stance that, surprisingly, shares certain structural features with the attitudes characteristic of colonizers of the nineteenth century. Such attitudes, argues Ahlmark, undermine democracy. To conclude, Ahlmark sketches what is at stake (for both Western liberals and Third World nations) in refusing to submit to the attractions of authoritarianism and in promoting democratic institutions.

While Ahlmark writes out of a specific place—the Swedish situation and its recent history—and suggests more general implications, lawyer Irwin Cotler links his inquiry into the status of human rights to two historic events: the fiftieth anniversary of the Nuremberg code and that of the founding of the state of Israel. These two shaping events—one legal, the other political—

are linked in that they embody a "revolution" in human rights; they are also linked because both have been assailed by a countermovement seeking to undo their accomplishments. To fortify against such counterforces, Cotler appends a series of lessons that distill the legacy of these twin revolutions, lessons that he links with the moral advocacy of Elie Wiesel.

Pnina Lahav also takes legal history as a starting point, linking this history to broader questions of Jewish identity and the legacy of the Holocaust. Reviewing two recent legal cases in which fathers struggle to establish the Jewish identity of their children, Lahav contrasts the paradoxical cultural implications brought out in an Israeli court, on the one hand, and in an American court, on the other. In both locales, a set of competing codes arbitrate the cases: in Israel, tradition and trauma; in America, plurality and the rights of the individual.

The democratic ideals that shape the decisions in American courts also, of course, shape other institutions, sometimes in disarmingly radical ways. Joshua Lederberg examines how the "extraordinary democratization of access" provided by the internet bears on a range of cultural concerns, particularly in terms of the challenge the internet brings to axioms of scholarly research (authenticity, accountability, authority) and to the pedagogy that is linked to it. In Lederberg's scenario, the vast enabling potential of the internet teeters on the edge of the absurd, an unbordered world in which standards and selection fail to apply. Yet Lederberg believes good teaching can avert what dangers may exist.

CONCLUDING MEDITATIONS

In "The Holocaust Experience as a State of Mind," Shlomo Breznitz explores the psychological residue that remains with a victim of vast trauma. More particularly, he interrogates the special mental status of survival, trying to discern what can and cannot be said and understood, what can and cannot be empathetically shared. Breznitz, also a child survivor of the Holocaust, has recently published his own distinguished memoir of those years, *Memory Fields;* even though reference to the memoir appears explicitly only in the final note of the essay, one can sense throughout the memoir's presence and the difficult experience that it evokes.

Elie Wiesel and Václav Havel are presently co-directing a series of seminars on morality. Theirs is a partnership linked by a direct experience of oppression, by an ongoing commitment to nurture their own wounded communities and people, and by a hunger to stir the world at large toward decency. Yet in terms of the Holocaust they occupy different ground: one writes from the inside, the other, from the outside; one is a Jew, the other a non-Jew; one draws his moral stature from within the nexus of the event, the other—as is demonstrated unequivocally in the remarks included in this volume—brings his moral stature to engage this event, arguing lyrically yet intensively that engaging the Holocaust at the most fundamental level is both foreboding and necessary. As with the most powerful moral commentators, Havel's voice is unflinchingly situated: as a Czech, as a humanist, as a human.

The seventieth verse in the Bible tells of God's punishment of the notorious snake, saying "upon your belly shall you go, and dust shall you eat all the days of your life." Once a student of the Kotsker Rebbe protested that the punishment of eating dust was not really a punishment; since dust was so prevalent, the snake would never go hungry. The Rebbe responded that, indeed, this was the snake's punishment: he would never know hunger, would always be complacent, always be satisfied. The life of our teacher, colleague, and friend, Elie Wiesel, is a protest against complacency; he teaches us to hunger for more: for ourselves, for others, for the world. May these contributions in honor of his seventieth birthday join in the act of protest and share in the task of teaching.

Fiction:
Stories and Critical Writing

AARON APPELFELD

As an Apple of the Eye

Translated by Hillel Halkin

I

"*V'YISROMAN V'YISNASEI V'YISHADAR,*"[1] stirred the words of the
ancient prayer. They fluttered and fell. An ultimate silence descended on the gathering and draped it in a gelid pall. Dusk va-
pored the windows. Slowly dropping snowflakes coated the earth
a dirty white. A storm was brewing on the horizon. The bare trees
stood shivering, their skin tinted blue.

My mother's mother had passed away. Since morning an army
of people huddled in the yard. She had spent her final weeks
talking about death with a kind of simple practicality. Though
she hadn't looked ill, she had talked all the time about the won-
drous world to which she was going. Her high forehead grew
translucent. On the last day of her life she still managed to taste
the new cherry liquor and to inspect the dairy cellar. Her life
ebbed with the day. Death found her sitting in the straw chair on
the glass-paned veranda.

Thick banks of mist rose up outside. Grandfather wore his old
winter coat and mother the brown jacket of her youth. We stood
surrounded by a crowd of unknown people who mumbled, whispered, and gestured with their hands to each other. The ancient
words drifted upwards once more, the voices led by a venerable
old man. Like shadows we stood in his fleeting world.

The snow stopped and a thin, cutting rain melted its white

3

remains. She had not been a person of transcendent religious faith but had lived with a kind of lucidity in each and every movement. "We'll just have to stop and consider it," she sometimes said to herself, as though listening inwardly, so that nothing should be done on a whim.

Clouds swept down over us. The horses plodded along. The unknown people dispersed in all directions. We stood in the old cemetery, an ancient tribe whose faith had been lost, whose customs had been forgotten. She, the last bearer of these hidden secrets, was gone.

Days of muffled silence descended on the house. Grandfather retreated to his attic. The great earth-brown cavalry horses were taken out to the lawn to be put through their paces. Occasionally, the regimental sergeant appeared and they drooped their heads as though in deference to their future master. Wood was sawed in the yard, coal unloaded. Wintry smoke spiraled on the horizon and soft mists padded the chill air. Unknown canvassers ran about the yard like animals that have scented a corpse. No one bothered to drive them away.

The winter light grew clearer, and distant churchbells pounded metallically, their mournful tones borne like blue waves on the shadows. It was as if time came to a halt. A frozen attentiveness could be seen in the eyes of the animals. There was nothing tangible about it, just a sluggishness, but to us it seemed that everything had stopped. An unearthly light put down its columns on the lawn.

The winter light rose up above us, and we felt small, like lost shadows seeking cover in the woods. What should we say, how should we be silent. How should we make the ancient words fit our own. Not a soul came to visit. The two white horses stood on the lawn like noble steeds whose cavaliers were gone.

The peasants were sleeping their winter sleep, as deep as the potatoes in their underground pits. The errant smoke spoke but faintly of their vigorous, rooted sleep. Yet whenever one of them died, the bells came metallically to life at once. The peasants emerged from their slumber, put on their fur coats, and followed the bells that summoned them to church. As soon as the chimes fell silent they reinterred themselves in their long sleep. But we, what should we say, what should we do.

The windows were like gates to a transparency that led to yet a further transparency. Father put a skullcap on his head and sat between the drawing room and the veranda with bewilderment in his eyes. The only one to cry was Karola. She had lived with us for so many years that her gentile face had taken on the color of the house. None of us cried. The long, lit, sky-fed nights piled up silently by the house. What should we do. We were like strangers in a house that came by way of an inheritance.

During the last year we sometimes saw her standing silently, thinking. She walked in the yard like a grand lady who knew a secret that could not be passed on. We knew that we were linked through her to a world nobler than our own. No one dreamed that such a mighty tree might topple. Winter came whitely with its snow and she stood unflinchingly in the doorway to greet it. No one knew that it was no longer she.

The servants remained outside, like forces of nature. Their movements diminished in winter and they became as torpid as bears, striking each other in slow motion, snoring rhythmically together, blowing fire into the coals when they were cold. How insubstantial we were by comparison, like moths whose antennae kept vibrating with a thin sadness. Uproot them all you might, they would still live the seasons, whereas we grew more sensitive, more anxious, always capable of surprise. We suddenly sensed that a distant melody was knocking on the shutters of the house—a melody without sound. We knew neither its name, nor how to chase it away, nor how to cloak ourselves in its whispered grief. We were like winter birds overtaken by some forgotten, unfathomed melody.

Many years earlier our heritage had fallen by the wayside. Even Grandfather was more a man of logic than belief, so that only Mother's mother had still known the secrets that the family had handed down. And she too had failed to transmit them. The secrets were thus forgotten. Our holidays were a tiresome reunion.

Father was always away in Vienna. Our country home that had come down to us as an heirloom was bare. Mother ordered peasant rugs for the floors and had the drawing room paneled in oak.

The snow stopped after a week and a steady frost covered the drifts. We sat in the drawing room. Karola served tea in thin cups. One didn't ask how it will be from now on. A draft hissed weakly through the storm windows. It was like the secret had touched us after all. Grandfather came down from the attic pale and wasted, as though returning from a long trip. The ironic glint in his eye had gone out. Tall tallow candles lit the room. Grandfather sat down at the table without a word.

But as he did the ancient melody seemed to start up by itself: *v'yisroman v'yisnasei v'yishadar.* We knew that these windy spirits were our own. The winter hadn't taken them in. The cold hadn't killed them. They were looking for some place to come to. Soon, it seemed, the large door would open, and lost shadows who had left us years ago would stand gaunt and naked in the doorway. No one dared to look. The door had really opened. The ancient, steadfast words rang out as though from noble metal. They hung there for a moment, then crumbled.

II

For days, no sound issued in the house. The forgotten melodies no longer stirred and a different silence took their place from out of the darkness. I looked at the family bookcase, a low piece in which a sensitive craftsman had subtly left his marks. I imagined him a tall, thin man who worked with the thinnest of chisels so as not to harm the precious wood. An unknown artisan who hadn't left a corner for himself.

The bookcase was open. I could have put a hand on the thin books but they seemed to tremble at the thought. A dark, self-created aura enveloped them. Mother sat reading a book by Franz Werfel. She read with great concentration, even when I stood by her side and said, "Mother." Father sat in the next room with his ledger, a long, narrow notebook with a red line down the middle to separate debits from credits. How many barges had been lost down the river. The train that never got to Danzig. Business could not have been worse. "Father," I said, my voice burning up in the stillness. I could have shouted and he still wouldn't have heard. A thin partition, transparent but soundproof, extended between us. The acacia tree was invading the window, a fact that made me realize more than anything else how much things had recently changed.

A peasant rug lay in the hall. The paper flowers that Aunt Tina had sent from the city were blooming again. The grandfather clock on the wall ticked away with languid movements like the shadowy fingers of a belltower.

Grandfather's face was unrecognizable. A beard had sprouted on it; his short, hiphugging coat had grown longer. A sublime melancholy graced his brow. Mother personally brought him his breakfast each morning. Everything had become as fragile as the china dishes that Father once brought from Danzig. Such paper-thinness could not last long. "It's almost Hanukkah," said Karola. The holidays always arrived in a last-minute panic. A thick, white snow was falling outside. The trees were accustomed by now to their white mantle; a fine feather of frost blossomed on the heads of the horses. The entire universe seemed sunk in meditation. You could stand at the window and take in the slow flow of it. Until a voice from out of the blue announced: Hanukkah.

The delicate web fell swiftly apart. Back came the same irritable spirits that assembled on every holiday. They were everywhere. You had only to lift a finger to find them standing in the doorway like starving beggars. A year ago a man had come to the house with a face as dry as shoe leather and clothes threadbare and moth-eaten. He carried a pack on his back and stood like a weeping willow, like an ancient remonstrance come to demand from us the return of some deposit. My name, said the man, is Alexander. I don't want a thing from you. I came just to see you.

"What is there to see?" said mother.

"I came to see if you still remembered."

"Remembered what?"

A trace of fatherly sorrow flitted over his face. Mother took stock. "Of course we're still Jews," she reassured him, less in apol-

7

ogy than in consolation. "Then I can go," said the man. "Why don't you have a cup of coffee first." But he was already outside, in the hands of the winds. In time we discovered that he was a vagrant in the area. An ex-lumber merchant whose business had failed and whose family had perished in the great plague. He had taken on himself the modest mission of reminding Jews when the holidays were near.

Such was the countryside in the cold of the year. The winds were a terror. The peasants burrowed deeper in their huts, leaving the unpredictable to us. Sometimes a stray horse reached our house, utterly gentle and with a look of supplication on its face as though begging for lodgings and a bowl of hot soup.

Who would come to remind us this year? The winter is clearing. The winds had lost their snow on their way to us. The doctor came to visit every day. Father no longer asked him any questions. They passed the time playing chess. Years ago the doctor had arrived to be the local savior. The peasants had scented his innocence and had badgered him incessantly ever since, rousing him from his bed even on the coldest of nights. Like a man stricken with guilt, he went whenever he was called.

If only he could catch his breath, if only he would learn. But each time he would answer the summons and arrive at our house in the evening, drained and exhausted. Karola would bring him tea. He would fondle the glass, stare at the chessboard in search of a move, and doze off.

III

Snow fell on top of snow. The village slept. A drunken blizzard howled outside while our servants staggered somnolently through the house. The ancestral cadences that drugged them at this time of the year were proving too much for them.

The river froze over. Bent gypsies skipped over it like emaciated grasshoppers maddened by hunger. What could they find to eat in this wilderness? Everything was buried in the snow, even the trees. It was suicidal to try. Yet they pressed forward, battling the winds, clawing up the slippery slope. They might have found something if not for the dogs. The dogs stayed awake in winter.

We too were awake, without words. In vain Karola tried cajoling us to sleep: sleep, children, sleep. Different words surfaced in her at this time of year, or rather, rhythmic murmurings that repeated themselves with a fatalistic monotony, purling silently like water trapped beneath ice.

Cariba threw off her blanket and said, "I had a bad dream, Karola. Help me with it, please."

"What did you dream?"

"I dreamt that I saw my mother, and that she was very sick."

"She must have been interceding for you with the saints."

"I hope so. I've sinned a great deal, my dear, a great deal."

"You've already confessed it all and been forgiven. You can sleep in peace."

"Listen to that storm."

Vaguely familiar objects lay on the table, as though placed there by an invisible hand. Old prayer books, bottles of brandy, white tallow candles. Days went by without visitors. Thin shadows crept along the walls and disappeared into the carpets. At night they mustered themselves by the table, opening the brandy bottles and humming under their breaths: *v'yisroman v'yisnasei v'yishadar.* A smell of damp hay reached my nostrils.

No sooner had the storm died down than the lumber clerks arrived. Short and thin, they seemed to grow even thinner as they entered the house. No one questioned their loyalty. It was their loyalty that had made clerks out of them. And that had kept them from getting ahead. Trees were in their blood. They couldn't live without forests. They stood before Father penniless and aghast, their faces plastered with pallor: the poachers. They were out of control. They were tearing up the forest, roots and all. Even Father's own lumberjacks were thieves; but worst of all were the storms. They had already destroyed a whole stand of trees. Trees as old as the hills.

Father sat listening. The fear froze in their eyes. Only now did they realize the error of their ways. Willingness was not enough. Loyalty was not enough. The forest needed different men, men who could keep an eye out. It was all very well to read and write, but you couldn't save a forest with it.

9

I was sure that Father would console them. But he said nothing at all, and a stillness like ultimate silence descended on them. At last he said: "The police are coming in the evening. I'll have a talk with them."

The winter refused to let up. The peasants' sleep deepened. The storms raged unchallenged. The days grew shorter and a crepuscular murk screened the sky. The clerks departed, leaving their amazement behind them. What about the spring deliveries?

"Come, Karola, help me with my dream," I heard Cariba say. "I saw my mother again. What does she want with me?" "She's interceding for you, my dear."

Sleep sought to swaddle us too. Shadows came and went at the table like uninvited but voracious guests. It was as though they hadn't had a square meal in ages. We sat there looking at them.

One evening, without asking permission, Karola gathered up the ritual objects on the table, placed them carefully in a white bag, spread out a new tablecloth, and in a somewhat dry voice said, "You can sleep in peace now, Cariba, no one's here."

It kept getting colder.

I V

Afternoons we sat on the paned porch and drank coffee. The long, quiet hours seemed to eavesdrop on the transparent cups. We watched the sun go down with a pang in our hearts.

The business deteriorated further. The canvassers circulated like evil spirits fleeing before a cruel God. Yet Father never swore at them once. His face kept growing thinner. A kind of spirituality glazed his eyes. From time to time, he leafed through a book by Lazarus. The light from the drawing room that cut across my bedroom during the long nights was more like silence than like light.

The holiday came. Mother took out the elegant Hanukkah menorah from the closet. Grandfather said the blessings. We had forgotten to celebrate his eightieth birthday. Karola served potato pancakes like Grandmother used to make. The elderly Karola remembered better than we did. Her repetitious insistence that one must never lose faith was a torture to Mother. God in heaven knew all. One must believe in Him. How little was expected of man. All that she had seen and heard in our household over the years was absorbed in her gentile soul. Whenever she spoke of Grandmother it was with the same holy reverence with which she spoke of the saints.

We sat around the table. The candles burning in the rooms seemed about to reveal our life histories to us, and the histories of unknown lives before us. The ancient, unfathomed words fell like leaves. Nothing was left. Nothing but a tunnel leading to another tunnel. Beneath our thin masks, so it seemed, we were getting to know each other better. To understand each other in a new way.

It was too much for Mother. She snatched up the thin china plates as if a visitor were at the door. But none was. The evening light and the silence in the windows were entirely our own. I saw Father as I never had before, a melancholy glow in his cheeks. He never traveled any more, as though reconciled to his losses. As for myself, I had given up my studies. My tutor, Thulin Grauber, had returned to Vienna. Mother had made a farewell banquet in his honor. Thulin Grauber lauded my aptitude for the humanities. It was a lugubrious evening. When he first came to the house, he had seemed the perfect cosmopolitan. The servant girls vied to seduce him until they discovered that he was a fraud; he was in fact still a virgin. After that they didn't stop poking fun at him. They called him Thulin the Druggist, an epithet bearing secret, coarse meanings that proved inexhaustible. He spent most of his time in his room, over his mathematics books. Yet he was a genius at other things too.

Now it was all over with. Father presented him with a thin gold watch and brought him to the railway station the next morning in the carriage.

The goodness of activity departed from us, as if on account of some forgotten sin. Even our little household quarrels ceased taking place. Whatever Karola put on the table was eaten. The cold weather eased a bit. Logs were sawed in the yard, coal was brought up from the cellar, just as they had always been. No one came to visit. We stood expectantly by the windows. If not for

Karola, we might have frozen to death there. She let out a cry of alarm. Something of Grandmother's voice had passed into her own. It isn't right, it isn't right, she said, and crossed herself.

V

Spring appeared, hale and headstrong. The peasants emerged from their huts and the heavy brown horses stood in the doorway of the stable. A vigorous quiet filled the air. The winter had faded before our eyes. The peasants' wives had grown fat. The poorest of the peasants had spent all their money on drink.

Vasil stood shading his eyes. The servant girls stepped outside to imbibe the new air. The snow had all but melted and muted burblings sounded through the night.

The phantasmagoric winter was over. Light reigned supreme. Long glances met each other, slid sideways and scraped. The eyes of the animals hazed with wonderment.

The mayor's wife had cheated on him. Vasil's sons had stolen horses. Someone had opened the sluicegates on the river and flooded the fields. Coincidence, one might say. But Cariba insisted that it wasn't. Man proposes, God disposes. And if you couldn't remember on that day, you would be reminded. Nothing would be forgotten. The peasants stepped gingerly from their huts as if the earth were mined, their wives trailing after them like bondmaidens.

In springtime deeds quickened and sprouted for all to see. It was too late to change very much, at any rate, not without risking more.

Does the bastard really think I didn't see? A sharp glance cuts the air. Another is hastily drawn and crosses swords with it. I was sleeping, I didn't do it, begs the woman for mercy. She is lying. Her voice is lying. It is clear that she won't be forgiven. Yet her punisher toys with her. I was sleeping, I didn't know what they were doing to me. It's true, he grudgingly admits, You can do what you want with a woman in her sleep. And now you want to kill me! I've brought orphans into the world.

The sentence was carried out by the river. The peasant whipped his wife while she squealed like a stuck pig. He beat her the same way each spring. She was used to it, like an animal. The other peasants mocked him. For twenty years he's been saying that he'll kill her. He hasn't got the guts.

The world is going to the dogs, Cariba stated piously. The two old women knew everything. The villages were woven into their brains. Nothing escaped them. And through them we too were linked to this fantastical world.

What am I sitting here for like an idiot? a peasant asks himself, wrapped in cobwebs of sleep, as though in a fur coat. He has drunk too much and is still half-asleep. The horse pulling the wagon is more awake than he is.

Suddenly the sacrificial knife flashes forth. The victim this time was the manager of the sugar mill. All winter long he'd had his nose in the mayor's gravy. Not just the mayor's wife. He emptied two silos as well. And stolen his horses. There had been accomplices, of course. But first he would have to pay for it himself.

Such was springtime every year. Only afterwards did an unnatural calm descend on the fields. The women dug away in the furrows. The peasants put spaces between themselves. Ask any one of them what happened and he'd play the innocent with you. Something has happened, then, has it? Funny I haven't heard of it.

Policemen swarmed around the sugar mill like blind dogs. Everyone could be bribed. The procedure was noisy but short. The murderer's assistants had already gotten away. Meanwhile, the skeins of winter kept unraveling and a green carpet rose out of the earth. The days grew longer, the horizons wider. Potatoes came up by the bucketful from their dark pits. The peasants came home every evening sated and satisfied. They and their animals gave off a persistent smell of earth.

Cariba announced that she meant to leave and go home to her family's farm. She had a plot of her own by the riverbank.

"What are you talking about?" Karola scolded her.

"My mother died in the fields. I want to die in them too."

"You mustn't talk like that," Karola silenced her, "you mustn't talk like that." Vasil was busy breaking the two horses his brother-in-law had sent from the mountains. He had learned to break horses in the army. He beat them without mercy, as if they were demons and not living things.

Suddenly a peasant stops his cart and says with murderous insouciance: Why did you cheat on me all winter?

No, says the terrified woman. The peasant gets out of his cart. In a second the lethal knife will be out. But the woman is too quick for him. Like a bird of prey she leaps from the cart, her husband after her with death in his hands. The books were not closed on the winter. Details would follow. In the faraway huts in the mountains the peasants were still wrapped in cold; but here, lower down, everything was thawing. The sunsets whispered softly. Cariba talked all the time about hell. What will become of me? our plump servant girl asked her. She had remembered her husband in the army. The other servants consoled her with the thought that her brothers-in-law would keep their mouths shut. They had boozed the winter away in town. Now spring had come and still they weren't back.

NOTE

1. "And exalted, and extolled, and honored." These Aramaic words are found in the middle of the *kaddish* prayer, the central prayer intoned by Jewish mourners.

ARIEL DORFMAN

What I Always Knew

Like a grain of wheat in the center of silence.
But from whom can you ask mercy for a grain of wheat?
—Pablo Neruda, *Residence on Earth*

NOW YOU ARE GOING down the stairs. Soon the sound of the door to the Embassy will be heard closing, your small figure will pass the gate, and then you will start to cross the street. That's where the two men come up to speak to you, on that curb. The conversation hardly lasts what it takes for a cigarette to be lit by the smaller man, the one with the checkered jacket. The other one looks you in the eyes, those eyes that must feel distant and startled. Then they invite you to get into the car. One of them takes your arm, but he does so with discretion, almost courteously. The motor is running, humming like a well-fed cat, but the car will not move. Now you're getting in, you and the smaller man in back, and the other one in front, pushing against the seat, those strong, decisive shoulders that contrast with his apologetic lips and the thin impoverished wisp of his moustache. It will not be possible to see you. Only, all of a sudden, your hand which accepts a cigarette and then cups the flickering flame of the lighter. Only, on one occasion, the other hand that can be seen for a moment fluttering on the top of the back seat, fingers that hesitate, the shine of a wedding ring. The man in the front, seated next to the empty driver's seat, is the one asking the questions. He can be seen, because that car is parked facing the Embassy.

Translated from the Spanish, "Siempre supe," by the author

15

Now, with his left hand, he turns off the motor and pockets the keys. That means they do not plan to leave right away. He will remain half hunched up against the door, one leg raised, the shoe pushing against the upholstery, fingers intertwined at the knee. Once in a while, he scratches under his sock, rubs the compressed skin. They will not be in a hurry. Children will pass by on bikes calling each other by the names their parents gave them many years ago, the mailman will cross this early summer day bringing news and ads and maybe letters from lost loves, mothers will go for a morning stroll and teach their kids how to stand up on both feet, take a step or two instead of crawling. Now a bird perches itself on the warm roof of the car and, without even a trill, flies off like an arrow. Maybe, inside, you've detected that slight presence, that slighter absence, like a leaf that falls from a tree out of season, a bit too late, maybe you didn't understand until it was too late and they were gone, that a pair of wings had opened up. An old couple will take some halting steps past the car, pushing an empty shopping cart. An hour later they'll be back, the cart packed with groceries. You will all still be there. The man extracts a small notebook from a pocket in his jacket, and then a pencil. He passes it to you. During the briefest wave of time, your hand can be seen receiving the pencil, the notebook. Then, as if you were not really there in the back seat of the car, that extension of your body disappears and nothing more can be seen. The man tosses his keys up into the air and catches them neatly. He smiles. He points a key at you and says something, it must be a question. Impossible to know what you answered. No passerby hesitates as his shoes shuffle by the car, nobody looks inside. A beggarwoman stumbles down the street, a flock of ragtag kids in her wake, she approaches the car to ask for something, and then she'll back off, half understanding or not wanting to understand. Now the car window opens and the swarthy face of the smaller man appears, the man who has been sitting next to you in the back. He hasn't slept much, hasn't slept well: there are bags under his eyes and his features are puffy. He blinks under that implacable daylight. Then he looks towards the Embassy for a while, giving the windows the once-over to see if there is somebody watching, if there is somebody behind half-drawn curtains trying to register and remember each movement, each gesture. He stays like that for a good while, his head motionless, as if he could guess what is happening behind those walls. He takes out a handkerchief and wipes it across his forehead, cleans the sweat from the rest of his face. He needs to shave, he needs to get home for a good shave. Maybe all night while he kept watch he's been thinking of the bath full of hot water waiting for him. The air dances with white spots, he blinks his heavy eyelids. The breeze has begun to fall asleep under the spell of the day's heat. He emerges from the car quickly. A stream of sunlight slides down his body. Now he gets back into the car, into the driver's seat. He holds his hand out so the other man can give him the keys. The sound of the back door that opened and closed, the front door that opened and closed, does not disturb the quiet. It's almost like a sound of harmony, sweet metal. But they will not take you away. The car accelerates, passes the house, passes the curtained windows of the house, for an eternal white instant your petite face can be seen, the way the shoulders breathe, that dress which presses to your body like the skin of a lover. You pass like a body of lightning that will never end, like a birth that will never end, you will pass without looking towards the house, your face will pass, your eyes sinking into the abrupt horizon of the street which connects with other streets. Now the car brakes a bit further on, sheltered under the generous shade of that tree you have come to know so well, that you have heard moaning and dancing its branches below the weight of the wind last night, it brakes half a block from the house. All that can be seen is the back part of the car, and in a hollow opened by the leaves gently swaying with the rays of this summer that has come too early, a blur of color that could be your hair or the neck trembling under your hair or the stubborn flurry of your head under your hair. If it were not for the leisurely and merciless progress of the minute hand on your wrist-watch, there where the slow blood inside your arm finds and flows with the mysterious blood inside your hand, if it were not for the imperceptible rotation of this planet, it might be thought that time had stagnated, that all movement is paralyzed, that silence is definitive, and that you will stay there forever, you, the men, the car, the street. No beggar will pass, the old couple will not go out again shopping. The children will have to put away their bicycles and go and eat lunch. When the sun begins to again invade the top of the car, when midday has finally concluded and the afternoon has finally begun, when once more the intolerable heat forces the driver to seek a new refuge, nothing in the world will be able to stop, neither the buzzing of bees nor the yellow cheerful burst of the flowers, nothing can stop that motor from being started up again, that car from inching away from the curb, and this time it will not pause under the shade or in the sun, this time the car will go on and on and on, nothing can stop it from losing itself there, faraway, down the street which connects with other streets, taking you to that place from where you will never return, that place you never returned from.

NANCY HARROWITZ

From Mt. Sinai to the Holocaust: Primo Levi and the Crisis of Science in The Periodic Table

PRIMO LEVI IS BEST KNOWN as one of the most widely read writers about the Holocaust, leaving behind an important legacy of memoirs, essays, and fiction. But Levi was also a chemist by trade, and his scientific perspective informs not only the philosophy of his work, but its content as well. The ways in which science informs Levi's work, however, are complex, as his own views on his discipline changed over time, from the writing of his very first publication to his last essays. The main complicating factor in Levi's own assessment of science, his place within it, and his self-identity as a chemist is the Holocaust itself, as an event which problematized the role of science and technology in society.[1]

In order to understand the role of Levi's *The Periodic Table* in relation to his philosophy of science, it is necessary to understand where this text stands in relation to his preceding works. Levi's first publication, which appeared in 1946, was a report that he and another survivor, the physician Leonardo Debenedetti, wrote detailing the conditions of death and disease in Auschwitz. Requested by the Soviet government, the report was then lengthened by its two authors and published in *Minerva medica*, an Italian medical journal. Levi's first authorship thus depended on his scientific persona for both its authority and its subject matter.

He then turned to the writing of his memoirs, *Survival in Auschwitz*, which appeared the next year, 1947. Followed by its sequel in 1962, *The Reawakening,* Levi began publishing stories that can best be characterized as science fiction, *Storie naturali* (Natural Stories) in 1966 and *Vizio di forma* (Structural Defect) in 1971. The subject of these science fiction stories ranges from machines that can write poetry and imitate life-forms to stories that are parables about the devastation done to science by the moral abyss of the Holocaust. Science as a discipline is put into crisis in some of these stories, in which scientific progress, achieved through human experimentation, is more important that the survival of the human subject.[2]

After these two collections of science fiction, Levi wrote *The Periodic Table,* published in 1975. The text can well be described as an autobiography of his life as a chemist, yet we also learn of his reactions to Fascist persecution of the Jews, to the early years of the war, and to his own identity as a Jew in Italy. Levi discusses his scientific vocation, which he felt at an early age, and details his experiences trying to become a chemist and graduate from the university despite the antisemitic racial laws of 1938. He describes his text in the following way in an interview published in 1984 in the journal *Prooftexts:* "the book goes beyond simple autobiography. Rather, it contains the story of a generation. . . . [T]he chapters entitled Argon, Zinc and Gold . . . refer to the situations and events preceding my deportation, and reflect my condition as a Jew in Mussolini's Italy: assimilated and integrated, but not Fascist. Argon is a gas which does not interact with other gases."[3]

Levi was most likely influenced by the fact that in the 1960s and 1970s, intellectuals in Italy and elsewhere were debating the role of science in society and the relationship between science and literature.[4] Given this, it is quite interesting that Levi chose to write his science fiction before writing the story of his life as a chemist. The science fiction allowed Levi to explore scientific issues in a fictive realm, perhaps preparing him to confront the real concerns about science he faced during his life, concerns which he explores in *The Periodic Table.* One sees the interplay of the literary mode and the scientific mode in Levi's writings, not only in terms of subject matter but in terms of his narrative strategies and literary outlook. As Cesare Cases affirms, "humanistic culture and scientific culture are at the base of that mixture of comprehension and of legitimate incomprehension that allowed Levi to write his best books."[5]

In *The Periodic Table*, the elements of the table function as catalysts for recalling historical moments in the author's life, often serving as metaphors for specific experiences. Science is thus both an organizing principle and a way to experience history. The text can be divided into three parts: the early years of the war before deportation, some fictive stories, and the postwar period. The first chapters deal with his education as a scientist, with the political atmosphere in Italy during the first years of the war, and with his first job as a chemist after his graduation from the university. There are two fictive stories which are found in the middle of the text, written during those years, then one more chapter which treats another early job, before deportation. The next chapter, "Gold," recounts his capture by Fascist militia, which led to his deportation. This event and his subsequent thirteen months in Auschwitz serve as a point of demarcation in the text, beginning with the chapter entitled "Cerium," which tells of his time working as a chemist in Auschwitz. The last stories, with one brief fictive interlude, confront his experiences as a working chemist after the war.

As the text is roughly chronological in composition, tension increases as the reader gets closer to the central event in Levi's life which marked him as a writer and as a philosopher. What is not immediately apparent in this text is the way in which deportation marked him as a scientist, and how the activity of science inscribed itself onto his philosophy. If we look for any overt philosophy of science in *The Periodic Table* as the most logical site for such a discourse in Levi's works, we are bound to be disappointed. The Nobel prize–winning physicist, Salvador Luria, in his review of *The Periodic Table*, goes so far as to say that "The book . . . is not about chemistry but about the personal and emotional development of the writer."[6] Nonetheless, because *The Periodic Table* uses science as its central theme and because we cannot separate chemistry from his development as a writer, it remains an important source for his philosophy on the discipline, expressed at times either indirectly or through a displacement of these concerns onto cultural and historical issues.[7] A close reading of *The Periodic Table* does reveal an obliquely articulated philosophy of science, a philosophy which permeates Levi's other works as well. In order to understand what is at stake for Levi in this philosophy and why it is that he does not articulate it more directly, it is necessary to look at the development of his ideas about science in this text, beginning with the early chapters.

The first chapter of the text, "Argon," does not discuss science at all, but rather consists of a discourse on Levi's ancestors and their difficult semi-assimilation into Piedmontese society. In this beginning to his text, Levi introduces nonscientific topics: antisemitism, tolerance/intolerance between groups, cultural mixes. "Argon," or "inert, noble gases," is defined as a scientific term, but then immediately appropriated as a metaphor to describe these relatives: "the little I know about my ancestors presents many similarities to these gases" (p. 4). Levi thus makes it clear from the beginning that science can be used metaphorically to shed light on other topics besides itself. It is in the second chapter, entitled "Hydrogen," where Levi will start to review his own involvement with science as a discipline. He discusses his early feelings about science in terms of a religious relevation:

> For me chemistry represented an indefinite cloud of future potentialities which enveloped my life to come in black volutes torn by fiery flashes, like those which had hidden Mount Sinai. Like Moses, from that cloud I expected my law, the principle of order in me, around me, and in the world. I was fed up with books . . . and searched for another key to the highest truths. (pp. 22–23)

Levi has situated his early sentiments about his discipline within a clearly Judaic context. This is a significant move for Levi, given his broad secular education within a strongly Catholic milieu. Elsewhere in his work, Levi in fact is much more likely to use Christian models such as Augustine and Dante rather than Jewish sources. Levi's view of science at this early age is relentlessly optimistic, as he believed that science could unlock the secrets of the universe. His view of science as that which can reveal the highest truths is a traditional one which posits science as not only able to discover those truths, but implicitly trusts science to handle the responsibility of that knowledge. The double simile of Mt. Sinai as the place from whence the revelation of scientific law and Levi's self-figuration as Moses, the recipient of the law, emphasizes this ennobling view of science and frames it within a religious, God-given experience that is unchallengeable from a secular point of view. Moses and Sinai occupy a primal position as a revelatory episode, a position which mimics the primal nature of the revelation for Levi as both the beginning of his career and the inspiration for it. The choice of the Moses-Sinai metaphor also establishes him as a Jewish scientist who takes his inspiration from a specifically Judaic revelatory moment.

Early in his education, Levi chooses chemistry as that revelatory science. In an episode he recounts that took place at the beginning of his studies at the university, Levi tries to communicate his enthusiasm about chemistry to one of his classmates, Sandro:

> Sandro was surprised when I tried to explain to him some of the ideas that at the time I was confusedly cultivating. That the nobility of Man, acquired in a hundred centuries of trial and error, lay in making himself the conqueror of matter and that I had enrolled in chemistry because I wanted to remain faithful to this nobility. That conquering matter is to understand it, and understanding matter is necessary to understanding the universe and ourselves: and that therefore Mendeleev's Periodic Table . . . was poetry. (p. 41)

Levi challenges his friend Sandro to think about chemistry as an antidote to Fascist lies, calling chemistry "the bridge between the world of words and the world of things" (p. 42).

Levi, however, will not maintain this concept of science as revelatory and untouchable. As his career progresses, his view matures and changes. Fascism as a backdrop to Levi's educational experience at the university has much to do with this metamorphosis. Levi's intellectual discoveries as a student are described on a trajectory that intersects at many points with the political environment of Fascism and the early years of the war. His life at the university was made difficult due to the antisemitic racial laws enacted in 1938 and 1939. These laws severely limited the rights of Jews in Italy: for example, Jewish students were generally expelled from public schools, including the universities. Levi did manage to remain, but his options were limited. The relationship between science and politics which so affected Levi in these early years will remain a concern for him throughout his career.

The chapter entitled "Potassium" is especially relevant to Levi's understanding that his beloved chemistry must exist in the world, rather than as a set of abstract concepts. This chapter begins with an assessment of the war in 1941 and the state of resistance to Fascism in Italy at that time, which Levi describes as only a passive resistance, rather than the active resistance which took root after the German invasion of Italy in 1943. At this point in his education, Levi begins to seriously question chemistry and its ability to be a source of certainty, to provide some answers to his questions:

> Chemistry, for me, had stopped being such a source . . . having reached the fourth year of Pure Chemistry, I could no longer ignore the fact that chemistry itself, or at least that which we were being administered, did not answer my questions . . . did chemistry theorems exist? No: therefore you had to go further . . . go back to the origins, to mathematics and physics. The origins of chemistry were ignoble, or at least equivocal: the dens of the alchemists, their abominable hodgepodge of ideas and language, their confessed interest in gold, their Levantine swindles typical of charlatans or magicians. (pp. 52–53)

Levi, with some difficulty, finds an instructor in astrophysics willing to take him on as a disciple. But even with his doubts regarding chemistry, Levi ultimately rejects physics and returns to chemistry. He clearly delineates this return as motivated by the political situation around him:

> During those months, the Germans destroyed Belgrade, broke the Greek resistance, invaded Crete from the air: that was the Truth, that was the Reality. There were no escape routes, or not for me.

24

Better to remain on the Earth, playing with the dipoles for lack of anything better, purify benzene and prepare for an unknown but imminent and certainly tragic future. (p. 57)

At the end of this episode, Levi has an accident when he tries to distill potassium hydroxide, a typical chemistry lab occurrence involving a burst flask, a small fire, and some panic. When he tells the instructor of the accident, the difference between science in the abstract and a more physical science becomes clearer to him:

> The assistant looked at me with an amused, vaguely ironic expression: better not to do than to do, better to meditate than to act, better his astrophysics, the threshold of the Unknowable, than my chemistry, a mess compounded of stenches, explosions, and small futile mysteries. I thought of another moral, more down to earth and concrete, and I believe that every militant chemist can confirm it: that one must distrust the almost-the-same (sodium is almost the same as potassium, but with sodium nothing would have happened), . . . the differences can be small, but they can lead to radically different consequences, like a railroad's switch points; the chemist's trade consists in good part in being aware of these differences, knowing them close up, and foreseeing their effects. And not only the chemist's trade. (p. 60)

Ending his chapter on this enigmatic note, Levi has articulated, however obliquely, his expectations of the scientific discipline he has chosen, as well as its weaknesses. Even though chemistry has failed his expectations as a discipline that could answer larger questions and satisfy his intellectual curiosity, Levi has chosen to return to it. Its hands-on quality attracts him precisely because of the imminent catastrophe of the war around him, even though he remains discontent in his search for bigger answers that could potentially explain the state of the world that created that war. At the same time, this discourse about the chemist's trade and the need to be able to distinguish the importance of small differences is crucial to Levi's philosophy about militancy and science. He uses the term "militant chemist" and "militant chemistry" several times in this text, as a way of attempting to bridge that gap he has identified between the social/political context and the world of ideas to which he is so strongly attracted. There is much at stake here for Levi, as he sees the kind of blindness and paralysis the astrophysicist demonstrates and advocates as dangerously apolitical in a dangerously political world.

Let us examine more closely this category of militancy that Levi depends on. Militant, from military, is a weaker term in Italian than it is in English: they share the same origin, "milus," or soldier, but in English, militant is stronger and more aggressive than in Italian, where there are two primary uses of the term. In Italian it can either indicate an active member of one's profession or group, like "la chiesa militante," the militant church, meaning an involved, active church. Levi's use of the term, however, is most likely modeled after the second meaning, "la critica militante," or militant criticism, a Gramschian term which became popular in Italy during the late 1960s and 1970s, and indicates involvement in the politics of the time, in other words "engagé." But neither definition really works very well in conjunction with chemistry. Even if we take the weaker meaning, as someone merely active within a profession, Levi has strayed beyond this definition by his oblique statement in this passage regarding the applicability of the method of militant chemists to "not only the chemist's trade." And "militant" in the sense of political involvement applied to chemistry makes even less sense. What resonance does that have after the kind of critique of chemistry and physics he establishes in *The Periodic Table,* a critique based largely on these disciplines' inability to interact meaningfully with the war?

When Levi ends his chapter with those enigmatic words about confusing likenesses and how important it is to be able to distinguish, and not just for the chemist, we begin to understand that his agenda is not so much the description of chemistry in his text as a certain kind of intellectual and practical activity, and his role in that activity. It is rather the importance of understanding the role of science in the world in which it operates, even though he has thematized a separation of science and the world in several places in his text. Yet chemistry has generally not been a politically engaged discipline. What then is Levi after here, in his use of a term which from several points of view doesn't make sense? A militant chemistry where militancy does not exist? It is my contention that Levi uses the term "militant chemist" to both point out this shortcoming, in an ironic way, and express his desire for this category to change, to become true: in other words, a call for his profession to become involved in times of need. He realizes that, as Mirna Cicioni has put it, "knowledge is the necessary but not sufficient condition to change reality."[8] And his timing is crucial: the chapter "Potassium" signals not only the end of his university career but the end of his quest for a profession. His disappointment about his science and the imperfect relationship of science to social issues which is particularly poignant in this episode of potassium influenced his writings about science throughout his career.

The next section of *The Periodic Table* deals with Levi's graduation from the university and his first jobs as a chemist. In the first of these jobs, entitled "Nickel," Levi works for a mine seeking to extract nickel from otherwise worthless rock. Levi dedicates himself to this thankless and ultimately unsuccessful task but only later, in other words after the war, realizes that any nickel he could have helped gather would have gone directly to Fascist Italy and Hitler Germany's war efforts. This is the first moment in which his own efforts within his chosen discipline could have had a resoundingly negative material and political effect. At this point in time, however, he is still thinking about science as a method of solving mysteries without taking into account long-term results. It will take his experience at Auschwitz to make the connections among industry, technology, science, and politics really take hold.

The chapter entitled "Gold" recounts Levi's brief experience as a partisan and his capture by Fascist militia before being deported to Auschwitz in January 1944. In the next chapter, "Cerium," Levi acknowledges the fact that he is now a different man

27

than the one whose life he has recounted in the early chapters of this book, and tells his readers that he has trouble recognizing the man who survived the Auschwitz experience:

> The fact that I, a chemist, engaged here in writing my stories about chemistry, have lived a different season, has been narrated elsewhere.
>
> At the distance of thirty years I find it difficult to reconstruct the sort of human being that corresponded, in November 1944, to my name, or, better, to my number: 174517. I must have by then overcome the most terrible crisis, the crisis of having become part of Lager system, and I must have developed a strange callousness if I then managed to think, to register the world around me, and even to perform rather delicate work, in an environment infected by the daily presence of death. (pp. 139–140)[9]

This beginning to the only episode he recounts of his time in Auschwitz reflects a rupture in Levi's narrative on several levels. At this point it becomes a more complicated conversion narrative. In *The Periodic Table*, Levi the mature chemist tells of his early life becoming a chemist. He is now referring to an absent narrative, *Survival in Auschwitz*, which narrates the fuller story of his time there, while he acknowledges that this was a different self whom he has trouble recognizing now. We thus have the early Levi, whose formation is discussed at length in this text, the mature Levi, who is the self who does the recounting, and the Levi who went through the concentration camp experience, to some degree unrecognizable to his more mature self. Yet the theme of chemistry links all three, and it is precisely the experience of the Holocaust, the existence of that third self, which accounts for much of Levi's formation as a thinker and as a philosopher about science. It is important to remember that Levi functioned as a chemist in Buna-Monowitz, a subcamp of Auschwitz, because of the Third Reich's selling of slave labor to major industries. Levi's chemical knowledge was put to work in the service of creating artificial rubber for IG Farben. The death or survival of their slave labor was a matter of absolute indifference to the civilian company. It is here that we see the politicization of science in its relation to industry for Levi, in a most problematic way. He attributes his survival of the concentration camp at least partially to the fact that as a chemist he was given a physically easy job, that helped him get through the second winter in the camp without backbreaking physical labor. At the same time, his knowledge of chemistry was exploited and had it been successful, potentially could have helped the German war effort. In the end, the artificial rubber was never produced. But the situation nonetheless left Levi in a state of moral and professional ambiguity, which his high level of personal integrity prompts him to acknowledge.

In the last section of *The Periodic Table*, there are two chapters which illustrate issues central to Levi's complex notion of science. One of these chapters demonstrates a successful moral, though failed science, and the other recounts a successful scientific experiment, but a failed moral one. Their differences and their interaction help fill out the complicated story of Levi's relationship to his discipline.

Significantly, the stories are both of the post-Auschwitz period. The first, entitled "Nitrogen," recounts one of the jobs that Levi undertook as a struggling young chemist after the war. He was asked by a lipstick manufacturer to find a substance that would make the lipstick's color stay on longer. The lipstick maker, described as a very sleazy character, wanted him to use a chemical, alloxan, that would impart a permanent color, rather than using a more expensive pigment. Levi discovers after doing some research that uric acid is the best source of alloxan, and that the most convenient source for uric acid is chickenshit, "la pollina" as the people in the countryside around Turin call it. He goes around and collects some, with notable difficulty and at a high price since it is valued as a fertilizer, goes back to his lab, and tries to separate the alloxan from the rest, which he describes as a filthy mixture of dirt, feathers, pebbles, and lice. The distance between that filth and the ultimate product does not concern him:

> The fact that alloxan, destined to embellish ladies' lips, would come
> from the excrement of chickens or pythons was a thought which
> didn't trouble me for a moment. The trade of a chemist (fortified,

in my case, by the experience of Auschwitz) teaches you to overcome, indeed to ignore, certain revulsions that are neither necessary or congenital: matter is matter, neither noble nor vile, infinitely
transformable, and its proximate origin is of no importance whatsoever. (pp. 180–181)[10]

In the end, Levi's discourse on the irrelevance of the origin
of the alloxan becomes irrelevant itself, as he recounts the results
of the attempt to separate the alloxan from the rest:

All I got were foul vapors, boredom, humiliation, and a black and
murky liquid . . . which displayed no tendency to crystallize, as the
text declared it should. The shit remained shit, and the alloxan and
its resonant name remained a resonant name. That was not the way
to get out of the swamps: by what path would I therefore get out, I
the discouraged author of a book which seemed good to me but
which nobody read? Best to return among the colorless but safe
schemes of inorganic chemistry. (p. 183)[11]

What Levi has produced here is a failed chemical experiment,
but framed in much larger terms. Twice he has referred to his
Auschwitz experience in these two citations: the first time when
he says that his trade as a chemist was fortified by his Auschwitz
experience, and the second by mentioning his authorship of a
book that at the time no one was reading. This is a reference to
the first edition of *Survival in Auschwitz,* turned down by Einaudi
and other major publishers in 1947 when Levi first completed it,
then published in a limited edition by a small publisher, and virtually ignored for several years. By evoking Auschwitz in connection with this experiment, Levi is raising the stakes considerably
on the meaning of this failed science. In looking at the relation
between Levi's Auschwitz experience and his other works, Cesare
Cases refers to "the dichotomy between the two spheres of 'foul'
and 'fair' that was at the base of Levi's first book."[12] Through his
mentioning Auschwitz, Levi reminds us of a world in which fair
is foul and foul is fair, the central figure of inversion through
which he attempts to understand his experience in the camp and
the Holocaust as a whole. In this lipstick episode, inversion is also

a main operating principle, as the charade of beauty attempts to cover up what is essentially foul.

But here at least there is an obstacle to the success of the experiment: "fowl" remains foul. Matter, according to Levi, is neither noble nor vile, yet in this experiment it remains vile. The origin of that alloxan *is* important after all, despite Levi's statement to the contrary, and despite the theory of the chemical textbook, which said that it should have crystallized, in other words *been separable* from its origins. Inversion, as the principle through which the chemist can bend or transform matter to his will, has failed him. Reading itself, as an activity that should be instructive, revealing either the secrets of the chemical world or those of Auschwitz, has failed too: the textbook was wrong and no one is reading his book.

At the same time, however, the ethical question in the story shares a different fate from that of the chemical question: Levi is unable to help the bully unethically solve his lipstick problem, and so a lipstick that would permanently stain is not possible because foul has remained foul, refusing to play the charade of fair. There is a certain built-in ambivalence about the ethical question, however: due to the exigencies of the economic situation after the war, Levi cannot afford to turn down any jobs and so he must work for this bully and his lipstick charade. Even though Levi claims that the origin of the alloxan does not bother him, the message regarding the failure of this experiment is mixed. Its very failure to some degree exonerates and distances him from its foulness and from the foulness of the character of the bully. Yet at the same time it is a failure of science to do what was expected, which generates disappointment on Levi's part. Because of failed science and a failed theory about science, the asked-for ethical compromise on Levi's part is not possible. At the end, he acknowledges defeat and states his desire to return to inorganic chemistry, away from the temptations of foul and fair, away from a confused world in which failed science can mean the reestablishment of ethical priorities.

In the chapter, "Vanadium," we have the opposite of what we found in "Nitrogen": namely, that successful science means failed

31

ethics. It is no accident that this penultimate chapter of *The Periodic Table* recounts Levi's epistolary encounter with Dr. Müller, who was the chemist that oversaw Levi's slave labor as a chemist in Auschwitz. This is one of Levi's most striking chapters, in fact Ruth Angress has called it "one of the most meaningful post-Holocaust survivor stories."[13] The way in which Levi discovers Müller speaks to Levi's abilities both as a close reader and as a detective: in his public relations position in a paint factory, Levi corresponds with a German company that made a defective resin. This resin is responsible in turn for ruining some varnish that Levi's factory makes. In analyzing the defect in the varnish, Levi writes to the German company, to a certain Dr. Müller:

> Müller. There was a Müller in my previous incarnation, but Müller is a very common name in Germany . . . and yet, rereading the two letters with their heavy, lumbering phrasing encumbered with technical jargon, I could not quiet a doubt . . . and then, all of a sudden, there rose before my eyes a detail of the last letter which had escaped me: it was not a typing mistake, it was repeated twice; it said "naptenate," not "naphthenate" as it should be. Now I conserve pathologically precise memories of my encounters in that by now remote world: well, that other Müller too, in an unforgotten lab full of freezing cold, hope, and fear, used to say "beta-Naptylamin" instead of "beta-Naphthylamin. (p. 213)[14]

Levi recognizes this idiosyncratic spelling as the same pronunciation anomaly that the Dr. Müller of Auschwitz used to make. He recognizes it, however, in a different word, which is what makes Levi's abilities as a close reader stand out, and he is able to translate it from a spelling difference to Müller's speech variant. The close reading sets the pace for the rest of this episode, in which his capacity to carefully read Müller, and Müller's intentions, becomes crucial. Continuing in the detective mode, he conducts discreet inquiries about the man and discovers that the two Dr. Müllers are one and the same.[15] A dual correspondence is begun: the first one Levi conducts in his official role as company representative, demanding retribution for the shipment of defective chemicals. The second correspondence is private, as

Levi asks Müller if he *is* the Müller from Auschwitz and sends him a copy of the German translation of *Survival in Auschwitz*. When he receives a reply to the affirmative, he writes to Müller again, setting up a kind of moral experiment. He asks Müller if he has accepted the judgments of his book, and he asks him as well his opinion of the role of IG Farben in the slave labor trade, and about Auschwitz itself. Müller's long reply to Levi's second private letter is full of self-deception and equivocations regarding most of these issues and demonstrates as well a need to protect IG Farben, since the company Müller now works for is an off-shoot of it:

> He attributed the events at Auschwitz to Man, without differentia-
> tion. . . . He affirmed that he had had a relationship with me almost
> of friendship between equals; that he had conversed with me about
> scientific problems and had meditated, on this occasion, on what
> "precious human values are destroyed by other men out of pure
> brutality." Not only did I not remember any such conversations
> (and my memory of that period, as I have said, is excellent), but
> against the background of disintegration, mutual distrust, and mor-
> tal weariness, the mere supposition of them was totally outside re-
> ality. . . . To my question about IG Farben he answered curtly that,
> yes, it had employed prisoners, but only to protect them. (pp. 219–
> 220)[16]

Müller even goes so far as to claim that the entire Buna-Monowitz installation that was part of Auschwitz had been created to pro-tect Jews and that orders to the contrary were a camouflage. He denies having had any knowledge of the huge numbers of people murdered nearby.

At about the same time Levi receives an official letter from Müller, dated the same as the private letter, announcing his com-pany's intention to assume blame for the defective varnish and to make reparations. The simultaneous epistolary resolution of both problems, at least from Müller's point of view, leaves Levi understanding more than just Müller's revisionist view on the Holocaust. The chemical issue has been settled, both in and out of the laboratory. The reason that the varnish would not harden has been found, the company with whom Levi's firm disputed the matter has given satisfaction, but the larger issues raised by Müller's response have not been put to rest, in fact they resist settlement.

Part of the problem is indeed the relationship between the wartime IG Farben, its postwar offshoot, and the role that Müller plays in both companies.[17] Müller functioned as a manager of slave labor for IG Farben and as a service representative for the offshoot company. Müller is a reflection of Farben's lack of remorse and inability to admit the truth vis-à-vis its wartime activities, not only through his repeating those myths to Levi in his letter regarding the company's purported efforts to protect the Jews, and its ignorance of mass murder, but through his settling of this paint dispute with Levi. In this episode, the relationship of the personal (Levi's private correspondence with Müller) and the institutional (the paint dispute) reflects Levi's concern with some larger issues, namely individual complicity and the role of personal and institutional responsibility during the Third Reich. The willingness of the offshoot company to settle a minor dispute over varnish is not indicative of Farben's willingness to accept responsibility for its own activities; it functions instead as a red herring. A small paint dispute is relatively easy to settle, agreements are easily reached once one company admits liability. But settling accounts on the part of companies engaged in exploiting slave labor during the Holocaust is a different matter, precisely because IG Farben admits no liability, minimalizing and lying about its own role, through its past and present accomplice/representative, Müller. The relationship of IG Farben to the postwar offshoot attempts to function as an unproblematic genealogical relationship whose logic of culpability becomes mutually exonerative: in other words, since the offshoot company readily admits liability, and the offshoot company is genealogically tied to its parent, IG Farben, then it stands to reason that had Farben done any wrong it would admit guilt, if there was liability to be admitted. Levi unmasks this false logic through his expert reading, thereby exposing Farben's self-representation as a socially responsible company as the sham it really is.

Is Levi demonstrating a failure of reading and writing, at least on matters larger than chemistry? Müller has evidently not understood Levi's book, and his letter about Auschwitz and IG Farben is constructed entirely to protect both himself and his company from blame. The mode of close reading with which Levi begins this episode leads to his uncovering a moral and ethical failure. Here chemistry can succeed, in other words he can figure out the origin of the defect in the varnish, but at the expense of a much more important resolution. The capacity of science to respond to an ethical dilemma is put into question, as it often is in Levi's science fiction. Even more remarkable here, however, is the way in which reading and writing are challenged, as those activities which connect the world of available information to that of action or moral resolution. But because Levi has uncovered the bad faith behind Müller and Farben's self-representation, reading as a mode of arriving at the truth, at least for us as readers if not for Müller, has been salvaged at least in part, even if reading is shown to be to a certain degree unpredictable and out of control. Reading and writing can be redemptive, through the potential of achieving a genuine understanding, but they can propagate falsehood as well, and the tension between the two extremes fuels Levi's tale.

Science in Levi's works serves as both an underpinning for his philosophy, and a way to get at ethical issues, even when science must fail in order to illustrate his concerns. The contradictions that arise from the scientific dilemmas that Levi recounts are not articulated vis-à-vis the nature of science itself, except in terms of the propensity of science to fail ethically. It falls upon us, as readers, to follow Levi's example in "Vanadium" and read closely and perhaps redemptively in order to understand the role of science in Levi's world and, on a larger scale, the problematic relationship of science to the Holocaust itself. These last chapters in *The Periodic Table* work to challenge science quite directly and to bring together concerns regarding the relationship between ethics and science and the history which has affected both.

Levi's views on science marked out in *The Periodic Table* continue to retain this ambivalence even into the period of his latest writings. Published in 1985, some ten years after *The Periodic Table*, a short essay entitled, "News from the Sky," further illuminates just how complex Levi's understanding is of the role of science in culture, through a statement which in part contradicts the readings of science he sets forth elsewhere. The essay begins with Immanuel Kant's belief that there are "two wonders in creation, the starry sky over his head and the moral law within him." As a Holocaust survivor, Levi takes some strong exception to the notion of a moral law within, but he affirms the wonder of the starry sky through the great potential of science. He ends his essay on this ambiguous note:

> The future of humanity is uncertain, even in the most prosperous countries, and the quality of life deteriorates; and yet I believe that what is being discovered about the infinitely large and the infinitely small is sufficient to absolve this end of the century and millenium. What a very few are acquiring in knowledge of the physical world will perhaps cause this period not to be judged as a pure return to barbarism.[18]

Cesare Cases states that Levi, deep down, believes that scientific rationalism can put back on track not only Levi himself, as a survivor deeply wounded by the events of the Holocaust, but society in general. The citation from "News from the Sky" supports that theory of an optimistic outlook on scientific potential only to a certain degree. Levi's use of the word "perhaps" at the end speaks volumes: he would like our age not to be judged as only barbarism, but he is not at all sure that this will in fact be the outcome. The desire, nonetheless, is there. As a man deeply committed to scientific rationalism, Levi is torn between a need to see science as unproblematic progress, motivated by his own professional allegiance to his discipline, and his own experience, in which science is deeply politicized and ultimately corruptible. This conflict emerges in Levi's writings as the varying ability of science to both destroy and to absolve human failings. These views are set up in opposition, if not always through his own statements on the matter, then in the sometimes contradictory and always complex examples he gives of the operations of science in the world. No reassuring, tranquil or easy response to the dilemma posed by science is possible on Levi's part, given the breadth of his reactions to scientific potential for harm.

NOTES

1. There have been several studies done on the role of medical science, genetics, and anthropology in the Third Reich. See, for example, George J. Annas and Michael A. Grodin, eds. *The Nazi Doctors and the Nuremberg Code* (New York and Oxford: Oxford University Press, 1992); Robert Proctor, *Racial Hygiene: Medicine under the Nazis* (Cambridge, Mass.: Harvard University Press, 1988); and Benno Müller-Hill, *Murderous Science: Elimination by Scientific Selection of Jews, Gypsies and Others, Germany 1933–1945* (Oxford and New York: Oxford University Press, 1988). Chemistry has also played a role in mass destruction. World War I was known as "the chemical war" because of the implementation of poison gas as a weapon for the first time. Chemistry played a role in the Holocaust as well, as the use of cyclon-B, the gas used in the gas chambers, was studied and decided upon as an efficient killing method. Levi refers to this choice in the preface to *The Drowned and the Saved* (trans. Raymond Rosenthal [New York: Summit Books, 1988]).

2. For example, see "Versamina," and "Angelica Farfalla," both in *Storie naturali*. For a discussion of medical experiments in "Versamina," see Nancy Harrowitz, "Primo Levi's Science as 'Evil Nurse': The Lesson of Inversion," in *Memory and Mastery: The Legacy of Primo Levi*, ed. Roberta Kremer, forthcoming.

3. Primo Levi, "Beyond Survival," in *Prooftexts* 4, no. 1 (1984).

4. For further discussion, see Mirna Cicioni, *Primo Levi: Bridges of Knowledge* (Oxford and Washington: Berg Publishers, 1995), ch. 3.

5. "La cultura umanistica e quella scientifica sono alla base di quel miscuglio di comprensione e legittima incomprehensione che ha permesso a Levi di scrivere i suoi libri migliori." (Cesare Cases, "Levi ripensa l'assurdo," in *Patrie lettere* [Milano: Einaudi, 1987], 145. My translation.)

6. Salvador Luria, review of *The Periodic Table* in *Science*, April 5, 1985.

7. Levi himself discusses the relationship of chemistry to his writing in *L'altrui mestiere* (Torino: G. Eiunaudi, 1985); English translation, *Other People's Trades*, trans. Raymond Rosenthal (New York: Summit Books, 1989). Page numbers for the English edition of *The Periodic Table* cited in parentheses refer to the translation by Raymond Rosenthal (New York: Schocken, 1984).

8. Cicioni, *Primo Levi*, p. 75.

9. Che io chimico, intento a scrivere qui le mie cose di chimico, abbia vissuto una stagione diversa, é stata raccontata altrove. A distanza di trent'anni, mi riesce difficile ricostruire quale sorta di esemplare umano corrispondesse, nel novembre 1944, al mio nome, o meglio al mio numero 174517. Dovevo aver superato la crisi piú dura, quella dell'inserimento nell'ordine del Lager, e dovevo aver sviluppato una strana callositá, se allora riuscivo non solo a sopravvivere, ma anche a pensare, a registrare il mondo intorno a me, e perfino a svolgere un lavoro abbastanza delicato, in un ambiente infettato dalla presenza quotidiana della morte (p. 558)

10. Che poi l'allossana, destinata ad abbellire le labbra delle dame, scaturisse dagli escrementi delle galline o dei pitoni, era un pensiero che non mi turbava neanche un poco. Il mestiere di chimico (fortificato, nel mio caso, dall'esperienza di Auschwitz) insegna a superare, anzi ad ignorare, certi ribrezzi, che non hanno nulla di necessario né di congenito: la materia é materia, né nobile ne' vile, infinitamente trasformabile, e non importa affatto quale sia la sua origine prossima. (Levi, *Opere*, vol. 1, pp. 597–98)

11. Non ottenni che vapori immondi, noia, umiliazione, ed un liquido nero e torbido che . . . non mostrava alcuna tendenza a cristallizzare, come secondo il testo avrebbe dovuto. Lo sterco rimase sterco e l'allossana dal nome sonante un nome sonante. Non era quella la via per uscire dalla palude: per quale via ne sarei dunque uscito, io autore sfiduciato di un libro che a me sembrava bello, ma che nessuno leggeva? Meglio ritornare fra gli schemi scoloriti ma sicuri della chimica inorganica. (Levi, *Opere*, vol. 1, p. 600)

12. "la dicotomia tra le due sfere del 'foul' e 'fair' che era alla base del primo libro di Levi" (Cases, "Difesa di 'un' cretino," in *Patrie lettere*, p. 141. My translation).

13. Ruth K. Angress, "Primo Levi in English," in *Simon Wiesenthal Annual* 3 (1986), pp. 317–330, citation from p. 324.

14. Müller. C'era un Müller in una mia incarnazione precedente, ma Müller é un nome comunissimo in Germania . . . eppure, rileggendo le due lettere dal periodare pesantissimo, infarcite di tecnicismi, non riuscivo a far tacere un dubbio . . . e poi, ad un tratto, mi ritornó sott'occhio una particolaritá dell'ultima lettera che mi era sfuggita: non era un errore di battuta, era ripetuto due volte, stava proprio scritto "naptenat," non "napthenat," come avrebbe dovuto. Ora, degli incontri fatti in quel mondo ormai remoto io conservo memorie di una precisione patologica:

ebbene, anche quell'altro Müller, in un non dimenticato laboratorio pieno di gelo, di speranza e di spavento, diceva "beta-Naptylamin," anziché "beta-Naphthylamin." (Levi, *Opere*, vol. 1, p. 630)

15. The way in which many chapters of *The Periodic Table* depend on a detective approach has been discussed by JoAnn Cannon in "Chemistry and Writing in *The Periodic Table*," in *Reason and Light: Essays on Primo Levi*, ed. Susan Tarrow (Cornell University Western Societies Program, Occasional Paper No. 25, 1990), pp. 99–111.

16. Attribuiva i fatti di Auschwitz all'Uomo, senza differenziare
. . . con me, affermava di aver avuto un rapporto quasi di amicizia fra pari; di aver conversato con me di problemi scientifici, e di aver meditato, in questa circonstanza, su quali "preziosi valori umani venissero distratti da altri uomini per pura brutalità." Non solo io non ricordavo alcuna conversazione del genere e la mia memoria di quel periodo, come ho detto, é ottima), ma il solo supporre, su quello sfondo di disfacimento, di diffidenza reciproca e di stanchezza mortale, era del tutto fuori della realtá. . . . Alla mia domanda sulla IG Farben rispondeva che sí, aveva assunto prigionieri, ma solo per proteggerli. (Levi, *Opere*, vol. 1, pp. 634–35, 37)

17. For a discussion of the role of IG Farben in the slave labor trade during the Third Reich, see Benjamin B. Ferencz, *Less Than Slaves: Jewish Forced Labor and the Quest for Compensation*, (Cambridge, Mass.: Harvard University Press, 1979).

18. "L'avvenire dell'umanitá é incerto, anche nei paesi piú prosperi, e la qualitá della vita peggiora; eppure io credo che quanto si va scoprendo sull'infinitamente grande e sull'infinitamente piccolo sia sufficiente ad assolvere questa fine di secolo e di millenio. Quanto alcuni pochi stanno audacemente acquistando nella conoscenza del mondo fisico fará sí che questo periodo non sará giudicato un puro ritorno alle barbarie" (from *L'altrui mestiere*, p. 175). English translation from *Other People's Trades*, pp. 23–24.

ALAN ROSEN

The Specter of Eloquence:
Reading the Survivor's Voice

Several years ago a visiting scholar of French women's history lectured at Bar-Ilan University on women's memoirs of the French Revolution. She asserted that in the immediate aftermath of the revolution few memoirs were written; the memoirs that we know of proceed rather from a significant span of years after the event. She accounted for the delay in the writing of memoirs by recourse to the Holocaust, suggesting that just as it took years for survivors of the Holocaust to testify about that event, so did those who lived through the trauma of the French Revolution need a similar distance from the event before they could articulate their response.

Such a comparison seems beset by serious methodological and conceptual questions. Be that as it may, it was striking that the guiding assumption that underlay the comparison between the memoirs of trauma was that in the immediate aftermath of the Holocaust survivors did not write and did not testify. There was, according to this view, no early testimony to speak of.

It is this common popular and scholarly assumption that Annette Wieviorka's recent work on testimony seeks to redress.[1] Wieviorka argues persuasively that survivors did testify extensively in the aftermath of the war, indeed to a degree far greater proportionally than those who, in Wieviorka's comparison, lived

through the trauma of World War I. This recovery of early survivor testimony on the Holocaust has led Wieviorka to schema-
tize the career of testimony in two phases, suggesting that early
and late survivor testimony serve two different yet complemen-
tary functions. Whereas early testimony provides information
regarding what happened during the Holocaust, late testimony
transmits the memory of the event to succeeding generations.
Notably, Wieviorka associates these different functions of testimony with different media: in the movement from the early to
the late phase, "print has been replaced by the tape recorder and
the video camera" (p. 24). According to this schema, print is
linked to knowledge, tape to transmission; the written and the
oral have their own precincts, and the evolution of testimony can
be defined by the dominance of one or the other.

Indeed, the relation between early and late testimony has elsewhere been coded as the opposition between written and oral
texts, an opposition usually accompanied by the privileging of
one over the other. Lawrence Langer's recent work, articulating
a poetics of survivor testimony, foregrounds this model, privileging recent video accounts over earlier written memoirs.[2] For
Langer, the authority of video accounts is essentially linked to
the fact that they are spoken, not written, testimony. Obsessed
with closure, imprisoned within a set of artistic conventions, writing mediates testimony of the Holocaust in a way that, according
to Langer, deflects the witness (and the audience) from entering
the unique universe of the Holocaust. In contrast, oral testimony
is not constrained by the conventions that govern written testimony. Under the best of circumstances and when read correctly,
this lack of restraint allows oral testimony to circumvent normal
heroic, artistic, and moral conventions. Consequently, recent oral
testimony, because it is spoken, acquires a kind of narrative authority that earlier written memoirs do not.

Art Spiegelman's remarkable graphic novel, *Maus*, also sets
early and late testimony in an adversarial alignment, and represents this adversity, as Langer does, through the tension between
written and oral testimony.[3] Whereas Langer locates the authority of testimony clearly, however, Spiegelman never does. Rather,

depending on context, authority devolves alternately on the early, written memoir, or on the later, oral one. Ultimately, I would suggest, *Maus* establishes the authority of its vicarious testimony through the vital interplay of the two.

Similarly, Cynthia Ozick's novella, "Rosa," interrogates the nature of testimony by opposing early and late testimony, an opposition that, again, is linked to that of writing and speech.[4] In addition to thematic affinities, *Maus* and "Rosa" share historical ones as well, for both Spiegelman and Ozick wrote and published in the late 1970s and in the 1980s, a period that, moreover, initiated crucial changes in the status and representation of the survivor and testimony in American society and letters.[5] This essay will elaborate the strategies that Spiegelman employs in *Maus*, and, more briefly and schematically, that Ozick deploys in "Rosa" in using early and late testimony to give authority to the voice of the survivor.

II

In *Maus*, Spiegelman portrays a series of interviews that he conducted with his aging and testy father, Vladek, a Polish-Jewish survivor of the Holocaust. His father's story, related in a heavily accented English, includes vignettes from Poland in the 1930s, incarceration in Auschwitz and other concentration camps, liberation from Dachau at the end of the war, and, finally, a reunion with Anja, his wife, shortly thereafter. Though Anja, also a survivor of Auschwitz, is no longer alive when the interviews take place—she had committed suicide some ten years previously— Art tries to obtain not only his father's story but that of his mother as well. *Maus*, then, centrally records Spiegelman's effort in obtaining the victims' story(s), decoding it, and finding the appropriate means to relate it.

From the outset, Spiegelman represents Vladek's testimony as both authoritative and problematic. Speaking in a fractured English, suffering from the distractions caused by ill health (Art's interviews begin, he tells us, after Vladek's two heart attacks have taken their toll), shifting regularly and abruptly from one year to another, Vladek makes it difficult for Art to piece the story together. The issue of chronological development comes in for particular censure. Initially, the realization that the narration lacks coherence is Vladek's own: "Ach! Here I forgot to tell something from *before* I moved to Sosnowic but after our engagement was made" (1:20). Further on, Art takes Vladek to task because he has skipped from 1941 to 1943: "Wait! Please, Dad, if you don't keep your story chronological, I'll never get it straight" (1:82). To be sure, these comments on the nature of narrative process are meant to be read somewhat ironically; at bottom, it is not at all clear that a chronological narrative is most fitting for representing the Holocaust, that we are meant to "get it straight." But the incoherence of Vladek's narrative is something established from early on and emphasized, implicitly as well as explicitly, throughout *Maus*.

Given this quest for chronological rigor, Vladek's incoherent oral testimony appears problematic especially when set against the specter of Anja's earlier written testimony. Though the details concerning Anja's notebooks are few, the kind of testimony that they suggest contrasts pointedly with Vladek's. First, Anja wrote "her whole story from the start," terms that suggest a comprehensive and coherent narrative. Whereas Vladek's oral account, as represented by Spiegelman, jumps from episode to episode and digresses frequently, Anja's written memoir seemingly told the story of what happened step-by-step, progressing methodically from beginning to end. The contrast figures not only in narrative rigor but also in the language in which the testimony is transmitted: for Vladek, a broken English; for Anja, a fluent, even eloquent, Polish. Indeed, early in *Maus* we learn that Anja's Polish prose was known for its beauty: "And then," says Vladek, "she started writing to me such beautiful letters—almost nobody could write Polish like she wrote" (1:17). Even though these sentiments are meant to convey the admiration Vladek felt for his wife, they also establish Anja's Polish as a language of eloquence. Later, when we learn that the notebooks were also written in Polish, the previous associations of eloquence shape our response to this writing as well.

Spiegelman foregrounds the challenge Anja's early memoir poses to Vladek's authority by incorporating the story of Anja's memoir into the story of *Maus* itself. During the war Anja kept a diary but, says Vladek, "her diaries didn't survive from the war." After the war, Anja rewrote her story in a memoir, and it is this memoir which comprised the "Polish notebooks." When Art learns that Anja wrote a memoir of her experience, he becomes preoccupied with finding it. As Vladek's story unfolds, the search for Anja's "Polish notebooks" unfolds as well. In the culminating moment of *Maus I*, when Vladek tells Art that he destroyed the memoir, the tragic tale of Anja's notebooks looms so large that it virtually displaces Vladek's own. Significantly, however, although the memoir is gone, Art's preoccupation remains. Even in *Maus II*, well after Vladek has revealed (or remembered) that he destroyed the memoir, Art, in response to Vladek's assertion that he has found something for him, calls out, "Mom's diaries!" Once again, Vladek has to work hard to convince Art that the notebooks are "no more to speak. Those it's gone, finished" (2:113). Though always absent, the memoir is shaped by Spiegelman into a haunting narrative presence.

If the absent memoir haunts the survivor's tale his father tells—and more than one critic has used the vocabulary of haunting to describe the relation of Anja's memoir to *Maus*—Spiegelman himself uses the language of specters to refer to Richieu, the first child of Vladek and Anja, who was born before the war.[6] Once the war began and the Nazi occupation of Poland threatened Polish Jewry, the Spiegelmans decided to place Richieu under the care of a relative with the thought that it would improve his chances for survival. But he perished nonetheless. For Art, who was born after the war, the first Spiegelman child exists as a kind of a specter: "My ghost-brother," Art tells his wife, "since he got killed before I was born. He was only five or six" (2:15). Sharing a vocabulary of specters and haunting, child and diaries also suffer the common fate of being consumed by the Holocaust.

Critics who comment on the rivalry between Anja's and Vladek's testimony in *Maus* generally frame the conflict in terms of gender, either, as Marianne Hirsh has argued, emphasizing the absence and destruction of Anja's memoir as the suppression of the mother's/woman's voice, or, as Nancy Miller contends, viewing *Maus* itself as Spiegelman's attempt to return to his mother a testimony that Vladek wished to obliterate.[7] While the narrative of *Maus* invites such a gendered reading, the terms in which Spiegelman represents Anja's memoir emphasize not gender but the memoir's status as early testimony.

The destruction of the memoir illuminates exactly how crucial is this early status. Clearly, the destruction of Anja's memoirs is significant because it eliminates what would have been a major source of information for *Maus*. Additionally, Vladek's destruction of the memoir repeats a destruction that occurred earlier, that is, that occurred to the earliest testimony that Anja produced. To whatever degree, then, that the interview Art conducts with Vladek attempts to fill the space created by the annihilation of Anja's testimony, it does what Anja herself has already been compelled to do in rewriting her story: it engages in an act of testimonial and memorial reconstruction.

Although the testimony contained in Anja's notebooks is reconstructed, Spiegelman nonetheless complicates its chronological status, tempting the reader to think that the notebooks contain the earliest kind of Holocaust testimony to be found. Indeed, the scene in which Vladek first tells Art of the notebooks seems designed to generate such a misreading. When asked if the Polish notebooks are the diaries that Anja wrote during the war, Vladek answers "yes and also no," then tells how "her diaries didn't survive from the war; what you saw [around the house when growing up] she wrote after" (1:84). Vladek's paradoxical "yes and also no"—perhaps his most philosophically nuanced statement in *Maus*—blurs the status of the notebooks, leaving us unsure of whether they are eyewitness accounts written during the war or a memoir crafted after it.

A similar blurring of generic and temporal boundaries results from Art's own nomenclature: throughout *Maus*, he refers to Anja's writings mainly as "diaries," occasionally as "notebooks," but never uses the seemingly correct term, "memoirs."[8] It is as if Art's insistent but inexact use of the term "diary" is meant to elevate the stature of the testimony, conferring on it an indisputable authority. This equivocation remains even when, at a certain point, Spiegelman, as narrator rather than as character, seemingly tries to clarify the terms, referring to the Polish notebooks as "a wartime memoir" (2:6). But this designation itself only serves to clarify in one way, to confuse in another. For what exactly is a "wartime memoir"? And when exactly has it been written: "during" or "after"?

By obscuring the terms used to nominate genres of testimony, *Maus* intervenes in the more general discussion regarding the distinction between Holocaust diaries and memoirs, between chronicles penned during the Holocaust and those that were written afterwards. On the one hand, some critics claim that the distinction is essential, arguing that proximity to the events brought the most authentic record; distance from it produced something less authoritative.[9] Other critics contend that, since all writing is interpretive and mediated, the distinction between diary and memoir is perhaps useful but not essential, the proximity to and distance from the events not conclusive in establishing the authority of any given form of testimony.[10] In *Maus,* Spiegelman engages the issue without resolving it, allowing the notebooks to exist simultaneously as diary and memoir, enabling them to double both as testimony emerging from the war and as that which was reconstructed after it.

The uncertainty about just how "early" Anja's testimony is, the fact that her writing represents two different efforts at chronicling her experience, the studied ambiguity concerning the relation between these writings—these strategies suggest that Spiegelman alternately promotes the authority conferred on early or late testimony. And this shifting sense of testimonial authority can be seen nowhere more strongly than in the authority with which Spiegelman invests Vladek's fractured oral memoir.

Paradoxically, it is through its very lack of eloquence that Vladek's testimony acquires its authority.[11] Clearly, Vladek's accented English is mimetically appropriate for a Polish Jewish immigrant to America, and critics have noted in this light that Spiegelman has a good ear.[12] Importantly, however, among the survivors in *Maus*, it is only Vladek whose speech is fractured; it is for him alone that Spiegelman reserves the distortions of syntax, the malapropisms, the quirky idiom—the stylistic correlates, as it were, of an accent. Additionally, Spiegelman's strategies differ when representing past and present. For episodes in the past, Spiegelman uses a fluent, colloquial English to represent the languages of Europe as spoken by their native speakers; for episodes in the present, Vladek's broken, accented speech serves as a constant marker.

Hence Vladek's tortured visualized prose (the phrase is Nancy Miller's) is not only meant to represent an English-speaking foreigner but is also meant to torture English into being a foreign language. Indeed, this quality of "foreignness" is the means by which Vladek's ineloquent oral memoir can become a language of testimony. By fracturing Vladek's oral testimony, and by making it the most foreign language in *Maus*, Spiegelman uses it to convey the foreignness of the Holocaust itself. In this light, it is not eloquence but brokenness, not coherence but incoherence, not fluent Polish but accented English, not the intentionality of writing but the spontaneity of speech, and, finally, not the desirable proximity of early but the enabling distance of late testimony that can most ably represent the Holocaust.

Powerfully authoritative though Vladek's broken account may be, there is yet another level of testimonial authority in *Maus*. For the graphic novel *Maus* is itself not a speaking voice but a written (and drawn) text. More precisely, it is a "speakerly text," to use Henry Louis Gates' evocative term,[13] a narrative that inscribes a spoken voice within a written text, constructing a written narrative which, paradoxically, constantly calls attention to its orality, to its spokenness. Indeed, *Maus'* graphic medium seems perfectly suited to calling attention to this "speakerly" dimension of the text, not so much registering speech through the usual novelistic convention of quotation marks but rather *showing* speech through the comix convention of balloons.

Conscripting this "spokenness" through the voice of his father, Spiegelman links his written text to that of his mother. In this case, however, the specter of her absent text does not undermine but rather confers authority on his own. Initially, the association is suggested at the linguistic level, for, just as Anja's testimony was contained in "notebooks," so Art records his interviews with his father not, at first, with a tape recorder but within a "notebook" (1:44).[14] Yet Spiegelman also associates the written texts of mother and son through a deft manipulation of narrative. At one point, for example, Vladek searches, as he tells Art, "for the things [i.e., Anja's notebooks] you asked me last time" (1:104). While not finding what Anja wrote, he does find what Art wrote—and drew—*about* Anja: the early comix that depicts Anja's suicide, entitled "Prisoner on the Hell Planet: A Case History." Attempting then to locate one hidden text, Vladek discovers another in its stead. And the narrative link suggests the link between these hidden texts; Art's early work stands in for his mother's early testimony, thereby claiming implicitly for itself the authority of Anja's. The eloquence that was once thought to reside only in his mother's absent text now informs his own as well.

I I I

The dynamics of early and late testimony in *Maus* can be helpfully, if here only briefly, gauged through comparison with Cynthia Ozick's "Rosa," a novella conceived, written, serialized, and finally published in book form in the same decade as *Maus*. Linked in the period of production, *Maus* and "Rosa" also share many elements of plot: the daily, routine events in the life of aging Polish Jewish survivors register the damaging effects of the Holocaust years after.[15] More specifically, both protagonists lost a child during the war, and, while after the war they emigrate to America and make a new life, they also clearly never recover from this loss.

Additionally, and central to my concern here, Ozick also structures her story through the oppositions of early versus late and written versus oral testimony. In the case of "Rosa," however, it is the early oral testimony that yields to a more eloquent written form of witness. Despite the evolution of testimony that occurs over the course of the story, the earlier testimony continues to register its influence. Eventually, and remarkably, the only direct narration of the events of the Holocaust in "Rosa" takes place by means of a retrieval of the earlier testimony. Ultimately, Ozick, like Spiegelman, invests her story with testimonial authority by forging a speakerly text, a written text informed by the voice of a survivor.

In Ozick's novella, the earlier testimony refers to how the protagonist, Rosa, also a survivor from Poland, tells every customer who enters her New York antique shop the story of her incarceration in the Warsaw Ghetto. Her customers, however, flee from her—she refers to them as "deaf"—and their intransigence provokes Rosa, after some thirty years, to destroy her store, move to Florida, and take to writing letters, which à la Herzog, she never mails.[16]

Like *Maus*, Ozick's epistolary tale culminates in a remarkable scene pivoting on the confrontation between early and late testimony. Whereas in *Maus*, Spiegelman dramatizes the confrontation in a conversation between father and son, Ozick deftly stages the confrontation in a Polish letter written by Rosa to her deceased daughter, the second of two such letters to appear in the story. Initially, these aspects of the letter seem calculated to oppose the strategies of Rosa's earlier testimony: native Polish displaces adopted English; writing displaces speech; the intimate audience of the daughter displaces the impersonality of the customer. In every way, then—language, media, audience—the vehicle of the letter appears to supersede the previous means of bearing witness. As we will see, however, the content of the letter itself challenges the way such oppositions are to be read.

In complement to the formal aspects of the letter, there are two crucial features of its content. First, it is the only place in "Rosa" that directly narrates the events of the Holocaust. Unlike in the companion story, "The Shawl," where the story is set in a concentration camp, in "Rosa" Ozick refrains from virtually any direct reference to the events of the Holocaust or to the settings (ghettos, trains, camps, or death marches) in which it generally and terribly unfolded.[17] There are, to be sure, frequent allusions to the war years and to the brutal treatment that Rosa was compelled to endure, including the murder of her baby daughter. But on the whole, the story intently focuses on what Irving Howe calls the "aftermath," the life of an aging, eccentric survivor some three decades after the war came to an end.

It is therefore arresting when, shortly before the end of the story, Rosa's Polish letter describes the fate of her family in the Warsaw Ghetto, the privations they were made to suffer, the shock the uprooting and relocating caused to her upper-class, assimilated family. Even here, admittedly, the descriptions stop far short of what we know that Rosa underwent and what Ozick ventured to represent in "The Shawl." But within the terms established by the story, the narration in the letter is exceptional.

Second, and strikingly, the letter narrates these events not mimetically but diegetically, that is, not by recounting directly experiences in the ghetto but by reporting the interaction between Rosa and the customers in her shop, including, and featuring, what she would tell them about the ghetto. "When I had my store," Rosa begins the letter to her daughter, "I used to 'meet the public', and I wanted to tell everybody—not only our story, but other stories as well" (p. 66). Moreover, the conditions that she faced in trying to testify in her store govern the mode of testimony itself: "I used to pick out one little thing here, one little thing there, for each customer. And if I saw they were in a hurry— most of them were, after I began—I would tell just about the tramcar" (p. 67). The rest of the letter intermingles a detailed description of the tramcar that ran through the Warsaw Ghetto with an odd assortment of information about her family. Yet the context for this account remains Rosa's shop; the end of the letter reiterates that this is a story about an attempt to tell the story: "I said all this in my store," concludes Rosa, "talking to the deaf" (p. 67). In being compelled to listen to what has never actually been heard, the reader of "Rosa" encounters the events of the Holocaust only by way of a written report of the earlier oral testimony, a testimony that, moreover, was in its oral version repeatedly condemned to failure.

It seems that the letter is the site for the convergence of the early and the late, the oral and the written, and, as such, is meant to transform the failure into success for the reader of Ozick's story. I want to suggest that Ozick chose the letter as the vehicle to represent the Holocaust because letters are a transparently written form. And it is preeminently by means of the written text, paradoxically, that the survivor's voice can finally be heard.

I V

As we approach the end of the millennium, there is a sense that what is left to hear has been heard before. Indeed, it is this observation that sets in motion Wieviorka's typology of testimony, that moves her to form categories of early and late testimony with differing functions. For although she begins her essay with a celebration of Lanzman's *Shoah,* Wieviorka also notes that for historians like herself the voices of the witnesses in the film are familiar; they have been "heard" before, mainly in books published years ago. Her recovery of early testimony, then, has its price: what comes later, while valuable, is nevertheless derivative, has been heard before.

Like Wieviorka's argument, *Maus* and "Rosa" make clear that survivor testimony emerged early and that this early testimony continues to have authority. Yet Spiegelman and Ozick also refuse to honor one mode of testimony over the other. To be sure, they are writing at a crucial and convulsive moment in the history of American efforts to locate and define the role of the survivor and his or her testimony. It is an era (Ozick's term for it is "aural culture") when technological, social, and critical trends imply that written testimony is becoming obsolete, or perhaps simply superseded. This is one way of accounting for the emphasis Spiegelman and Ozick place on the capacity of the written form—in *Maus,* Anya's diaries or memoirs, in "Rosa," Rosa's Polish letter—to testify with unparalleled eloquence.

This polemical stand does not, however, lead Spiegelman or Ozick to demonize the oral memoir; it is rather the formidable powers that reside in written texts that they hope to celebrate and harness to the task of testimony. Yet they do this deviously, layering, as it were, voices on texts, texts on voices, so that one absorbs and enriches the other. Ultimately, through the remarkable convergences I refer to as a speakerly text, they seek to inscribe a survivor's voice within the medium of writing itself, and to draw upon the distinctive authority invested in early and late testimony to sustain, obliquely yet insistently, the claims that those voices make upon us.

NOTES

I would like to thank Ruth Clements, Rita Horwath, Kinereth Meyer, Joseph Polak, and Emmy Zitter for helpful readings of and comments on various stages of this manuscript.

1. Annette Wieviorka, "On Testimony," in *Holocaust Remembrance: The Shapes of Memory,* ed. Geoffrey H. Hartman (Oxford and Cambridge, Mass.: Blackwell, 1994), pp. 23–32.

2. Lawrence Langer, *Holocaust Testimonies: The Ruins of Memory* (New Haven and London: Yale University Press, 1991). Langer's study generally exalts oral testimony while pointing out the shortcomings of (even the best of) written memoirs: "when literary form, allusion, and style intrude on the surviving victim's [written] account, we risk forgetting where we are [in the abyss of the Holocaust] and imagine deceptive continuities" (p. 45). Oral, videotaped testimony, on the other hand, possesses "a freedom from the legacy of literary form and precedent"; this freedom allows oral testimony to "plunge deeper" into the "abyss" than is granted to authors of written memoirs. It needs to be pointed out that, in a footnote (p. 208), Langer counters what his own text implies, and claims that he does not wish to privilege one form of testimony over another. For a review of Langer's book and approach that engages these issues see David Roskies, "Through a Lens, Darkly," *Commentary* (Fall 1991): 58–59.

3. Art Spiegelman, *Maus: A Survivor's Tale* (New York: Pantheon, 1986); *Maus II: A Survivor's Tale* (New York: Pantheon, 1991). Unless otherwise indicated, all subsequent citations are to these editions. Admittedly, to foreground the narrative and rhetorical strategies of *Maus* seems perhaps to miss what is most singular about its approach to the Holocaust: the cartoons. But as I hope to show, this graphic novel compels attention to the shaping of its words.

4. Cynthia Ozick, "Rosa," in *The Shawl* (New York: Knopf, 1989). All subsequent citations are to this edition. Published initially in *The New Yorker* in 1983, "Rosa" was later issued together with Ozick's story, "The Shawl," in book form in 1989. But according to Ozick both stories were originally written in 1977. On the composition of the stories, see Ozick's remarks in Francine Prose, "Idolatry in Miami," review of *The Shawl,* by Cynthia Ozick, *New York Times Book Review,* 10 September 1989, p. 44. Spiegelman's project also began to take shape in the 1970s: he

53

based *Maus* on a series of interviews of his father conducted in 1972 and 1978. The first published installment of the Maus project appeared in 1972, but in a form substantially different from what was to become the book. The narrative that eventually became *Maus I* and *II* had its first airing in Spiegelman's underground comix, *Raw*, beginning in 1980 and continuing in periodic installments through 1991. See Art Spiegelman, *The Complete Maus*, CD-ROM (New York: Voyager, 1994). Both *Maus* and "Rosa," then, were projects that unfolded gradually over more than a decade, during which time each appeared serially prior to book publication.

5. Virtually all commentators observe this transformation; how they account for it varies considerably. For one of the best attempts by a literary historian to chronicle these developments up through 1980, see Sidra Ezrahi's "History Imagined: The Holocaust in American Literature," in her *By Words Alone: The Holocaust in Literature* (Chicago: University of Chicago Press, 1980). More recently, Alvin Rosenfeld, taking what he calls a "typological" rather than "chronological" approach, reviews what he sees to be some of the changes occurring in American representation of the Holocaust from the 1940s to the 1990s. See "The Americanization of the Holocaust," *Commentary* 99, no. 6 (1995): 35–40.

6. See, for instance, Nancy K. Miller, "Cartoons of the Self: Portrait of the Artist as a Young Murderer, Art Spiegelman's *Maus*," M/E/A/N/I/N/G 12 (1992): 47.

7. Marianne Hirsh, "Family Pictures: *Maus*, Mourning, and Post-Memory," *Discourse* 15, no. 2 (Winter 1992–1993); Miller, "Cartoons of the Self."

8. See *Maus I*, pp. 84, 93, 105, 123, 158; *Maus II*, pp. 89, 113.

9. For a clear statement of this position registered in a polemical context, see David Roskies, "The Holocaust According to the Literary Critics," *Prooftexts* 1, no. 2 (1981). More recently, Roskies argues this point in "The Library of Jewish Catastrophe," in *Holocaust Remembrance*, ed. Geoffrey Hartman. With a different emphasis, Sarah Horowitz wants to argue that diaries and memoirs consistently present a radically different view of the Holocaust. See "Voices from the Killing Ground," also in *Holocaust Remembrance*.

10. See, for instance, James E. Young, "On Rereading Holocaust Diaries and Memoirs," in his *Writing and Rewriting the Holocaust: Narrative and the Consequences of Interpretation* (Bloomington: Indiana University Press, 1988).

11. I develop this argument at greater length in my article, "The Language of Survival: English As Metaphor in Spiegelman's *Maus*," *Prooftexts* 15, no. 3 (1995). For a helpful review of the context in which to

read the connotations of Yiddish-accented English, see Kathryn Heller-
stein, "Yiddish Voices in American English" in *The State of the Language,*
ed. Leonard Michaels and Christopher Ricks (Berkeley: University of
California Press, 1980).

12. As Alice Yaeger Kaplan phrases it, "One of the many extraordi-
nary features of *Maus* is that Spiegelman gets the voices right, he gets
the order of the words right, he manages to capture the intonations of
Eastern Europe spoken in Queens" (in "Theweleit and Spiegelman: Of
Mice and Men," *Remaking History,* ed. Barbara Kruger and Phil Mariani
[Seattle, 1989], p. 155).

13. Henry Louis Gates, *The Signifying Monkey: A Theory of African-
American Literary Criticism* (New York and Oxford: Oxford University
Press, 1988), p. 170 ff.

14. Indeed, Art relies exclusively on the notebook for the first half
of *Maus I.* Even after he buys a tape recorder ("writing things down is
just too hard," p. 73), he continues to use a notebook to log non-inter-
view comments (p. 133) as well as to interview Vladek while walking on
the street (pp. 105–127). Vladek's story in *Maus I,* then, is mainly mediated not by the tape recorder but by Art's own notation. Moreover,
Spiegelman often draws the notebook and its accompanying pencils,
making them a common feature of his visual vocabulary.

15. Sidra Ezrahi refers to these narratives as "survival novels," in *By
Words Alone,* p. 94; Alvin Rosenfeld as "a fiction of post-Holocaust implication" in *A Double Dying: Reflections on Holocaust Literature* (Bloomington: Indiana University Press, 1980), p. 71; Irving Howe as the "aftermath" in "Writing and the Holocaust," *Writing and the Holocaust,* ed.
Berel Lang (New York: Holmes and Meier, 1989).

16. Ozick addresses the significance of letter writing and notes the
specific effect of Bellow's novel *Herzog* on her notion of the self in Elaine
Kauvar, "An Interview with Cynthia Ozick," *Contemporary Literature* 26,
no. 4 (1985). Janet Altman discusses the innovations of Bellow's epistolary strategy in the context of setting forth a theory of epistolary writing
generally, in *Epistolarity: Approaches to a Form* (Columbus: Ohio University Press, 1982). Though she does not extend the discussion to Ozick,
Altman's comments on *Herzog*—letters obsessively written but never
sent—are germane to "Rosa." Despite Ozick's attention to letter writing
in several works in addition to "Rosa" (for example, *The Cannibal Gal-
axy*), critical commentary on epistolary writing—even that specifically
interested in women and epistolary writing—has not integrated Ozick.
See for instance Linda Kauffman, *Special Delivery: Epistolary Modes in
Modern Fiction* (Chicago: University of Chicago Press, 1991), and Eliza-
beth Goldsmith, *Writing the Female Voice: Essays on Epistolary Literature*

Alan Rosen

(Boston: Northeastern University Press, 1989). Mary Favret's revision of commonplace assessments of woman and the epistolary tradition, emphasizing not the private dimension of female correspondence but rather the intervention of women's letters in the public realm, intersects with my discussion of the private/public realm in Rosa's Polish letters. See *Romantic Correspondence: Women, Politics and the Fiction of Letters* (Cambridge: Cambridge University Press, 1993).

17. The first part of "The Shawl" represents a march to an unnamed concentration camp; the second part is set in the camp itself. Throughout the story, Rosa, faced with the trials of excruciating hunger and the special vulnerability of children, desperately endeavors to preserve the life of her toddler. The story ends with the murder of the child and the anguish of the mother. Thus in "The Shawl" the reader directly and unrelentingly confronts many of the most brutal aspects of the Holocaust.

Kafka and Kundera:
Two Voices from Prague

In a comment on my book, *The Problematic Rebel,* Martin Buber wrote:

> The theme is the revolt of man against an existence emptied of meaning, existence after the so-called "death of God." . . . One must withstand this meaninglessness, must suffer it to the end, must do battle with it undauntedly, until out of the contradiction experienced in conflict and suffering, meaning shines forth anew.

The destruction of meaning through the encounter with evil has placed us squarely before the absurd. After this encounter, meaning cannot be recovered through a retreat to a standpoint of innocent immediacy. Still less can it be recovered through a fall-back to some general worldview or overall design from the perspective of which evil is to be affirmed. As Buber intimates, meaning can only be recovered by going through and beyond the absurd to the place where one can endure the tension between affirming where one can affirm and withstanding where one must withstand.

No one puts this tension before us so honestly and compellingly as Franz Kafka. In every line that he has written, whether in finished stories, unfinished novels, diary, or letters, this is his

57

central concern. To say this is not to dismiss the wealth of aspects and levels in Kafka's writings which have received so much attention from his interpreters. Rather, it is to indicate the wholeness that gives his work its central significance.

If concern for human existence in its concrete reality makes one an "existentialist," then Kafka is more of an existentialist than most of those who today are called by this name. He does not start with any absolute or with the assumption of the death of God, but with human existence itself. Those who seek to understand and interpret Kafka through some allegorical key, whether religious, psychoanalytic, or sociological, miss the simple fact that, paradoxical as it is, Kafka's world is not a transparent one through which we can glimpse some other, more familiar reality. It is just what it is in its irreducible opaqueness and absurdity. "The only really difficult and insoluble problems are those which we cannot formulate," writes Kafka, "because they have the difficulties of life itself as their content."[1] Kafka, however, is not a philosopher but an artist. His writing cannot be reduced to abstract philosophical concepts any more than it can be reduced to religious or political allegories, mystical symbols, or psychoanalytic case histories. Yet his stories and novels have a curiously abstract quality. Kafka's heroes are never full-dimensional, concrete human beings, and his stories never have the ring of everyday reality, no matter how detailed and circumstantial they may be.

The key to Kafka, perhaps, is that sense of caricature which is borne in on us again and again. If one feels that one recognizes reality in Kafka, one always feels at the same time that it is a reality that is somehow caricatured. Though this caricature is of the nature of an abstraction from concrete reality, it does not point outward to some still more abstract concept but back to an altogether concrete way of seeing—a perception of reality that again and again lays bare the absurdity inherent in Kafka's particular relationship to it, if not in reality itself. Kafka's stories do not suggest a really open response to the unique reality of person and situation such as we find again and again in Dostoievsky. In Kafka, as a result, the romantic grandeur of Melville and the profound realism of Dostoievsky is replaced by an almost ascetic restriction in subject matter and perspective that makes his creations more thoroughly unromantic, unheroic, and nonpathetic than even the most "realistic" and sordid of portrayals.

Kafka's heroes move from self-sufficiency to ever more anxious isolation and exile. Some of them experience the world's breaking in on the self, destroying its security and calling it to account. Others are engaged in a hopeless and unceasing striving for a contact with reality that they can never attain, a call that they can never clearly hear, and an uncertain calling that will "answer" that call. The result is guilt and anxiety. The conclusion is that there is a goal, but there is no way; the "way" is only a hesitation or wavering. "The true way goes over a rope which is not stretched at any great height but just above the ground," reads a Kafka aphorism. "It seems more designed to make people stumble than to be walked upon."[2]

As important as the question of Joseph K.'s guilt in *The Trial* is the frighteningly irregular and corrupt bureaucracy that has him in its clutches. This bureaucracy wraps its tentacles around the whole of Joseph K.'s reality until it finally crushes him to death—with his compliance! Most of the workings of the Law are removed from sight and understanding, while what can be seen offers a spectacle of disgusting dirt and disorder. The goddess of Justice is portrayed by the court painter as "a goddess of the Hunt in full cry." K. accepts his guilt in the end and reaches out at the same time for help. Yet neither of these attitudes save him from dying grotesquely and cruelly, "like a dog!" All this may seem simply absurd, yet if we put it together with the problem of existential guilt that lies at the heart of *The Trial,* we discover that what Kafka is really pointing to is what I call in my books on the human image the "Dialogue with the Absurd." This is a position which I see developed in both Kafka and Camus. "Everything is not summed up in negation and absurdity," says Camus in *The Rebel.* "But we must first posit negation and absurdity because they are what our generation has encountered and what we must take into account."[3] Camus moves toward and Kafka, for all his negation, stands at the position that in *Problematic Rebel* I have called the Modern Job—the person whose contending still includes the trust that meaning may be found in Dialogue with the Absurd.

In *The Trial*, Kafka is clearly as concerned about the grotesque absurdity of the world that K. encounters as about K.'s existential guilt. But he is concerned most of all about the confrontation of these two, about what happens when the world breaks in on the self as it does on K. Although the world that confronts the self is absurd, it places a real demand on the self that the latter must meet. The self can find meaning in its existence neither through rationalizing away the absurdity of the world nor through rejecting the world's demand because of this absurdity, but through answering with its existence the demand that comes to it through the absurd and that can reach it in no other way.

Kafka's last and greatest novel, *The Castle*, is the story of the attempt of K., "a disreputable-looking man in his thirties," to get some foothold in the village which he has just entered as a total stranger and to make some contact with the Castle which stands above the village. Though K. at first glance seems to be the lone exile in a community of secure and settled villagers, it becomes clear that the villagers too are in exile at the very place where it seems most unthinkable, namely, in their relation to the Castle. The mutual distrust which exists between the villagers and the Castle officials belies the assertion that there is no gulf between them and nothing to be bridged. Despite all this, practically everyone in the village has a childlike trust or dogmatic faith in the officials that rules out categorically all possibility of error and evil on their part. The Castle official is presumed to be right, even when he seems wrong, while the villager must presume himself wrong even when he seems right.

K. looks on the Castle as happy and free in itself but as threatening and cruel in its relations with him. K.'s relation to particular officials tends to follow a pattern of hope followed by disappointment ending finally in indifference. Above all, K. seems to be prevented from getting anywhere in his own suit because of his impatience. Yet his impatience is the result of his anxiety—the anxiety of the exile and the stranger who has no sure ground on which to stand. Even if there were such a thing as a "true way,"

K. could not find it, or if he found it, he could not follow it. He does not have any access to immediate existence that would make it possible for him to live the moment for itself or relate to another person for the sake of the relationship alone. Throughout the novel, K. remains in transition, while trying in vain to leave this condition by every means possible.

K. is constantly assured from all sides that he was not called and not needed and that his "calling" is no real "calling." He is left to establish his calling himself, yet this is exactly what he cannot do. Before he can be accepted in the village, and still more important, before he can begin his work as Land-Surveyor, he needs the confirmation of the Castle—a confirmation which he never receives in any unequivocal or really effective way. What we have here, therefore, is a sort of inverted calling—the need to be called coupled with the impossibility of proving that one is called and the improbability that anyone else will prove it for one.

If K. needs a call to confirm his calling, he also uses his "calling" as a way of answering whatever it is in this "desolate country" that has called him and that makes him want to stay. Whatever this call is, it does not come from other people, no matter how much K. gets himself involved with them in the course of the novel. He sees people as a means to the end of contacting the Castle or as a trap to sidetrack him and prevent his reaching it. He hardly ever sees his relationship to others as a value in itself.

Kafka could live only as a writer, not because he wished to escape from life but because in his writing alone could he find meaning in his existence and *understand* the meaning of his existence. In partial analogy to this, K.'s calling as Land-Surveyor makes him a person who seeks, in one way or another, to find, understand, and respond to meaning, and the meaning that he finds is not some essence of existence but concrete existence itself, the irreducible "given." An in-depth study of *The Castle* suggests that K.'s calling as Land-Surveyor is already in the truest sense a seeking to answer a call—the call of existence itself. K. wants some assurance that he is not *merely* presuming (The German meaning of *vermessen*—the verb from which *Vermesser* [Land-

Surveyor] derives—is 'to presume') that he has the right to separate himself from the calling of ordinary people and take on the
unique task of finding and defining meaning.

K. does not look on the Castle as the means to living in the
village, as Max Brod suggested.[4] The village, rather, is the means
of reaching the Castle. Social reality is either a means or an obstacle for K. It is not a goal. K.'s call is not a call to life in relation
to people. It is a call to a unique and lonely relation to the Castle.
But for all K.'s desire to by-pass the village and reach the Castle
directly, he never does so and, in the nature of things, never can.

Kafka's world differs from Kierkegaard's on the most essential
point of all, namely Kierkegaard's belief that it is possible for the
Single One to say "Thou" to God without saying "Thou" to man.
Despite his aphorisms about the eternal and the indestructible,
Kafka knows no ultimate reality that can be reached apart from
the world.

If we may apply this insight to *The Castle* (from my dialogue
with which it was, in fact, derived), the tension between the self
and the social is complemented by the tension between social
reality and ultimate reality. This border realm of the social may
offer us a key to K.'s problematic. Through this double tension
we can understand K.'s alternation between stubborn rejection
of all mediating social forms and his clinging to even the smallest
social connections with the Castle. Ordinary social life is fundamentally boring to K., as it was to Kafka, yet only through some
connection with the social can he hope to reach his goal. His
goal, however, always remains unclear, both in itself and as to the
way of reaching it, and this is because his goal is neither the village nor the Castle but an immediacy from which he is excluded
in the former and which he tries in vain to reach through the
latter. Again: "There is a goal, but no way: what we call the way
is only hesitation."[5]

To sum up, K. has to prove that he has been called by the
Castle to be a Land-Surveyor before he can practice his calling
and survey the land. To do this he must make contact with the
Castle, which he cannot do. The paradox of his calling is that he
can never know who calls or how to answer, yet he must establish

his calling in order to exist as a person and is accountable for the inauthenticity of his personal existence if he does not. Confronted by an absurd reality which seems by its very nature to offer no personal meaning, he is, nonetheless, not free to run away to any "higher" reality or to abandon his search as hopeless.

In *The Castle* the social is an amorphous realm between the self and the call, a neutral strip, or "no man's land," whose borders on either side are constantly fluctuating. The fluctuation of these borders constitutes the central problematic of *The Castle*. The problem of the calling, as we have seen, is not merely that a calling is only meaningful as a response to a call and that a call is needed to confirm the calling, but also that the confirmation needs to be personal as well as social, social as well as personal. The impossibility of identifying social and personal confirmation, on the one hand, and of separating them, on the other, is paradigmatic of the whole situation of the self. K. is a masterful portrayal of the confusion of the anxious and at the same time reflective person who fights for freedom and independence yet recognizes both the necessity of social binding and the extent to which one is not so much an individual as a social unit.

The other border is between the social and the ultimate reality—what we might call "ontological reality" in order to distinguish it in some way from the social without erecting it into a separate metaphysical or theological realm. Here too the self experiences great confusion, this time from the side of the call. The call seems to come through the social, yet in such a way that it not only becomes indistinct but often highly dubious. It tempts one to believe, as a result, either that there really is no call or that it comes to one from some metaphysical, religious, or eternal realm quite outside the social. The problematic of the social, as a result, becomes essential to understanding both the self and the call.

In the world of *The Castle* the self finds meaning not through identifying society and social confirmation with the call nor through turning away from them to some pure call that one hears apart from the world. It finds meaning, rather, through answering with its existence the call that comes to it through the absurd—through the bigoted villagers and the endless, senseless hierarchies of Castle officials, the call that can reach it in no other way. K. never sees any "ultimate reality," he never hears the call except as it is mediated through social reality. He hears the call in such a way, what is more, that he can neither separate social and ultimate reality, on the one hand, nor accept social reality as simply reality, on the other.

K. is in some respects a Modern Job, if a lesser and less passionate one. Like Job, K. demands direct contact with ultimate reality. As Job is not content just to hear about God but wants to see God face to face, so K. is not content with Klamm's environment: he wants to see Klamm face to face and go beyond Klamm into the Castle. Like Job, K. does not feel impelled to choose between the self and what transcends it. "He may well slay me. I am ready to accept it," says Job. "Yet I shall argue my ways before His face." Although K. recognizes that he may not be able to face Klamm, this is no reason for refraining from the attempt. "If I only succeed in holding my ground, . . . I shall at any rate have the satisfaction of having spoken my mind freely to a great man."[6] Like Job, too, K. contends. "I am here to fight," he says in the variant of the opening. Like Job, K. dares what others do not and is condemned by the upholders of tradition as proud and presumptuous. Although "he had arrived yesterday, and the Castle had been here since ancient times," K. demands what Job demands and what every person alive has the right to demand—the opportunity to confront the Castle directly and with the whole of one's existence.

Insofar as he stands his ground and contends, K. is like Kafka himself. To Kafka, our task is not to escape from the absurd into inward contemplation but to stand and withstand, to hear and contend. Kafka fights against the transience of the world, not by leaving the world for some immutable, metaphysical realm but through perceiving and creating, hoping and despairing. Kafka discovers the human again and again in the very heart of the bewildering social hierarchy, personal meaning in the midst of the impersonal absurd. Kafka possesses a trust in existence which not all the terror and conflict of his life can destroy. It is a trust that the world will come to you unsummoned. But it is no less a trust that the world calls you and that you can call the world. Life's splendor lies forever in wait, writes Kafka, veiled but not hostile, reluctant, or deaf. "If you summon it by the right word, by its right name, it will come."[7]

Kafka depicted the course of the world in gloomier colors than ever before, wrote Martin Buber in *Two Types of Faith*, yet he also proclaimed trust in existence anew, "with a still deepened 'in spite of all this,' quite soft and shy, but unambiguous." Kafka's modern Kabbala stressed the exile of the soiled and suffering immanence of God from the hidden transcendence, in place of the traditional kabbalistic reunification of God and the world. Kafka offered us only this "trust in spite of"—the complaint of a Modern Job who will not give up struggling to find meaning in his suffering but who can never affirm that meaning in the unqualified fashion of the biblical Job to whom God has come near again. "So must Trust change in a time of God's eclipse in order to preserve steadfast to God, without disowning reality," comments Martin Buber, and adds, "The contradiction of existence becomes for us a theophany."[8] Such "theophany" as Kafka experiences comes not apart from but through the very heart of "the contradiction of existence," holding the tension between affirming and withstanding.

MILAN KUNDERA'S *IMMORTALITY* DECONSTRUCTING THE ILLUSION OF PERSONAL UNIQUENESS

In one of Kafka's short sketches a man comes into the room of another man, gets out a case of knives, and starts sharpening one, announcing at the same time that he is going to execute the other man. "You can't do that," the victim protests. "There can be no execution without a hearing and a trial." "You are thinking of fairy tales," the executioner replies, "but this is no fairy tale." And he continues sharpening his knife.[9] The beginning of the absurd, as Camus defines it, is the expectation of a rationality which is not present. Yet further along even that expectation disappears. Ishmael in Melville's *Moby Dick* finds evil in indifference. "Is it by its indefiniteness that it shadows forth the heartless voids and immensities of the universe and thus stabs us from behind with the thought of annihilation when beholding the white depths of the milky way?" Ishmael asks.[10] But when Meursault is about to be guillotined in Camus' novel *The Stranger,* he expects so little of the world that he speaks of "the benign indifference of the universe." For Meursault the "partnership of existence," to use my phrase, is just that benign indifference, or even, so he may feel less lonely, the shouts of hatred and contempt that will greet his execution![11]

Kafka, even less than Camus, expected rationality, yet moving from Kafka to Kundera is moving to a world where the Absurd is so much the expected that it is no longer seen as Absurd. Kundera's world is not so opaque as Kafka's, yet in some ways it is even more curious. In his recent novel *Immortality* Kundera not only inserts his own philosophizings on various subjects, as in previous novels, but even enters the novel himself as author and character combined, accompanied by Professor Avenarius, a friend who serves a similar bridge function. Thus the point of view does not come to us through the tensions of points of view, as in Kafka. But neither can we say with any sureness what Kundera's point of view is, despite his all too numerous authorial interventions.

Kundera wants the novel to be a form that cannot be paraphrased in any other media, and he certainly succeeds with this one. He also wants it to be an end in itself and not a movement of plot toward some dramatic conclusion, and in this too he succeeds. Can *Immortality* be subsumed under what I have in the past called the "Dialogue with the Absurd" and what I now call "Holding the Tension between Affirming and Withstanding"? Here too we cannot be sure. All we can do is juxtapose Kafka with Kundera as one might juxtapose "the modern" with the "postmodern." In doing this we shall certainly not be misled, for much of this novel seems to fit the spirit of deconstruction: from the attack on the connection between self and face to the attack on the uniqueness of the self and the insistence that our gestures possess us rather than we them since there are many more people in the world than there are gestures to go around.

The book begins with the youthful gesture of an older woman at a swimming pool, a gesture witnessed by the author and one that leads him to invent the central character Agnes and, in time, her father and mother, her sister Laura, and her husband Paul. Agnes is compared on the cover to Madame Bovary and Anna Karenina, and this seems apt in light of the fact that her whole life seems to be a withdrawal from relationship with anyone but her dead father. It is, in fact, exactly what the American psycho-analyst Leslie Farber called "a life of suicide." Yet this very with-drawal places Agnes in the superior, impregnable position that leaves her husband Paul at a total loss. This is symbolized by the mysterious smile on her face after she has been killed in a truly absurd automobile accident. This smile has no reference at all to Paul, who has shown up fifteen minutes too late as a result of Professor Avenarius' absurd slashing of the tires of automobiles while he is jogging. Paul faints, but the reader holds up since, in contrast to Madame Bovary and Anna Karenina, one can see no tragedy here at all. Death was exactly what Agnes wanted, and as she lay dying she prayed that she would succeed in dying before Paul reached her, a "prayer" which is granted.

Agnes' sister Laura is of some secondary interest in her affairs with the television announcer Bernard Bertrand (son of the leg-islator politician Bertrand), with Professor Avenarius, and, after Agnes' death, with Paul, whom she marries in an ultimate inces-tuous fulfillment of her lifelong desire to imitate, overtake, and catch up with her older sister Agnes. Laura even steals from Agnes the gesture that gave rise to the novel, after which Agnes refuses to use it herself. It is this gesture which ends Laura's part of the novel when Laura takes her farewell of Kundera, Professor Avenarius, and Paul, who are having lunch together. Although married to Paul and mother of his child, she leaves him for a long period without explanation and when she returns is hardly there for him. Paul is visibly shrinking and aging under our eyes until the gesture, which he mistakenly sees as for himself when it is really for Professor Avenarius!

What I want to draw attention to in *Immortality* is not the absurd plot but the leitmotifs with which the book abounds, either in the form of reflections of the characters or of brief authorial essays. The first of these is a thought Agnes' father shares with her when she is a child and on which she meditates after she is grown up, namely that the world is the Creator's computer. In this thought God is compared not to the deist's watchmaker who started the machine and then left it to itself nor to the traditional notion of an all-powerful God who predetermined everything but to someone who programs a cosmic computer. "This does not mean that the future has been planned down to the last detail, that everything is written 'up above'."[12]

This image sets a realistically absurd and impersonal tone for the book which is amplified by the first actual leitmotif: the denial that there is any link between the face and the uniqueness of the self or for that matter that there actually is any uniqueness of the self. Agnes sees the face as an "accidental and unrepeatable combination of features" which "reflects neither character nor soul, nor what we call the self." Yet without a passionately held basic illusion that the face represents the self we cannot live.[13]

The contemporary French philosopher Emmanuel Levinas says that it is the face of one's fellow human being, more than anything else, that presents one with the reality of otherness, of alterity and "puts a stop to the imperialism of the same and the I."[14] Martin Buber could not go back to Germany to give a public lecture as long as the Germans had become for him "faceless," as they did as the result of Nazism.[15] In Part Five on "Chance" Kundera, who consistently confuses individuality and difference with uniqueness, defines ugliness as "the poetic capriciousness of coincidence." Beauty, in contrast, comes when the "play of coincidence happens to select the average of all dimensions"—"the unpoetic average."[16]

Agnes is not unaware of the faces of Paul and her daughter Brigitte, and she even cares enough about them that she would

want to know that they are alive and all right, but when the chips
are down, she would not want to be reborn as the soulmate of
Paul or the sister of Laura or the mother of Brigitte, and she acts
this out by accepting a position in Switzerland that would have
effectively removed her from all of them even if she had not been
killed in the accident.

It is the memory of her father, whom she later realizes is the
only person she has ever loved, that delivers Agnes from her hatred—by way of total detachment from the world: "I cannot hate
them because nothing binds me to them; I have nothing in common with them." When Agnes' father is dying, he asks Agnes not
to look at him anymore. Agnes obeys and lets "him leave slowly,
unseen, for a world without faces." Agnes' sense of detachment
goes so far that, although she knew that it was absurd and amoral,
she accepted it as produced by feelings beyond her control. Actually it is the product of a growing attitude which might be described as just the opposite of Donne's famous Meditation #19
with its statement that we are a "part of the mainland." Agnes
had nothing in common with these two-legged creatures with
heads and mouths. Their wars and celebrations were none of her
concern.[17] We cannot, of course, ascribe this point of view to
Agnes' author; for if Kundera shared it, he would be incapable
of writing novels!

There is one thing, we are told, that can wrench Agnes out of
her attitude of "no solidarity with mankind," and that is "concrete
love toward a concrete person." If she truly loved one person, she
could not be indifferent to the fate of humankind since "her beloved would be dependent on that fate." But even this concrete,
personal love seems to be absent from her life. She sees her love
for Paul as nothing more than the will to have a happy marriage.
"If she eased up on this will for just a moment, love would fly
away like a bird released from its cage."[18]

In conversation with the stranger from another planet who
comes at the end of Part One, "The Face," to tell Agnes and Paul
that they will not return to Earth in their next incarnation, Agnes
is reassured to learn that "Faces exist nowhere else but here." In
answer to the visitor's question whether they wish to remain to-

gether in the next life, "Agnes gathers all her inner strength" and answers, "We prefer never to meet again." She knows that in doing so she is ruining everything between them; for this amounts to saying, "No love ever existed between us and no love exists between us now." "These words are like the click of a door shutting on the illusion of love," ends Part One. What makes these deconstructions absurd is that there is no suggestion that the world is totally *maya,* or illusion, as in the non-dualistic philosophy of Hinduism. Rather, like a latter-day Sartre or Camus, Kundera is left with the irrational longing for what he knows cannot be possible—uniqueness, personal meaning, love.

In Part Three, "Fighting," "Addition and Subtraction" are set forth as a key to the two sisters and their opposite yet equally hopeless attempts to preserve their uniqueness in the face of the essential facelessness of the self. Agnes subtracts everything from herself in order to come to a sheer essence which she hopes is unique. Laura adds more and more attributes in hope to identify with them. In *The Knowledge of Man* Buber distinguishes between the "being" person and the "seeming" person. The latter is concerned with how he or she appears to other people and tries to assume a face that will lead others to confirm him. The being person, in contrast, is able to withstand this temptation to false confirmation. He or she responds differently to different persons, but his or her concern is not with how he or she appears but with the other person, the relationship, or the situation and the common task. By this Buber does not mean some "essence of the person" that could be distilled out of the individual as gold is mined out of ore, but the stamp of personal uniqueness on every action, utterance, and attitude. Seeming threatens the authenticity of the interhuman, according to Buber, and therefore of the human. Man's essential courage is to resist the temptation to seeming; his essential cowardice is to give in to it.[19]

It is not surprising, given the deconstructionist reflections on the absence of personal uniqueness that we have seen above, that Kundera puts into the mouth of Paul the notion that we are all nothing but seeming persons. "As long as we live with other people, we are only what other people consider us to be." In a remarkably superficial reflection, which it would almost be embarrassing to ascribe to Kundera himself, Paul asks whether any kind of direct contact between oneself and others exists except through the eyes.[20] This too takes us back to Sartre with his universe of intersubjectivity based upon the way each sees the other and turns them into an object (*en-soi*) or a subject (*pour-soi*) under one's own domination.

It is striking how much the above analysis is dependent upon essentially outmoded notions of "inner essence" and "outer manifestation" as the basic realities. Inner and outer, as I have written elsewhere, "are *not* primordial human reality but secondary elaborations and constructions arising from a human wholeness that precedes them both."

> The inner is psychic in the sense that we do not perceive anything with our senses, the outer physical in the sense that we do. And these divisions are useful for a certain ordering of our lives, such as the distinction between what we see, what we dream, what we envision, and what we hallucinate. . . . Yet if we think about human existence in its wholeness, we realize that a true event in our lives is neither inner nor outer but takes up and claims the whole of us. . . . Our existences interpenetrate. Inner versus outer is thus not only a distortion of the primordial human wholeness of the person, but also a distortion of the reality of our existence as person *with* person.[21]

Yet in the midst of all this denial Kundera contrasts the being in love with love, which Laura embodies, and having a real interest in the person with whom one is in love. "The emotion of love gives all of us a misleading illusion of knowing the other." In *I and Thou* Buber insists that real love is not a feeling, which is at best only an accompaniment, but the responsibility of an *I* for a *Thou*.[22] It means "knowing" the other in the full meaning of the biblical use of the term: knowing the other in mutual relationship. In his critique of Laura, Kundera understands this at least in the negative sense.

In Part Four Kundera launches an attack against feeling as *the* touchstone of reality that is quite close to Buber's critique and my own:

> Homo sentimentalis cannot be defined as a man with feelings (for we all have feelings), but as a man who has raised feelings to a category of value. As soon as feelings are seen as a value, everyone wants to feel; and because we all like to pride ourselves on our values, we have a tendency to show off our feelings. . . . As soon as we *want* to feel . . . , feeling is no longer feeling but an imitation of feeling, a show of feeling.[23]

Again feelings are at best the accompaniment. As soon as we make them an end in itself and aim at them, as the romantics did, they lose their reality. Yet Kundera singles out feeling as the one thing that gives any individual uniqueness, although it is a uniqueness that is not essentially dialogical, like Buber's, but is shut in itself: "The basis of the self is not thought but suffering, which is the most fundamental of all feelings. . . . In intense suffering the world disappears and each of us is alone with his self."[24] This is a brilliant half-truth. Kundera understands the unmaking of the common world that suffering and pain bring us but not the remaking of that world that can come in what Aleene Friedman calls "The Healing Partnership."[25]

In this same part, in one of our last glimpses of Agnes, we also get a taste of an impersonal, anti-individualistic, and by implication antisocial mysticism that opts for "being" in place of "being one's self." Cleansed of the dirt of her self Agnes participates in the "primordial being that was present even before the Creator began to create, a being that was—and still is—beyond his influence."[26] This is reminiscent of the ancient Gnostics with their distinction between the *deus absconditus*—the true God who transcends creation entirely—and the *demiurgos*—the evil God that created this evil world.

In moving from the "modern" literature of Kafka's novel *The Castle* to the "postmodern" literature of Kundera's novel *Immortality* we have not moved closer to but further away from the Dialogue with the Absurd. While the postmodern contemporary may feel more at home in Kundera's world, there is no evidence that it combines the trust and contending of the "Modern Job" or that it holds the tension in the face of each new situation, affirming where it can affirm and withstanding where it must withstand.

NOTES

1. Quoted in Maurice Friedman, *Problematic Rebel: Melville, Dostoievsky, Kafka, Camus,* 2nd ed., enlarged (Chicago: University of Chicago Press, 1970), p. 286.

2. Franz Kafka, *Dearest Father,* trans. Ernst Kaiser and Eithne Wilkins (New York: Schocken Books, 1954), "Reflections on Sin, Suffering, Hope, and the True Way," p. 34, #1.

3. Albert Camus, *The Rebel: An Essay on Man in Revolt,* trans. Anthony Bower (New York: Vintage Books, 1956), p. 45.

4. Max Brod, "Additional Note" to Franz Kafka, *The Castle,* trans. Edwin and Willa Muir, 1st ed. (New York: Alfred A. Knopf, 1946), p. 330 ff. See also Max Brod, *Franz Kafka: A Biography* (New York: Schocken Books, 1963), pp. 171–85.

5. See Friedman, *Problematic Rebel,* Part IV, chaps. 13–17, pp. 285–410 and Part VI, pp. 449–51, 475–91.

6. Franz Kafka, *The Castle,* definitive edition, trans. Willa and Edwin Muir (New York: Alfred A. Knopf, 1956), p. 65.

7. *The Diaries of Franz Kafka, 1914–1923,* ed. Max Brod, trans. Martin Greenberg in co-operation with Hannah Arendt (New York: Schocken Books, 1949), October 18, 1921, p. 195.

8. Martin Buber, *Two Types of Faith,* trans. Norman P. Goldhawk (New York: Macmillan, 1951), p. 168 f.

9. *The Diaries of Franz Kafka, 1914–1923,* "A Singular Judicial Procedure," July 22, 1916, p. 162 f.

10. Herman Melville, *Moby Dick,* Chap. XLII "The Whiteness of the Whale" (different editions have different page numbers).

11. Albert Camus, *The Stranger,* trans. Stuart Gilbert (New York: Vintage Books, 1958), p. 154 ff.

12. Milan Kundera, *Immortality,* trans. Peter Kussia (New York: Harper & Row, Harper Perennial, 1992), p. 11.

13. Ibid., 12.

14. See Emmanuel Levinas, *Totality and Infinity,* trans. Alphonso Lingis (Pittsburgh: Duquesne University Press, 1969), pp. 42–49, 87.

Maurice Friedman

15. Maurice Friedman, *Martin Buber's Life and Work: The Later Years—1945–1965* (New York: E. P. Dutton, 1984), p. 105 f.

16. Kundera, *Immortality*, p. 248.

17. Ibid., 39.

18. Ibid., 40.

19. Martin Buber, *The Knowledge of Man: A Philosophy of the Interhuman*, ed. with an Introduction by Maurice Friedman (Atlantic Highlands, N.J.: Humanities Press International, 1988), "Elements of the Interhuman," trans. R. G. Smith, pp. 65–68.

20. Kundera, *Immortality*, p. 127.

21. Maurice Friedman, *The Human Way: A Dialogical Approach to Religion and Human Experience* (Chambersburg, Pa: Anima Books, 1982), pp. 79 f.

22. Martin Buber, *I and Thou*, 2nd rev. ed., trans. Ronald Gregor Smith (New York: Chas. Scribner's Sons, 1958), p. 14.

23. Kundera, *Immortality*, pp. 194 f.

24. Ibid., 200.

25. Aleene Friedman, *Treating Chronic Pain: The Healing Partnership* (New York: Plenum, Insight Books, 1992), chap. 20, "The Healing Partnership and the Common World." One of the theoretical bases of Aleene Friedman's integration of pain therapy and healing through meeting is her recognition that, more than any other experience, pain involves us in the unmaking of "the world"—in Martin Buber's sense of that common "cosmos" that we build together through our common "logos"—that common speech-with-meaning to which we contribute, each from our own unique place, in a strenuous "tug of war." Recognizing this, Aleene Friedman understands how it is the healing partnership alone that can bring the chronic pain sufferer back into the common world.

26. Kundera, *Immortality*, p. 258.

JEFFREY MEHLMAN

Translation and Violence: Legacies of Benjamin

AT A RECENT VISIT to the Translation Seminar at Boston University, Harry Zohn, the first translator of Walter Benjamin into English, gave disarming evidence of how enigmatic a presence the German thinker continues to be. When queried about the ultimate import of Benjamin's classic essay on "The Task of the Translator," he quipped: "After all these years, I am still waiting for someone to explain to me what it really means."[1] Zohn had been taken to task—for his translation of "The Task"—by Paul de Man in one of his last essays, a piece intent on demonstrating that Benjamin on translation was much closer to Nietzsche "than to a messianic tradition he spent his entire life holding at bay." Responsibility for the "misinterpretation," moreover, was clear to de Man: the culprit was Gershom Scholem, who "deliberately tried to make Benjamin say the opposite of what he said for ends of his own."[2] Now what makes de Man's essay remarkable is that in tracking down alleged errors in Zohn's translation, the medium through which his argument about the Nietzschean, anti-messianic Benjamin was to be clinched, de Man failed to observe that Zohn's most blatant error was the omission of the word messianic: *bis ans messianische Ende ihrer Geschichte* is rendered "until the end of their time."[3] This was a stunning oversight on de Man's part, attributable, no doubt, to his will to de-messianize (or de-Scholemize) Benjamin's thought, and the editors of the

75

new Benjamin edition are to be congratulated for having restored the phrase in their first volume.[4]

Contra de Man, then, we are presented with a messianic reading of the phenomenon of translation. What might that mean? Given the Benjamin-Scholem understanding that the messianic (like revolution itself) was not to be gradualist or progressive, but abrupt and catastrophic, we are left to wonder what in the phenomenon of translation, the redemption or rebuilding of Babel, might correspond to such catastrophe. By the end of Benjamin's essay we find meaning in Hölderlin's Pindar translation plunging madly "from abyss to abyss until it threatens to become lost in the bottomless depths of language."[5] The tone is manifestly catastrophic, though enigmatically so. We are left, in sum, with the unresolved question of the relation between translation and catastrophe—or rather, between an inherent ideal translatability of all texts, independent of empirical considerations, on the one hand, and, on the other, catastrophe.

It is in this context that a short Benjamin text written for children's radio takes on interest.[6] Its subject is the flooding of the Mississippi in 1927 and its premise is that we are all prey to an illusion. In assuming that the fundamental and legendary movement of the Mississippi is from source to mouth, north to south, we fail to see that there is a more fundamental movement of the river, as it floods its own bed and displaces itself alternately or simultaneously to the east and the west. That horizontal movement (on the map) with all the destruction it wreaks would have a certain priority over the obvious irreversible movement to the mouth (or delta), and thus would be akin to the "carrying *across*" which translation etymologically is. Moreover, the catastrophe of the Mississippi floods of 1927 leads Benjamin to recount a tale of a flood victim who dives desperately, suicidally into the flood tide just before rescue boats arrive unexpectedly on the scene to save his fellow victims. For anyone familiar with the circumstances of Benjamin's death on the Spanish border it is a movingly prescient narrative.

We thus have a version or metaphor or translation of translation—the violent displacement of the river's bed to the east and the west—that is linked to catastrophe. But in order to better gauge that catastrophe, we would do well to displace our focus laterally, carrying it across to a second Benjamin text of 1921, the "Critique of Violence." Or rather to a contemporary reading of it. The text is steeped in a reading of Georges Sorel on the politically revolutionary potential of myth, and specifically of the violent myth of the general strike. But myth in this case does violence to revolutionary violence itself: according to Benjamin, it diminishes the "incidence of actual violence in revolutions."[7] It is violent non-violence—or mythic—in opposition to the actual everyday violence of governmental or legal coercion. Now toward the end of his essay, Benjamin compounds his distinctions by one between Greek violence, which founds law, and Hebrew or divine violence, which sweeps it away. The model of Hebrew violence, moreover, is God's punishment of the Levites in Numbers 16 in a massacre "without spilling blood."[8] The killing without blood is like the violence without violence of the general strike, the model *par excellence* of divine or revolutionary violence. Here then is a divine catastrophe of messianic proportions being evoked by Benjamin in the same year as he publishes his essay on the messianic import of translation. It is almost as though the true understanding of translation might lie in building a bridge, elaborating a translation from the text on translation to the messianic excursus on divine or "expiatory" violence, a bridge we will make it our business in these pages to construct.

It is worth observing, then, that the reference we have evoked to Numbers 16 should serve as something of a crux for Jacques Derrida's reading of Benjamin.[9] Specifically it provokes the critical equivalent of a panic attack: "When one thinks of the gas chambers and crematoria, how can one hear without trembling this allusion to an extermination that would be expiatory because non-bloody? One is terrified at the idea of an interpretation that would make of the holocaust an expiation and indecipherable signature of the just and violent wrath of God."[10] Whereupon Derrida shuts the book on Benjamin, whose text he finds here "resembling to the point of fascination, of vertigo the very thing one must act and think against." Benjamin stands condemned at this juncture of "possible complicity" with the "final solution."[11]

We have, then, evoked the world of deconstruction in terms of two botched confrontations with Benjamin 1921:

1. De Man misreads the import of messianism in a flawed reading of an admittedly erroneous translation of "The Task of the Translator."

2. Derrida slams the book shut on Benjamin's evocation of divine or expiatory violence—without bloodshed—lest he partake in what appears to be an anticipatory endorsement of the Holocaust.

For those familiar with the history of contemporary criticism, this resonance or short circuit we would establish between what I have called these two botch-ups, one in de Man, one in Derrida, cannot but evoke a whole chapter of the recent past that I have written about elsewhere and shall not discuss in these comments.[12] Instead I would like to address the resonance between these two texts of Benjamin 1921 (on translation and on violence), between the two readings or misreadings they have occasioned, as it comes to structure the work of one of the most intriguing poets and surely the greatest translator in contemporary Britain, a worthy heir to Benjamin, Tony Harrison.

Relatively unknown in the United States, he is something of a phenomenon in England. Widely regarded as the man who has restored verse drama to English, he has compounded that scandal by successfully making the case for rhymed verse. A school anthology of Harrison's work refers to him blithely as "our greatest theatre poet since Shakespeare."[13] At the same time Harrison has managed to provoke a tempest in Parliament where a Tory campaign was launched some ten years ago to keep a poem of his, seething with what the British call "working-class aggro" (or aggression), from being read on television for reason of obscenity.[14] Harrison's response to his accusers was signed, on official stationery, Tony Harrison, President of the Classical Association of Great Britain.[15] In sum, an altogether fascinating case.

Let us turn to his work as a translator, specifically of two classical French plays, Molière's comedy *Le Misanthrope,* and Racine's tragedy *Phèdre.*[16] Indeed, I will be arguing that the path leading us back to the node in Benjamin with which we began will constitute something of a genealogy of the opposition between the genres of tragedy and comedy. Here is Harrison, in his preface to *The Misanthrope,* on translation: "If we were to expand a usual organic metaphor for a work of art, we could say that, like the rose, for example, in a state of nature, a work is constantly throwing up new growths. Into these new growths it gradually directs its sap, and the older growths become starved out. The activity of pruning, in our case the historical consciousness at work in the mind of the director or translator of the classic, is to hasten the rejection of the old wood and to encourage the instincts for producing new growths *especially* (the gardening manuals tell us) *from the base of the plant.*"[17] What dies in the language of the work must be pruned through what anthropologists of oral cultures nicely call an instinct for "structural amnesia." Harrison continues: "Translations are not built to survive though their original survives through translation's many flowerings and decays. The illusion of pedantry is that a text is fixed. It cannot be fixed once and for all. The translation is fixed but reinvigorates its original by its decay. It was probably along these lines that Walter Benjamin was thinking when he said in his 'The Task of the Translator' that 'the life of the original reaches its ever-recurring, latest and most complete unfolding in translation.'"[18]

It will be perceived that what Harrison, via Benjamin, adds to the normally spatial model of translation is temporality. The translator will modify the work to make it conform to the linguistic conventions of another geographical region, yes, but also to those of another historical period. A Richard Wilbur translation of *Le Misanthrope* (or *Phèdre*), for instance, is imaginable as the surface of an ideally polished mirror, recasting the details of the French work with maximum precision onto another surface. To which one may oppose Harrison's metaphor of translation as a variety of growth in the life of a rose or plant.

But here additional attention to the precise temporality of a

Jeffrey Mehlman

Harrison translation will prove rewarding. His *Misanthrope* is set in 1966, three hundred years after the play's first performance— and two years prior to the political revolt of May 1968. Why that transposition? Molière's play tells of the fury of the dissident or misanthropic Alceste at being unable to draw the woman he loves, the duplicitous Célimène, out of the infinitely frivolous salon she presides over. Now concerning this play, Harrison noted a quadripartite structure. On the one hand, synchronically, the fundamental dishonesty and jockeying for power in Célimène's salon resembled the dynamics of Louis XIV's court as evoked by Saint-Simon. On the other hand, diachronically, the world of Louis's court served as a model for a celebrated satirical series on de Gaulle's Elysee Palace, entitled "La Cour" (by André Ribaud), in *Le Canard enchaîné*. What remained was to forge the fourth element in the structure, a translation of *The Misanthrope*, following the Molière text line by line, but situating it three centuries later, on the eve of the would-be insurrection of May 1968 and raising the question of how the dissident or misanthropic Alceste might have reacted to those events. The result is quite dazzling. With Célimène corruptly playing her every suitor off against the other, and that duplicity taken as a metaphor of the internal politics of the Gaullist "court," Harrison gives us a portrait of Fifth Republic politics fully as devastating as that served up by Régis Debray in his recent political memoir *Loués soient nos seigneurs*, and one essentially identical in its structure.[19]

Harrison's translation establishes a short circuit between the seventeenth and twentieth centuries, whose spark is ignited just prior to a would-be revolution. The fact that there is nothing random in that configuration (or "tiger's leap" into the past, to quote a tag from Benjamin) becomes clear upon consideration of Harrison's next play, a translation of Racine's *Phèdre*, transposed to the British Raj just prior to the Indian Mutiny of 1857, and performed in 1975 under the title *Phaedra Britannica*.

Euripides' *Hippolytus*, from which Racine derived his play, is a tragedy of misogyny punished: Hippolytus, son of the slayer of the Minotaur, the compulsive womanizer Theseus, is punished by Aphrodite, to whom he refuses to pay homage, by having him

80

brought to ruin through the instrument of the criminal love of Theseus' wife, Phaedra. *Racine's* play tells of Hippolytus's failed emergence from the closet of his heterosexuality: he has fallen in love with Aricie, but this only further exacerbates Phaedra's criminal passion. At play's end Racine's newly heterosexual Hippolytus suffers exactly the same fate as Euripides' militant misogynist. Phaedra's jealousy, that is, is as potent as Aphrodite's resentment.

Harrison's *Phaedra Britannica* focuses on Theseus the transgressive civilizer, the womanizing British Governor of India. Phaedra-Memsahib is taken with his halfbreed son, who in turn is in love with the daughter of the Rajput family leading what will turn into the rebellion of 1857. The best readings of Racine have always been intrigued by the fact that Aricie is politically tainted from Theseus' point of view, but have tended to interpret that taint psychologically. To the extent that Hippolytus' guilty passion resembles Phaedra's, to the extent, that is, that he appears to be a shadow of her, his would-be liberation from her is plainly illusory and doomed from the start.[20] What such readings have never managed to do is infuse life into the political taint of Aricie and her clan. By recasting Racine in British India, just prior to a native revolt or mutiny, this is precisely what Harrison engineers in the text.

Once again, then, translation becomes a citation of the past, a short circuit with revolutionary potential, a "tiger's leap" of Benjaminian pedigree which indeed this time will turn the fabled "bull from the sea" into a man-eating tiger. From Harrison's version of the celebrated *récit de Théramène:*

The forest begins heaving like the sea,
and seems to open up, and, suddenly,
we see, festooned with seared lianas, IT,
some horrifying, monstrous, composite,
like one of those dark concoctions that one sees
in dark recesses on a temple frieze . . .
The whole earth shudders as it moves its feet
and shambles forward through the shimmering heat.

An epidemic smell, the beast exhales
a stink like cholera from its golden scales.[21]

Translation becomes a redemptive—or revolutionary—citation of the past (in the terms of Benjamin's "Theses on the Philosophy of History"). *Le Misanthrope* just prior to the events of May 1968 and *Phèdre* just prior to the Sepoy Rebellion of 1857 become what Benjamin refers to as "memories flashing up as they are seized in a moment of danger."[22] Let the tiger just "translated" out of the last Act of Racine's *Phèdre* stand for the bond between translation and catastrophe with which, in Benjamin, we began.

Harrison's *Theatre Works* begin, then, with a tragedy (Racine) and a comedy (Molière). Subsequently Harrison would come to claim that the heart of his activity as a translator might lie in dismantling that opposition. Specifically, he would undertake to translate Sophocles' one extant satyr play, *The Trackers*. This time the resonance or short circuit between past and present is between a (relatively) modern framing plot and the ancient plot that it frames. The frame, set at the beginning of the century, gives us "trackers" Greenfell and Hunt, the "Holmes and Watson of Oxford papyrology," tracking down the papyrus of the sole extant Sophoclean satyr-play, *The Trackers*, with the help of their *fellaheen* at Oxyrinchus in Egypt.[23] The *framed* plot (Sophocles' subject) involves a series of obscene satyr trackers commissioned by Apollo to track down his stolen herd. The satyrs eventually discover that Silenus, a fellow satyr, has killed the herd and used its guts to make a—sublime—instrument: the first lyre. Eventually Apollo will seize the instrument for himself, and pay off the obscene satyr-sleuths with what appear to be gold bars. They are to be excluded from the tragic stage, indeed from noble aesthetic endeavor generally as the play turns into a meditation on the repression of the Dionysian (satyrs) by the Apollonian: Apollo himself.

Apollo makes reference to the crucial episode of the flaying of Marsyas: after Athena throws away the first flute (*aulos*) lest she be seen with her cheeks puffed out, Marsyas, a satyr, dares

play and master the instrument. For that act of hubris, he is
flayed:

> It confounded the categories of high and low
> When Caliban outplayed Prospero.[24]

Apollo becomes the arch totalitarian torturer, who drowns out
the shrieks of his victims with renditions of the "Marsyas theme":

> Wherever the losers and the tortured scream
> the lyres will be playing the Marsyas theme.[25]

"There is no document of civilization," in the language of Benjamin's "Theses on the Philosophy of History," "which is not at
the same time a document of barbarism."[26]

Return to the framing conceit, the papyrology motif, for it too
is marked by the satyric element: the high culture of the ancient
text is constantly threatened by reabsorption into the disintegrating muck of the Egyptian rubble heap. The fellaheen, moreover,
are all too aware that disintegrating papyrus makes excellent fertilizer. In Greenfell's words: "They ferret for fertilizer, and Hunt
and I track/ for philosophy and drama in nitrogenous *sebakh*"[27]
Greenfell (as Apollo) must keep the papyrus (and its text) pure
of satyric contamination.

Now the framing conceit of *The Trackers*, fertilizer (manure)
and those who would, in the name of spirit or the core curriculum, pretend—disastrously—to save us from it, serves as a transition to Harrison's play of 1992 *Square Rounds,* a play which, to
the extent that it is readable as a transformation of *The Trackers,*
may be viewed as a satyr-play about the Holocaust. More specifically, it is about the World War I context in which (poison) gas
warfare was developed by a Nobel Prize–winning German Jewish
scientist, Fritz Haber.

The play effectively begins with a nineteenth-century German
chemist, Justus von Liebig, blaming Britain for its promotion of
the toilet on a planetary scale:

> Your nation, Britain, has left the world less green
> by making universal the use of the latrine.[28]

With human waste washed into the rivers and the oceans, the soil has become depleted:

> Each pull of the chain is like a Noah's Flood
> taking in its cataracts so much nutritious good.[29]

As in *The Trackers,* the British would save us from life-enhancing manure. With the result that the British regularly resorted to replenishing their soil with the bones of the dead from the battle-fields of Waterloo, Leipzig, and the Crimea. There is something positively grisly in the British will to purity as evoked by Harrison—a fate from which the world may be saved in this case by von Liebig's development of the first artificial fertilizer.

At the play's center, we find a tragedy surrounding the invention of a new instrument, not the lyre, as in *The Trackers,* but Fritz Haber's Gas Detector, an instrument that sounds two different notes, depending on whether the gas it tests is nitrogen or oxygen. Haber, a Jew, having developed "nitrogen fixation," has become a valued German, but his wife rejects the Faustian aspect of his discoveries. Given the war of attrition that the Great War had become, Haber's humane solution was to develop a murderous weapon that would "break the deadlock": poison gas. He sings of the benefits of the intact corpse, thus joining up with the paean to killing "without spilling blood" in Benjamin's "Critique of Violence." Here is Harrison's Haber:

> Without gas the Maxim gun[30] could not exist
> and no need for me to counter his mechanics with my mist.
> . . .
> One gas blows to pieces, one manages to choke
> its unsuspecting victims with its greenish yellow smoke.
> If I were a victim's mother. Imagine being her
> I know which of the two fates for my son I'd prefer . . . [31]

Haber's wife, trying to dissuade him, invokes the Kaiser's anti-Semitism, suggests he is "supping with the devil." He dreams of serving "the Prussians as their Prospero," winning their "surprised gratitude" with his science, and proceeds to develop his gas: "putting to sleep / the unsuspecting enemy entrenched at Ypres."[32] In short order, however, things go awry. The Germans lose their advantage when they refuse to call on the talents of a second Jew, the inventor of the gas mask. A new and more deadly deadlock results, whereupon Clara, the inventor's wife, commits suicide and is transformed surreally into a musical (i.e., note-based) gas detector:

> Remember the whistle you invented that pulsates
> in the presence of poisonous gases underground?
> I am a human whistle and your dead wife's fate's
> to be your new invention's warning sound.[33]

Like the Sophoclean *Trackers*, then, *Square Rounds* deals at its center with the murderous politics surrounding the invention of a new instrument: satyr Silenus separated from his lyre, Marsyas flayed for his mastery of the flute, and Jewish Clara Haber dying in the song—of the irony of her husband's fate—she sings:

> He'll never live to see his fellow Germans use
> his form of killing on his fellow Jews.[34]

The English scientist Hiram Maxim develops a perfect gas mask, the rounds are squared (in the sense of evened), and the Gas Alarm Music (the equivalent of flute or lyre in *The Trackers*) ends with the sublimely intoned words: "HYDROGEN CYANIDE— ZYKLON B."[35]

Perhaps it is time to interrupt these remarks and see where they have taken us. We began with two remarkably idiosyncratic readings of two passages in two important texts published by Benjamin in 1921. Paul de Man, for all his complaints of flaws in the translation of "The Task of the Translator," failed to note the omission of a strong reference to messianism in Harry Zohn's version and affirmed the critical urgency of de-messianizing the interpretation of Benjamin's text. Jacques Derrida appeared to recoil in dread from Benjamin's invocation, in his "Critique of Violence," of a massacre without bloodshed in Numbers 16 as the beneficent prototype of divine violence. For Benjamin's endorsement of that strangely "non-violent" violence appears to Derrida to be tantamount to a welcoming of the sort of violence (without bloodshed) of the Nazi gas chambers. A horrendous prospect which has in its favor little more than the authority of Derrida's imagination.

Two quirky readings, then, by two masters of deconstruction of two key fragments of Benjamin. Yet might there not be more to the juxtaposition of these passages than the quirkiness of those readings? If translation, ideally understood, is in some sense messianic in its horizon, and if messianism in Benjamin is quintessentially cataclysmic, then to read Benjamin 1921 might mean to articulate the link between the messianic dimension of translation in "The Task" and the prototype of divine violence without the spilling of blood in the "Critique."

At this point we turned to the work of Tony Harrison, arguably the leading practitioner of verse drama in English, and his efforts, in Benjamin's wake, to historicize the act of translation. In the case of a Molière comedy and a Racine tragedy, we observed the status of his translations as "tiger's leaps" into the past, short circuits established between classical works and pre-insurrectionary circumstances: the events of May 1968 in Paris, the Sepoy mutiny of 1857 in India. Benjaminian configurations that seem directly inspired by the "Theses on the Philosophy of History."

To pursue his work as a translator, however, meant somehow dismantling the (very French) distinction between tragedy and comedy. Whence the version of Sophocles' sole extant satyr-play, *The Trackers,* with its investment in the spectacle of "the bloated celebrant following hard on the heels of the sufferer."[36] As Harrison deepens his relation to translation, the dominant trope of translation as/or drama ceases to be the rose or plant, as in the remarkable image we have quoted from the preface to *The Misanthrope* which leads directly to his reference to Benjamin, and becomes fertilizer or manure. The Sophoclean papyrus must be preserved from its disintegration into fertilizer, even as the nobility of the Apollonian lyre must be retrieved from defilement at the hands of the satyrs. That cruelly pure solution appeared to work. Silenus was bought off, humiliated, and consoled himself with drink:

> Some sort of pattern seemed to exist
> Get a bit pissed on then go and get pissed.[37]

So much for what remains of the Dionysian. But the insurrectionary impulse remains constant in Harrison. By the end of the play *The Trackers*, the satyrs—become football hooligans—will be spray-painting the name Marsyas (in Greek!) across the theatre and threatening, in dactyls, to "stuff the papyrus down Sophocles' throat."[38]

But what is most remarkable in the present context is that this deepening of Harrison's relation to translation, *The Trackers of Oxyrhinchus*, should be readable as a transformation or translation of Harrison's play about the ironies of a Jew's unwitting contribution to the horrors of the genocide, precisely through brandishing the exemplary non-violence of massacre without bloodshed. For that, we have seen, was Derrida's idiosyncratic reading of a key passage in Benjamin's "Critique of Violence." The congruence between the "translation" of the satyr-play and the proto-Holocaust drama is clear: in the frame, the productive decay of fertilizer is pitted against the baneful effects of British aspirations to classical culture (Sophocles) and sanitation; at the core, the invention of a new instrument (the lyre, the note-based gas detector) and the human devastation (the ostracism of satyrs, the genocide of Jews) it will lead to.

In the fullness of his *oeuvre*, the translator Harrison has effected the bridge or translation between the fragments of Benjamin 1921 to which we were drawn by what one wants to call the misreadings of de Man and Derrida. Misreadings? Derrida's panic—at massacre without bloodshed—is not that different from Clara Haber's distress at the infernal consequences of her husband's invention. And Clara is the most prescient character in the play. Shall we say, concluding our montage, that literary history, in the work of Harrison, has generated the truth of what we took to be de Man and Derrida's errors? The opening stage directions of *Square Rounds,* enigmatically, all but invite such a conclusion: "A

87

Jeffrey Mehlman

circle of white surrounded by a black circle. It could be read as
a 'deconstructed' top hat."

NOTES

1. February 21, 1997. "The Task of the Translator" appears in *Illuminations* (New York: Harcourt, Brace & World, 1968), introduction by Hannah Arendt, pp. 69–82.

2. Paul de Man, *The Resistance to Theory* (Minneapolis: University of Minnesota Press, 1968), p. 89.

3. For a refutation of several of de Man's "corrections," see my "Prosopopeia Revisited," *Genealogies of the Text* (Cambridge: Cambridge University Press, 1995), pp. 131–38.

4. The fact that they did so without consulting Zohn, who is still listed as translator, is a separate problem of editorial ethics. Walter Benjamin, *Selected Writings*, vol. I, ed. Marcus Bullock and Michael Jennings (Cambridge, Mass.: Harvard University Press, 1996), p. 257: "If, however, these languages continue to grow in this way *until the messianic end of their history*, it is translation that catches fire from the eternal life of the works and the perpetually renewed life of language." My emphasis.

5. *Illuminations*, p. 82.

6. "Die Mississippi-Uberschwemmung 1927" was broadcast over Berlin radio on 23 March 1932. It has been published in *Aufklärung für Kinder* (Frankfurt: Suhrkamp, 1985).

7. "Critique of Violence," *Selected Writings*, I, p. 246.

8. Ibid., 250.

9. Jacques Derrida, "Prénom de Benjamin," *Force de loi* (Paris: Galilée, 1994).

10. Ibid., 145.

11. Ibid., 146.

12. I refer, of course, to the controversy surrounding the revelation that Paul de Man, during World War II, had served as an exuberant cultural commentator in the Brussels collaborationist press. My own comments on the subject appear in "Perspectives: on Paul de Man and *Le Soir*" and "Prosopopeia Revisited," both reprinted in *Genealogies of the Text*.

13. Tony Harrison, *Permanently Bard: Selected Poetry*, ed. Carol Rutter, p. 11.

14. The poem, "v," is in important ways a recasting of Gray's "Elegy": the poet enters into imaginary dialogue with one of the vandals who has just spray-painted Harrison's parents' graves. From the *Daily Mail*,

12 October 1987: "Broadcasters are lining up for a head-on clash with the political establishment over a planned Channel 4 programme featuring a torrent of four-letter filth. . . . " Bloodaxe Books assembled the press file in an appendix to a reprinting of the poem in 1994.

15. "v," (Newcastle: Bloodaxe, 1994), p. 69.

16. *The Misanthrope* (1973) and *Phaedra Britannica* (1975) appear in Tony Harrison, *Theatre Works 1973–1985* (London: Penguin, 1985).

17. "Preface to *The Misanthrope*," in *Tony Harrison*, ed. Neil Astley (Newcastle: Bloodaxe Books, 1991), p. 145.

18. Ibid., 146.

19. R. Debray, *Loués soient nos seigneurs: une éducation politique* (Paris: Gallimard, 1996), pp. 332–34, presents François Mitterrand in Molièresque terms. His strength lay in confiding incompatible "truths" to different "intimates" and making sure they could never confront each other in a frank exchange. "Ainsi l'imbroglio devint-il à l'Elysée une culture collective." Such are the dynamics of Célimène's mendacious court as well.

20. See, for instance, Charles Mauron, *L'Inconscient dans l'oeuvre et la vie de Racine* (Gap: Ophrys, 1957).

21. *Theatre Works*, p. 120.

22. *Illuminations*, p. 255.

23. *The Trackers of Oxyrhynchus* (London: Faber and Faber, 1990), p. 9.

24. Ibid., 64.

25. Ibid., 64.

26. *Illuminations*, p. 256.

27. *The Trackers*, p. 10.

28. *Square Rounds* (London: Faber and Faber, 1992), p. 12.

29. Ibid., 13.

30. The Maxim was the principal gun used in World War I.

31. *Square Rounds*, p. 43.

32. Ibid., 48.

33. Ibid., 51.

34. Ibid., 52.

35. Ibid., 56.

36. *The Trackers*, p. x.

37. Ibid., 69.

38. The flaying of Marsyas thus comes into contact with the vandal "skin" desecrating the cemetery in "v." In another Harrison poem, "The Gaze of the Gorgon" (1992), addicts getting "stoned" in the shadow of

a Frankfurt statue of Heine ("or maybe Europe doesn't care / there's junkies' blood in Heine's hair") are similarly brought into contact with the mythological motif of petrification: ("The Gaze of the Gorgon" in *The Shadow of Hiroshima and other film/poems* [London: Faber and Faber, 1995], p. 35).

Commentary

JOSEPH A. POLAK

Interpreting Catastrophe: Insights from the Halachic Literature on the Prague Fire of 1689

I

We begin with a discussion of the Jewish tradition of *qri'ah*, the act of rending one's outer garment upon hearing certain kinds of evil tidings.[1] In the parlance of Jewish law this rending is referred to as "tearing *qri'ah*." One tears *qri'ah* most commonly upon *hearing* of the death of certain principals in one's life—parents, siblings, children, rabbis, and rabbinical leaders of the community. One tears *qri'ah* if one is present at the death of another person, even if that person is a stranger; one tears *qri'ah* in the presence of blasphemy, and most importantly for our purposes here, one tears *qri'ah* upon witnessing the malevolent burning of a Torah scroll.

In 1689 a fire raged through the Jewish community of Prague, destroying most of its structures, and certainly its Torah scrolls and sacred scriptures. The rabbi of the community, Jacob ben Joseph Reischer[2] (known in the lore of Jewish law not by his name but by that of his *magnum opus*, the book of responsa entitled *Shvut Ya'akov*), is asked by his congregants whether they are permitted to tear *qri'ah*. The rabbi, in a tortured responsum in which he makes it clear that he is both a victim of the tragedy and witness to it, replies in the negative, and at least in his writing on this subject, offers his community no spiritual direction for

93

dealing with this catastrophe. Two hundred years later, the saintly Hassidic Master, Rabbi Haim of Zans, gives nothing but spiritual direction on this topic, in response to a question about a similar fire which he neither experienced nor witnessed, and in which responsum, utterly unlike *Shvut Ya'akov,* he ignores all matters halachic. This study will explore these and other responsa on this topic with the hope of exposing *from specifically legal* Jewish sources a theological understanding of certain kinds of catastrophe.

In order to fully appreciate the nuances of the responsa we will look at, it is necessary to explore the biblical and talmudic texts on which they are based, and it is to these that we first turn our attention.

II

In the thirty-sixth chapter of the book of Jeremiah, Jehoakim, an evil King of Israel, has become aware of a new series of prophecies uttered by the prophet and recorded by his scribe Baruch ben Neria. Jehoakim asks for the scroll containing the prophecies, and has it read to him by his courtier, Jehudi:

> And it came to pass, when Jehudi had read three or four columns, that he [the King] cut it with a penknife, and cast it into the fire that was in the brazier, until the entire scroll was consumed by the fire which was in the brazier. Yet they were not afraid, *did not rent their garments,* neither the King nor any of his servants that heard all these words.[3]

The Talmud engages in an extended examination of these verses as it seeks to isolate the conditions under which *qri'ah* is halachically mandated. It does so by offering the following dialogue between the King and his courtiers on the one hand, and the representatives of the prophet and the people on the other. "What is the meaning [asks the Talmud, with respect to the verses just quoted from the book of Jeremiah] of the phrase "three or four columns?"

> [The Talmud replies:] They said to [the King] Jehoakim: "Jeremiah has written a book of lamentations."

"What is written in it?" he replied to them.

Eicha Yashva Badad—How alone sits [Jerusalem].

"I am the King," Jehoakim replied to them [i.e., there is nothing in this verse that unsettles me, that challenges my authority].

They said to him [continuing from the Book of Lamentations], *Bacho tivke baLayla*—she [Jerusalem] weeps, she weeps into the night.

"I am the King," he replied.

Galta Yehuda me'oni—Judah is gone into exile because of affliction . . .

"I am the King."

Darkhei zion avelut: The ways of Zion do mourn . . .

"I am the King."

Hayu tzareha leRosh—Her *adversaries*[4] have become her head [i.e., her leaders] . . .

Said [Jehoakim] to them: Who said that?

Ki HaShem hoga 'al rov pesha'eha—For [as the verse just quoted continues] the L-rd hath afflicted her for the multitude of her transgressions.[5]

[The King] began at once to cut all the Divine names out of the scroll and [then] burnt them.

And that is why [i.e., because Jehoakim desecrated the divine names of the scroll of Lamentations by burning them in a moment of malevolent rage] it is written [in the Jeremiah verses cited at the beginning of this section] "Yet they were not afraid, did not rent their garments [neither the King nor any of his servants that heard all these words"]. [The purpose of this verse is to teach that even as they did not tear their garments when they witnessed the burning of a Torah scroll,] so are we *required* to tear . . .[6]

Here finally, the Talmud has ferreted out the parameters which mandate *qri'ah*. The behavior of King Jehoakim is a negative model: this burning of the divine name, cut out of sacred scripture, and, of particular importance, emerging from his deep, contemptuous rebelliousness against the G-d of Israel—this *specific* combination of act *and* intention is what halachically mandates the performance of *qri'ah*.

Joseph A. Polak

The Talmud, now sensing, so to speak, the critical role of intentionality in forming the legal apparatus around *qri'ah*, explores this theme more closely, considering a bizarre yet pertinent episode:

> Rabbi Abba and Rav Huna were sitting [and studying]. Rabbi Abba arose to relieve himself and [accordingly, first] removed his phylacteries [which are sacred objects and do not belong in the privy] and placed them upon a pillow. An ostrich came along and wanted to swallow [the phylacteries]. Said R. Abba: Surely we would here have been obligated to tear . . . ! Replied Rav Huna . . . Don't be so certain—[7] Something similar happened to me, and I [brought the matter] before Rav Matna, who had no tradition about this, so I came before Rav Judah, who said: Thus said Samuel: [Tearing *qri'ah* for a burning Torah scroll] was only permitted[8] where there was *coercion*,[9] and where the *situation resembles that incident* [wherein King Jehoakim malevolently burned the Torah scroll].[10]

The Talmud cites this discussion around the strange incident with the ostrich and the phylacteries in order to illuminate, and better define, the notion of coercion. By foregrounding an episode in which a Torah scroll (or, in this case, its stand-in, phylacteries) is destroyed but in which *qri'ah* is not a legitimate response, one learns (or learns better) that coercion is an essential criterion. Unless, that is, one can prove malevolence, there is no option for *qri'ah*.

It is the nature of the development of Jewish law for the legal *interpretations* of the Talmud to end up as a part of the halacha itself. Thus, when over the course of time, an interpretation becomes definitive, either because of the compelling nature of its argument or because of the authority of its author (or, obviously, both), then the text in which this interpretation is contained is transformed from its originally intended status as a secondary source to a primary text. This is what happened to many of the rishonic analyses of the talmudic texts we have just cited, and it is essential that we examine some of these however briefly.[11]

- Rashi is preoccupied with the witness. He explains "with coercion" to mean, remarkably, "where [the witness] was unable to save [the Torah scroll]," as in the case of the witnesses watching Jehoakim burn the scroll-fragments, where they are powerless to intervene in the activities of the king. Rashi supports this interpretation by saying that this precisely was the point of the Talmud citing the incident with the ostrich, where the phylacteries, in fact, were saved, and *that* is why *qri'ah* was unnecessary.
- Ritva is preoccupied with the act of *qri'ah* itself. He specifies that *qri'ah* is called for because of the destruction of the divine name. This interpretation has been taken to imply that *qri'ah* would be appropriate in the burning of any text in which the divine name is found, not merely in a Torah scroll. This assertion is supported by the fact that the ostrich went after R. Abba's *phylacteries,* in which the divine name is certainly found; moreover, the tale with Jehoakim centers around the biblical book of Lamentations (which is not in a Torah scroll) and not around the Pentateuch (which is).
- Nimukei Yosef is interested in the perpetrator: He limits the law to be derived from our talmudic passage to a case where a Torah is destroyed "out of rage," as with Jehoakim. His position, and indeed that of Ritva, as well as the positions of RaN, the Codes, and later decisors, thus differs significantly with the unique interpretation of Rashi.[12]

We are now ready to examine the *Shvut Ya'akov*'s responsum written in reaction to the Prague Fire of 1689.

III

Question: During the major fire that occurred here where hundreds of Torah scrolls and other countless books and phylacteries were seen burning—is there or is there not an obligation for the one who witnesses to tear *qri'ah*?

Answer: . . . I was of course unable to consult [the legal literature] . . . at the time of the conflagration—there was none [which survived, and in the absence of such sources] I had the thought that we were indeed obligated to tear, even though I was well aware [that the two talmudic criteria for tearing, viz.,] "coercion and where the situation resembled that incident" [were clearly inapplicable here]. [Yet I thought tearing *qri'ah* was still appropriate because] I was nonetheless struck by [another talmudic countertext which says] "whomever is present at the expiration of a soul is required to tear *qri'ah*, for to what may this be compared but to a Torah scroll being burned."[13] . . . Thus when a Torah is burned by Heaven, then this is comparable to a person dying [and we would certainly want to tear *qri'ah*]. This is also supported by Rashi's interpretation of "coercion" as our being powerless to save, which is as applicable to a burning Torah as it is to a dying person . . . [and which would reinforce the notion that even as we need to tear for a dying person, so do we need to tear for a burning Torah]. This would then be entirely applicable in our situation [in Prague] with a conflagration so massive that many were able to save neither their lives nor their fortunes, and in which the Torah scrolls, phylacteries and holy texts could not be saved. This indeed transpired in my personal case as well—[I speak of] an unclean [*bilti tahor*] event, wherein during my efforts to save my books, a consuming fire surrounded me, forcing me to flee with hands empty of all sacred texts—woe upon what has been lost—leaving me only my body as the spoils. . . .[14]

Shvut Ya'akov, in the end, rejects his own analysis. He understands that this ruling, were he to require *qri'ah*, would be based on Rashi's interpretation, which was the minority opinion,[15] and the halacha always follow the majority.

For some reason—whether it be support, public pressure, a paucity of legal sources at his disposal, at this point we simply do not know—R. Reischer felt compelled to address this problem to an authority greater than himself, and for this he chose R. Zvi Hirsh Ashkenazi, known in the histories of Jewish law after the name of his *magnum opus, Hakham Zvi.*

Hakham Zvi answers rather definitively:

. . . I see no room in which to rule that there is some obligation for *qri'ah*, for there is absolutely no obligation to tear unless one

actually witnesses the [scrolls themselves to be] . . . burning, as
was the case with the King of Judah . . . and I do not believe that
you will find people in Prague who literally stood and watched
[either] a Torah scroll proper burning, or [for that matter] a single
phylactery.[16]

He argues that a fire can often be extinguished—it is not inevitable that it will burn everything in its path, and that additionally, things are often saved from fires. If this is so, then it is not
inevitable—it is not necessary to the character of fires as domestic accidents—that they consume. In this way, the fire of Prague
actually resembles the ostrich incident in the Talmud more than
it does the Jehoakim story (i.e., sometimes ostriches swallow phylacteries and sometimes they do not; sometimes fires burn everything nearby, and sometimes they do not).

Hakham Zvi continues, seeking to prove that this analysis supports both *Shvut Ya'akov*'s decision not to tear, *and* Rashi's position. He extends his argument to say that since the connection
between ostrich and phylactery on the one hand, and between
fire and Torah scroll on the other, is not causal—neither the ostrich nor the fire are understood to have been agents of the divine—there is therefore no inherently necessary powerlessness
on the part of the witnesses; it was, in other words, possible for
the witnesses to act to prevent the destruction. And just as *qri'ah*
was not required for R. Abba in the case of the ostrich so is it not
required for the victims of the Prague fire. In any case, *Hakham
Zvi* maintains, Rashi when speaking about powerlessness did not
mean powerlessness as a *sufficient* category for *qri'ah;* there is nothing in what he says in the critical text in *Mo'ed Qatan* to believe
that he discarded the Talmud's second criterion, viz., that the
situation needs clearly to resemble the event around Jehoakim.
Rashi's interpretation is not the problem you are making of it,
he tells *Shvut Ya'akov,* concluding that

. . . in any case, those citizens of Prague running into their homes
to rescue their effects certainly did not have the opportunity to
head towards the synagogue to see what became of the Torah

scrolls, and so they did not see them burning, and are without question exempt from *qri'ah*.[17]

The questions that these legal giants leave with us are greater than the ones that they answer. If the issue surrounding tearing *qri'ah* is that of *hilul HaShem*—desecration of the divine name[18]—then does it really matter what the cause of the fire is? Why can we not argue that the burning of sacred scripture, including the divine name, *is* such a desecration, and that all witnesses, horrified as they would be by such a fire, be *allowed* to tear *qri'ah?* In other words, if we can assume that *Shvut Ya'akov* was plagued by his congregants for a ritual which would do justice to the mortification they must have felt at the incineration of all their Torah scrolls, phylacteries, and sacred books, why could he not have allowed them to tear? Moreover, I am tempted to ask: what would it have hurt him to let them tear? True, there is no *obligation* to tear, but is it equally *forbidden* to do so?

The immediate halachic answer to this question is simple: Tearing *qri'ah* is a rabbinic ordinance (as opposed to a biblical injunction), and halacha does not *allow* the law to be interpreted stringently in the case of a rabbinic ordinance. The legal thinking goes as follows: When a Torah scroll is burnt accidentally one could perhaps *presume* that there has been desecration of the divine name. A stringent interpretation of this presumption would require *qri'ah*, while a lenient interpretation would not. Thus, were the law of *qri'ah* of biblical origin, *qri'ah* would be required in the case of the Prague fire. But since it is rabbinic in origin, the need to interpret the law leniently falls into place, and *qri'ah* is not available as a legal option. Interestingly, neither *Shvut Ya'akov* nor *Hakham Zvi* offer this argument.[19]

The absence of this argument, then, leads me to propose something else: that in the absence of intentionality, none of our scholars, earlier or later, are prepared to consider sacrilege (*hilul HaShem*) as having transpired. In a later section of this paper the truth of this claim will be examined.

But there is a second, more subtle issue at play here, apparent not from the nature of the halachic reasoning (as has been our methodology until now) but from its phenomenology. Let us return to the language of *Shvut Ya'akov's* responsum: "I had the thought," he writes, "that we were indeed obligated to tear, even though I was well aware [that] 'coercion' and 'where the situation resembled that incident' [was inapplicable here] . . . when a Torah is burned *by Heaven*,[20] then this is comparable to a person dying. . . . " Clearly, "by Heaven" is a phrase not used by the Talmud. This passage suggests, I believe, that *qri'ah* meant much more to *Shvut Ya'akov* than acknowledging *hillul HaShem;* it meant ascribing some kind of meaning to the catastrophe whose victim and witness he was, it meant taking the fire out of meaninglessness and locating it in some kind of theological context—at the very least, into a context which suggests that the burning Torah scrolls have been desecrated by the fire.

Furthermore, his use of the phrase "by Heaven" suggests that he wanted desperately to posit a divine role in the fire. The notion, I believe, of this catastrophic conflagration having no meaning other than that it was an accident was extremely difficult for him as both victim and witness to accommodate. Being permitted to tear *qri'ah* here would have meant that at the very least, there was some desecration of the divine name, and the tearing of the garment would have allowed his community and him to at least cathartically ascribe some higher meaning to the fire. What both *Shvut Ya'akov* and *Hakham Zvi* understood, it seems to me, is that neither notion—*hillul HaShem* nor a divine role in the accident—could honestly be posited from the available halachic sources around the burning of a Torah scroll.[21]

All this is not to argue that a divine hand in an accidental fire is out of the question in Jewish theology. This would run counter to one of the most fundamental of Jewish beliefs. Thus Maimonides, perhaps the most rationalist of all the Jewish philosophers, in his halachic *opus:*

It is a positive commandment in the Torah to sound . . . horns whenever tragedy such as drought [and plagues] befalls the community. This tradition is among the paths of repentance viz., that when tragedy strikes and the horns are sounded, the community may know that it is all because . . . of its evil ways. . . . And if horns be not sounded, and the community says that this [tragedy] is simply a natural event, that it is mere happenstance, then this is [sheer] arrogance, and would cause the [community] to continue adhering to its evil ways, and then further tragedies would befall it. . . . And we [further] have it as a scribal tradition[22] to fast on the occasion of any tragedy that befalls the community in order that Heaven visit compassion upon it. . . . [23]

We are forbidden, Maimonides is saying, to utterly de-theologize catastrophe. Yet when he refuses to characterize sounding the horn and fasting in the face of catastrophe *as obligations,* and locates these actions instead, as "ways of repentance," he falls short, it seems to me, of saying that every catastrophe is "because of our sins." What he is asking is that we be alert to this possibility, perhaps even to behave as if it were the case, and to use the occasion for examining our ways.

What is striking is that neither of our decisors (*Shvut Ya'akov* and *Hakhem Zvi*) saw fit to mention this highly familiar Maimonidean passage. What I take this to mean quite simply is that neither was prepared to make a *definitive* causal connection between the sins of the people and a fire ignited by accident. Our decisors are thus displaying a profoundly conservative theological tendency, and it is to this tendency that we now turn our attention.

IV

What is remarkable, first of all, is how this conservative tendency has been subdued in our own times. One needs merely to read the popular press daily in Israel to appreciate the scope of this development: someone gets killed in a car crash, and his rabbi announces that it happened because his *mezuza* was in a state of ill-repair; a synagogue in Kiryat Shmoneh is hit by a katyushka rocket, yet its inhabitants miraculously survive—the miracle, the rabbi announces, is due to the increase in Torah-study in this community in the last few months. What is interesting is the *shift:* whereas *Shvut Ya'akov* and the *Hakham Zvi* show the greatest reluctance to engage in this kind of interpretation, today there is no such reluctance. Explaining events as causal miracles, as divine responses to our deeds with almost prophetic certainty, has become *de jure.*

This leads us to three questions: (1) When did this shift begin? (2) What triggered it? (3) Has it affected halacha itself? Answering each fully here would be beyond the scope of this essay; it would require a vast perusal of three hundred years of literature; yet there are, I think, some directions that present themselves.

In 1955 R. Zvi Eliezer Waldenberg (today the chief justice of the Jerusalem rabbinical court) wrote as follows:

> In recent times there transpired here in the Holy Land several . . . terrifying instances of Torah scrolls burning, some from the hands of Heaven, others from the hands of men. So also [the scrolls have been known] to . . . fall from the hands of their bearers onto the ground, Heaven-forfend. . . . From time to time I have been approached by those who caused [these catastrophes] for some advice on how to appease their Maker, for the fear of the L-rd was in their eyes and in their suffering, and they sought to be comforted, for they did not want [these catastrophes] to remain with them as sins. . . . And the custom of all Israel (which is binding[24]) from days of yore is well known, viz. to be required in such cases to establish fast days, and to yield up the sin to the giving of charity.[25]

R. Waldenberg sets as his task here to fully examine the literature on the response to the burning of Torah scrolls, and to come to some resolution on these matters. Of great significance, I believe, is his decision to remain true to the rulings of *Shvut Ya'akov* and *Hakham Zvi,* and for that matter, to the Jewish Codes: tearing *qri'ah,* he rules, is only possible when there has been "coercion and where the situation resembles that incident," and he defines these criteria as obtaining where there were human players with malevolent intent. He therefore cannot condone tearing *qri'ah* in the case of accidental burnings of Torah scrolls, arguing further, as we have already seen, that this would be *adding* strictures to a *rabbinic* ordinance, a legal procedure which is itself prohibited in Jewish law. And yet, he writes,

> Notwithstanding all this, we find among the writings of the decisors [those] who required fasting of [the community where a Torah scroll was burnt] even where there was no malevolence,[26] even where there was no human hand [involved in setting the fire], and even if no one [there] saw the conflagration.[27]

The responsum he has in mind was offered by the great nineteenth-century Hasidic master, R. Haim of Zans, who wrote as follows:

> in a certain house of study, one of the candles lit in honor of the Sabbath was left burning . . . even after members of the congregation returned to their homes. [The candle] was tipped to its side, and was [left] on the reader's desk adjacent to the Holy Ark. The [community] neglected to straighten the candle, which would certainly have been permissible had it been done with [the help of] a gentile. Neither was the sexton [less negligent in this matter]—he who was appointed to pay attention to all matters pertaining to this community. He, too, left for home without checking and seeing what might proceed from all this. And thus did the flame from the candle lick the wood of the reader's desk, which together with the Ark and four Torahs scrolls were burnt [in their entirety that evening].

R. Haim replied to them to do as follows:

> 1. They donate forthwith from the communal treasury the sum of ten rubles of silver, to be distributed to the gentile poor.
> 2. That all the worshippers in this house fast a full communal fast, following to their full stringency the legal requirements of the four [existent] communal fasts, including reading the *vayekhal* passage from scriptures morning and afternoon.[28]
> 3. The women need not fast.

4. The sexton must fast four times in the year, once in each season.

5. Each worshipper should further contribute to charity according to his capacity; G-d forbid that even a single person, be he wealthy or poor, exempt himself from this. These funds should then be distributed to a pious orphan, the daughter of a scholar, to enable her to marry a scholar, and in order to clothe both of them in garments of dignity.

6. The ashes must be disposed into an earthenware vessel, and laid to rest next to the grave of a man pure and fearful of Heaven.[29]

What R. Waldenberg finds of special significance in this reponsum is that the Rabbi of Zans causally links the fire to the fact that this synagogue had been rented out, during an interim period, as a barracks for the billeting of the military (with its attendant immoralities).

[From the fact that the fire destroyed the prayer stand, the ark, and its four Torah scrolls] and that it [amazingly] did not affect the walls of the house and they remained intact . . . we see that the fire was a punishment from Heaven . . . [perhaps] because of their negligence, or certainly that of the sexton, or [perhaps] because the house had been used to billet troops. . . .[30]

R. Waldenberg does not find the basis for this ruling compelling, and he goes to some pains to show additionally that all subsequent rulings of this nature base their (in his opinion, misguided) authority on the Zans responsum. The Zans responsum, then, appears to be the historically pivotal one; it is only *after it is published* that the shift is made to permitting the tearing of qri'ah for the burning of a Torah scroll.[31]

We also need to point out—as R. Waldenberg fails to do—the complete absence of any halachic discussion in the Zans responsum. No sources are cited, no polemics are brought forth, no authorities traced. The implications of this are, I believe, quite serious, because it allows us to conclude that what the Rabbi of Zans was writing was not a responsum, but the reply of an Hassidic master to a beleaguered community. A pastoral letter, perhaps, which we might locate in a newly identified Hassidic literature of *hanhagot*,[32] but certainly not (as is R. Waldenberg's instinct) as the basis for rulings in Jewish law. If R. Haim had been interested in writing a legal responsum, he would, at the very least for example, have cited the passage from Maimonides quoted above.

Moreover, the evolution of this kind of thinking—attributing direct divine consequences to human behavior—as the norm has also been traced in some depth by Moshe Idel, who shows it to be one of the major characteristics of Hassidic mysticism, and to have emerged with renewed vigor in the eighteenth and nineteenth centuries.[33]

V

What we see in all this, of course, is a dialectic. On the one hand, the major halachic authorities continue to restrain their interpretations of the accidental burnings of Torah scrolls. On the other, a host of decisors, starting with R. Haim of Zans, are zealous in calling all such events a desecration of the divine name, requiring if not *qri'ah* itself, then certainly grave penitence.

It is possible that given his considerable spiritual powers, R. Haim knew things about the fire and the community that led him to believe that here there had in fact been a desecration of the Divine name. Yet, insofar as R. Waldenberg is the most recent spokesman on the issue and its final authority, halacha itself remains inviolate to the spiritual sensibilities, however great, of R. Haim of Zans. And given, as we have seen, the non-halachic literary nature of his "responsum," it is altogether possible that where pure halacha is concerned, R. Haim might well have agreed with R. Waldenberg.

Rabbi Waldenberg concludes his essay by saying that where the desecration of Jewish holy objects has taken place, there is little basis *in Jewish law* for rabbis to *require* their communities to engage in acts of public and private contrition, and in support of this statement he points to the rather loud absence of such a practice in the Code of Jewish Law. He nonetheless concludes that there is still enough in halachic literature to permit them to so decree at their discretion.

And yet in the end, there is more halachic ground to support R. Haim of Zans than his opponents have allowed, and it is to this that we now finally turn.

V I

One of the instances requiring *qri'ah* mentioned at the opening of this essay was when the divine name is employed in blasphemy—the case of the *megadef:*[34]

> The *megadef* is not liable [for capital punishment] until he articulates [*piresh*] the divine name. Said R. Joshua ben Qarha: Each day the witnesses [to this blasphemy] are judged [i.e., cross-examined] employing [not the divine name itself but] a substitute [*kinuy*]. . . . After the sentence has been passed, [the defendant] cannot be sentenced [with the court merely having heard[35]] the substitute. Rather, all are sent out of the courtroom, and [the judge addresses the eldest of the witnesses, saying] "Say what it is you heard." [The witness] says it, and the judges rise and tear *qri'ah*. . . . The second witness says ["thus did I hear as well"], and so . . . the third witness.[36]

The question this mishna poses, of course, is why do the *judges* tear *qri'ah*? Surely there is no intention whatsoever on the part of the witnesses to blaspheme, surely they are merely repeating with great loathing an expression halacha requires them to repeat so that justice can be had. And what we see here is precisely that *intentionality is not necessary for desecration of the divine name to take place*. *Qri'ah* can thus be required even where there is no malevolence, contra *Shvut Ya'akov*, contra *Hakham Zvi*, contra R. Waldenberg.[37]

And if we move from the strictly legal to the phenomenological, as did R. Haim, another question presents itself from this mishna: why is the courtroom emptied before the witness repeats the blasphemy? The significance of this, I believe, is not merely to prevent the blasphemy from being heard yet again in society,[38] but is a move to isolate the judges themselves, so that they stand alone, representatives not of society, but of G-d's justice, and by extension, of G-d Himself.[39] Thus, when G-d hears the blasphemy through the ears of His judges, when it is confirmed that this is indeed what emerged from the lips of a son or daughter of the covenant, then G-d himself, as it were, tears *qri'ah*.

It is possible that R. Haim of Zans is alerting us to the existence of yet another Audience, in addition to the mortal community of victims. It is possible that G-d sees Himself, per the mishna about the *megadef*, as a victim of the fire, and locates Himself among the victims. Perhaps He knows of perpetrators where mortal victims see none, perhaps He does not. Yet surely the mishna is suggesting that G-d needs to tear *qri'ah*, as it were, and needs the community to tear with Him.

Or, perhaps, there is no intended continuity between the *qri'ah* of the *megadef* and that of the witnesses to the burning of a Torah scroll; that we may not learn the laws of the one from those of the other. And therefore the issue of whether one can ascribe theological significance to events of accidental destruction is best left as a dialectic.

NOTES

This paper profited greatly from early readings by Professors Adam Seligmann and Alan Rosen, to each of whom I herewith register my appreciation.

1. A full discussion of this practice is found in B. *Mo'ed Qatan*, 25a ff. What follows in the text is a partial rather than an exhaustive discussion of *qri'ah*.

2. Also known as Jacob Backofen (*c.* 1670–1733). See the article about him in the *Encyclopedia Judaica*, vol. 14, p. 61. See also Gutmann Klemperer, "The Rabbis of Prague: A History," in *Historia Judaica*, vol. 13, 1951, pp. 55–82. I am indebted to Professor Hillel Kieval for sharing with me his knowledge of the history of this period.

3. Verses 23–24.

4. My emphasis.

5. The translations here are from the 1955 Jewish Publication Society Bible. The verses cited are from the beginning of the first chapter of the Book of Lamentations.

6. B. *Mo'ed Qatan* 26a. My emphasis.

7. Lit.: How do you know this?

8. Lit.: was not said.

9. Lit.: "use of forearms": *biZro'a.* The more contemporary word is "violence." My emphasis.

10. Lit.: "And like the tale that took place." My emphasis. Note that the Jersualem Talmud has three significant variations with this Bavli text: 1) There is no mention of the destruction of the divine name being necessary in order to make *qri'ah* mandatory. 2) *Zro'a* means that a king of Israel must burn it with his hands. 3) Rav Huna actually hunted the ostrich and strangled it with his hands. The Jerusalem Talmud concludes: "Said Rav Yirmiya in the name of Rav: We tear *qri'ah* only over a Torah scroll burnt by the forearms of a King of Israel, as with Jehoakim the son Josiah, King of Judah, and his friends." See Tosafot here, s.v. *lo.*

11. The sources for all the rishonim cited are in their standard editions, commenting on B. *Mo'ed Qatan,* op. cit.

12. RaN, *Mo'ed Qatan,* op. cit. R. Haim Yosef Azoulai writes: "And we have it received from the early and later decisors [*rishonim ve'achronim*] that whomever sees a Torah scroll burning has no obligation to tear, because "coercion" is required, and not spontaneous burning" (Responsa *Haim Sha'al,* standard editions, #12). See also R. Eliezer Waldenberg, *Tzitz Eliezer,* vol. 5, Responsum #1, chapter 1:6 (standard editions), where he interprets Maimonides and the Codes to support Ritva and not Rashi.

13. B. *Mo'ed Qatan,* op. cit.

14. Responsa *Shvut Ya'akob,* #84, Lemberg, 1861.

15. He refers to it as *da'at yahid,* a solitary opinion in a sea of counter-opinions.

16. Responsa *Hakham Zvi,* #17, standard editions.

17. Ibid.

18. This is the presumption of virtually all the authorities we have cited, and is stated explicitly by the major seventeenth-century authority, R. Joel Sirkes; see BaH on Code *Yoreh De'ah* 340.

19. This is the position of R. Waldenberg; see n. 12 above, and the text below.

20. My emphasis.

21. It is important to note that the burning of the parchment itself is not attributed any theological significance, perhaps because of the magical overtones of such interpretation.

22. *midivrei sofrim.*

23. *Yad, The Laws of Fasting,* 1:1 ff. For a contemporary review of this position see Israel Meir Kagan, *Mishne Brura* on Code *Orach Haim* 576: 1, note 1.

24. *minhag yisroel Torah:* lit., the custom of Israel is Torah.

25. This responsum is cited in note 12 above.

26. *hach'asah;* lit. anger.

27. Waldenberg, op. cit.

28. The reference is to Exodus 32:11ff, read on the regular Jewish fast days of 17 Tamuz, 9 Av, 3 Tishrei, and 10 Teveth. Only on the 9th of Av is this read twice a day; the Rabbi of Zans is thus lending a special note of somberness to his prescriptions.

29. Responsa *Divrei Haim,* vol. 2, "Collections and Omissions," chapter 1.

30. Ibid. The word used in the responsum for troop barracks is written in Yiddish, unlike the rest of the responsum which is in Hebrew. I transliterate the word as "kasseren." Both Professors Solomon Poll and Arnold Wieder advise me that the word means military barracks, and stems from the Hungarian "kaszar nyi."

31. The full list of the decisors who permitted this is contained in the Waldenberg responsum, where the origin of their ruling in the Zans responsum we have cited is also traced.

32. See Ze'ev Gries, *Conduct Literature (Regimen Vitae): Its History and Place in the Life of Beshtian Hassidism* (Jerusalem, 1989. Hebrew). See also Moshe Idel, *Hasidism: Between Ecstasy and Magic* (Albany, N.Y.: State University of New York Press, 1995), p. 25.

33. Idel, *Hasidism,* pp. 29–30 and p. 65ff. Idel refers to this kind of thinking as "magic"; to my mind, the term "magic" is not the best to characterize this phenomenon. Be that as it may, these are not the only times "magical" thinking of this type appears. R. Waldenberg himself identifies R. Isaac ben Hayim of Bruenn (*c.* 1400–1480) ("Ri Bruna") as writing a responsum regarding a man who dropped his phylacteries. The responsum argues that this signifies a call to repentance, even as the accidental reversal of his phylactery strap inspired the talmudic Rav Huna to extensive fasting (B. *Mo'ed Qatan,* op. cit). R. Waldenberg sharply criticizes this argument, saying that the sole purpose of this talmudic illustration is to depict Rav Huna's piety, and not to legislate behavior for anyone else—i.e., it has no place in a halachic responsum. Why this kind of thinking appeared at this time is, of course, beyond the scope of this essay.

34. See Leviticus 24: 11–16. The obligation for the witness to tear *qri'ah* on such an occasion is cited in B. Sanhedrin, 60a.

35. Lit.: on the basis of.

36. B. Sanhedrin 55b, 56a. My translation.

37. This view, however, is perhaps consonant with that of Ritva, presented earlier.

38. Indeed, one could argue with some eloquence that uttering the blasphemy for the purposes of achieving biblical justice is itself noble and acceptable. Why then send everyone out?

39. The Bible itself refers to the judiciary as Elokim—G-d—(see, for example, Exodus 21:6, and Rashi here, citing Mekhilta).

HILLEL LEVINE

Rabbi Yose's Laundry:
The History of a Flagrant Voice
and the History of an Idea

MY DIALOGUE WITH Elie Wiesel began in the mid-1960s. Entering his solitary garret, perched over New York's Riverside Drive, was entering a garden of enchantment as much as it was experiencing that shock of ultimate reality. Legend and quotidian existence abided. Telephone calls from distressed people in distant lands, sudden appearances of semi-mythical characters at the door provided interludes to conversation spanning the personal and the cosmic. Piles of books and manuscripts obscured lower parts of windows overlooking the Hudson River.

It was a time of reflection and activism and a few young Jews, *as Jews*, wanted to be involved in both. We were shaped by what might be described as a golden age of American Jewish security and achievement. Americans, it seemed, had learned one most important lesson of the Holocaust—the dangers of antisemitism—though American Jews themselves would partake in the collective forgetting and repression of the details. The doors to the suburbs, the academy, the professions were largely open even as the windows of memory were closed. Some of us had that uncomfortable feeling that not everything truly was getting "bigger and better."

The man whose writing and inexhaustable lecturing were beginning to stir a much delayed confrontation with the Holocaust, who was presenting the first reports that elegies for an additional

three million Jews behind the Iron Curtain were altogether pre-
mature, who was challenging Jews and their neighbors to engage
Israel with more than charity and political support was himself
never too busy to be with those in search and to share his inimi-
table melancholy mirth. The Jewish sacred festivals in Hebrew are
identified with feet. Yet, in the spiritual ascent to Jerusalem or,
as associated centuries later with the visit to the Hasidic Master,
feet indeed would be an unnecessary apparatus of conveyance. I
would enter and leave the presence of a teacher with that floating
sensation. Those visits transformed my life.

More than anyone in our times, on several continents and
among people of different religions and backgrounds, Elie Wiesel helped sundry "Jews of Silence" explore the depth of their
silence and thereby discover their truest voices. He adjured us to
"hear the voice of the oppressed" while teaching us the language
of the oppressors. His intellectual and moral leadership are
unique. With more gratitude than I could possibly express for
decades of inspired friendship, I offer thoughts about a worthy
antecessor.

Rabbi Yose, the son of Halafta, lived in the middle of the second century, CE, in a time that succeeded a major catastrophe, a
time not unlike ours. This was the generation that witnessed the
abortive Bar Kokhba rebellion ending in mass destruction. Yose's
beloved teacher, Akiva, and other rabbis chose martyrdom. During the relatively calm period that followed the abrogation of the
Hadrianic decrees of the Roman Emperor, Rabbi Yose and his
colleagues fostered a renaissance which mightily shaped nearly
two millennia of diaspora Judaism.

In Rabbi Yose's lifetime and after, his authority was unrivaled.
His opinions are conveyed several hundred times in the Mishnaic
literature. Though Yose was not an uncommon name among the
rabbis, rulings cited in that name without a patronym were un-
hesitatingly attributed to him as if to say with this familiarity that
"everyone knows who is Rabbi Yose." And those rulings would
prevail among his contemporaries as much as among his successors. Yet, this rabbi who enjoyed such prestige was himself known
to be temperate and modest, a mediator who despised contro-

versy and division, distanced himself from extreme positions, and was gentle towards others. Yose the son of Halafta was altogether willing to defer to the opinion of his colleagues.

But there is one enigmatic discourse—it is about a matter seemingly as mundane as laundry—in which the response of Rabbi Yose wholly challenges these characterizations. The discussion between Rabbi Yose and the rabbis is cited in three different collections of early rabbinic literature.[1] The variations for our purposes are not significant. Let us examine the presentation, narratively most developed in the *Babylonian Talmud, "Nedarim"* 8ob:

> With respect to a well belonging to townspeople, when it is a question of their own lives or the lives of strangers, their own lives take precedence; their cattle or the cattle of strangers, their cattle take precedence over those of strangers; their laundering or that of strangers, their laundering takes precedence over that of strangers. But if the choice lies between the lives of strangers and their own laundering, the lives of the strangers take precedence over their own laundering. Rabbi Yose ruled: Their laundering takes precedence over the lives of strangers.

Here we have a variant on the case involving the tragic choices that must be made in the allocation of scarce resources. In this instance, typical then and typical now for the Land of Israel, the discussion relates to the responsibility of members of a particular community who depend on a limited water source to the downstream "strangers" who are as much dependent on any water that might remain undiverted. Two sets of principles inform this text: One relates to social geography; the other to hierarchy. Individuals have special obligations to members of their own community. As the Rabbis put it, *"aniyei irkha kodem,"* the needy of your own city take precedence. Consequently, the townspeople seemingly have the right to consume the water without concern for others. But this must be qualified by another principle. The parameters of moral concern are established by spatial proximity as long as the consumption represents the same category of need. The rabbis present an inverted hierarchy—human life, animals, and material possessions which provide the basis of triage. They rule in accordance with what appears to be commonsense morality that the preservation of human life, even of animal vitality, outweigh the solemn responsibility that one has for the material welfare and comfort of others, even the "needy" who are closest.

It is on this point that Rabbi Yose surprises his contemporaries as well as us by the seemingly intransigent tone and unfeeling substance of his position. We think we hear him propose that members of a community have the right to do their laundry though this same water could be used to save life—the mortals who happen to be outsiders and their animals. This ruling is more than surprising. It is shocking in view of this emphasis generally placed on the absolute sanctity of life—not only of the *me* and of the *we* but even of the *other*, of the stranger. To cite but one example of the stringency of interpersonal obligation that would influence his thinking: would not Rabbi Yose surely have imagined himself among the elders of his town who would have had to trouble themselves considerably, taking measurements to the site of an unknown victim, in accordance with biblical law (Deuteronomy 21:1–9)? The Bible is so very explicit about the technique for establishing responsibility in the instance of a total stranger found dead in the field where there is no other basis to account for the death. Here proximity becomes a formal measure for attributing fault, guilt, and moral responsibility, it being assumed that the people closest to the dead person were inadequate in the hospitality and protection that they rendered to a wayfarer. And would he not have had to expiate the community declaring, "our hands have not spilt this innocent blood?" Where the risk to others is known, could this same Rabbi Yose be sanguine about doing laundry while his neighbors and their animals are dying of thirst?

Hyperbole or even humor are not foreign to rabbinic rulings, though they are not necessarily a stylistic device of this Rabbi Yose. Neither is enlightened self-interest uncharacteristic of the rabbis. Is Rabbi Yose an early version of Bernard Mandeville or Adam Smith, who saw in avarice a privileged passion? While this explanation has some plausibility, it clearly does not answer all of our questions. We are still left with a sense that there is as yet something unaccounted for going on here.

There is internal evidence in this version of the text that we are not the first to have difficulty in understanding Rabbi Yose. The Talmud continues on the next page (81a):

> Isi, the son of Judah, did not come for three days to the academy of Rabbi Yose. Wardimus, the son of Rabbi Yose, met him and asked, "Why have you Sir, not been for these last three days at my father's school?" He replied, "Seeing that I do not know your father's grounds [for his rulings], why should I attend?" "Please repeat, Sir, what he told you," he urged, "perhaps I may know the reason." Said he, "As to what was taught, Rabbi Yose said: Their laundering takes precedence over the lives of strangers, whence do we know a verse [to support this]? Said he, Because it is written, *And the suburbs of them shall be for their cattle, and for their goods, and for all their beasts* [*hayyatam*]. Now, what is meant by *hayyatam:* Shall we say, "beasts"—but beasts are included in cattle? But if *hayyatam* means literally "their lives," is it not obvious? Hence it must surely refer to laundering, since [neglect of one's clothes] causes the pains of scabs.

In this vivid, even touching exchange between disciple and son, we capture some of the emotions that Rabbi Yose's rulings must have evoked in his long career. The specific names and the identification in particular of the disciple assures us, indeed, that this *stam* or anonymous Rabbi Yose is the Yose whom we believe he is, notwithstanding our difficulties in reconciling this ruling with his reputation. Isi was Yose's beloved student, well known for his piety. The disciple's bewilderment over his teacher's flagrancy leads to his passive protest: Isi absents himself from the academy. But the son eased matters by averring that Rabbi Yose did not, could not possibly have said what he indeed seems to have said—that my laundry is more important than your life.

Whether the disciple was convinced by the son's defense of his father and returned to the academy, whether Isi and others really believed that when Rabbi Yose was making what seems to be such an audacious and counter-intuitive argument about laundry, he was in actuality merely affirming the importance of saving lives, we do not know. Textually, it certainly was useful to suggest this interpretation. It supports wholly other issues that the redactors of the Talmud were trying to clarify; it also makes Rabbi Yose appear to be less flagrant. But how did generations of Jews who read this text respond?

Rabbi Yose took a position that was opposed to the ruling of other rabbis. In this beautiful *sugya* and transgenerational debate, they appeared to have scriptures, logic, and commonsense morality on their side. What he said and how he said it were so out of character for Rabbi Yose that generations of indignant rabbis used their well-developed rhetorical skills to convince themselves and others that laundry was not laundry, that Rabbi Yose could not possibly have meant what he seemed to be saying, that there were mitigating circumstances to his ruling. When all else failed they even ignored Yose's ruling. And yet we sense that Rabbi Yose really meant—*laundry*.

One commentator does establish the law in accordance with Rabbi Yose. The Gaon Aha of Shabha cites that ruling in connection with a discussion that he presents on the boundaries of compassion and generosity. In the *She'iltot* (Deuteronomy 15:7), he emphasizes the importance of charity, an obligation from which even the recipients of charity are themselves not exempt. And yet there are limits to that generosity, particularly where it jeopardizes the welfare of the individual. He cites the equivocal meaning of the scriptural prooftext for generosity, *vehai ahikha imakh* (Leviticus 25:36), that your brother may live with you. Some interpreters emphasize the "live," the obligation to help the other; some foreground the "with you" meaning that charity should not be sacrificial. Nevertheless, whatever the focus of the specific interpreter, this biblical precept was taken to support calculated moderation. Though the Gaon Aha lived half a millennium after Rabbi Yose, may he have sensed the actual context of Rabbi Yose's flagrancy? In ruling with Rabbi Yose, we soon discover, the Gaon Aha ultimately believes that Rabbi Yose is merely reiterating the uncontroversial statement that laundry thinly conceals life-threatening dangers. Under these circumstances, people have no obligation to share their limited water supply with their neighbors. We are still left with the question: if Rabbi Yose truly meant life, why did he make such a fuss about laundry?

Yet still other interpreters, including a relatively recent commentary upon the *She'iltot*, the *Haamek Sheaila* of the late nineteenth-century Rabbi, Isaiah Berlin, with the super-super commentary of his son, Rabbi Naftali Berlin, suggest that this discourse must be related to still another and better known controversy involving the aforementioned Rabbi Akiva, Rabbi Yose's teacher, and the distinctions that this controversy elicits.[2]

> If two are travelling on a journey, and one has a pitcher of water; if both were to drink they will die. But if one only drinks, he can reach civilization. The Son of Patura taught: it is better that both should drink and die, rather than one should behold his companion's death. Until Rabbi Akiva came and taught: "That your brother may live with you." Your life takes precedence over his life.

The mysterious and unidentifiable son of Patura adumbrates what seems to be a reasonable ethical stance evoking compassion and avoiding indirect causality of serious harm. There certainly should be room for ben Patura's ruling in what might be identified as Jewish lifeboat ethics. And indeed, the very language by which this exchange is presented—the "until Rabbi Akiva came and taught"—seems to echo more than a measure of residual plausibility which others found in ben Patura's ruling. But it also might register confusion and resistance to this same ruling that two should die when one could be saved. Why was Rabbi Akiva rushing to the scene, as it were, with such determination to set things straight?

Rabbi Akiva's position was related to the discourse on *pikuah nefesh* and *sakanot nefashot,* on the degree of risk which should be assumed in rescue situations. While saving the life of another is deemed particularly meritorious—and the Talmud abounds in discussions of the hierarchy of social obligations in situations of conflicting demands (e.g., priests vs. scholars, teachers vs. fathers)—serious constraints against self-sacrifice were placed upon would-be rescuers. Rabbi Akiva seems to rule that even in the instance of *safek sakonot nefashot,* that a potential rescuer is only in uncertain danger and *vadai pikuah nefesh,* that a potential victim is in incontestable mortal danger, the rescuer must be circumspect. This is what underlies Rabbi Akiva's position.[3]

This strident opposition to self-sacrifice might be a strange ruling for Akiva who in fact martyred himself.[4] That *even* Rabbi Akiva, the martyr *par excellence,* takes a most anti-sacrificial stance might provide precisely the context in which we hear the substance and style of Rabbi Yose's statement. Issued only a few years after his teacher, Rabbi Akiva, suffered martyrdom, might not Rabbi Yose's ruling regarding laundry actually have been directed toward contemporary Jews who were themselves survivors of the Hadrianic persecutions, and particularly to those who were finding themselves emotionally drawn to the early preachers of syncretic Jewish-Christian ideas? Might not some of these survivors have developed enthusiasm and alacrity for martyrdom exceeding the situations for which there was consensus that martyrdom was appropriate behavior?[5]

We must transpose the discussion from the hierarchy of obligation to the degree of risk. Precisely when clean laundry is a matter of comfort, even of self-indulgence, and when dirty laundry is the carrier of vermin and disease and is life threatening can never be clearly established. But that is the real point about risk: its assessment is, at best, precarious. In defining the domain of interpersonal obligation, charity should be clearly differentiated from usury, as the Bible does, in that it should not grant any benefit. But charity must also be clearly distinguished from sacrifice in that risk and the emotional pleasures that may accompany it are not acceptable. The same *avak ribit,* the great concern that money lending as a mode of charity be free of the most subtle "dusting" of usury or any benefit to the lender, may have its parallel in Rabbi Yose's disparagement of the slightest degree of self-sacrifice.

Rabbi Yose, indeed, might have meant laundry. In a hyperbolic manner he may have been trying to denegrate self-destructive giving that is ultimately centered on the donor and the donor's otherworldly benefit rather than on generosity which places the needs of the recipient at its center. Additionally, self-sacrifice often provides the legitimation for harming others, and in so doing sets in motion a vicious and tragic cycle. We know of cultures, for example, in which gifts—subtle forms of self-sacrifice—are modes of aggression, even of violence in another key; potlatch initiates fierce competition over the bestowal of gifts and ultimately the flaunting of brazenness in destroying one's own property.[6] As this example suggests, self-sacrifice is undesirable and even dangerous because on some psychological level and among some people, it is used to justify the sacrifice demanded of others in the form of the violence that is perpetrated against those others. Indeed, during Rabbi Yose's youth, and perhaps with the participation of his father, a rabbinic assembly convened in Usha. Among the very *takkanot* [reforms] promulgated in Usha was the imposition of limits on the percentage of an individual's wealth that could be bestowed upon charity. At that time, as this edict would indicate, self-sacrificial generosity was a problem.

Rabbi Yose's flagrant voice was, perhaps, a response to the same murky motives of self-sacrifice that prompted those rabbis to impose limits on generosity. In using this domestic image of laundry, the rabbi who was, after all, so very amiable was utilizing flagrancy to say more than what was obvious to his contemporaries. For a generation emerging from a great catastrophe with unspent zeal—zeal reserved for dangerously worldly nationalistic provocations, on the one side, and otherworldly flights into martyrdom, on the other—Rabbi Yose's message about obligations to God and one's fellow human was clear: "*Vehai bahem' velo sheyamut bahem,*" and you should live by those teachings, as the Torah repeats in so many ways, and not that you should be consumed by them—a temptation against which the rabbis, among them Rabbi Yose, at many times felt it so very necessary to warn.

NOTES

This *sugya* and its implications for Jewish attitudes towards rescue were brought to my attention through many discussions with teachers, friends, and family. These include David Kazhdan, Adin Steinzaltz,

Emily Rose, Elie Wiesel, Ron Garet, Anita and George Lasry, Gila Rau-mus-Rauch, David Gordis, Jeff Spitzer, Walter and Tova Reich, Ronit Meroz, Peter Stark, Shulamith, Hephzibah, Tiferet, and Haninah Levine.

1. *Tosefta, "Baba Metsia,"* Ch. 11; *Palestinian Talmud, "Nedarim,"* ch. 11; *Babylonian Talmud, "Nedarim,"* 80b–81a.

2. *"Baba Metsia,"* 62b.

3. Is it conceivable that this emphasis on endangerment could undermine the moral obligation of rescue in situations such as the Holocaust? It well might raise questions about the 1953 Israeli Parliamentary legislated definition of a "righteous gentile" that emphasizes the mortal risk taken by the rescuer as a qualification for particular approbation. Moreover, could it be that the Jews would maintain a double moral standard, as they were so often accused of doing by their enemies, in harboring expectations for self-sacrificial and heroic rescue from the "Town beyond the Wall" while advocating self-preservation and the most prudent risk taking where Jews are involved? In this particular discussion, there is no distinction being made between obligations to a Jew and non-Jew; where there is, the rabbis ultimately obliterate that distinction to advance concordial relations. It could be that the reticence towards self-sacrifice weighs so heavily, precisely in situations such as "two walking in the desert," where the threat comes from a *force majeure.* But in observing humanly perpetrated murder, the standard of obligation between human beings, even towards the murderer, is such that in order to stop the slaughter, the rescuer falls under different obligations. These might include the rules of preemptive response to the *"rodef,"* the person threatening another with violence or even an extension of the very few situations in which an individual is obligated to act self-sacrificially, in order to avert murder, where the rule "he must risk being killed but not transgress" applies.

4. While the rabbis narrowed the circumstances under which a person is obligated to surrender life for principle, the second-century religious persecutions, perpetrated by Roman rulers whom Akiva sought to defy, justified his self-sacrifice in the acceptable rabbinic terms.

5. This again was the situation in medieval Ashkenaz when the rabbis expressed reticence towards martyrdom. See Jacob Katz, *Exclusiveness and Tolerance* (New York: Schocken Books, 1962), pp. 82–92.

6. See, for example, the study of Melanesian millennial movements by Peter Worsley, *The Trumpet Shall Sound* (London: MacGibbon & Kee, 1968).

NEHEMIA POLEN

Coming of Age in Kozienice: Malkah Shapiro's Memoir of Youth in the Sacred Space of a Hasidic Zaddik

Professor Elie Wiesel has shown us how to face with unblinking
candor, with dignity and courage, the enormity of what has been
lost. He has also shown us how to treasure that which survives,
even if only in memory. He has been an illuminating teacher,
a wise mentor, and an inspiring guide. It is a signal privilege
to dedicate this essay in his honor.

CHILDHOOD AND THE RECOVERY OF SACRED SPACE

Childhood memories are intimately intertwined with our sense
of self, our feeling of place in the world. Especially for the sensitive soul, the persons, locations, and moods of childhood continue to haunt us, to form and shape our perspectives on life,
our ways of looking at and perceiving the lifeworld we inhabit.[1]
But what if the place of one's childhood no longer exists? How
does the mature individual continue to nurture a sense of one's
place in the world when the locus of one's youth is no longer
physically present? For some individuals this issue arises because
the bucolic settings of childhood were overtaken by the encroachment of industry and technological civilization. But there are
those for whom the question is even more painful, since the disappearance of the sites of youthful memories was caused by malevolent acts of willful destruction. For such individuals, the re-
constitution of their childhood memories is not only retrieval of
the early parts of the self; it is an act of conjuration, the recrea-

tion of a world destroyed, a religious statement of faith, an imaginative reconstruction of sacred space.

If this is so for individuals, it is, mutatis mutandis, true for nations and peoples, especially the Jewish people. The Bible can be viewed as the record of humankind's diverse and multifaceted relationship to place.[2] On the one hand, Genesis 1 emphasizes the protean universality of human dominance over the earth as a whole. But starting with Genesis 2, where God places the earthling in one particular location, from which in short order the human pair is exiled, the human condition is a story of the quest for home, for the place of one's origins. Abraham's journey from his homeland in quest of the land that God will show him is a reversal of the natural desire to live in one's birthplace and to embrace one's patrimony. At the same time, it enables Abraham and his descendents to replace a blood-and-soil ideology with a more spiritual notion of acquiring one's land in response to the divine Word. The entire narrative sweep of the Bible centers on this Land, but much of the action takes place outside of it: in Egypt, in Babylonia, in the desert.

The book of Genesis retains traces of an archaic ideology of sacred place expressed by the Hebrew word *makom,* denoting a special location, typically a site of cultic activity.[3] The *makom* is a center of sacred energy, a window that opens to heaven.[4] Typically associated with events in the lives of the patriarchs, the *makom* invokes the memories of the great individual who lived or worshiped there, and enables his descendents to recall those memories and access that sacred energy.

A different notion of sacred place is developed in the book of Deuteronomy. There it is stressed that the place that is to be the central site of worship in the Land is sacred not because of any tellurian power or ancient associations, but because it is the "place that the Lord your God will choose to cause His name to dwell there" (12:11). That is, the chosen place (Jerusalem, as we will be told subsequently in Scripture) is unique not because of any inherent quality of place, but simply because God has chosen it. This philosophical notion is clearly in some tension with the idea of *makom* in Genesis, which suggests that certain sites are endowed with essential sacred qualities.

Yet another perspective on sacred place might more properly be called "sacred space," and is not fixed to a particular location at all. Sacred space is movable, a portable domain created by partitions which are erected by human agency, eventually to be disassembled and reerected somewhere else. The prime example of this kind of sacred space is the desert Tabernacle of the Books of Exodus and Leviticus. Here too there is a contrast to the *makom* of Genesis, where a sacred spot is discovered, encountered, chanced or stumbled upon (consider Jacob at Bethel), but is never created by humans. On the other hand, Exodus and Leviticus largely avoid the word *makom*, but repeat again and again the word *va-ya'as* in its grammatical variations: he made, they made, Israel made, Bezalel made. It is humans who erect the partitions which circumscribe the boundaries of sacred space, and who fashion the utensils which furnish it.

All of these notions of sacred place/space converge in the biblical portrait of Jerusalem, and especially in the Temple erected by Solomon, which manages to combine aspects of deuteronomic theology of divine choice, with *makom*/place theology rooted in Genesis, along with a floor plan whose basic schematic design is modeled after the desert Tabernacle of Exodus and Leviticus. Given the cumulative force of these perspectives, combined with the theology of Davidic kingship, it is not hard to see why many people in Judea considered the Temple eternal and impregnable to attack, and why the events of 587 were seen as an incomprehensible disaster.

Along with the return to Zion and the slow and ultimately incomplete restoration of the Second Commonwealth, a new theology arose in which the notion of sacred space was projected, at least in part, onto the Torah scroll itself. By the time of the rabbinic period, it was clear that Jews dwelled in their sacred books as much as in their nominal places of residence. They settled in and built homes within the extraterritorial space provided by Scripture and tradition. If the content of their religion consisted of the words inscribed in black ink on parchment and paper in scrolls and books, their geographical borders were the white margins surrounding the words.[5]

These diverse notions of sacred space/place are all part of the heritage of classical Judaism. The kabbalistic and hasidic traditions add one very significant feature to this picture: the idea of the zaddik as sacred center.[6] The hasidic master is the pivot around which the world turns, the bridge between heaven and earth, the channel through which blessing flows from its supernal origin to its human destination.

MALKAH SHAPIRO AND HER WORK

We have presented this brief survey of the history of ideas of sacred place/space in Jewish thought as a framework for analyzing the writings of Malkah Shapiro (1894–1971). Born Reizel Malkah Hapstein, Shapiro grew up in Kozienice, a small provincial town about fifty miles southeast of Warsaw, where her father Rabbi Yerahmiel Moshe Hapstein (1860–1909) was the incumbent Kozienicer Rebbe, in a line begun by the famed Kozienicer Maggid (d. 1814), one of the founding fathers of Polish Hasidism. In 1927 she left Poland and emigrated to Palestine. In the 1950s and 1960s several collections of her Hebrew writings were published in Israel. [7]

Much of Shapiro's work consists of autobiographical memoir describing her life in rural Poland at the beginning of the twentieth century. The narrative often unfolds from the perspective of a young girl at the threshold of maturity (11–12 years old) named Bat-Zion,[8] the author's literary persona. The members of Shapiro's family, women especially, are the major characters in her stories, and a major theme is the role of women in Hasidism. Women are depicted not only as performing acts of service, kindness, and charity, but also as scholars of Torah, transmitters of sacred traditions, and as spiritual beings who attain holiness and strive for elevated and sublime states of personal, inner piety.

Shapiro's work fills a gap left by almost all other collections of hasidic tales and traditions from Eastern Europe. In her stories we find a specificity of detail simply not to be found in most hasidic writings, which tend to focus on the anecdote, the wise saying, the Torah discourse or insightful comment, but do not provide sustained descriptions of people and places. With her richness of expression Malkah Shapiro recreates the taste and texture of Eastern European hasidic piety from within, presenting Hasidism as a devotional path. Her stress is always on the interior life and the cultivation of sublime states of awareness and reflection. She depicts all the members of her family, women and men, as attending to inwardness with loving, reverential care. In addition, her portrayal of rural Polish Hasidism and its male and female personalities in the late nineteenth and early twentieth centuries contains much material valuable for social and religious history: descriptions of family relationships, girls' education, Polish-Jewish interaction, local customs, folk healing practices, as well as an extensive exploration of the complex dynamics of a Rebbe and his community.

Shapiro's portrayal of the meticulous care which her family members shower upon matters of the spirit finds a parallel in her own loving attention to matters of style and language. Her stories are written in a poetic literary Hebrew which reveals broad knowledge of biblical, rabbinic, and kabbalistic sources. She obviously cared deeply about the literary and aesthetic value of her work, and placed as much emphasis upon the grace of her style as upon the substance of what she had to say.

While Malkah Shapiro's works received some favorable notice in the Hebrew press during her lifetime and at the time of her death,[9] they are today largely forgotten to Hebrew readers, and are almost entirely unknown to the English language reader. In Shapiro's day, Hebrew literary circles were often ambivalent about the efforts of women writers.[10] In the traditional hasidic circles of Shapiro's own community, such writing was virtually nonexistent. Apparently, neither secular literary critics on the one hand, nor her own hasidic community on the other, knew quite what to make of her. As someone whose very act of writing transgressed traditional boundaries, her work emerges as a bold and essentially unprecedented creative achievement. At a time when the history of Jewish women's spirituality and literature is a subject of intense academic and popular interest, it is appropriate that the rich oeuvre of Malkah Shapiro be redeemed from obscurity and studied for its many riches.

KOZIENICE AND SACRED PLACE

While depicting her family and the Hasidism of her youth, Shapiro describes the place where she grew up—the town of Kozienice, whose Jewish community no longer existed when her books were published.[11] She traces with love the world of her childhood, a world of profound tenderness, exquisite beauty, and enveloping holiness, filled with individuals whose aspirations were directed entirely to the domain of the sacred.[12] In this world, the domestic and natural environment is not merely an arena for the unfolding of events, but rather a vital and active contributor to the story. Her home and surroundings are suffused with the rhythms of nature and the cycle of the Jewish sacred calendar. Kozienice not only reverberates with holiness, it yearns for it, coming alive in its own voice. The natural world in which the town is situated is alive with metaphysical and kabbalistic forces, so that humans and nature join together to celebrate the sacred days. Kozienice, in other words, is a sacred place with a personality and a soul. Our goal in this essay will be to explore this sacred place, which can fruitfully be compared to the modes of spatial sacredness in the Bible.

Let us begin with sacred place as *makom*, the biblical site associated with the life and deeds of a revered ancestor. In Shapiro's memoir, entitled *Mi-Din le-Rahamim* (From Justice to Mercy), *makom* is defined by locations associated with her famous ancestor, R. Israel Hapstein (d. 1814), known as the Maggid of Kozienice, a founder of Polish Hasidism. A master of Talmud and legal codes, as well as the practical and theoretical Kabbalah, he was sought out for blessings and amulets, which were reputed to assist barren couples in having children. His fame attracted Christian Poles as well as Jews, and prominent figures from the Polish nobility such as Adam Chartoryski, Josef Poniatowski, and Prince Radziwil came to seek his blessing. He used his influence and prestige in Polish ruling circles to mitigate the effect of prejudicial regulations and to protect his people from outbreaks of anti-Jewish violence. The author of twenty-three works in all areas of rabbinic literature, he was active in sponsoring the publication of kabbalistic manuscripts. He transmitted his teachings to scores of disciples, many of whom became leading figures of the hasidic movement in Poland and Galicia throughout the first half of the nineteenth century. The Maggid of Kozienice thus combined in one person all the ideals of the early hasidic master: selfless devotion in service of God and other human beings; mastery of traditional rabbinic literature while cultivating an inner life of ecstatic prayer and mystical practice; a reputation for paranormal powers, especially the ability to grant efficacious blessings; and finally, saintly prestige and influence in the Gentile as well as the Jewish world, deployed for the benefit and protection of his community.

The fame of the Maggid continued in succeeding generations. Throughout the nineteenth century and into the twentieth, the small and otherwise undistinguished provincial town of Kozienice was celebrated as the home of the Maggid. Christian residents of the town as well as Jews revered his saintly memory. The street he lived on, and upon which his house still stood, was named Magitowka in his honor.

The Maggid's shtibel, his personal room which had been left just as it was during his lifetime, one hundred years earlier, was revered as a shrine. As Shapiro describes it,

> The canopied bed, upon which the Maggid slept; the upholstered chair upon which he sat; the high and narrow table, upon which he wrote the amulets and Torah esoterica: these all were still in their places. Silently they absorbed the laments of people who came to pour their hearts out in this sacred place.[13]

The Hapstein family and the hasidim apparently believed that the spirit of the Maggid was still present in the room. On the eve of Shabbat, Shapiro's father would enter the room with great respect, say "*Gut Shabbos,*" and leave. At the end of the Sabbath, he would come with his violin and play the special Kozienitzer melody for *Eliahu Ha-Navi*. During times of illness, the room would be used for prayers and the chanting of Psalms.

Another place associated with the memory of the Maggid was his *bes-medresh*, or study hall, which was used for study, prayer, and other sacred activities. This is Shapiro's description of an evening Hanukkah celebration led by her father, Rabbi Yerahmiel Moshe Hapstein (1860–1909), the incumbent Rebbe of Kozienice in the days of her childhood:

> Midnight. The songs began to ring out from the old bes-medresh of the Maggid that was filled with veteran hasidim. The Rebbe kindled the lamp in the Hanukkah candelabrum; with the old silver tongs, he kept adjusting the wick. He began singing psalms and songs of praise, to which the hasidim joined in responsively. The wick from the Holy Land, which had been fashioned to the accompaniment of esoteric contemplations, rose in flame from the pure oil. The bes-medresh was afire in songs of praise, in melodies, and in the glow of the candies affixed in silver candlesticks on the long tables. Under the beams of the low ceiling poured out the notes of the Great Hallel and psalms. They stretched out and enveloped the courtyard, its buildings, its rooms and its trees seized by slumber. . . .

> The ambience of the bes-medresh, bathed in an ancient light and saturated with melodies drawn from the font of the Primordial One, warms the spirits of the hasidim, who stand crowded in, breaking out responsively to the verses. . . . The Master begins playing a melody on the violin. The notes tremble and shake, they flow out like the current of a river that has burst its dam, enveloping the room uniting with holy longing in the song that bursts out of the heart of the hasidim: "A PSALM, A SONG OF DEDICATION." The room reverberates, as if singing of its own accord. The notes of the melody combine with the pounding of feet as the hasidim join hands and begin to dance, swept away by the spirit. The dancers circle round, chained hand in hand. The eyes are closed; only the heart is open. The Master puts down the wondrous violin. With the silver tongs he adjusts the Hanukkah lamp. He begins dancing; he

leaps with the others; his mouth utters songs of praise incessantly. The shadows of the dancing hasidim prance on the whitewashed walls, which, worn out from age, tell stories of bygone times. (ML, pp. 29–30)

In Shapiro's depiction, Hanukkah is being celebrated not only by the master, her father; by the hasidim, his disciples; but also by the bes-medresh itself, which bears and reverberates with the spirit of all the sacred melodies that ever were sung there, as far back as the days of the holy Maggid.

Perhaps the most important of all the *makom*/locations is the Maggid's sepulcher. Known as the *Ohel* ('Tent'), the Maggid's burial place would be visited for petitionary prayer and during Yahrtzeits, the anniversary dates of the passing of the saintly family members interred there. Shapiro describes one such occasion, a visit around the time of the Yahrzeit of Rabbi Elimelekh of Grodzisk, her grandfather. The Ohel is being visited by her father, Rabbi Yerahmiel Moshe, by her mother and grandmother (the two Rebbetzins), and by other hasidim.

The Rebbetzins stayed a long while in the holy sepulchre, as they followed the intense outpouring of spirit that emanated from the Rebbe's heart. He was dressed in a sable Shtreymel, standing totally absorbed in contemplative communion with the spirits of his ancestors. His pale, noble face was illumined by the light of hundreds of candles lit in this sepulchre of his holy ancestor the Maggid and his holy descendents, generation after generation, who rested here in the cemetery between the pine trees in back of the great synagogue. (ML, p. 122)

In this scene of prayer and reverential devotion, there is a communion, a touching of the spirits of the current members of the dynasty, with earlier generations, going back to the founder, the Maggid himself. Direct contact with the souls of the deceased is greatly facilitated by one's physical presence at the location where their bodily remains are buried.

If the places associated with the Maggid of Kozienice and his descendents determine the *makom*-sacredness of Bat-Zion's world, there was also a sacredness of domestic residence, like the Tabernacle of the Bible, defined by partitions and home to the Shekhina, the tenting-Presence of the divine. In this case it was the family compound, a complex of buildings which housed the Rebbe's immediate and extended family, as well as a much wider circle of workers, household staff, hasidim in permanent residence, guests, and visitors. The large numbers of hasidim who would visit during holy day periods required a permanent staff of cooks, domestic workers, service personnel of various kinds, who in turn required overseers and managers. Ultimate responsibility for the workings of the household and the staff rested with Bat-Zion's grandmother Sarah Devorah, and to a lesser degree, her mother Bracha Tzippora Gitl. Here too one can trace an analogy to the biblical tabernacle, with its large staff of Levites to maintain the House of God, and a cadre of priests to supervise the Levites and engage in the sacred service which provided, as scripture puts it, "the food of God." One might consider this analogy a bit strained, given that much of Shapiro's description revolves around domestic activity: cleaning, cooking, sewing, embroidering. But precisely these activities were considered sacred in Exodus and Leviticus. And Shapiro's reverent and finely detailed descriptions of the work of the household make it clear that she views it all as consecrated activity, genuinely sacred work in every sense of the word.[14]

The family compound had two courtyards, an outer and an inner. Significantly, the outer courtyard was "open," that is, not entirely fenced in, whereas the inner courtyard was completely closed off, accessible only by a wooden gate that was always kept shut. As Shapiro describes it,

> The open courtyard is near the large kitchens which were constantly in use for preparing food for large numbers of people. There was a small garden planted with cedar trees—between the servants' rooms and the woodshed. (ML, p. 127)

Not far from the kitchens were a wine cellar and the horse stables. The open courtyard led through a small gate to the inner, closed courtyard, defined by a few modest buildings: the residence of

the Rebbe and Rebbetzin; his study; and residences for the boys
and girls of the family. In the center of the courtyard was a cop-
per sundial on a small pedestal, which testified to the Rebbe's
interest in astronomy as a religious discipline.

The courtyards are living personalities resonating with spirit.
This is Shapiro's description of how sunset fell upon the courtyard on the eve of Hanukkah:

> The courtyards of the Maggid, surrounded by ancient buildings—
> in which dwell his descendent and heir Rabbi Yerahmiel Moshe and
> his family—are intoxicated with the flaming elixir of the sunset,
> and are veiled in the deepest secrets. . . . The shrubs in the garden
> are bedecked with crimson fire, as if they have stolen a whiff of the
> mysteries. . . . (ML, p. 18)

The two courtyards correspond to two nested domains of association: the outer circle of guests and staff, and the inner circle
of family and veteran hasidim. The inner domain was hidden to
casual view. An intimate place of delicacy, grace, and familial
love, it was protected and isolated from the winds of change.

The two courtyards were deployed for the household's communal preparations for Passover, a task which took many weeks
and which involved all members of the community. Most activities took place in the outer courtyard and the surrounding buildings. These included grinding Passover flour, preparation of bar-
rels to store raisin wine, and making the kitchens and their many
vessels kosher for Passover. The inner courtyard was used for airing out clothing, linens, and the many sacred books. In the context of these Passover preparations, Shapiro conveys the symbolic
meaning of the two courtyards and their spiritual relationship in
the following words:

> The tumult of the workers, the chirping of the birds, the rustling
> of the trees, which announced in the open courtyard the coming
> of spring and of freedom: all these were concentrated in the inner
> courtyard, condensing in a mantle of sound which bespoke holi-
> ness. From that sublimely ethereal mantle, the Passover burst forth
> on all sides. (ML, p. 126)

That is, the inner courtyard was a lens of holiness which absorbed the pastoral energies of the outer courtyard, intensifying and transmuting them at the pulse of sacred time known as Passover.

If the courtyards are sacred, the ambience inside the family's rooms is even more sacred:

> The light projected by the stained glass in the nickel oil-lamp covered the palpable silence. The double windowpanes, etched in frost, . . . sealed out the tumult of the outside world. Even the tall cedar trees, which banged against the windowpanes, appeared as if attempting to break into the room, but remained outside in the frozen garden, behind the window. Here in this cozy pensive space, wrapped in murmuring silence, here was the goal and purpose of the universe. (ML, pp. 28–29)

All of this brings to mind the desert Tabernacle (and the Jerusalem Temple), with courtyard, Sanctuary, and Holy of Holies. The Holy of Holies was the energy center for the entire system, the point where the divine Presence erupted into the realm of the physical, as well as the focal point for all acts of Israelite sacred service. Its position at the inner core of nested rectangles assured its complete hiddenness, and protected it from desecration or encroachment by interlopers.

Let us now turn to examine the metaphoric significance of Shapiro's descriptions from a biographical perspective. Born in 1894, Shapiro is eleven years old in 1905, the year in which her memoir is set. The time is one of crisis for all Jews living in Imperial Russia. 1903 is the year of the Kishinev pogrom, an event which shook Russian Jewry and aroused the conscience of the world. While the pogrom of Kishinev is the most well known, it was only a foretaste of a much wider wave of anti-Jewish violence associated with the First Russian Revolution of 1905. The events of 1905, which forced Nicholas II to promise basic political rights to the Russian people, adumbrated the fall of Imperial Russia in the next decade. Thus 1905 could be considered a watershed year, where the incipient collapse of the old order could already be foreseen. For Jews this meant the disappearance of the shtetl and its way of life, a process which would soon be accelerated by the Great War and its aftermath. To be sure, the new century held out much hope, but the dangers of the new age, both physical and spiritual, were already very much in view. For Kozienice specifically, these events had already brought stagnation and the seeds of decline, which would accelerate in the decades to come, as more and more Jews left either for the economic opportunities of large cities such as Warsaw, or emigrated to Palestine in a wave of Zionistic idealism. The sacred memory of the Maggid of Kozienice had surrounded the town with a protective field, largely shielding it from hostile activities motivated by anti-Jewish sentiments. The ongoing shelter of the Maggid's memory had held firm for over a century, but eventually it too would not be able to overcome the overwhelming cultural and political forces which assailed it, and the sheer military brutality which would soon sweep the town away.

Parallel to these forces besetting the sacred space of Kozienice were the changes taking place for young Malkah ("Bat-Zion") herself. Standing at the threshold of maturity, she is deeply embarrassed (her memoir tells us) by the biological changes that are taking place in her body. She notices men looking at her. She is about to lose the private inner space of childhood. In fact, by age fourteen the author was to marry her first cousin, Abraham Elimelekh Shapiro of Grodzisk (who was about the same age at the time of the wedding). Not long after, she moved to Warsaw to escape the ravages of World War I. In the densely settled and diverse religious culture of Warsaw she encountered and studied with figures such as Hillel Zeitlin, a religious seeker and mystic fully acquainted with the diversity of both western and eastern spirituality.[15] By 1927 she is in the Holy Land, first in a tiny hasidic settlement near Haifa founded by her brother, and later in Jerusalem. Most members of her family who remain in Poland are eventually killed in the Holocaust. Malkah Shapiro never returns to the site of her childhood. By the time of World War II, the town as she knew it ceases to exist. The implicit question posed in her work is how to situate all the memories of sacred space/place—which by their nature are seemingly immutable, eternal, indestructible, and not transferable—in a circumstance where their physical referent is inaccessible, and in some sense no longer exists. The question is adumbrated in the work by the emphasis placed on the issue of building a new mansion to replace the elegant family home which was destroyed in a fire around 1900. The issue is a major point of contention between Bat-Zion's grandmother, Rebbetsin Sarah Devorah, and her son— Bat-Zion's father—Rabbi Yerahmiel Moshe Hapstein, who is the incumbent Kozienicer Rebbe. R. Yerahmiel Moshe believes that it is improper to build elaborate edifices outside of Eretz Yisrael; even when hasidim specify that donated funds should be used for his home, he immediately distributes the funds to the poor. Eventually the new house does begin to rise, due to Sarah Devorah's indefatigable marshaling of architectural, financial and managerial resources.

Yet there is a sense in which the Rebbe was right to oppose the construction. Perhaps he foresaw that the days of Kozienice, and the kind of irenic rural hasidism it embodied, were numbered. As we have noted, in the next few decades most of his own descendents were either to emigrate to Eretz Yisrael or were to die in the Holocaust. The dynastic center of the House of Kozienice was to become a kingdom of memory.

Shapiro faces the challenge by shifting the focus to the Holy Land, an exile from the sacred space of Kozienice and Polish Hasidism, which is a homecoming to the sacred land of the Bible. In a story entitled "Ambience of Eretz Yisrael,"[16] a visitor tells the family that the souls of the Seer of Lublin, of the Holy Jew of Pshyshche, and of the zaddikim of the dynasties of Kozienice, Stolin, and Chernobyl have been seen at the Western Wall and other holy places. These visions no doubt adumbrate the historical reality: the hasidim who revered and made pilgrimages to the sacred sites of Polish Hasidism, and many of the sites themselves, were to be swept away. Only by a spiritual move to the Holy Land would the souls of the zaddikim find their true home; only by a physical move to the Holy Land would the living hasidim be spared the destruction.

This return to the Holy Land in Shapiro's work (as well as in her life) expresses a hard fact: for all that the Hapstein family, beginning with the Maggid himself, had vested the town of Kozienice with sacredness, in the end it was not enough to prevent the cataclysm. By virtue of the saintly personalities who made it their home, Kozienice had indeed been endowed with the qualities of sacred place/*makom*. For generations its boundaries and partitions had also created a protected domain where a quiet and unhurried hasidism could flourish, luxuriating in a sacred space far from the pace and pressures of urban life. But Kozienice could never become "the place that the Lord your God will choose to cause His name to dwell there." In the nature of things, there could only be one such place, one Eretz Israel and Jerusalem. Shapiro herself wrote in mandatory Palestine and the State of Israel; she knew her life was saved by her decision to leave Poland in 1927. Thus the love of her birthplace, so much in evidence in her writing, must have competed with a still greater love for the Holy Land, which was not only the land of biblical Israel, but the land where she found refuge, raised her own family, lived most of her adult life; where she was to die.

The saintly figures of Shapiro's family now live in her own works. The sacred space of Kozienice, like the memory of biblical Israel, is inscribed in the word. But here the parallel breaks down: unlike the Bible, Malkah Shapiro's stories capture a sacred place which, on the stage of history, will never be recovered. For Kozienice, there will never be a return from the Babylonian exile.

For the delicate, spiritually sensitive child Bat-Zion, the sacred space of Kozienice once enabled her to commune with her deceased ancestors. It provided an entry into the world of hasidic holiness; it afforded a measure of protection from the terrors without (hatred and political instability in Imperial Russia and Poland) as well as the terrors within (the changes brought about by the onset of adolescence and her forthcoming marriage at age fourteen). But for the empirical author Malkah Shapiro, in the image of Sefer Yetzirah, letters are stones. Memory inscribed as text creates a domain of the sacred which can never be destroyed, but lives eternally.

NOTES

This essay is part of a larger work which aims to produce a literary biography of Malkah Shapiro, situating her in the context of Polish Hasidism, with special focus on the role of women in the hasidic movement. The project involves translation of a significant portion of her work into English. All translations that appear herein are mine.

1. Cf. Louise Chawla, *In the First Country of Places: Nature, Poetry and Childhood Memory* (Albany: State University of New York Press, 1994).

2. Cf. Michael Fishbane, "The Sacred Center: The Symbolic Structure of the Bible," in *Texts and Responses: Studies Presented to Nahum N. Glatzer on the Occasion of His Seventieth Birthday by His Students,* ed. Michael A. Fishbane and Paul R. Flohr (Leiden: Brill, 1975), pp. 6–27.

3. Cf. Nahum Sarna, *The JPS Torah Commentary: Exodus* (Philadelphia: Jewish Publication Society, 1991), p. 116.

4. See Gen. 28:10–22.

5. Cf. Emanuel Maier, "Torah As Movable Territory," *Annals of the Association of American Geographers* 65, no. 1 (1975): 18–23; N. Wieder, "'Sanctuary' as a Metaphor for Scripture," *Journal of Jewish Studies* 8, no. 4 (1957): 165–76.

6. Cf. Arthur Green, "The Zaddik as Axis Mundi," *Journal of the American Academy of Religion* 45, no. 3 (1977): 327–47.

7. These include *Sheneinu Be-Maginim* (Tel Aviv: Dvir, 1952); *Be-Lev ha-Mistorin* (Tel Aviv: Netzah, 1956); *Mi-Din le-Rahamim* (Jerusalem: Mosad Harav Kook, 1969). Shapiro's poetry is collected in *Shiri Li Bat Ami* (Tel Aviv: Netzah, 1971).

8. The name Bat-Zion was added during childhood at a time of critical illness. See *Mi-Din le-Rahamim* [= ML], pp. 35–37.

9. See, e.g., A. Sharvit, "Be-Ma'agalei ha-Hasidut ve-ha-Musar," *Mabu'a* 7 (1970): 141–49; M. Ungerfeld, "Le-zikhrah shel Meshoreret ha-Hasidut," *Ha-Do'ar* 51 (March 17, 1972): 293.

10. For attitudes toward women's literacy in Yiddish, Hebrew, and other languages, in the context of Eastern European Haskalah, see Iris Parush, "The Politics of Literacy: Women and Foreign Languages in Jewish Society of Nineteenth-Century Eastern Europe," *Modern Judaism* 15 (1995): 183–206; Shmuel Finer, "The Modern Jewish Woman: A Test-Case in the Relationship Between Haskalah and Modernity," *Zion* 58, no. 4 (1993): 453–99; Shaul Stampfer, "Gender Differentiation and Education of the Jewish Woman in Nineteenth-Century Eastern Europe," *Polin* 7 (1992): 63–87. For the situation in Palestine during the first two decades of the twentieth century, see Dan Miron, "Why Was There No

Women's Poetry in Hebrew Before 1920," in *Gender and Text in Modern Hebrew and Yiddish Literature*, ed. Naomi B. Sokoloff, Anne Lapidus Lerner, and Anita Norich (New York and Jerusalem: The Jewish Theological Seminary of America, 1992), pp. 65–91, which argues for the overwhelmingly suppressive influence of male stars, especially Bialik. In the same volume, the introductory essay by Anita Norich is very informative and helpful. Note for example her remark that the world of modernity and its literature "emerge from a complex relationship to tradition, which eventually opened the cultural world to women but which, paradoxically, may have initially left them with less of a footing in a coherent cultural universe then they had previously been able to claim" (p. 13). See also Deborah S. Bernstein, ed., *Comments on Pioneers and Homemakers: Jewish Woman in Pre-State Israel* (Albany: State University of New York Press, 1992). It is interesting that a work by David N. Myers, *Re-Inventing the Jewish Past: European Jewish Intellectuals and the Zionist Return to History* (New York and Oxford: Oxford University Press, 1995), which focuses on the intellectual climate at the Hebrew University's Institute of Jewish Studies, where Shapiro sat in on courses, hardly makes mention of women at all.

11. Extensive information on the history of the Jewish community of Kozienice, including the period of the Holocaust, can be found in Barukh Kaplansky, ed., *Sefer Kozienice* (Tel Aviv, 1969) [Hebrew and Yiddish]. This memorial book includes photographs, personal reminiscences, as well as much material about the family of Malkah Shapiro.

12. It is notable that Shapiro displays an overwhelmingly positive attitude toward her childhood, family members, and community. In contrast with many other memoirists who emerge from the world of the shtetl into modernity, she is concerned to stress continuity rather than discontinuity. It is illuminating to compare her work with those discussed in Alan Mintz's *"Banished from their Father's Table": Loss of Faith and Hebrew Autobiography* (Bloomington: Indiana University Press, 1989). Shapiro wishes to show, among other things, that despite the geographical and existential distance she has traveled from Kozienice, she was not "banished from her father's table." Shapiro's fully embracing appreciation of the world of her childhood distinguishes her from other writers deeply rooted in the world of tradition such as S. Y. Agnon, whose attitude, as Arnold Band has put it, stood "between nostalgia and nightmare." Shapiro's effort to link herself to the world of her childhood in an apparently unconditional manner sets her apart from another woman writer who left the shtetl, Devorah Baron. See Anne Lapidus Lerner, "Lost Childhood in East European Hebrew Literature," in *The Jewish Family: Metaphor and Memory*, ed. David Kraemer (New York and

Oxford: Oxford University Press, 1989), pp. 95–112. See also Anita Norich's remarks on the autobiographical writings of Esther Singer Kreitman—sister of Isaac Bashevis Singer, in "The Family Singer and the Autobiographical Imagination," *Prooftexts* 10 (1990): 91–107.

In light of this material, Malkah Shapiro appears to be quite exceptional, giving support to her own view expressed in her memoir, that her parents—with special emphasis on her father—truly encouraged the daughters of the family to become accomplished scholars of Hebrew and the classics of Judaism. On the broader issue of attitudes towards women in Hasidism, see Nehemia Polen, "Miriam's Dance: Radical Egalitarianism in Hasidic Thought," *Modern Judaism* 12 (1992): 1–21.

13. *Be-Lev ha-Mistorin*, pp. 119–20.

14. A clear exposition of the perspective on domestic life which emerges implicitly from Shapiro's writing may be found in Kathryn Allen Rabuzzi, *The Sacred and the Feminine: Toward a Theology of Housework* (New York: Seabury, 1982). See esp. chapter 1, "Home As Sacred Space."

15. See Arthur Green, "Three Warsaw Mystics," in *Rivkah Shatz-Uffenheimer Memorial Volume II* ed. Rachel Elior and Joseph Dan (Jerusalem 1996), pp. 1–58.

16. "Avira de-Eretz Yisrael," ML, pp. 52–61; the specific passage is on pp. 56–57.

Ethical and Religious Reflections

JOHN K. ROTH

Helping Others to Be Free: Elie Wiesel and Talk about Religion in Public

> To be free is important. To help others to be free
> is even more important.
>
> Elie Wiesel to Oprah Winfrey

TALK ABOUT RELIGION is often disagreeable and divisive, contentious and dogmatic, or worse. Could those outcomes be corrected? Could those circumstances be improved? With particular reference to American life, but also with implications that reach beyond those boundaries, I have been exploring such questions. Elie Wiesel inspires my inquiry. He does so because his work includes emphasis on two key concerns: (1) the importance of talking in public about fundamental issues in religion and ethics, and (2) how public discourse and dialogue about religion can be made more sensitive and humane. This essay draws on Wiesel's example to suggest ways in which talk about religion in public might contribute to move us beyond contradiction and dissonance and into territory that people can identify as common ground that they want to share with care.

To set the scene for this inquiry, I need to mention a ritual that captivates millions of Americans every weekday afternoon. I refer to the watching of television "talk shows." In the United States, nobody does "the talk show thing" better than Oprah Winfrey. For a week in the summer of 1993, Oprah varied the format of her immensely popular show. The guests were special people, she said, whom she had long wanted to interview face to face. Maya Angelou was among them. On Thursday, July 15, so was

143

Elie Wiesel—the author of more than thirty books, winner of the 1986 Nobel Peace Prize, and a Jewish survivor of Auschwitz.

Oprah wanted to interview Wiesel because she had been deeply moved by reading *Night,* Wiesel's classic memoir about the destruction of his family during Nazi Germany's Final Solution and his survival of Auschwitz and Buchenwald, where he endured the Holocaust from 1944 to 1945. Wiesel accepted Oprah's invitation. The setting for the interview was not, however, the usual television studio but Wiesel's apartment in New York City. Oprah was not on her own turf in more ways than one. Perhaps the topics she needed to cover made her uncertain. How could they not? Maybe she was not quite sure how to approach a Holocaust survivor like Wiesel. How could she be? In any case, Oprah appeared less self-assured than usual. She seemed unable to draw Wiesel out as she might have thought she could. When, for example, she asked Wiesel to describe how he felt when he saw his mother forever separated from him at Auschwitz, Oprah got back a look that she had not anticipated. Wiesel's silence spoke more than words could say.

A captivating storyteller, Wiesel is a charismatic orator and a spellbinding teacher as well. He asks questions as insightfully as he fields them. He often talks publicly about religion in one way or another. But he is not a garrulous man by any means. He respects language too much to waste words in chit-chat and small talk. Often dwelling in the silences of memory and meditation, Wiesel seemed an incongruous talk show guest. Yet the reason for Wiesel's appearance on the *Oprah Winfrey Show* was not incongruous at all. For decades—through books, conferences, public lectures, teaching, and humanitarian acts—Wiesel has tried to "tell the tale," as he puts it. Talking and acting in public, he bears witness for the dead and the living as he protests against the wasting of human life, particularly but not only during the Holocaust. He warns especially against the indifference that permits such evil, regarding that indifference as worse than evil itself. Haunted by the fact that humankind seems to have learned so little from the Holocaust, Wiesel refuses to give up despite having, as he told Oprah, "six million reasons" to do so. Instead he strives to expose the anatomy of hate and to give people the courage to care. "To be free is important," he explained to those who heard the *Oprah Winfrey Show.* "To help others to be free is even more important."

A conversation with Oprah Winfrey was another way to "tell the tale." Specifically, it was a way to reach a huge audience of daytime television viewers who might not otherwise listen to what Elie Wiesel hopes they will hear. Among that audience, in fact, there probably were people who contributed to a Roper Organization poll, whose disturbing results were released by the American Jewish Committee (AJC) just three months earlier.[1] When the pollster asked American adults, "Does it seem possible or does it seem impossible to you that the Nazi extermination of the Jews never happened?" one third (34 percent) said either "it seems possible" (22 percent) or "don't know" (12 percent). For American high school students, the poll's results for the same question showed that over one third (37 percent) said either "it seems possible" (20 percent) or "don't know" (17 percent). Moreover, as confirmed by the filmed interview segments that Oprah used during her interview with Wiesel, large numbers of American high school students (39 percent according to the Roper Organization's findings) could not identify the historical event that is called the Holocaust. Apparently many of them (10 percent) had never even heard the word.

Although such skepticism and ignorance would be welcome news for the pseudo-historians who deny that the Holocaust ever happened, it is important to note that two subsequent polls discredited the initial results of the AJC/Roper inquiry. The wording of the original key question—"Does it seem possible or does it seem impossible to you that the Holocaust never happened?"—was less than crystal clear. When the Gallup Organization conducted a poll in January 1994, it used a clearer wording—"Do you doubt the Holocaust actually happened or not?"—and found that only 9 percent of the respondents expressed doubt about the Holocaust's happening. Two percent believed that the Holocaust definitely never happened. These results led the AJC to do another Roper survey, one that asked more clearly, "Does it seem possible to you that the Nazi extermination of the Jews never happened or, do you feel certain that it happened?" Analysis of responses to this second survey showed that only 1 percent of Americans believed it was possible that the Holocaust never happened. An additional 8 percent indicated that they lacked enough knowledge to answer one way or the other.[2]

The follow-up poll results suggest that Holocaust education has had some success, but those findings were unknown when Elie Wiesel appeared on the *Oprah Winfrey Show*. Rightly determined to prevent the manipulation and falsification of history, committed to overcoming ignorance about the Holocaust, "ethnic cleansing," and every other kind of suffering that people inflict on one another, Wiesel talked in public with Oprah, making use of the vast forum that only her show could provide.

Oprah and Wiesel talked about his experiences in "the kingdom of night," as he calls it, a creation that Nazi Germany produced alongside God's. It was hell. Perhaps it was even worse than hell if chaos rules there, said Wiesel, for in Auschwitz there was order. In that place and others like it—Treblinka, Majdanek, and Belzec to name just a few—things happened as they were planned, and the plans called for suffering and death to continue until the Final Solution was complete.

As Oprah and Wiesel spoke, questions were raised about God and religion, too. What, she asked him, was the first thing you did after you were liberated? We prayed, Wiesel replied. The survivors said Kaddish, the prayer for the dead. They did so for the sake of the dead, and perhaps for God's sake as well, but most of all, Wiesel stressed, the survivors prayed to show themselves that they still could pray—that is, to show themselves that they were still fully human. What about God? Oprah wanted to know. In Auschwitz, Wiesel told her, bread was more important than God. That statement did not mean, however, that God was unimportant. Rather it was a way of saying how much human life was reduced to the pain of an empty stomach. He had not rejected God in Auschwitz, Wiesel disclosed. His religious upbringing was too deep-seated for that. But he had rebelled against God, although most of his dissenting questions, including the anger and inability to understand God, became more focused and intense later on—partly because Wiesel was only fifteen when he arrived at Auschwitz. Laced with protest, his religious questions persist to this day as Wiesel sustains his quarrel with God and with humankind as well.

Their conversation continued. Wiesel and Oprah talked about serious, horrible, and, at times, hopeful things. They did so with civility and respect. Oprah posed her questions and offered her own observations tentatively. Sometimes she struggled for the right words and, faltering, did not always find them. Other times, she sensed that her own experience was inadequate for penetrating Wiesel's world. For his part, Wiesel reassured Oprah by acknowledging the limitations of his own perspectives. He did not know well enough how to describe, let alone to understand, what he had experienced during the Holocaust and continued to experience after Auschwitz in memories, dreams, and reflections.

If the interview was not entirely successful—interrupted by commercials as it was—there were moments when two very different people communicated with each other. Oprah had discovered that she was born on the day Wiesel was liberated from Buchenwald. As she talked with him, it became apparent that her encounter with Wiesel affected how she thought of herself. Wiesel spoke of the gratitude that he and other survivors feel when people try to fathom what happened, and when they are moved to be more sensitive in spite or even because of the fact that full comprehension of the Holocaust eludes them.

By talking in public, Wiesel and Oprah touched others in ways that went far beyond the privacy of Wiesel's New York apartment. The next day, for instance, while browsing in a bookstore, I overheard a young woman asking a clerk if the store had any copies of Elie Wiesel's *Night*. He looked and found one. We had quite a few yesterday, he told the woman, and now this is the last one. The day before, Oprah had told her viewers that they should all read *Night*. I am not sure, but I would bet that the young woman in the bookstore had been watching and listening carefully, too.

Some additional reflection on Wiesel's ways of thinking can show further how our talking about religion in public might help to mend the world. Consider, then, six of his major insights—two sets of three that focus, first, on understanding and then on doing. Simple and yet complex, complex and yet simple, each point is central, I believe, to Wiesel's way of thinking and living. None of his insights is an abstract principle; all are forged in fire that threatens to consume. For those reasons, these themes from Wiesel have integrity, credibility, and durability that make them worthy guidelines for all seasons. Each of them, I also believe, speaks indirectly but powerfully respecting how best to talk about religion in public.

Understanding: Wiesel seeks it but not too much. While wanting people to study the Holocaust, he alerts them to the dangers of thinking that they do or can or even should know everything about it. While wanting people to meet as friends, he cautions that such meetings will be less than honest if differences are glossed over, minimized, or forgotten. While wanting humankind and God to confront each other, he contends that easy acceptance is at once too much and too little to bear. Wiesel's understanding is neither facile, obvious, nor automatic. Nevertheless its rhythm can be learned. Three of its movements follow.

"The Holocaust demands interrogation and calls everything into question. Traditional ideas and acquired values, philosophical systems and social theories—all must be revised in the shadow of Birkenau."[3] Birkenau was the killing center at Auschwitz, and the first lesson Wiesel teaches is that the Holocaust is an unrivaled event because nothing exceeds its power to evoke the question: Why? That authority puts everything else to the test.

Whatever religions, and reflections or criticisms of them, that have existed, whatever dreams human minds have produced, they were either inadequate to prevent Auschwitz or, worse, they helped pave the way to that place. The Holocaust insists, therefore, that how we think and act needs revision in the face of those facts, unless one wishes to continue the same blindness that eventuated in the darkness of *Night*. The needed revisions, of course, do not guarantee a better outcome. And yet failure to use the

Holocaust to call each other, and especially ourselves, into question diminishes our chances to mend the world.

"The questions remain questions."[4] As the first lesson suggests, Elie Wiesel does not place his greatest confidence in answers. Answers—especially when they take the form of religious certainties and theoretical systems—make him suspicious. No matter how hard people try to resolve the most important issues, questions remain and rightly so. To encounter the Holocaust, to reckon with its disturbing Whys?—without which our humanity itself is called into question—that is enough to make Wiesel's case.

Typically, however, the human propensity is to quest for certainty. Wiesel's urging is to resist that temptation, especially when it aims to settle things that ought to remain unsettled and unsettling. For if answers aim to settle things, their ironic, even tragic, outcome is often that they produce disagreement, division, and death. Hence, Wiesel wants questions to be forever fundamental.

People are less likely to savage and annihilate each another when their minds are not made up but opened up through questioning. The Holocaust shows as much: Hitler and his Nazi followers "knew" they were "right." Their "knowing" made them killers. Questioning might have redeemed them and, more importantly, their victims.

Wiesel's point is not that responses to questions are simply wrong. They have their place; they can be essential, too. Nevertheless questions deserve lasting priority because they invite continuing inquiry, further dialogue, shared wonder, and openness. Resisting final solutions, these ingredients—especially when they drive home the insight that the best questions are never put to rest but keep us human by luring us on—can focus concern toward the common good in ways that answers alone rarely can.

"And yet—and yet. This is the key expression in my work."[5] Elie Wiesel's writings, emerging from intensity that is both the burden and the responsibility of Holocaust survivors, aim to put people off guard. Always suspicious of answers but never failing for questions, he lays out problems not for their own sake but to inquire, "What is the next step?" Reaching an apparent conclu-

sion, he moves on because there is always more to consider, more to warrant our concern and care. Such forms of thought reject easy paths in favor of hard ones.

Wiesel's "and yet—and yet" affirms that it is more important to seek than to find, more important to question than to answer, more important to travel than to arrive. Just as it is dishonest not to focus our thinking as self-critically as we can, the point is also that it can be dangerous to believe what you want to believe, deceptive to find things too clear, destructive to cling too tightly to one tradition alone, divisive to interpret the American Dream in only one way, and dumbfounding to fail to talk about these matters in public. He cautions that it is insensitive to overlook that there is always more to experience than our theories admit, even though we can never begin to seek comprehension without reasoning and argument. So Elie Wiesel tells his stories, and even their endings resist leaving his readers with a fixed conclusion. He wants them instead to feel his "and yet—and yet," which provides a hope that people may keep moving to choose life and not to end it.

Elie Wiesel's lessons about understanding urge one not to draw hasty or final conclusions. Rather his emphasis is on exploration and inquiry. It might be objected that such an outlook tends to encourage indecision and even indifference. To the contrary, however, one of Wiesel's most significant contributions runs in just the opposite direction. Thus, dialogue leads not to indecision but to an informed decisiveness. Tentativeness becomes protest when unjustified conviction asserts itself. Openness results not in indifference but in interdependence that helps all of us to be free. Wiesel's doing is demanding, but it, too, has a rhythm that can be learned. Here are three of its movements.

"Passivity and indifference and neutrality always favor the killer, not the victim."[6] Elie Wiesel will never fully understand the world's killers. To do so would be to legitimate them by showing that they were part of a perfectly rational scheme. Though for very different reasons, he will not fully understand their victims, either; their silent screams call into question every account of their dying that presents itself as a final solution.

Wiesel insists that understanding should be no less elusive where indifference—including its accomplices, passivity and neutrality—prevails. Too often, indifference exists among those who could make a difference, for it can characterize those who stand between killers and victims but aid the former against the latter by doing too little, too late. Where acting is concerned, nothing arouses Wiesel more than motivating the inactive. Inactivity, indifference, passivity, neutrality—concerned about the places where they can lead, Wiesel's understanding should help us to understand that, where religion in public is at stake, those traits prevail at our peril.

"As a Jew I abide by my tradition. And my tradition allows, and indeed commands, man to take the Almighty to task for what is being done to His people, to His children—and all men are His children—provided the questioner does so on behalf of His children, not against them, from within the community, from within the human condition, and not as an outsider."[7] Some of Elie Wiesel's most forceful writing involves the Jewish tradition known as Hasidism.[8] Many features impress him as he traces this movement from its flowering in the Jewish shtetls of Eastern Europe during the eighteenth century to its presence in the death camps, and to its continuing influence in a world that came close to annihilating Hasidic ways, root and branch. One of the rhythms of understanding and doing stressed by Wiesel derives, at least in part, from a Hasidic awareness of the relationships between "being for—being against."

Hasidism, in particular, combines a genuine awe of God with direct and emotional reactions toward God. It finds God eluding understanding but also as One to whom people can speak. The Hasidic masters argue with God, protest against God, fear, trust, and love God. All of this is done personally and passionately, without compromising God's majesty and beyond fear of contradiction. Levi-Yitzhak of Berditchev, for example, understood his role as that of attorney-for-the-defense, reproaching God for harsh treatment the Jews received. Joining him was Rebbe Israel, Maggid of Kozienice, author of one of Wiesel's favorite Hasidic prayers: "Master of the Universe, know that the children of Israel are suffering too much; they deserve redemption, they need it.

But if, for reasons unknown to me, You are not willing, not yet, then redeem all the other nations, but do it soon!"[9]

Nahman of Bratzlav holds another special place in Wiesel's heart. Laughter is Nahman's gift: "Laughter that springs from lucid and desperate awareness, a mirthless laughter, laughter of protest against the absurdities of existence, a laughter of revolt against a universe where man, whatever he may do, is condemned in advance. A laughter of compassion for man who cannot escape the ambiguity of his condition and of his faith."[10] And a final example, Menahem-Mendl of Kotzk, embodied a spirit whose intense despair yielded righteous anger and revolt so strong that it was said, "a God whose intentions he would understand could not suit him."[11] This rebel embraced life's contradictions both to destroy and to sustain them. Short of death, he found life without release from suffering. At the same time, he affirmed humanity as precious by living defiantly to the end. Wiesel implies, too, that the Kotzker hoped for something beyond death. His final words, Wiesel suggests, were: "At last I shall see Him face to face." Wiesel adds, "We don't know—nor will we ever know—whether these words expressed an ancient fear or a renewed defiance."[12]

Anything can be said and done, indeed everything *must* be said and done, that is *for* men and women. Wiesel understands this to mean that a stance against God—against religion—is sometimes enjoined. But he hastens to add that such a stance needs to be from within a perspective that also affirms God and that respects the importance of religious traditions. Otherwise we run the risk of being against humankind in other ways all over again. Those ways include succumbing to dehumanizing temptations which conclude that only human might makes right, that there is human history as we know it presently and nothing more, and that, as far as the Holocaust's victims are concerned, Hitler was victorious.

For . . . against: that rhythm involves taking stands. Spiritually, this means to be against God and against religion when "being for" would put one against humankind. Spiritually, this also means to be for God and for religion when "being against" would put one against humankind by siding with forces that tend, however inadvertently, to legitimate the wasting of human life. Elie Wiesel is fiercely humanistic. His humanism, however, remains tied to God and to religion, specifically to the Jewish traditions that inform his understanding and his refusal to understand both. The lesson here is that, without discussing, enlivening, and testing those ties in public, and, in particular, their ways of being for and against humankind, a critical resource for saving life and mending the world will be lost.

"By allowing me to enter his life, he gave meaning to mine."[13] Elie Wiesel's 1973 novel, *The Oath*, tells of a community that disappeared except for one surviving witness. It is a tale about that person's battle with a vow of silence. Azriel is his name, and Kolvillàg, his home in Eastern Europe, was destroyed in a twentieth-century pogrom prompted by the disappearance of a Christian boy. Ancient animosity renewed prejudice; prejudice produced rumor; rumor inflamed hate. Indicted falsely by the ancient, hateful accusation of ritual murder, Azriel and his fellow Jews were soon under threat.

Moshe, a strange, mystical member of the community, surrenders himself as the guilty party though no crime has been committed. But he does not satisfy the authorities and "Christians" of the town. Madness intensifies. The Jews begin to see that history will repeat, and they prepare for the worst. Some arm for violence; most gather strength quietly to wait and endure.

Permitted to speak to the Jews assembled in their ancient synagogue, Moshe envisions Kolvillàg's destruction. He knows the record of Jewish endurance, its long testimony against violence, but this seems to have done little to restrain men and women and even God from further vengeance. So Moshe persuades his people to try something different: "By ceasing to refer to the events of the present, we would forestall ordeals in the future."[14] The Jews of Kolvillàg become Jews of silence by taking his oath: "Those among us who will survive this present ordeal shall never reveal either in writing or by the word what we shall see, hear and endure before and during our torment."[15]

Next comes bloodshed. Jewish spirits strain upward in smoke and fire. Only the young Azriel survives. He bears the chronicles of Kolvillàg—one created with his eyes, the other in a book entrusted to him for safekeeping by his father, the community's historian. Azriel bears the oath of Kolvillàg as well. Torn between speech and silence, he remains true to his promise.

Many years later, Azriel meets a young man who is about to kill himself in a desperate attempt to give his life significance by refusing to live it. Azriel decides to intervene, to find a way to make the waste of suicide impossible for his new friend. The way Azriel chooses entails breaking the oath. He shares the story of Kolvillàg in the hope that it will instill rebellion against despair, concern in the place of lethargy and indifference, life to counter death.

The oath of silence was intended to forestall ordeals in the future. Such forestalling, Wiesel testifies, must give silence its due; it must also break silence in favor of speech and action that recognize the interdependence of all human actions. "By allowing me to enter his life, he gave meaning to mine." Azriel's young friend echoes the insights that Elie Wiesel has shared with those who hear what he has to say. He also sums up the most valuable gain that could occur if we learned to talk well about religion in public: "By allowing me to enter his life, he gave meaning to mine." Rightly understood, that understanding becomes a mandate for doing unto others what Azriel did for the boy he saved.

In October 1966, Wiesel began a series of public lectures at New York's 92nd Street Y, a prestigious Jewish cultural center. Each autumn since then, he has returned to that place where, among other things, he talks about religion in public. As he explores the many questions that his talks always raise, Wiesel's words are governed by themes that include the six I have identified.

When Wiesel speaks at the 92nd Street Y, he focuses especially on biblical men and women, Talmudic interpreters and interpretations of biblical stories, and the masterful teachers of the Hasidic tradition that informs so decisively the Jewish perspective where he "sees it from." Finding them "close to us everywhere and always," he picks these subjects because they are "intriguing and demanding of attention."[16] They have that quality because their stories are also ours. Just as the flaws and weaknesses of their characters can be seen in us today, so their hard-won wisdom and hard-earned dreams can provide vision for us now.

In 1991, Wiesel published a book called *Sages and Dreamers: Biblical, Talmudic, and Hasidic Portraits and Legends.* There are twenty-five of them, one from each of the annual series of lectures that Wiesel had given at the 92nd Street Y since 1966. The last chapter in the book is about "The Ostrowtzer Rabbi." It talks about a Hasidic dynasty that lasted for only two generations.

The dynasty's founder, Yehiel-Meir Halevy Helstock was born in Poland sometime in the early 1850s—the exact date is uncertain. His learning and powers of memory were awesome, his humility and compassion legendary, his desire to eliminate injustice and suffering impassioned. Rabbi Yehiel-Meir, says Wiesel, "ascribed all evil to come to the cardinal sin of gratuitous hatred."[17]

Again and again, Rabbi Yehiel-Meir returned to the biblical story of Joseph, who was victimized by his brothers' hate. In every way he knew, the Ostrowtzer rabbi encouraged people to stop hating each other. "Let us stop claiming that we alone are right, and all others are wrong," he implored. "Only then will redemption come."[18] Weakened by long years of fasting as well as by illness, Rabbi Yehiel-Meir died a few days after Purim, a joyous Jewish festival that celebrates redemption. But especially toward the end of his life, he had been increasingly tormented by nightmares.

The first Ostrowtzer rabbi had rejoiced when his people were happy. "When they were sad," Wiesel adds, "he brought them consolation. He gave meaning to their lives."[19] The same might have been said of Rabbi Yehezkel, the son who succeeded him. He was known for his weeping. "When he prayed, when he delivered sermons, when he studied, people would see tears streaming down his face," Wiesel says of him. "He too saw the dark clouds covering Europe and he spoke about them."[20]

In the summer of 1942, the Germans liquidated most of the ghetto they had established in Ostrowtze. Along with a few hundred others, Rabbi Yehezkel and his immediate family remained alive for a time. By the end of year, however, the Germans had murdered them, too. The Ostrowtzer dynasty had come to an end.

The Ostrowtzer rabbis' yearning for things to change, for things to improve, was as intense as their dynasty was brief. Redemption eluded them, but their spiritual authority and Elie Wiesel's remains. Although the shadow of Birkenau cannot be removed from the earth, its darkness may be lightened by public expressions of religion that "stop claiming that we alone are right, and all others are wrong," that encourage us to "stop hating one another," and that drive home this truth: "To be free is important. To help others to be free is even more important."

NOTES

1. For the complete results of this poll, see Jennifer Golub and Renae Cohen, *What Do Americans Know About the Holocaust?* (New York: The American Jewish Committee, 1993). The AJC commissioned the poll in late 1992. The findings were released in April 1993 to coincide with the fiftieth anniversary of the Warsaw ghetto uprising and the opening of the United States Holocaust Memorial Museum in Washington, D.C.

2. For information on these follow-up surveys, I am indebted to Lawrence Baron, "Holocaust Awareness and Denial in the United States: The Hype and the Hope," in *Lessons and Legacies III,* ed. Peter Hayes (Evanston, Ill.: Northwestern University Press, forthcoming).

3. This statement is from Elie Wiesel's foreword to Harry James Cargas, *Shadows of Auschwitz: A Christian Response to the Holocaust* (New York: Crossroad Publishing Company, 1990), ix.

4. Elie Wiesel, "Telling the Tale," in *Against Silence: The Voice and Vision of Elie Wiesel,* 3 vols., ed. Irving Abrahamson (New York: Holocaust Library, 1985), 1: 234.

5. Elie Wiesel, "Exile and the Human Condition," in *Against Silence,* 1: 183.

6. Elie Wiesel, "Freedom of Conscience—A Jewish Commentary," in *Against Silence,* 1: 120.

7. Elie Wiesel, "The Trial of Man," in *Against Silence,* 1: 176.

8. See, for example, *Souls on Fire: Portraits and Legends of Hasidic Masters,* trans. Marion Wiesel (New York: Random House, 1972); *Four Hasidic Masters and Their Struggle Against Melancholy* (Notre Dame, Ind.: University of Notre Dame Press, 1978); *Somewhere a Master: Further Ha-*

sidic Portraits and Legends, trans. Marion Wiesel (New York: Summit Books, 1982); and *Sages and Dreamers: Biblical, Talmudic, and Hasidic Portraits and Legends,* trans. Marion Wiesel (New York: Summit Books, 1991).

9. Wiesel, *Souls on Fire,* p. 133.

10. Ibid., 198.

11. Ibid., 245.

12. Ibid., 254.

13. Elie Wiesel, *The Oath,* trans. Marion Wiesel (New York: Random House, 1973), p. 16.

14. Ibid., 239.

15. Ibid., 241.

16. Wiesel, *Sages and Dreamers,* p. 13.

17. Ibid., 434.

18. Ibid.

19. Ibid., 431.

20. Ibid., 438.

DOROTHEE SÖLLE

The Languages of Mysticism:
Negation, Paradox, and Silence

Translated by Ruth Morris

For Elie Wiesel
who frequently speaks through silence

Spricht die Seele, so Spricht, ach! die Seele nicht mehr.
(If the soul speaks, then—oh!—the soul no longer speaks.)
—*Friedrich Schiller*

IN A SEMINAR on mysticism that we always began with a short meditation, I criticized a group which had fobbed us off with some, in my opinion, shallow music and then, on top of that, simply left us alone with our thoughts and feelings. One of the students objected to my criticism, saying, "What's the problem? After all, feeling is *always* something that you do *alone.*" I thought this was a terrible thing to say, for it implied a kind of hopelessness, a profound mistrust of the possibility of sharing feelings with others. When Jesus, I countered, had succeeded in feeding the five thousand, they all felt closer to the Kingdom of God. Disbelief, despair retreated. There were shared feelings of oneness, hope and solidarity.

But there still remained the student's objection, born out of despair over the possibilities of our language. She grounded her objection in what Martin Buber called *Getriebe:* the commotion, or hustle and bustle of life, the "confusion of feelings and objects."[1] According to Buber, language duplicates *Getriebe,* the hustle and bustle, and therefore is incapable of communicating the actual experience of Oneness; *cognitio Dei experimentalis,* the encounter with God conveyed not by books or teaching but by experience, is not provided for in normal speech. As in an image from the Sufi mystic Rumi, words are simply dust on the mirror that we call experience, a form of dust to which the broom of "tongue" gives rise.

All mystics have had to suffer from this dust of words. They can describe in images but can never put a name exactly as it was—*tel quel*—to what happened to them. If it is true that all human beings are capable of ecstasy, can experience mystical moments of "wholeness," then all human beings also share the helplessness of the language which we generally use. How can we make ourselves understood about something which does not represent the objective reality surrounding us? Can one explain the fragrance of a rose to a creature with no sense of smell? Can one convey to someone who has not been in love the condition of being in love? The intoxication of the Divine to someone sober?

Literary scholars speak of the topos of the unspeakable, but this form of helplessness is more than a literary device. It is a basic experience that language is too little, too narrow, too dusty, too meaningless, too misleading to express the mystic condition. How could God be named? Are not all names necessarily too petty? Is it not an erroneous assumption, not to say an arrogant conceit, to put into language that which is—the one being that is—neither one thing nor the other? And how can those who are sick with the longing to completely bury and lose themselves even acquire speech if the self-negation of the person speaking belongs to the very heart of their experience?

Most mystics knew: whatever you say about the Divinity is untrue. Their position on this basic question oscillated between an acknowledged helplessness of language (sometimes, in tension with the topos of the unspeakable, a helplessness deplored in an abundance of words) and a radical despairing thereof. A Franciscan mystic in Italy, Angela von Foligno (1248–1309), calls her own highly precise descriptions of what she has experienced "blasphemies"![2] How can one take the word, that uncomprehended *logos,* and "throw it to the [common] words for grub," as Buber similarly expresses his loathing of trivialization. He refers to the contradiction "between the experience and the hustle and bustle

(*Getriebe*) from which they soared upwards and into which they collapse again . . . between the ecstasy, that does not enter memory, and the longing to save it for memory, in image, in speech, in confession."[3] In every mystical sensitivity there lives something which struggles against the humdrum and is not willing to settle down tamely in it. The fact that what utterly affects us should not be utterable nourishes our mistrust of language as such and isolates us, as the student mentioned at the beginning rightly felt.

But nobody can really feel comfortable with unspeakability. Working on the impossible cannot be given up—the soul *cannot* renounce speaking of it. Nothing induces speakers to talk as much as the unspeakable; in a variation on Schiller's comment, one might say, "If the soul is silent, then—oh!—the soul is no longer silent." It is striking that nothing makes speech so flat, so trivial, so banal as the assumption in talk shows that people can talk about anything and everything. Speech develops on the margins, the outer edges, not in the interior, not at home.

Mystical sensitivity, with its exuberance, its *cognitio Dei experimentalis,* its longing for Oneness cannot be communicated because language itself, as Buber reminds us, partakes of the variety, the hustle and bustle, the confusion and tumult. Language reflects it and consequently, even if those who speak struggle against confusion and tumult, language remains tied to this supremely nonmystical domain: a domain in the service of purpose, calculation, and power.

THE "*SUNDER WARUMBE*": WITHOUT WHYS AND WHEREFORES

Why is our language so helpless, why can we not share through communicating that which we most need? I have learned most about this question from Meister Eckart. His concept of "*sunder warumbe*" (without whys and wherefores) constitutes in my eyes an indispensable expression of mystical existence; Eckart's notion also introduces an existential quality into the understanding of language. In the German sermon, "*In hoc apparuit caritas dei in nobis*" (John I: 4, 9), Eckart writes:

For this most innermost reason you should perform all of your deeds without whys and wherefores. I say in truth, as long as you perform your deeds for the sake of the kingdom of heaven or God or your eternal salvation, in other words for an external reason, things are not truly well with you. You may well be accepted, but it is certainly not the best way. For verily, if somebody imagines that they will receive more in warmth, devotion, sweet rapture, and in the special grace of God than by the hearth or in a stable, all you are doing is taking God, placing a coat round his head, and pushing him under a bench. Because the person who seeks for God in a particular way takes the way and misses God. But the person who seeks for God without a way will find Him, as he is, in Himself; and such a son lives with the Son and He is life itself. The person who for a thousand years asked the question of life, "Why do you live?" could provide the answer, the only answer: "I live because I am alive." The reason for this is that life is lived for its own reasons and emanates from its own sources; hence it is lived entirely without any whys or wherefores, because it lives for itself.[4]

What is the meaning of this "without any whys or wherefores" in which we should live and in which life itself lives? It is the absence of all purpose, all calculation, all quid pro quos, of all something for something else, all power which makes life into service. Whenever we are torn between being and acting, feeling and doing, at that point we are not living "*sunder warumbe*," but are reckoning expenditure and success, calculating probability and benefit, or obeying fears which are not understood. I say this with a view to the purpose-oriented rationality that grows massively in our highly technological world, prohibiting any experience, any "being there," for which there is no reason: we eat certain foods in order to lose weight, we take dance lessons in order to keep fit, we pray in order to work out with God the fulfillment of certain wishes. The rose is no longer "without a why or a wherefore" or "because it blooms," as Angelus Silesius put it; instead, in the market-oriented world in which we today live, the blooming rose is an article for sale like all other items.

Eckart uses an amusing comparison to make vivid this pathology of calculation: "But many people want to look upon God with the eyes with which they look upon a cow, and they want to love God the way they love a cow. Which you love because of the milk and the cheese and your own benefit. This is the behavior of all those people who want to love God because of external wealth or inner comfort; but they do not love God properly: rather, they love their self-interest" (Quint, 227, Fox, 207).

The *"sunder warumbe"* is what underlies all mystical love of God. It settles the immense difficulties in mystical language between that which cannot be uttered and being dumb. For our relationship with language is actually not much better than that of those who love God like a cow. Our language is part of our life in the world of purposes and intentions. I say something in order to achieve something or to receive something. I stand as a subject face to face with objects and use them. I still have what Meister Eckart calls the mind of a merchant, the "this for that" attitude. I promise something in order to receive something in return, quid pro quo. I use language in the spirit of purpose-oriented reification. In contrast, in the experience of Oneness, I would not speak in order to appropriate something for myself. Then language would not be a means of appropriating the world for myself. It rather could celebrate joy or bewail pain. It does not aim at something that I can capture, but gathers me in the Now.

The basic mystical idea of what language can do (not just can, but cannot renounce under any circumstances) follows the lines of pure praise. Praise may indeed have its reasons (and also may combine with thanks in liturgical language) but in reality it always has the character of the *"sunder warumbe."* In praising the moon as it rises, or a beloved person or the source of all good things, the purpose-obsessed ego with its thirst for domination has vanished. It has gone out of itself. It has sunk itself.

The merchants' mind has been renounced and we have lost what Eckart called *"Eigenschaft"* (literally "own-ness"). When Eckart uses this word, it has a number of connotations: it means possession and the desire to possess, originality in the sense of the modern word "attribute," characteristic features and singularity, and finally also egotism and egoism. Living without *Eigen-*

schaft is therefore practically inconceivable—and yet at the same time it is an expression of the ultimate freedom that we can attain. We become free if we are unencumbered by fears and constraints in God's presence, if we are there *sunder warumbe.*

For Eckart, all authentic actions are those which emulate the original action of the Creation: they spring forth from life and love. In this sense, they have no whys or wherefores. The Creation is not pressed into the causal context to which we are subject in the everyday world. Why should God have created giraffes, wonderful stones seen by nobody, and also beings like myself? The mystical spirituality of Creation relates to the world through a principle different from that of the instrumental.

God too loves us without whys and wherefores. "But love has no why, no reason. If I had a friend and loved him because good things happened to me because of him and my entire will, then I would love, not my friend, but myself. I should love my friend for the sake of his own goodness and his own virtue and everything that makes him uniquely him" (Quint, 299). If our actions emulate the original action of the Creation, then our language must also be without whys and wherefores. Like the rose, love has no why; "it blooms because it blooms" (Angelus Silesius).

If the sentence "I love you" means I would like to sleep with you or I want you to marry me, it still lies within the realm of purposes. If "I love you" means your proportions are ideal or you have a good job, we are still in the realm of reasons, a realm destructive to love. Purposes and reasons differentiate between me and my motivation, between the person speaking and his or her language. I cannot then "be what I do." The language of "this" world, from which the mystics distance themselves with such passion, is arranged along hierarchical lines and excludes authentic Oneness. Egotism, rationality of purposes, and hierarchical order are reflected in our normal language. Linguistically, we take our bearings from distinctions, from genus and *differentia specifica,* which we use to classify things. We make ourselves into lords of the world and use language as an instrument of reification. We appropriate the world to ourselves, make it "our own," and use it as something that belongs to us.

Nowhere at present is this so clear as in the bioethical debate in which the distinction between "invention" and "discovery" is obliterated and the biogenetic codes which have been discovered are made into the private property of those who possess the world. The attempt to patent everything living elaborates on the power of control over everything that was formerly called Creation, and today is genetic material. From this perspective, the *"sunder warumbe"* and everything that is not controlled, dissected, used, possessed, or cannot be further utilized and exploited does not exist. Yet it is precisely this mystical knowledge of freedom from the "why" that enables people to resist. "If they should question a truthful person who acts for his own reasons, 'Why do you act as you do?' he should answer correctly, saying simply, 'I act because I act'" (Quint, 180).

FORMS OF MYSTICAL LANGUAGE: NEGATION, PARADOX, AND SILENCE

In the mystical traditions there are linguistic elements which are clearly indispensable and occur in the most diverse cultures. I shall here consider the three most striking forms of mystic language: negation, paradox, and silence.

The stylistic figure of negation belongs to the experience which is unspeakable. It is not this, it is not that, it is not that which you have already known or seen or what somebody quoted to you before. The negation of the "this" in the interest of the absoluteness of the absolute is the response to this danger: this linguistic act provides a knowing through unknowing.

Let me use an example to explain this knowing through unknowing, a kind of mystical knowing that, it might be added, Dionysius the Areopagite introduced to the Christian tradition. The example, I believe, also charts a path that leads from mystical theology to practical spirituality. The New Testament story of the Good Samaritan (Luke 10) can be interpreted in mystical terms such that the question of the knowledge of God becomes its focus. The priest and the Levite who pass by the man that fell in with robbers who seriously injured him are pious God-fearing men. They "know" God and his laws. They have possessed God as the man who knows possesses that which is known. They know what God wants of them in being and in doing. They also know where God is to be found—in the Scriptures and in worship at the Temple. For them, God is mediated through the institutions that exist. They have their God—and he cannot be found on the road between Jerusalem and Jericho. What is wrong with this knowledge of God? Neither the knowledge of the Torah nor of the Temple! (It is clearly misguided to introduce, as many interpreters have done, an anti-Jewish point into this story of Jesus the Jew! It could just as well come from Hillel or another Jewish sage). What is wrong is a knowledge of God which does not allow for any unknowing, any negative theology. Because the two actors know that God is "this" they do not see "that." Hence the Good Samaritan is the antifundamentalist story par excellence.

"And so I ask God to rid me of God" says Eckart. The God who is known and familiar is too small for him. To know God like another object of our knowledge means making Him or Her into a thing which is usable, available. The call to leave God for God's sake can be heard at many places in mystical piety. The priest and the Levite in the story in Luke could have heard it. In this sense they could have learned to leave the object of God with which they were familiar, in order to find the God who has assumed the form of a battered poor man. To leave God for God's sake means giving up a form of God, a way of God—as well as a manner and style of talking about God.

To give an example typical of our culture, this would mean letting go of the God of childhood, or the God of one's native country, or the God of one's own family. The fundamentalist pride in which we hold fast to the childhood God often gets in the way of live experience. The process of letting go would be a process of "annihilation" of the Self that has evolved, a process which is necessary in order to know God in the unknown. Getting rid of the "I" fits consistently into the apophatic tradition. The Samaritan is doing just this in the story of the Gospel according to Luke, and the mystical theologist from Nazareth is recounting just this.

The second element present in all mystical language is paradox. Clearly, images, comparisons, and parables arise on all levels of religious language. But it is only the mystical language of paradox, with its attempt to remain close to the "religion vécue," that time and time again achieves a glowing, explosive language in complete contrast to the cold language of theology. An excellent stylistic device of explosive language is the oxymoron, the deliberate combining of two contradictory or mutually exclusive concepts into a new unit, as in "light-dark" (chiaroscuro), "sad-happy" (Hoelderlin), "bitter-sweet," or "eloquent silence." The coincidence of concepts that are contradictions in logical or substantial terms—*coincidentia oppositorum*—occurs when a single statement contains words which are not adequate on their own and are juxtaposed with each other, producing the paradox, the unexpected, a statement which runs counter to the general opinion or what is generally known. From the viewpoint of the philosophy of language, the paradox is an attempt to come closer to a fact which cannot be perceived or understood, by approaching it from two opposing sides.

In the introduction to *Ecstatic Confessions,* Martin Buber speaks of the "language which bustle (*Getriebe*) once laboriously called into being for itself to be its errand girl and which, since it has existed, has ever desired the one thing which is impossible—to set its foot on the neck of bustle and become pure poetry—truth, purity, poetry." Paradox is the clearest expression of this desire and this struggle. Buber quotes Meister Eckart: "There I heard without sound, there I saw without light, there I smelled without moving, there I tasted that which was not, there I felt that which did not exist. Then my heart lost its reason, my soul its love, my spirit its form, and my nature its essence" (Buber, 15).

The third, and perhaps most crucial, element of all mystical languages is silence, the end of speaking that, at the same time, produces an expanse of silence. Starting from day-to-day experience, a distinction can be drawn between two kinds of silence. One is a dull, listless, apathetic silence, a wordlessness arising out of poverty, such as exists in cultures of poverty between people who have nothing to say to each other. But in addition to this pre-speech silence there is also a post-speech version, which arises out of an abundance which transcends language as a means of communication. This silence after speaking does make use of words, but only in order to relinquish them. The sought after mediation is no longer necessary, its instrument is laid aside—or more precisely, it falls from one's hand, because in the place of mediation there has come an association, which no longer needs language as a tool. Being silent together is a higher degree of being together and of oneness. Just as listening to music can bring people closer together than words, so too can the spoken or written word come closer to its limit and boundary, silence, by falling silent independently and of necessity. Paradox and apophatic speech are indicative of this "silence arising out of abundance." Being cast out from this form of silence is a bitter experience, because we then find ourselves thrown back to the apathetic silence of pre-speech, and left all alone.

The authenticity of mystical texts arises from its proximity to the border that runs between speech and speechlessness. In the best of cases such texts are able to create an expanse of tranquillity, a time of silence. The living and ineffable light withdraws from language, it is experienced in the physical-spiritual (*leib-seelisch*) transformation that it effects. I assume that within a mystical (or sometimes even a poetic) text there occurs time and time again this possibility of not only naming or calling for (*fordern*) silence, but of producing it, so that a reader allows the book to drop as she reflects on it, or a speaker of the text speaks with the silence, or a listener sinks into it. Silence here is not only conjured; it occurs.

All religions, above all the non-theistic ones, have practiced and sought out silence. Buddhism in particular lives in silent contemplation; for Buddhists, silence is more prayer than the word can ever be. Orthodox Christians enter a ceremonial silence "in order to let God speak." The Quakers begin their prayer meeting in a lengthy silence. And in the reorientation of the Catholic liturgy following Vatican Council II, the view became accepted that speech must be rooted in silence. In philosophical terms Wittgenstein—going far further than the famous final sentence in the *Tractatus*—made the following observation in connection with the mystical experience: "There is something which is unspeakable. Not as the result of a syllogism, but as that which shows itself. It shows itself as reason, not in the sense of a causality, but as transparency of the sayable in a sense which is simply the other side of this thing which is sayable, outside the world."[5]

Silence has a double meaning as part of the mystical experience: on the one hand, silence is the ascetic praxis of preparation, a kind of fasting with words; on the other hand, it is the self-expression of the living light. Religious orders, communities of monks and nuns, have built praxis and periods of silence into their rules. Many distinguish three degrees of attaining tranquillity: the silence of the mouth, the silence of the spirit, and the silence of the will. They based themselves on biblical quotations such as, "the effect of righteousness [shall be] quietness" (Isaiah 32:17) where the word "quietness" also refers to "peace." In Luther's translation, justice brings forth eternal quietness and confidence. The essence of the Carmelite rules also derives from Isaiah: "In quietness and in confidence shall be your strength" (Isaiah 30:15).

Teresa of Avila (1515–1582), who in 1970 was the first woman on whom the pope conferred the title of "teacher of the Church," introduced two hours of silent prayer daily as the most important reform in her small newly founded convents. This silent or "inner meditation" was contested in the world of the Counter-Reformation. For the Church authorities, it was perfectly reasonable to hold oral communal prayers in the words of canonical tradition, shaped by its dogmatic knowledge. That people could pray without moving their lips and without murmuring words appeared strange—indeed, threatening. Even Ignatius Loyola was eyed with mistrust by the Inquisition authorities because of this "praying within," in which they suspected subjectivity and heresy precisely because of the emotional intensity known to be involved.

In addition to this general suspicion of heresy, which was directed against brothers and sisters of the Illuminati free-thought movement and the Alumbrados (Enlightened Ones), there also prevailed a sexist ideology common to mystical movements that asserted women's mental and spiritual inferiority. The University of Salamanca was dominated by the school of thought which held that a woman by her very nature was incapable of silent meditation. Her constitutional temperament could all too easily drive her to heresy. Hence "inward," genuinely spiritual prayer should be the exclusive province of men, with their intellectual lucidity. An erudite theologian could advance up the theological ladder from concepts and conclusions to truly spiritual prayer. Women, who grew up without Latin and often illiterate, would do better to listen to the instruction of clerics and to remain within the tradition of oral prayer. They were allowed obedience, but mysticism and the way to the Inner Citadel—the path that Teresa herself showed and lived—were forbidden.

Yet the language of mysticism includes a resisting silence, a silence which learns to listen and risks sinking in the dark night of the soul. This silence belongs to Teresa's life-work of reform, reform which strove to free women from the confines of minority status and from an absence of spirituality characteristic of their existence. Teresa's silence had to contend with powerful foes: the Inquisition's hostility to women's education went so far as to ban not only the Spanish translation of the Bible, but also all books about matters of faith and religious life written in the vernacular. Accordingly, Teresa's autobiography (*Vida*) was also confiscated by the Inquisition and for a long time made inaccessible. She nevertheless remained undeterred, continuing her project of reform and thereby setting an example of how a language beyond words can give rise to a new form of freedom.

Today, silence plays a similar role in some of the most important religious movements that focus on justice and peace. Activists in these movements are often so politically powerless that their idiom is not understood: an unarmed God is ridiculous. This resisting silence also has had its tactical expression: since the beginning of the 1980s, people have been observing silence jointly in the shopping centers of our major cities in protest against human rights violations or on behalf of peace. Since these protests are in the public arena, there are frequently abusive reactions on the part of onlookers. Yet in these new forms of a piety that lives with its own powerlessness and does not hide in churches or other sequestered places, there is a mystic kernal. For the silence is that which comes after all information, analysis, knowledge. Simply by standing there, then, the silence of these activists speaks, almost mystically, of God's presence.

NOTES

1. Buber, *Ekstatische Konfessionen* (Berlin, 1928), pp. 19–20.

2. Peter Dinzelbacher, *Christliche Mystik im Abendland. Ihre Geschichte von den Anfängen bis zum Ende des Mittelalters* (Paderborn, 1994), p. 246.

3. *Ekstatische Konfessionen,* pp. 19 and 20.

4. Meister Eckart, *Deutsche Predigten und Traktate,* ed. J. Quint (Munich 1969), p. 180. English version: *Breakthrough. Meister Eckhart's Creation Spirituality in a New Translation,* with introduction and commentaries by Matthew Fox (Gorder City, N.Y., 1980), p. 201.

5. Cf. Schweigen/Stille (silence/quiet) in *Praktisches Lexikon der Spiritualität,* ed. C. Schütz (Freiburg, 1988).

JOHN SILBER

From Thebes to Auschwitz: Moral Responsibility in Sophocles and Wiesel

IN THIS ESSAY, I wish to challenge the ancient and enduring view now represented by H. L. A. Hart and others that responsibility and guilt are not only distinct and separable concepts, but that one cannot be guilty, either morally or legally, unless one can act otherwise than one does and unless one has *mens rea*, recognition of the wrongness of one's act. Our understanding of the highly complex nature of human volition can be deepened, I believe, by the examination of the works of two great writers—one ancient, one modern—who preserve in their writing the mystery and full complexity of human action and volition. I shall use their work to illuminate varieties and degrees of responsibility and guilt and the effect of fate—an ancient concept almost totally ignored by contemporary moralists—by which responsibility and guilt are conjoined in the absence of the conditions conventionally held to be required for their presence.

The reader should know from the outset that I do not proceed in the examination of Sophocles's *Oedipus Tyrannus* the way literary folk have been taught to do. I realize the play is not a realistic drama or an antique detective story. I believe, nevertheless, that much can be learned about human nature, especially about the nature of freedom and responsibility, by viewing the play as a drama in which Oedipus, ignorant of his origins, undertakes a relentless search for the murderer of Laius that leads to the discovery of his parentage and his hand in the death of his father.

I must also note that in seeking to illuminate the concept of fate, I do not intend by fate some deterministic and hence predictable outcome that defines the person in a way essentially external to him. I have in mind, rather, *moira*, the Greek word for fate. It simply means one's portion, what is given in life. This is precisely what I intend by fate: all the circumstances in which one plays out his hand in life, the contexts that to a considerable degree limit or define the scope of one's freedom. So understood, *Oedipus Tyrannus* is not the tragedy of a man fated in advance to commit dreadful acts, but rather a tragedy of *moira*, of the given circumstances Oedipus meets and the way his own nature, his temperament, talents, and character lead him to deal with them.[1]

I

As students of Elie Wiesel's spoken and written words, we discover observations and statements that seem both compellingly true and bafflingly incompatible. Among these are his reflections on responsibility and guilt. I have heard him say that "In war no one is innocent," thus recognizing the possibility of collective responsibility and guilt. Yet he has consistently rejected the idea of collective guilt. He has written that the zeal and brutality with which Hungarian police implemented plans for the extermination of the Jews "will forever remain the dishonor of the Hungarian army and nation."[2] How can a nation be dishonored unless it is to a degree both collectively responsible and collectively guilty for the actions of some of its people? In his volume of memoirs Wiesel speaks of a peasant woman, Maria, who tried to save his family. By her courage and compassion, he writes, this "simple and devout Christian woman . . . saved her town's honor."[3] But how is this possible unless one individual can atone collectively for the moral failure of an entire town? And how can the town be dishonored if there is no guilt other than that of individuals?

Without collective virtue and collective guilt, how could a nation or town be either saved or dishonored?

In *Dawn*, Elisha, the young terrorist who must kill a hostage, at first says, "All I knew was that he was an Englishman and my enemy."[4] As Elisha grows in his understanding of what he must do, he observes that "[a]n act so absolute as that of killing involves not only the killer but, as well, those who have formed him. In murdering a man I was making *them* murderers."[5] "Them" includes parents, teachers, all who had an influence upon him, and especially the child he once was. Through his action he makes all of them murderers. Does this not suggest Wiesel's acceptance of individual and collective responsibility and guilt? One might argue that it could not be collective responsibility or guilt with regard to the child since Elisha is the same person as the child. But Elisha is not the child; he is rather the adult the child has, to a degree, been fated to become. Yet, by committing murder Elisha compromises the innocence of the child and makes the child a murderer. The child is not only father to the man; the man is father to the child by compromising its innocence.

The clearest statement of collective guilt in *Dawn* is voiced by Elisha when he says, "All enemies are equal. . . . Each one is responsible for the crimes committed by the others. They have different faces, but they all have the same hands. . . . "[6] All are clearly guilty if all are responsible.

The sense of community and collective responsibility and guilt found in *Dawn* is in striking contrast to the views of the author of *Night*, a record of the growing sense of isolation from town and friends, from family members, from comrades, from God—even from one's father—bleakly summed up by a doctor's remark: "Everyone lives and dies for himself alone."[7] Wiesel never reached that degree of isolation as long as his father was alive. But when at the threshold of starvation he gave the remainder of his soup to his father, he added, "it was with a heavy heart . . . [and] against my will."[8] Wiesel the man blames Wiesel the child, and in despair thinks himself no better than Rabbi Eliahou's son who, on a forced march, abandoned his father.

After his father's death, Wiesel's isolation became total. In his bitterness, he acknowledges more faith in Hitler than in God, for Hitler, unlike God, "kept his promises, all his promises, to the Jewish people."[9] He observes that, after his father's death, "nothing could touch me anymore."[10] To eat was his only desire, and he reports that he no longer thought of his father or mother.[11] When, after liberation from the camp, he finally saw himself in a mirror, he could not recognize himself, but neither could he forget the face with which he now addressed the world.

That state of isolation which Wiesel describes in *Night* allows neither collective guilt nor collective responsibility. In isolation all guilt, even all reality, is individual.

It may seem strange that in *Dawn*, which appeared only two years after *Night*, Wiesel himself writes from the perspective of communal responsibility. But Wiesel wrote *Night* out of the horror of his and his family's experiences in 1944 and 1945. *Dawn*, by contrast, was written with a sense of renewed spirit, a renewal achieved not in two years but over a period of fifteen years, almost half the life of the author. This sense of renewal was inspired by the determination of the people of Israel to fight for their survival.

In *All Rivers Run to the Sea*, Wiesel continues to express that reborn sense of community. He recalls with pride that his father, in refusing to accept the refuge offered by Maria, said "[A] Jew must never be separated from his community: what happens to everyone else will happen to us as well."[12] Wiesel affirms his father's stand: "My father was right."[13] If what one does will be done by all, and if what happens to one will happen to all, does that not only involve suffering and death, but also responsibility and, consequently, innocence or guilt?

Wiesel's concern for community and collectivity is not only expressed by characters whose views may not express his own, but by his own statements as well. In conversation with Harry James Cargas he said,

> Let's take the problem of suffering because it's one of the elements that moves me to write. . . . If we envisage literature and human

destiny as endeavors by man to redeem himself, then we must admit the obsession, the overall dominating theme of responsibility, that we are responsible for one another. . . . If not, we are condemned by our solitude forever and it has no meaning.[14]

Wiesel recognizes, as did Plato, Aristotle, Kant, Hegel, Husserl, and Wittgenstein before him, that community is essential for meaning. And community is built on mutual responsibility. But if, as Wiesel suggests, the community is one in which each is responsible for all, and if it fails in its duty, how can there fail to be communal guilt?

Wiesel does not limit responsibility or guilt for the Holocaust to those who were directly involved. He notes the responsibility and therefore—though he does not draw the conclusion—the guilt of others: "The silence of the accomplices was a destructive one because it destroyed our future."[15] By "accomplices" he includes not only participants in the crime but also those near and far who knew of the crimes but did nothing. Does this not involve degrees of collective responsibility and guilt that may extend even to nations who abhorred the extermination of the Jews?

So where does he stand? He writes that his non-Jewish neighbors and the Hungarian people are dishonored and guilty, but that a single individual, Maria, is the redeemer of their honor or at least that of her town. The confusion of ideas increases when Wiesel, in applauding his father's decision not to separate the family from the rest of the Jewish community, goes on to say, "We wanted to stay together, like everyone else. Family unity is one of our important traditions, as the enemy well knew."[16]

Understandably, Wiesel endorsed the decision not to separate the children from the parents. But Maria had not proposed to break up the Wiesel family; she offered her isolated cabin not to one but to all its members. So how was Wiesel's father right to reject her proposal? He was concerned to hold together not only his family but also the entire Jewish community.

Concerning the solidarity of Jews, Wiesel records in *Night* the way in which at Auschwitz torture, beatings, hard labor, and especially extreme sickness and hunger so isolated Jews from one another that, eventually, a boy beat his father to death for a morsel of bread, and "starving men fought each other to the death for a few crumbs."[17] Their obligation as Jews to stand together as one people was not canceled, however, by their inability to do so in those tragic, brutalizing circumstances. In such circumstances no one could speak with any justification of guilt or even moral failure. But none who suffered this brutalization would deny the fated and pitiable wretchedness of their condition.

This apparent confusion of ideas and observations offers an important lesson for the philosopher. Theories should be held with tentativeness and subordinated to all the facts. One must, of course, seek consistency, but a theory is never adequate if its affirmation requires the denial of factual complexities. True philosophy seeks a comprehensive system of thought in which all that is relevant is accounted for in an *Aufhebung* (a picking up and saving) of all facts and concepts.

One of the uses of literature is to save us from the reductionisms that often compromise scientific, legal, sociological, psychological, and moral theorizing. Wiesel notes the frequent occurrence of reductionism in discussions of the Holocaust:

> First of all, they say, "The whole world suffered and [Jews] suffered too." Then they say, "All Jews were survivors, even those who weren't there were survivors." And at the end they say, "What was Auschwitz? Man's inhumanity to man." It is all reduced to a formula. Thus, all of a sudden all the suffering of people, Jewish people, is gone.[18]

The substitution of a cliché for mind-numbing reality does not provide understanding; rather, the tragedy is lost in the reduction.

II

Elie Wiesel's understanding of responsibility is richly complex. And so is that of Sophocles, particularly as set forth in *Oedipus Tyrannus*. This remarkable and sometimes puzzling masterpiece treats the subject of responsibility and offers insights that illuminate Wiesel's thought.

The story of *Oedipus* is well known. Laius and Jocasta are king and queen of Thebes. An oracle has told them that Laius will die at the hand of their son. Laius has the infant's ankles pierced and bound and then hands the boy to Jocasta, who tells a herdsman to expose the child on a mountain. Taking pity on the child, the Theban herdsman gives him to a herdsman from Corinth.

The Corinthian shepherd presents the child to King Polybus and Queen Merope, who adopt him. As a young man, Oedipus, hearing a rumor that he is not his parents' true son, goes to Delphi to consult the oracle, who, ignoring his question, says he will kill his father and lie with his mother. Oedipus proceeds to Thebes, and at a crossroads encounters an older man in a carriage. He quarrels with the coachman, who strikes him. Oedipus then kills both the coachman and his master.

Next Oedipus encounters the Sphinx, who has been posing a riddle to the young men of Thebes and devouring them when they fail to solve it. Courageously and decisively he challenges the Sphinx, solves her riddle, and destroys her. Arriving at Thebes, he is acclaimed as savior and king. He then quickly marries the widowed Queen Jocasta.

All this action is prior to the opening of the play, which starts some years later. A plague has come upon Thebes. With characteristic courage, impulsiveness, and determination, Oedipus commits himself to ending the plague. He sends Creon, Jocasta's brother, to Delphi to seek an answer to their problem.

Creon brings back the news that the plague will be lifted as soon as Thebes expels or kills the murderer of King Laius. Oedipus orders all to cooperate in the search to discover the killer's identity. Creon recounts what Thebes knew about the murder of Laius, who was reported to have been killed by bandits. Concerned at the time to rid themselves of the Sphinx, the Thebans were distracted from solving the crime, but the oracle has said that both the witness and perpetrator of the crime are still in Thebes. Oedipus promises that if the murderer confesses, he will be sent into exile unharmed. He then invokes upon the murderer, and upon himself, a curse: "if he is at my hearth/and in my home, and I have knowledge of him,/may the curse pronounced on others come to me."[19]

The blind prophet, Tiresias, sent for by Creon to assist in solving the mystery, accuses Oedipus himself of the crime. Oedipus accuses Creon of paying others to kill Laius in order to take the throne, and of now plotting his overthrow with Tiresias.

Tiresias's words begin to sink in and Oedipus demands to know the identity of his parents. But Tiresias taunts him by pointing to his reputation as a solver of riddles.

The tension between Oedipus and Creon mounts as Creon objects to the charge of treason, while Oedipus calls for his death. As their quarrel intensifies, Jocasta insists that Creon depart to his home and that Oedipus believe his denials, guaranteed as they are by his powerful oaths.

In quiet, Jocasta reviews with Oedipus the charges made against him. She is exasperated that he takes seriously the words of Tiresias or any prophet, for she insists that no mortal can prophesy.

Jocasta, wishing to reassure Oedipus by offering direct proof of the falseness of Tiresias's accusation, tells Oedipus that Laius was told that he would be killed by their son. But robbers who were no kin to him killed Laius at a place where three roads meet. And to be sure the prophecy would never be fulfilled, Laius had his son's ankles pierced and bound together and three days after its birth the infant was put on a mountainside to die.

Although offered as reassurance, Jocasta's words have the opposite effect, as Oedipus, whose ankles bear scars of some unremembered wounds,[20] recalls his encounter with an older man where three roads meet. Oedipus is troubled further when Jocasta identifies the crossroads as the place where the road from Delphi joins the road from Daulia. Oedipus now fears the worst, and recognition is almost complete once Oedipus learns that Laius was a large man of middle age whose hair was just beginning to gray.

Oedipus recounts his doubts about his parentage to Jocasta, but he has not yet grasped their portent. He knows that if Laius is the stranger he killed at the crossroads, he himself is the murderer he is seeking, and that by his own curses he has banished himself from Thebes. Oedipus sees that everything turns on whether Laius and his party were attacked by one or by several men. Oedipus, true to his duty, pursues the answer. He sends for the surviving witness.

Jocasta, despite her early protestations of skepticism, now proposes to go as supplicant to Apollo to seek cleansing that will relieve the plague but not pollute Oedipus. At this point a messenger from Corinth announces the death of Polybus. On learning that Polybus has died of old age, Oedipus then echoes Jocasta's rejection of prophecies and omens. Jocasta exults in her assertion that true foresight is impossible. But Oedipus is cautious, noting that Merope, his mother, still lives and that he must be concerned to avoid her bed.

In his search for the truth, despite what it may reveal to his cost, Oedipus interrogates the Corinthian messenger with the same relentless thoroughness with which he examined Tiresias and Creon. Oedipus learns that he was saved from death by the messenger himself, who as a shepherd on Mount Cithaeron had received Oedipus, lamed with pierced ankles, from a shepherd of King Laius. The importance of the pierced ankles would appear to be obvious when the messenger explains that it was those pierced ankles that led to naming the child Oedipus, "Swollenfoot," but Oedipus seems oblivious to the implications. Oedipus's initial response is rage at the parents who had so mistreated him.

Jocasta, who now knows the dreadful truth, still tries to shield Oedipus from it and urges him in vain not to seek the shepherd who gave the child away.

When the shepherd arrives, he is relentlessly interrogated by both Oedipus and the messenger. Like Tiresias, he is reluctant to speak. Only under threats to his life does he confess that he took the child of Laius and Jocasta from its mother's own hands and was ordered to kill it. Oedipus is incredulous; he asks if Jocasta ordered his death. The shepherd leaves no room for doubt. Oedipus pronounces unwavering judgment on himself.

Oedipus, enraged, then searches for a spear to kill the cruel mother. Charging the doors of her chamber, he tears them from their hinges, and finds Jocasta already dead by her own hand. He tears the pointed brooches from her gown and blinds himself with them.

The action of the play is done, and only its assessment by the chorus, messengers, and Oedipus himself remains. The chorus says, "Time, all-seeing, surprised you living an unwilled life."[21] A messenger differentiates between Oedipus's unwilled parricide and incest and the willed acts of Jocasta's suicide and Oedipus's self-mutilation. The messenger concludes that "[g]riefs hurt worst/which we perceive to be self-chosen ones."[22] But which of these ills was worse: Jocasta's suicide or her complicity with Laius in the mutilation and attempted murder of their child; Oedipus's self-mutilation or his killing Laius and marrying Jocasta? And which of these ills was self-chosen? Laius and Jocasta voluntarily disposed of their baby; Oedipus did not kill Laius involuntarily, nor was he forced to marry Jocasta and sire her children.

Commentators have described these elements as fated. But were they? They were prophesied and they came to pass. Not by virtue of the prophecy alone, however, but also by the voluntary complicity of Laius, Jocasta, Laius's herdsman, Polybus, Merope, the Corinthian messenger, and Oedipus himself.

The Thebans asked, "Doer of horror, how did you bear to quench/your vision? What divinity raised your hand?"[23] *Daimon,* the word Sophocles uses here for "divinity," can easily be confused or misunderstood by modern readers. When Greeks spoke of a *daimon,* or of their *daimon,* they were referring to something not entirely external to themselves. Rather, by attributing their action to a *daimon,* they were offering a partially psychological explanation. At his trial, Socrates explained his inability to engage in politics by referring to an inner force, his *daimonion,* which never commanded him to do anything but often forbade a prospective act. A modern Socrates might have said, "My conscience won't let me." So saying, neither the ancient nor the modern Socrates would mean that his conscience was a separate force directing him from without. Rather, each would insist that his conscience is also an expression of his own personality. Socrates, however, may have believed his conscience was not only an expression of his personality, but also an inner voice stimulated by an external deity.

When Socrates speaks of his inner voice, he does not refer to it as his *daimon*, although translations have used that Greek word. Rather, he refers to his *daimonion*, his diminutive *daimon*, not a god but his personal *daimon*, something so personal, private and modest that other persons would not know about it. As Charles Griswold has observed, "For Socrates to claim to have a *daimon* in him would be a bit like claiming that one had a God in one rather than, say, the spirit of God." Avoiding the error of hubris, Socrates claimed no more than some sort of "guardian angel" to guide him. Or we might say that he was guided by his conscience. Socrates' claim was unusual, perhaps unique, and another measure of the extent to which he advanced our knowledge of the ethical dimension beyond the limits of conventional morality.

Similarly, when Greeks in the *Iliad, Odyssey,* or *Oedipus Tyrannus* attribute their actions to gods or goddesses, the attribution is again offered in part as a means of explanation. William Arrowsmith holds that "A Greek god is *experienced;* his name is the name of that experience."[24] It is doubtful that Phaedra believed simply that Artemis had possessed her and created in her an uncontrollable passion for Hippolytus. Phaedra tried to explain herself by attributing to a goddess the passion which suddenly and mysteriously overwhelmed her. Her experience of the passion was her experience of Artemis.

It is difficult to believe that all the talk about gods and *daimon* was taken literally among educated fifth-century Athenians. Such talk was important, nevertheless, as pointing to the mystery of human motivation, to forces within the personality that clearly and directly influence what a person does.

In answering the question "What *daimon* raised your hand?" Oedipus replies:

> It was Apollo there, Apollo, friends,
> who brought my sorrows, vile sorrows to their perfection,
> these evils that were done to me.
> But the one who struck them with his hand,

that one was none but I, in wretchedness.
For why was I to see
when nothing I could see would bring me joy?[25]

Oedipus assumes full responsibility but not guilt for his blindness, for under the circumstances he was right to blind himself. But it is also clear that he is responsible for his insistent search for the truth, for his unflagging pursuit of insight into both the cause of the plague and his true identity, and finally for the light of self-knowledge that compels him to enter the dark world of the blind by his own hands. In blinding himself, Oedipus dispenses justice by punishing himself for his intellectual blindness, in scorning and accusing Tiresias and Creon, in ignoring the evidence of his ankles and his name and the uncertainty of his parentage.

Oedipus is also right to say that all but stabbing out his own eyes is the work of Apollo. Apollo is not only the god of light, reason, and understanding—virtues manifest in Oedipus—Apollo is also, as Arrowsmith observes,

> a light-bringer, a god whose quality is the radiance he confers. . . . Whenever we feel our mortal darkness illuminated, whenever we feel sudden clarity stabbing into our darkness—as when we are literally *enlightened* by poetry, or music, or logic, or prophecy, or insight—then Apollo is the name of what has happened to us.[26]

Apollo is at the same time a cultural force in Theban life, and we recognize the mischief caused by his prophets. If Laius had not been told by Apollo's oracle that his son would kill him, he would never have collaborated with Jocasta and the herdsman to cripple and abandon the infant. He and Jocasta, like many Greeks, were well aware of the ambiguity of prophecies and skeptical of them. Nevertheless, they chose to believe this prophecy and, by acting to avoid it, contributed to its fulfillment. Voluntarily and intentionally, they attempted to kill the child. Oedipus on two occasions comments on their cruelty. Jocasta, so vehement in her denunciation of prophecies, must also have felt that guilt. That she and Laius went to such pains to avoid directly murdering the child indicated their clear recognition that to do so would have made them guilty of murder. The dodge of indirection could not excuse them either in the moral universe of pious Thebans—as shown by Oedipus's outrage—or in terms of modern moral and legal standards.

Oedipus, on hearing rumors that he was not the true son of the king and queen of Corinth, did not demand the truth from his supposed parents. Instead, he intentionally went to Delphi to learn the truth from a far less reliable guide. Even though the oracle failed to answer the only question he asked, Oedipus voluntarily and intentionally decided not to seek the truth from his adoptive parents but to flee from them.

Thus, it was Oedipus, not Apollo, who kept him in the dark.

And the adoptive parents, who had heard the rumor that created doubts in Oedipus's mind, failed to put those doubts to rest by telling Oedipus he was adopted. Here again, Apollo was not involved.

Neither did Apollo cause Oedipus to fight and kill at the crossroads. Just as pedestrians would normally get out of the way of an automobile, Oedipus might have been expected to step aside at the crossroads for a carriage. Instead, Oedipus, acting out of a concern for his *timē*, his own estimation of his worth relative to the worth of others, intentionally asserted his rights and ended by killing both the coachman and Laius. Since Oedipus saw that the man in the carriage was old enough to be his father, was he not also reckless in killing him?

It was not an external Apollo, but the inner nature and character of Oedipus—his courage, his daring, his intelligence, his shrewdness, and his capacity for outrage—that led him to challenge and destroy the Sphinx. His ambition may also have played a part since his victory over her made him king of Thebes. So too he freely and intentionally went to Thebes where he freely and intentionally entered the royal family by marrying the widowed queen. Here his shrewdness in consolidating his position by marrying his predecessor's widow contrasts with his reckless intentionality in marrying a woman old enough to be his mother. And what of Jocasta's responsibility for her incestuous marriage?

Shouldn't Oedipus's youth and his unusually scarred ankles have triggered some memory of similar wounds? Was there no voluntary element in her denial of the obvious?

Oedipus abandoned Corinth to avoid incest with his mother. But the failure of Apollo's oracle to identify his mother left her identity a mystery. Nevertheless the ambition, cunning, and blind impatience that prompted his reckless marriage to Jocasta are all central elements in Oedipus's character.

All these are also elements of Oedipus's greatness, the traits that directed his actions as king of Thebes, establishing him as a great and worthy king, venerated by his people and compassionate and decisive in confronting the plague. He does not wait in vain hope for the plague to be lifted; rather, he seeks the remedy and is relentless in his pursuit of the answer no matter what the cost to himself. His ambition not only to be a king but to be a good king, his impatience to find an answer, his courage to proceed to discover the truth despite the warnings and objections of Creon, Tiresias, Jocasta, the chorus, and the herdsman reveal his greatness.

When he demanded the truth of Tiresias, when he angrily accused him and Creon of treason, when he called down curses upon the killer of Laius and the polluter of Thebes, when he dismissed the warnings of Jocasta and forced the herdsman to speak, he acted freely with full intentionality and in character. Thus, while Apollo may in some sense be said to have brought Oedipus's sorrows to perfection, it was Oedipus himself who not only put out his own eyes but who killed Laius, destroyed the Sphinx, married Jocasta, cursed the polluter of Thebes, and proceeded with courage and determination to discover his true identity as that man and then to call down the curse upon himself.

The complex role of fate begins to intrude on our understanding when we recognize that while Oedipus intended to kill the old man at the crossroads, he did not intend to kill his father. If, by hypothesis, we hold that it was wrong for Oedipus to kill the old man (and we can only speculate on this issue since Sophocles gives us no clue as to the justification for Oedipus's challenging the coachman's right of way), then since Oedipus killed the old man, would he not also be guilty of killing Laius, King of Thebes? But if Oedipus is guilty of killing King Laius, even though he did not know his identity, is he not also guilty of killing his father? Is he not guilty at once of murder, regicide, and parricide? But if provocation were sufficient and he killed in self-defense as seems probable, there being no law outside of the polis, he would not be guilty of murder or any wrong. Still he killed his father.

Sophocles was right not to tip his hand regarding the right of way at the crossroads. In the absence of evidence on which to find Oedipus responsible for wrongdoing, we lack evidence of a wrongful act (*actus reus*) or a guilty mind (*mens rea*) required in order to find Oedipus criminally liable by current standards for murdering an old man, the king of Thebes, or his own father. Neither, however, can we find him innocent. It is a Scotch verdict—not proven.[27] If by hypothesis the killing was wrong, we could find both *actus reus* and *mens rea* not merely for murder but also for regicide and parricide. We can go no further than the Scotch verdict only because we are left in doubt about the rightness or wrongness of Oedipus's violent act at the crossroads.

A similar analysis applies with regard to Oedipus's marriage to Jocasta, although here there is no question concerning the propriety of the marriage. There would seem to be no basis for criticizing Oedipus either from a moral or a legal point of view since there was no wrongful act or guilty intent.

These are hasty conclusions, however, for in our analysis of the fight at the crossroads and the marriage, we have not sufficiently considered Oedipus's recklessness. Even according to the Model Penal Code, a verdict of guilty to a lesser degree may apply when, for example, a person recklessly or negligently fails to heed a stoplight. This finding depends, however, on a prior determination of the wrongness of the act. Oedipus was reckless or negligent in killing the old man and in marrying Jocasta, but it could be argued that he had no reason to believe that either act was wrong. To argue in this way, however, obscures the central point. In ignorance of his parentage, he should have questioned the rightness of killing any man or marrying any woman of an age to be his parents. Perhaps the provocation at the crossroads offered no time for reflection about the age of his assailants, but he was clearly reckless in failing to note that Jocasta's age was consistent with the age of his mother.

If questioned, Oedipus might have answered that insofar as killing Laius and marrying Jocasta were concerned he was reckless, but that without recognizing that these acts were wrong he could not exhibit wrongful intent. In these reckless acts, he had reason to know, however, that they might be wrong. If we take seriously his ignorance and doubts concerning the identity of his parents and the degree to which these doubts were of continuing concern to him, we cannot avoid the conclusion that he was reckless to a culpable degree in the marriage and perhaps in the killing. It is his character, moreover, and not Apollo, that accounts for his recklessness. Or, with more precision, we might say that Apollo is present in Oedipus's character, that the god "moves in him, blazes in him," that "the course of Oedipus's life incarnates the god's."[28] Oedipus's character determines his fate in part even as it is buffeted by it.

The element of *moira,* or fate, in the life of Oedipus is now clear: his fate is neither entirely under Oedipus's voluntary control nor entirely or even predominantly the work of Apollo. Oedipus is morally outraged by the father who mutilates his healthy child and by the mother who orders a herdsman to abandon it to die on a remote mountainside. But he has no less wrath for the herdsman who, disobeying that cruel order, let the life of that ill-fated child unfold.[29]

> Were it not for the herdsman's compassion [Oedipus continues],
> I'd not have returned to be my father's
> murderer; I'd not be called by men
> my mother's bridegroom.
> Now I'm wretched,[30]
> child of a polluted parent,
> fellow progenitor with him
> who gave me birth in misery.
> If there's an evil that

surpasses evils, that
has fallen to the lot of Oedipus.[31]

Now we face life in its full complexity and uncertainty. Oedipus is ashamed of his very nature as a human being, morally tainted by what he has freely and intentionally done within a fated context beyond his control. His *moira,* this fated context, includes in major part Oedipus's own character.

The herdsman, too, is compromised by fate. He did not seek this moral dilemma; it was thrust upon him. When Oedipus asked the herdsman if he gave Jocasta's child to the Corinthian shepherd, the herdsman answers, "I did. I wished that I had died that day!"[32] The herdsman's intent was clear. He gave the child to the Corinthian shepherd "so he would take him home,/to another land. But what he did was save him/for this supreme disaster."[33] The herdsman and the Corinthian shepherd had only the best intentions; nevertheless, they voluntarily contributed fatefully to the disaster that was Oedipus's life. By their voluntary acts they defined in significant part Oedipus's *moira.*

Oedipus does not blame his blinding on Apollo or anyone else, but accepts it as the fullest and most appropriate expression of himself in the circumstances to which he has been fated. Oedipus's self-blinding would be totally inappropriate apart from his acceptance of responsibility for the entire course of his life. He forcefully, perhaps angrily, rejects the observation of the chorus that it is "[b]etter not to be than live a blind man."[34] His response in justification of his self-blinding reveals the full dimension of his personality. In reflection he says, with extraordinary compassion for Laius and Jocasta, who have so cruelly wronged him,

Should I descend to Hades and endure
to see my father with these eyes? Or see
my poor unhappy mother? For I have done,
to both of these, things too great for hanging.
Or is the sight of children to be yearned for,
to see new shoots that sprouted as these did?
Never, never with these eyes of mine![35]

Oedipus will not be an ignorant victim. Although he had lived in ignorance, devoid of self-knowledge, he acted swiftly, decisively, impulsively and angrily in his moral blindness. He now sees clearly the full scope of his own responsibility. Without flinching, Oedipus heroically sums up his nature and his acts: "Evil my nature, evil my origin."[36] In the summation of his life, he sees and accepts his own nature. He reviews what he—and Apollo in him—have done, noting that at the crossroads, the soil drank the blood of his father from his own hands and that his marriage was an abomination. He even acknowledges his wrong in falsely accusing Creon of treason. Rising to his full greatness Oedipus asks Creon to fulfill the sentence he decreed: "To drive me from the land at once, to a place/where there will be no man to speak to me!"[37] We see him, as Carne-Ross observes, "marching straight up against a great cliff-face of divinity."

In assessing his life, Oedipus is aware of its uniqueness and its greatness: "I'd never have been saved/when left to die unless for some dread evil./Then let my fate continue where it will!"[38] Before leaving, Oedipus requests that Creon protect his daughters but asks again for banishment.

Oedipus recognizes his self-identity, his nature and being, in what he has done, and in recognizing what he has done, he discovers his true identity. He does not limit his moral responsibility to voluntary and intentional acts. He knows that he killed Laius voluntarily and that, although he did not know the identity of his victim, he intended his death. When he discovers that the victim is not only Laius but his own father, that does not relieve him of responsibility, nor does it place the blame on Apollo.

His sense of responsibility is not seriously dissimilar from our own. If I set out to poison a rat but fail adequately but not unreasonably to assess the ingenuity of the children's cat and kill the family pet instead, the responsibility is mine. If I lacked any sense of guilt, the children of the family would promptly and rightly fix the blame. In American law, the doctrine of transferred intent will fix the blame for the consequences of an act on one who voluntarily initiates the causal chain, even if his initial intent is thwarted and the wrong done is not initially intended.

But the basis for assigning transferred intent in such cases rests on the assumption that the act, being voluntary, could have been avoided. This assumption addresses the gravamen. Can we assume that all of Oedipus's voluntary acts were acts that he could have avoided?

It is commonly held that one is not morally responsible for an act unless one could have done otherwise than one did, that is, unless the act could have been avoided. But is it true that one is morally responsible only when one could have done other than one did? An affirmative answer turns on the assumption that one can always do other than one did. Hence, one is assumed to act voluntarily as long as one is not prevented by external forces or by psychological or physiological pressures, such as addictions, from doing so.

This assumption ignores entirely the internal restraints on action due to one's character and the totality of one's being. Could Oedipus have encountered the Sphinx and, while being Oedipus, failed to challenge her? If he were Creon, he could easily have avoided the confrontation, for Creon was prudent, not subject to bursts of anger, not overly ambitious, caring more about his comforts than his *areté*, his achievement of genuine excellence or nobility.

Did Oedipus voluntarily make himself into an intelligent, courageous, impulsive, risk-taking individual determined, like Achilles, to achieve greatness beyond the lot attainable by ordinary men? Hardly. Nor did Achilles. Did not Oedipus's fate, like that of Achilles, include all those qualities of character either given at birth or developed by nurture and by habit to the point that their expression in action was in fact unavoidable? We substitute a moral and legal fiction for reality if we insist that all elements of a mature personality are voluntary in the sense that they are totally malleable and without a powerful vector expressive of character and habit. It is a fiction to suppose that when we assess someone's responsibility for his acts, it is always relevant to ask, "Could he have acted otherwise?" When Martin Luther said, "Here I stand; I can do no other," he was not in the least suggesting that his actions were not free. Rather, his actions were made necessary and inevitable by his own free nature. His actions were both voluntary and inevitable.

How could Oedipus accept his victory over the Sphinx, the kingship of Thebes, and the veneration of his people unless he took credit not only for his voluntary acts but for those physical and mental properties that, fused with the given elements of his character, made it necessary for him not only to dare the Sphinx but to dare to find the truth necessary to relieve the suffering of Thebes?

The given elements of Oedipus's character also include his being reared as a prince: he enjoyed many advantages which greatly enhance the development of the strong, intense, and highly intelligent boy. Growing up in privilege, the subject of high expectations, he naturally develops a sense of exalted worth, fiery ambition, and desire for command based not only on extraordinary abilities but on anticipation of one day becoming king.

All these define his being and are summed up in every expression of his personality—in all he does or fails to do in consequence of who he is. His being, thus defined as the totality of his personhood, is an aspect of his fate which he has shaped in part by his actions—the doing that is the expression of his being.

Fate encompasses much more of his life, however, than merely those given elements out of which Oedipus forges his personality in voluntary action. Fate also intrudes to impose unforeseen and unwilled contexts in which Oedipus is forced to act, contexts that limit or expand alternatives, impose obligations or offer temptations. Fate makes both generous and cruel intrusions in the life of everyone, as in the life of Oedipus, but rarely at such magnificent and tragic extremes. Things similar to what happens to Oedipus can happen to any of us.

Despite the infrequency of our use of the term "fate," each of us confronts *moira*, fated elements, in our daily lives. When a doctor comes unexpectedly on the scene of an accident—and, ready or not, must operate to save a life or scurry away hoping that he has not been seen—he meets his fate. Whether he fulfills or fails in his duty, his action reveals his person, including the fated elements of his being that made it possible for him to become a doctor. The moral character of the doctor is defined in a situation he neither intends nor can escape. And what he does in that situation is a necessary expression of himself.

Young prince Oedipus was not inclined to yield at the crossroads to persons he perceived to be less worthy than himself. He willed neither the meeting at the crossroads nor the attack upon him. This much was fated. But Oedipus voluntarily fought back and deliberately killed Laius. It was his *moira*, his fate, however, that he do much more. By killing Laius, even in fully justified self-defense, Oedipus has, albeit unknowingly, killed his father and avenged the wrong done to him by his father, who was guilty of maiming and abandoning his infant son.

Could Oedipus have done otherwise? Or was his act the necessary and free expression of a forceful, confident, impetuous, presuming personality, one quick to find insult or moral offense and angrily to answer it? Oedipus was fated, without intending it, by both internal and external factors to punish Laius for a crime deserving punishment both legally and morally. By Oedipus's act, the just moral order invoked by the Theban chorus was confirmed.[39]

Oedipus is defined by his being, and his being is revealed in his doing. All his physical and mental qualities, experiences, memories, aspirations, and social and political status define him and direct his moves. Having married Jocasta, Oedipus is now fated to punish the crime of a cruel mother by her abasement and defilement. This just punishment of Jocasta, although the consequence of their voluntary acts, was not intended by either. It was, nevertheless, the fated consequence of both the given contexts and the voluntary acts that led to her bed.

Why should we find it strange to recognize Oedipus as Apollo's avenger—as one who restores justice by rewarding crimes with appropriate punishments? We do not question the claim that Sir Alexander Fleming discovered the antibiotic properties of penicillin even though his discovery was a serendipitous accident. Fleming's fate included, of course, the well-trained mind and the habit of careful observation that enabled him to recognize the significance of an unplanned and unintended experiment. He was not seeking what he found and neither was Oedipus, but both were responsible for their discoveries. Being who they were, however, neither could have done other than he did.

While Fleming properly rejoiced in his fate, Oedipus could only despair. Who would not despair if, in the cause of justice and morality, one must destroy one's parents? Can one be human and attuned to the full dimensions of one's being without recognizing that one's moral innocence has been compromised by the role of avenger? Is it not relevant to ask, "Am I pure enough to cast the first stone?" Is it not indeed inseparable from the human condition that none of us can fully avoid the experience of fated guilt and moral taint—guilt that could not be avoided given one's character and one's *moira?*

If this conclusion seems implausible, it is only because we have artificially reduced the dimension of morality by supposing that no guilt can follow from discovering who and what we are in consequence of what we do, unless we accept the fiction of being always capable, by acting voluntarily and/or intentionally, of doing otherwise than we did.[40]

As king of Thebes, Oedipus had responsibilities that followed from his special status. Obligations were imposed upon him as king which he could not voluntarily dismiss. When a king or a commander-in-chief sends soldiers into battle, he must assume responsibility for their lives and even for the crimes they may commit while soldiering. He intends neither their wounds, their deaths, nor their crimes. But in fulfilling the duties of his station, he is voluntarily responsible (but not perhaps criminally) by transferred intent for these consequences. He may not even have the option of avoiding these consequences, for the safety or indeed the survival of the state may depend upon his committing forces to battle. The commander thus confronts fated responsibilities no matter what he decides; this responsibility and any consequent guilt are the inevitable results of his status.

We need only recall the My Lai massacre or the bombing and killing in Lebanon of hundreds of sleeping Marines to recognize the dereliction of duty by subordinates, or the unintentional misjudgment by those in command that compromises their innocence. That the law may not or cannot be invoked in all such cases does not obscure a degree of guilt for which *mens rea* is not required.

E. R. Dodds, in this connection, compares Oedipus's feelings to those of a motorist who runs down and kills a man:

> I think he *ought* to feel that he has done a terrible thing, even if the accident is no fault of his: he has destroyed a human life, which nothing can restore. In the objective order it is acts that count, not intentions. A man who has violated that order may well feel a sense of *guilt,* however blameless his driving.[41]

Consider the tragic fate of the captain of a ship who, to save the ship, must seal off a flooded compartment and thus condemn to death the men who are trapped there. He voluntarily orders the death of innocent men—men as good as those who are saved. His guilt is fated. But is it any less genuine? His act, though lacking *mens rea,* is both voluntary and intentional; but if he is a good captain, could he have done other than he did? If not, does that make his act less free or him less responsible? And because his act in one sense is right, is that any reason to deny that in another relevant sense it is wrong? Could he be a good captain if he did not have in his innermost being a sense of guilt for not saving all his men? By his voluntary act of accepting command, he colors with voluntariness all the consequences of his acceptance.

These are examples of status responsibility.[42] This is why Shakespeare has Henry V say:

> Upon the king! Let us our lives, our souls,
> Our debts, our careful wives,
> Our children, and our sins, lay on the king![43]

The status responsibility and guilt of the ruler are mirrored in the collective responsibility and guilt of the subjects. When the people of Thebes select Oedipus as king, by their allegiance establish his authority, and in response to his remarkable leadership and concern for their welfare come to venerate him, they participate collectively in responsibility for his decisions. They not only prosper and suffer collectively with him, but they share collectively his virtue and his vice, his innocence and his guilt.

Although they did not intend it, they selected as their king not only the celebrated killer of the Sphinx, but also the killer of their former king and the despoiler of their queen. Do they not share collectively in the killing and the defilement? Are they not rightly debased in their own eyes? Might not one interpret the plague as nothing more than a symbol or embodiment of that defilement?

Not only are there degrees of responsibility and guilt, but there are, I wish to argue, kinds of guilt other than those recognized by lawyers and moralists. The differences and degrees of guilt are revealed in the responses appropriate to each degree and kind. Punishment by law to varying degrees is the appropriate means of dealing with the guilt arising from crimes recognized by law. Various degrees of moral indignation, from ostracism to disappointment, may be appropriate responses to moral failure and guilt.

But abhorrence, horror, shame, and pity may be the appropriate response to guilt of such complexity and moment that it lies beyond the remedies of the law or conventional morality. It is tragic guilt, whether personal or collective, incurred by the participation of the individual or group but without their conscious intent or their ability to avoid it.

To hold that Oedipus is not guilty requires one to ignore the unitary fabric of his being. He is the man who does these wonderful and terrible things as a consequence in part of the prophecies, but also in part because of who he is: as a consequence, that is, of his being as defined by what he has done. To ignore the guilt of the people of Thebes, moreover, is to ignore their selection and support of Oedipus. How can they escape their share of his guilt and shame?

Prophecy does not presuppose determinism or predestination either in *Oedipus* or in Christian theology. Neither Sophocles, St. Paul, St. Augustine, nor Calvin supposed that the foreknowledge of God limited the freedom of man. Neither Oedipus, Laius, nor Jocasta is a puppet on Sophocles's string, and their voluntary reactions to the prophecies of their fate contribute causally to the fulfillment of those prophecies.

Because Oedipus is not a puppet, we must consider his responsibility. If one recognizes degrees of responsibility (including responsibility for allowing oneself, despite one's intelligence and shrewdness, to be deceived), it is by no means clear that the objectively horrible acts of Oedipus are subjectively innocent. Oedipus accepts responsibility for *all* his acts precisely because they are *his* and because they reveal to him and to others his true being.

III

Wiesel and Sophocles, like all great writers, protect us from our natural tendency to simplify and reduce human experience to easily understood categories and clichés. They confront us with the complex wonder of human nature—its nobility and magnificence, its depravity and meanness, its courage, compassion, and sacrifice, its cowardice, indifference, and cruelty. In their writings we witness the beauty and power of truth and enlightened self-knowledge, the ugliness of deception, and the inscrutable darkness of our innermost being. In them we feel the exhilaration of decisively free acts and the oppressive, enervating constriction of fate. They help us to a fuller realization of our true dimension—the heights to which we may climb and the depths to which we may fall—and throughout the adventure of life they reveal the tragic stage on which we play.

The works of these authors reveal the fuller dimensions of responsibility and guilt: their alteration by status, their increase or attenuation by degrees, and their presence as a component of shame when we are morally tainted by fate, not only by what happens to us but by who we are.

These degrees and kinds of responsibility and guilt found in *Oedipus* can also be found in Wiesel's writings. At fifteen, Wiesel was witness to the outer limits of human depravity. He had seen what no one in human history should ever have seen—the final, horrible limits of human cruelty and guilt. Figuratively speaking, he blinded himself: he fell silent before remembered visions of the unspeakable until more than a decade later François Mauriac restored his vision and his voice.

Wiesel and his family, like the characters in Sophocles's play, confronted their fate. Without the fated elements of time and place, Shlomo Wiesel, Elie Wiesel's father, would have lived out his life as a devout Jew, devoted husband and father, and a pillar of wisdom and strength in Sighet. But fate decreed otherwise.

He did not choose to put his wife and children on a train to Auschwitz. Or did he? Maria offered an alternative: shelter in her secluded cottage. But was that a choice for Shlomo? He refused to split up the family; but he did not have to, for Maria was prepared to take all of them to her refuge. Why didn't he accept her offer? He was constrained not by the SS or their Hungarian accomplices but by his essential identity as a Jew who was committed to the solidarity of the Jewish community. How could he leave his family with Maria while he entrained with the rest of the Jewish community? Could he thus violate his duty to wife and children? And how could he accept Maria's offer—an escape for himself and all his family—without accepting an advantage denied to the rest of the community? What right had he and his family to this special treatment? Was he a modern Noah whose family alone was to be spared the flood of barbarism? God had not told him so.

Shlomo also had to be cautious. While he might trust the good will of Maria, how safe was her proffered refuge? Were there no neighbors who would see them there and report them? Spies were everywhere. Wouldn't there be greater safety for his family among the numbers of the entire Jewish community than if, after the community had departed, they alone were discovered in their forest hideaway?

These were Shlomo's fated choices. He chose what he, Shlomo, had to choose: solidarity with the Jewish community. But in Auschwitz, as he observed along with his son the gradual decay of solidarity and the mounting isolation, had he no second thoughts? As he looked into the face of his son—hollow-eyed and ravaged by starvation—was he not troubled by a growing sense of guilt for the decision that brought them to ruin in Auschwitz? Could not, did not he imagine the fate of his wife and his other children? Was he not oppressed by the thought that he might have spared them this suffering had he not been committed to Jewish solidarity?

Could he have done other than he did? Did he do his best? Only the conventional, superficial observer would say that Shlomo could have been who he was and done otherwise. And who would deny that he had done his best? He was the father who, with the best will in the world, rejected an offer to save his family and by that decision delivered them into the hands of the exterminators. No matter how innocent his intent, this was his voluntary choice. A tragically fated choice.

Moreover, a prophet might have foreseen it all. Some latter-day Amos could have said: *Thus sayeth the Lord of Hosts: Hitler, having declared his hatred of the Jews and his evil determination to exterminate them, will create situations in which many devout Jews will face the choice of abandoning their Jewish neighbors or going with them to the death camps.* What difference does it make whether the prophecy comes from Apollo's oracle or from a discerning Jew who, like a prophet of old, heard the lion's roar and understood its meaning?

I suppose, even in his intentional innocence, Shlomo felt the pain of tragic guilt as a father defeated by his own choice in his efforts to save his family. Such tragedy and such tragic guilt should befall no one. But fate is neither compassionate nor just.

And what of Maria? Did she feel no guilt? Wiesel says that her offer of refuge for his family redeemed her town. But did she feel redeemed from the taint of participation as a citizen of Hungary and a townswoman of Sighet in the pogrom that took the property and the lives of most of her Jewish neighbors? Did she work as a servant only for the righteous? Did not her services, modest as they were, contribute to the well-being of other citizens of Sighet? Did not a person as compassionate and devout as she recognize her own guilt as a member of that morally tainted town? Did she not share to a minimal degree in the collective guilt of the citizens of Sighet just as the people of Thebes were to a degree morally tainted by their contribution to the fulfillment of Oedipus's dreadful fate?

As Hamlet says, "There's a Divinity that shapes our ends,

John Silber

Rough hew them how we will." Wiesel and Sophocles make us acutely aware of the profound current that, unknown to us in our present blindness, carries us to our fated ends. Only later do we discover our truer natures for good or ill depending not only on who we are and what we have done, but also on *moira*, the context in which we are born and in which we have lived.

Sophocles and Wiesel are united in affirming the complexity and mystery of human existence both in its grandeur and its depravity. In contemplating the outrage of Auschwitz, Wiesel writes:

> It forces us to question everything. The very foundations of culture, of faith, of science. Educated men and women, gifted, refined lovers of literature, music, and art, were able to commit those most hideous crimes. . . . How can we explain such an abdication of culture and morality? I have tried to understand for forty years without success. For me the mystery of Auschwitz remains intact.[44]

And although the world makes sense for Sophocles, it does not make sense in a way we can understand. Sophocles would have agreed with the lines of Aeschylus near the end of his *Suppliants:* "But who can scan the mind of Zeus?/What eye can fathom that abyss?"

NOTES

1. I am indebted to my friend and colleague Donald Carne-Ross for this clarification.

2. Elie Wiesel, *All Rivers Run to the Sea,* trans. Jon Rothschild (New York: Alfred A. Knopf, 1995), p. 62. Originally published as *Tous les fleuves vont à la mer* (Paris: Éditions du Seuil, 1994).

3. Ibid., 70.

4. Elie Wiesel, *Dawn,* trans. Frances Frenage (New York: Bantam Books, 1982), p. 2. Originally published as *L'Aube* (Paris: Éditions du Seuil, 1960).

5. Ibid., 58. Emphasis added.

6. Ibid., 95.

7. Elie Wiesel, *Night,* trans. Stella Rodway (New York: Penguin Books, 1981), p. 122. Originally published as *La Nuit* (Paris: Éditions de Minuit, 1958).

8. Ibid., 118.

9. Ibid., 92.

10. Ibid., 123.

11. Ibid., 124.

12. Ibid., 69.

13. Ibid., 70.

14. Harry James Cargas, *Conversations with Elie Wiesel* (South Bend, Ind.: Justice Books, 1992), p. 7.

15. Ibid., 8.

16. *Sea,* p. 70.

17. *Night,* pp. 111–113.

18. Jerrold Hickey and Michael B. Shavelson, "A Time to Speak: Elie Wiesel on Literature, Presidents, Belief, and Memory," *Bostonia* (Summer 1995): 19.

19. Sophocles, *Oedipus the King,* trans. Thomas Gould (Englewood Cliffs, N.J.: Prentice-Hall, 1970), lines 249–51.

20. Although Oedipus had been wounded in both ankles, his name in Greek means Swollen-foot (for *oida,* I swell). Despite the wounds, Oedipus is no cripple but a powerful, able-bodied man as befits a great king.

21. Ibid., line 1213.

22. Ibid., lines 1230–31.

23. Ibid., lines 1327–28.

24. *Sophocles' Oedipus the King,* ed. William Arrowsmith, trans. Stephen Berg and Diskin Clay (New York: Oxford University Press, 1978), p. x.

25. *Oedipus,* lines 1329–30.

26. Arrowsmith, *Oedipus the King,* p. x. Here my interpretation follows that of William Arrowsmith. Donald Carne-Ross holds that while in the later fifth century, particularly in the plays of Euripides, a Greek god may be the name of an experience as, for example, Artemis is a way of expressing the uncontrollable passion of Phaedra, it is a mistake to impose this later interpretation on Sophocles. For Sophocles, Carne-Ross insists, "the gods or god (Greek uses singular or plural with no trouble) are blazing, all-powerful, terrible divinity." When, for example, at Colonus, old Oedipus says: "The gods are slow to mark but they mark surely when a man rejects divinity and turns to madness" (lines 1536–37), Carne-Ross insists that Oedipus, in speaking for Sophocles, "is not speaking of gods who are names of human experience." I rely more heavily on Arrowsmith's interpretation, in part because I find it difficult to believe that Euripides' and Sophocles' views of the gods were so radi-

cally different. They were contemporaries, lived long lives through a disastrous period of Athenian history and died in 406, only seven years prior to Socrates' death.

27. For purposes of contemporary understanding I am introducing legalisms that perhaps classical people would find inappropriate. An Athenian jury when finding for a defendant could acquit by a "vote off" which meant the defendant was not to be punished but not necessarily that he was innocent. See Kenneth Dover, *Marginal Comment* (Duckworth, 1994), p. 157.

28. Ibid., xi.

29. *Oedipus,* lines 1349–55.

30. Gould observes in his translator's notes (p. 153) that line 1360, "Now I'm wretched," literally translates Sophocles' text. Gould departs from it for rhythmic consideration; he substitutes, "Now I'm without a god." I have inserted the exact meaning.

31. *Oedipus,* lines 1357–66.

32. Ibid., line 1157.

33. Ibid., lines 1178–80.

34. Ibid., line 1368.

35. Ibid., lines 1371–85.

36. Ibid., line 1397.

37. Ibid., lines 1436–37.

38. Ibid., lines 1456–58. Surprisingly, at no time does Oedipus express pride or even satisfaction in having saved Thebes.

39. Sophocles believed in a just moral order confirmed by such actions; similarly the ancient Hebrews believed in a providential history in which God's will was always confirmed. This view is presented with great clarity by Milton in *Samson Agonistes.* There is also a line from a lost play of Sophocles: "The gods' dice always fall right side up."

40. For an extended discussion of these issues, see my "Being and Doing," *University of Chicago Law Review,* XXXV, 1 (Autumn 1967): 47–91 and H. L. A. Hart, *The Morality of the Criminal Law* (1965), pp. 8, 27.

41. E. R. Dodds, *The Ancient Concept of Progress* (Oxford: Clarendon Press, 1973), p. 72.

42. For a further discussion of status responsibility, see references listed in note 40.

43. Henry V, IV.i., ll. 234–36.

44. Elie Wiesel, Opening Address, Forum 2000, Prague, September 1997.

REINHOLD BOSCHKI

Towards an Ethics of
Remembrance after the Shoah

"DEAR ELIE WIESEL . . . ":
LETTERS FROM SIXTEEN-YEAR-OLD
GERMAN HIGH SCHOOL STUDENTS

"Dear Elie Wiesel: When we received your book *Night* from our religion teacher, Dr. Boschki, I thought: 'Not National Socialism, Judaism, concentration camps again. We had dealt with them so often in other subjects.' I did not know, however, how captivating the book would be. It is something completely different to be confronted with this topic through precise accounts, descriptions, and observations by a person who lived through all of this, than to read about numbers and statistics. I often had to put the book away for some time because I did not dare turn to the next page." (Claudia)

"Since reading the book *Night* I have decided to always be open to dealing with this topic, no matter if it is talked to death or not spoken about. You are perfectly right with your statement: 'Only if we remember do we have the strength to make the present and the future humane.' And I want to try that!" (Karin)

"Your words are burned into my memory." (Michaela)

"While reading your book I shed many tears. Afterwards I wrote the following poem":

You come into a town,
It is lonely.
You go through the streets,
They end in a dead end.

You look into a window,
You see people.
They are all the same,
They are made of cardboard.

You want to scream,
But something constricts your voice.
You want to cry,
But something holds back your tears.

You want to escape from this town,
But something ties you down.
You dream about,
Finding your own fire
But that is only a dream.
(Svetlana)

OPENING QUESTIONS

The strange, unknown town that the student describes in her poem, the town that never lets its visitors go, that constricts their screams, and holds back their tears—is that the "kingdom of memory" that Elie Wiesel talks about?[1] Is the fire that one seeks there a *Night*mare of remembrance? Is it that "memory that burns, but never consumes itself"?[2]

As we will see, Germany still has difficulties with the memory of the Shoah, the destruction of European Jewry. However, the young German students who wrote the above letters are somehow able to identify with the event's consequences. They can do so because, as these letters suggest, they are not "flooded with numbers and statistics" or confronted with accusations of guilt. They also identify because they do nothing but listen to a witness. Herein lies the power of narrated memory: it affects the listener, opens him up to the pain of others in the past and present, and sensitizes his thoughts and actions in the future.

This ethical sensitization is what the philosopher Theodor W. Adorno demands in his famous essay, "Education after Auschwitz," in which he argues that education always has to deal with the prevention of a repetition of Auschwitz.[3] Therefore, the goal of education is an ethical sensitization by means of memory. Neither classical pedagogy nor classical ethical theory, however, provides a framework for Adorno's vision. The purpose of this essay is to provide a prolegomena for such an "ethics of remembrance." The thesis may be stated as follows: *The memory of concrete historical events, especially the singular event of the Shoah, is vital for our humane social existence. Without such memory society becomes inhumane. Ethical theory must not only be led by a rational reason, but also by a recollecting reason.*

The essay will proceed by four steps: (1) an analysis of the culture of remembrance and attempts at recollection in present-day Germany; (2) a review of the place (or absence) of the concepts of experience and memory in the history of philosophy; (3) an attempt at articulating the beginnings of an ethics of experience and remembrance; (4) a summary of the foundation of an ethics of remembrance.

1. RECOLLECTION IN GERMANY AT THE END OF THE TWENTIETH CENTURY

Before taking up the theoretical issues this essay proposes to address, it is both honest and necessary to make clear the standpoint from which I think and write. I therefore begin the essay by reflecting on the current situation in Germany. These reflections emphasize how Germany confronts its past, the past here referring especially, but not only, to the Holocaust. Such a starting point is necessary because an ethics of remembrance always is based on the actual historical situation. In Germany today history is so present that the past sometimes seems to be the twin brother of the present.

The country in which I was born, live, and write is also the country of the perpetrators of the Shoah. One can ascertain the climate of remembrance in Germany by various means: asking young and old Germans about the era of national socialism as well as by listening to public reaction and agitation concerning the Third Reich.[4] This approach enables the following thesis to be set forth: *the memory of the event and period of the Shoah is a central moment in the collective consciousness and, even more, in the collective subconscious of the German people at the end of the twentieth century.*

This thesis may seem surprising, since many studies talk about a culture of forgetting and a hostility towards remembrance of the Shoah in Germany. Yet it is true that most Germans are, in one way or another, conscious of the Nazi times. To be sure, many who are aware of this period also would prefer to see it as something finished. The poll taken by the Emnid-Institute, Bielefeld (Germany), together with the Gallup-Institute, Tel Aviv (Israel) revealed that at the beginning of the 1990s, 62 percent of the people of Germany want to lay to rest the memory of national socialism.[5] Adding the 16 percent who answered with "I do not know," one could assume that almost three-quarters of the German population do not want anything to do with the most terrible and devastating event in German history.

Additionally, general knowledge of the barbarism of those days—the background, dimensions, and implications of the Shoah—is extremely schematic and vague. Indeed, already in the 1980s a "historical illiteracy" was diagnosed in German society.[6] But the notion of historical illiteracy does not represent the issue of memory of the Shoah with complete accuracy. Even an illiterate person, someone who cannot read or write, can be exemplary in his sensitivity in unjust situations and in his commitment to sensitize people. A few examples highlight the ambiguous status of this form of illiteracy: In a small village near my hometown of Tübingen, right-wing groups wanted to open a center for frustrated youths. The official advertising campaigns of the "National Youth," the group sponsoring the center, declared that German youth were to be led back to a national way of thinking, and thus would be encouraged to travel to the "German homeland areas" in Poland and the Czech Republic, to broaden "their knowledge of German history and culture" and to "further develop the moral concepts of past generations." Surprisingly, many young people, some who would be classified as illiterate, came together to demonstrate against the center and what it stood for. Strikingly, the groups that faced off at the demonstration, illiterate though they may be, were characterized and even motivated by a certain way of recollecting recent German history.

The centrality of remembrance of the Nazi period reveals itself as well in a number of arenas of public discourse: for instance, an unexpectedly strong emotional reaction to Spielberg's *Schindler's List* in 1994 showed concern for the fate of the Jews during the Holocaust. And there are other increasing signs of commemoration: the great number of survivor memoirs published recently in Germany;[7] the unceasing effort of nationwide groups and organizations that are committed to the memory of the Shoah (e.g., the eighty institutes for Christian-Jewish cooperation; the "Fritz Bauer Institute"; the many teachers who focus their attention on the "Third Reich"; the so-called "history workshops" and local initiatives that deal with the Nazi past in specific villages and towns; and numerous memorials to Nazi injustice). Such memory also surfaces in another manner: from time to time public figures make extremely insensitive comments about Jews in Germany, evoking sharp reactions and counter-reactions. All this and more exposes the double standard of remembrance in Germany: memory of the Shoah is either consciously or unconsciously looked after or averted.

The bifurcated response of one of my students to Wiesel's *Night* symbolizes Germany's double memory: "This is one of the most important books that I have ever read. Every student should read it. But it is also important finally to consider the past to be over." This statement embodies the ambivalence of the German approach to the Nazi past.

This review of the current situation regarding memory of the Shoah in Germany attests to the need for a systematic ethics of remembrance. As we have seen, memory is shot through with ambivalence. Some people—in Germany as well as elsewhere—justify hatred, racism, and violence on the basis of memory. Hence, memory cannot be naive; it must rather be scrutinized and articulated within the context of the history of ethics. This approach must be taken even if, as the following section argues, the history of ethics is itself in need of rehabilitation when it comes to interrelated notions of experience and memory.

2. THE ABSENCE OF THE CONCEPT OF HISTORICAL EXPERIENCE IN CLASSICAL ETHICS

In its classic formulations, ethical theory has excluded the notion of memory because it also has excluded the notion of historical experience. This means that philosophical and theological ethics, by definition, has excluded the range of human experience, and therefore—as explained below—has excluded the memory of concrete historical events. The traditional methodology of the theory of ethics foregrounds rationality or, theologically, deduction from revelation. Empirical facts, drawn from human behavior, from successful and unsuccessful forms of human coexistence, have generally been relegated to ethical example, moral praxis, and pedagogy. What is drawn from experience, according to a classical philosophy, is not relevant for theory.

The reason for the lack of experience lies not only in the history of ethics but also at the center of the history of philosophy itself. Though pre-Aristotelian sources refer to the concept of experience, it is Aristotle who defines it as a technical term. Aristotle introduces the concept of *empeiria* in philosophy; his definition continues to hold sway even today.

Empeiria means in Aristotle's *Metaphysics* the acquired abilities of human being, a skill, a familiarity with certain objects or tools.[8] This understanding of *empeiria* as a skill in contact with things of the environment is quite different from the modern scientific understanding of empirical observation and research, but the new use is especially in one respect already laid out in the Aristotelian use: the concept of experience is henceforth used philosophically without ethical reference.

Medieval and scholastic thinkers such as Albertus Magnus and Thomas Aquinas deploy the term as Aristotle did. Not until modern times does Francis Bacon give the concept of empiry a technical-practical sense,[9] and coins a new term for it: *experientia*. However, he does not by this notion mean human skills, but the process of their acquisition. For Bacon, observation becomes the basis of *experientia,* the practice of which makes the knowledge of nature possible. A century later, empiricism (Locke, Hume) refined Bacon's notion of experience; it is this notion that ultimately informs Carnap's logical empiricism, where sentences are only given reason if they are verifiable, and are either verifiable through logic or through scientifically based inquiry. Consequently, though it would appear that, given the triumph of the empirical method, the concept of experience has come into its own, this is not the case. Rather, in the twentieth century the concept of experience is viewed almost exclusively under the rubric of science, where experience does not mean human experience but experience as verifiable by means of scientific method.[10]

It is true that Kant's use of the concept "experience" or "empirical recognition" is complex and ambiguous. Nevertheless, Kant, a major influence on all further ethical theory, still excludes all forms of human experience from the ethical knowledge of reason. In his epochal "Foundation for the Metaphysics of Morals" (1785), he demands that the autonomous ethics "is fully cleansed of anything that could be empirical and that belongs to anthropology."[11] All insight gained from anthropology, theology, physics, from experience and human nature cannot be the source of ethical knowledge. Only in reason, specifically in practical reason, do the ethical concepts have "completely a priori . . . their seat" (see p. 411). Thus Kant successfully constituted freedom as independent from experience, positing that the categorical imperative of action is absolutely autonomous. But the negative side to this achievement is that experience—and thus memory and its authority—are dismissed from ethical consideration and are left to scientific empiricism.[12]

Thus, one can, after this admittedly brief sketch of the notion of experience in the history of ethical theory, formulate a conclusion: *Almost nowhere in classical philosophical ethics did concrete human experience and concrete historical events serve as the basis for ethical theory and as the ground for ethical principles.*

What exactly, then, does "experience" and "historical experience" mean and how can these concepts be foundational for ethics? I now consider three twentieth-century movements—existentialism, critical theory, and contemporary theology—that have challenged the peripheral status of experience in Western philosophy and Christian theology.

3. TOWARD AN ETHICS OF EXPERIENCE

a. Existential Philosophy

Influenced by the nineteenth-century philosophers Soren Kierkegaard and Friedrich Nietzsche, German and French existentialism in the twentieth century moved experience to the center of philosophy (see Pieper 1996). Yet Kierkegaard and Nietzsche's influence had a down side as well, since their emphasis on subjectivity simultaneously excluded collective historical experience.

Kierkegaard already understands experience to be the *subjective* acquisition of self. That self is a "relationship that relates to itself."[13] Existence is defined by conflict between the self and itself and in relationship with God. German existentialism remained in Kierkegaard's debt; both of his major successors, Martin Heidegger and Karl Jaspers, continued to look at the human being in extremity: they wrench the human being free from the superficiality of everyday life, and bring him face to face with himself through a confrontation with borderline situations. Yet each thinker also went his own way. While Jaspers was fully aware of the times in which he philosophized, Heidegger thought of time as fundamentally "timeless." As is well known, his refusal to address the implications of the Shoah continued even after 1945 and lasted until his death. Heidegger's problematic stance in relation to Nazism was, as George Steiner correctly notes, the consequence of his ontology, which does not contain or implicate ethics.[14]

In contrast to Heidegger, the French existentialists, Albert Camus and Jean-Paul Sartre, opened their philosophy to social and ethical issues. The present was the object of their commitment. The individual I-experience was extended by them into an "Us-experience,"[15] and concepts such as justice, solidarity, and freedom became central.

But, strangely, Camus and Sartre do not foreground the history of the Nazi rule in Europe and the extermination of the Jews. Yet despite these shortcomings, existential philosophy has played a major role in liberating the concept of experience from a narrow scientific and empirical interpretation. Experience now becomes *human* experience, the concrete and daily life experience of people.

b. Critical Theory

It was, however, the Frankfurt School which in the 1940s and 1950s first linked the concept of experience with collective historical experience. I cannot focus here on the heterogeneous developments in the philosophy of critical theory,[16] but I do want to highlight two thinkers who clearly point the way to a better estimation of the concept of experience. For Walter Benjamin, historical and aesthetic experience form the center of his entire work; the concept of experience is the fertile soil of all philosophical theory.[17] In an early essay from 1917, "About the Program of the Coming Philosophy," he voices his criticism of the narrowness of the concept of experience in Kant's epistomology, and demands a revision of this timeless, unhistorical way of thinking.[18] Benjamin believes in the dignity and authenticity of concrete human experience and links this historical experience with the aesthetic one. In his later, remarkable essay, "The Storyteller" (1933),[19] Benjamin suggests that a story is vitally linked to the notion of experience: "Experience that travels by word of mouth is the source that all storytellers have drawn from" (p. 440). Benjamin's essay turns around the contrast between the novel and the story. Whereas the novel is a modern form of fiction that isolates the writer and reader alike, the story is rooted in collective experience: "the storyteller takes that what he tells from experience—his own or that reported by others." Experience is both the basis and the inspiration for stories. Moreover, stories are the vehicle by way of which human experience circulates, allowing one person's experience to take root in another: "And [the storyteller] in turn," continues Benjamin, "makes [the story] the experience of those who are listening to his tale" (p. 443). Benjamin did not develop a full-blown ethics out of these re-

211

flections; it may be that his tragic death did not permit him to do so. Even so, Benjamin's notion that the story is taken out of experience and, when told, changes the listener has implications for ethics. For such experience turns into remembrance—a notion that, as we will see, itself has great promise for the unfolding of a post-holocaust ethics.

Like his friend Benjamin, Theodor W. Adorno also did not formulate an explicit ethics. He had planned a broad exposition on moral philosophy but never carried it out. Still, one can understand his whole thinking as a "practical philosophy," and can trace a "negative ethics" in his work.[20] Adorno uses the term "Negative" because he assumes in his thinking the viewpoint of the "damaged life," and thus foregrounds the negative side of things. The philosophical eye is focused on the horror and terror that humans have brought into the world. Adorno makes central negative experience: the suffering of humans, the barbarism of the perpetrators, and the oppression of the victims of history. This is how Adorno became the philosopher who thought through the meaning of the Shoah, because all suffering experiences of humanity culminate in it. His whole work, from the "Minima Moralia" (written between 1944 and 1947) to the "Dialectics of Enlightenment" (published in 1947), to finally the "Negative Dialectics" (1966) originates in the world historical catastrophe that is Auschwitz (Claussen 1988, p. 57). With regard to ethics Adorno's new formulation of the Kantian categorical imperative is especially meaningful. In his book "Negative Dialectics" Adorno is convinced that the perpetrators of the extermination of the Jews (Hitler, but also his accomplices) have forced a new categorical imperative on humankind: "To arrange their thoughts and actions in such a way that Auschwitz does not repeat itself, [that] nothing similar ever happens again."[21]

This imperative for human thinking and acting is based not on a Kantian theory of knowledge but on history. The *memory* of the terror of the extermination of Jews should protect people in the present and future from a repetition of Auschwitz. The practical consequence of the ethical imperative is Adorno's demand that education always has to be "education after Auschwitz."

This brief discussion of some aspects of critical theory can be summarized as follows: Late twentieth-century philosophy (or at least a part of it) is at the point of recognizing and integrating historical experience. Only by taking such a step can philosophy also come to terms with the Shoah and turn into a "Philosophy after Auschwitz," a philosophy which will never forget the extermination of the Jews.[22]

c. Postmodern Christian Theology

Not only philosophy excludes the notion of experience and the collective historical event: Christian theology, the tradition out of which I think, suffered from this, too. The theological deficit does not stem from the fact that experience had not been an object of theological reflection; on the contrary, the history of theology is full of references to experience.[23] But theology means by this primarily *religious* experience, and "religious" here means the direct relationship of the person with the saint or God. Christian mystics for instance understand experience to be a mystical experience of God. Martin Luther later concentrates his thinking on the experience of confession through the Gospel and the existential recognition of God in Jesus Christ. F. D. E. Schleiermacher understands religious experience as a feeling of absolute dependency on God. Theological reasoning is often chained to the scheme in which a person in particular "religious" situations experiences the presence of God: "What theology calls 'revelation' . . . is on the part of the receiver always a specific form of experience."[24]

Outside of this narrowly understood religious area, Christian theology, from the Middle Ages to modern times, has subscribed to a surprisingly limited notion of experience.[25] Only in the twentieth century have theologians begun to address the meaning of daily life experience and especially of historical experience. While Karl Barth rejects the tracing back of religious experience to daily life experience on the background of his dialectical theology, other major Protestant theologians (Tillich, Ebeling, Pannenberg, and especially Moltmann and Sölle) have begun to engage seriously concrete existential and historical-political experience. In Catholic theology, the French "Nouvelle théologie" as well as Karl Rahner and Edward Schillebeeckx shift toward anthropology, i.e., the care for the human subject as the center of theological reflection. All anthropological facts in this theological approach are per se theological facts. But the "experience of the Holy Spirit" that can be gathered out of fundamental human experiences,[26] remains linked to the transcendental sphere and does not emphasize history enough.

Whatever the limitations, progress has been made worldwide toward integrating the notion of historical experience into theological reflection. Edward Schillebeeckx and Dietmar Mieth did the pioneering work in Europe,[27] the theologians of liberation in Latin America and in other parts of the world.[28] Despite this pioneering work, however, Christian theologians took considerable time before attending to the catastrophe of the Shoah.[29] Yet, when reflection came, it proved crucial: for reflection on the annihilation of the Jews in the Shoah not only made central the concept of experience but also led to a related yet powerfully new concept: memory.[30] This is the first time in the history of Christian theology that an "unreligious" historical event became the object of genuine theological reflection. But it was to take half a century—hence more than the biblical forty years—until confrontation with the Shoah would change theological ethics.

4. TOWARD AN ETHICS OF MEMORY

This adumbrated review of the history of the philosophical and theological concept of experience was necessary to show how the influence of Aristotle and empirical and scientifically oriented understanding have made historical experience peripheral to ethical theory. If one does not perceive the experiences of people, then they cannot be remembered. *The lack of a role for experience in philosophy and theology results in a lack of remembrance.*

Strikingly, but not surprisingly, attention to the beginning of European philosophy shows that the concept of memory endured a fate parallel to that of experience. Plato interpreted the concept of memory metaphysically, as the repeated memory of the existence of the soul in the everlasting world of ideas. All insight is *anamnesis,* repeated memory, of that what one always already unconsciously knows.[31] In the Platonic system there is no new human insight, no new learning, no teaching—one can say, no ethical value to memory—but always and only metaphysical remembrance. Just as Aristotle later did with the concept of experience, so Plato's influential model located memory in metaphysics and out of ethics, establishing a philosophical tradition bereft of a concept of ethical memory.[32]

However, the shock that came in the aftermath of the Shoah and the slow realization of the dimensions of this event demonstrated the need for a concept of memory in philosophy and theology that would make it possible to face real history. Here, the reference to the *Jewish* concept of remembrance is especially important.[33] Johann Baptist Metz has argued that the ancient Greek philosophical reason that until today is dominant in the Western world has to a large extent driven Jewish reason out of the history of reason. The latter is the remembering reason, the "anamnetic reason" as Metz calls it,[34] that has lived in the Jewish historical consciousness since biblical times. Mind and memory belong together in Judaism. To think always means to remember. Culture and religion have an "anamnetic profundity," because everything that a person does and believes is intertwined with what was done and believed in earlier generations.

With this, we have reached the central thesis of the exposition: *If human reason itself is led by memory, then ethics, which receives direction from reason, has to be led by memory.* Only recently has it become clear that the ethical question, the question of human behavior, has to be embedded in historical memory.[35] An ethics of remembrance has to expand the philosophical and theological concept of experience through the concept of memory. This kind of remembrance has the following aspects:

a) Experience is ethically relevant because it reflects the suffering of the respective times that has to reflect ethics (existentialism). Ethically relevant means that no ethical theory can be developed without these experiences "to remember." Classical ethics is not crushed but enhanced by the addition of memory. The anamnetic reason is that faculty which connects the autonomous, empirically free reasoned ethics with human experience. This means that the memories of people that have experienced suffering have to form the starting point of ethical and pedagogical efforts.

b) The Shoah has to be present in collective memory (critical theory). How people have to act today becomes clear by means of and reflection on the negativity of past suffering. Adorno's formulation articulates the starting point of negative ethics: Auschwitz cannot be repeated, nothing similar can happen again. Whoever says "Auschwitz" has to know what he is talking about. That is why he has to concretely remember what happened. One needs to recollect the historical facts but also the testimonies of the victims (diaries, memoirs, and other records of the disappeared and the survivors). Such testimony is the basis of philosophical, theological, and ethical insight after Auschwitz.

c) A theology of remembrance contains the dimension of hope. The memory of suffering is theologically always linked to the remembrance of the proximity of God. The memory of the catastrophe and the recollection of the experience of liberation in history (e.g., the Exodus) go hand in hand for the religious person. It is clearly not easy to reconcile these two memories (catastrophe and liberation) and often only despair and bitter complaints against God remain as the single possible path. But ethics depends on hope, because it wants to convey the vision of a humane world. Therefore, memory is, as Elie Wiesel says, always hope. And hope depends on remembrance.

FINAL QUESTIONS

The claims of memory are demanding and paradoxical: How can I be asked to remember that which I did not experience? The paradox is seemingly even greater when attending to the Holocaust, for how can I be asked to "remember" a trauma to which I was not subjected and which lies in a realm virtually outside my experience? The paradox remains insistent. Yet, following the ethical direction pointed to by Buber and Levinas, one can say that we never exist without the being of others. The words and silence, the presence and absence of the other dominates my life and thinking. Therefore the memory that belongs to the other—even the absent memory of the victim—needs to become part of my memory if I want to act human.

This basis for this ethics of memory can be found in Elie Wiesel's work, message, and commitment.[36] He has elaborated it in many different forms: in stories and novels, in essays, in drama, and in biblical, talmudic, and Hasidic commentary.[37] Even after forty years, Wiesel's elaboration of an anamnetic ethics goes on uninterrupted. He never wearies of warning people about an "understanding" of Auschwitz and a misuse of the victims of the Shoah. He rightfully resents talk of the "lessons of Auschwitz," because they subsume individual fate—the small child that dies holding its mother's hand, lovers separated forever, the screams of a person in despair, the silent tears of a father, and the pains of the tortured—under an impersonal "Program for the Future." Do we "use" the victims of the past as a "road" on the way into the next millennium or do we have the strength to remember them in silence and—as Wiesel says—to remember their silence?

Finally, let us return in our thoughts to the German high school students that were existentially affected by reading *Night*. I do not believe (as some do) that they are using the victims to gain a certain attitude or philosophy of life. Their first act is simply and purely to remember the victims; hopefully they will remember them for the rest of their lives. Exactly in such an initial act of remembrance a sensible reasoning of ethical principles also occurs; such a process is at the center of every ethical theory. Simultaneously an ethical sensitization takes place; it is the goal of every ethics. Is ethics ready for the challenge posed by memory?

NOTES

With this essay I thank my teacher Elie Wiesel for what he has taught me. In truth, his influence and example affect everything that I teach and write. I also wish to thank my friends in Europe, in the United States, and in Israel that I have met through our mutual interest in

Wiesel's work and message; these friends enrich me again and again in every conversation and contact that we have. Finally, I wish to thank Miss Claudia Asch for the initial translation of this essay.

1. Elie Wiesel, *From the Kingdom of Memory: Reminiscences* (New York: 1990).

2. Elie Wiesel, "Wiederbegegnung mit Auschwitz," in *Auschwitz-Birkenau: "Eine Erinnerung, die brennt, aber sich niemals verzehrt,"* ed. A. Bujak (Freiburg, 1989), pp. 5–8.

3. Theodore W. Adorno, "Erziehung nach Auschwitz," in *Erziehung zur Mündigkeit,* (Frankfurt/M., 1971), pp. 88–104.

4. For example, the discussions about the exhibit on war crimes of the German army during the Nazi period shown in major cities in Germany in 1996 and 1997 or about Daniel J. Goldhagen's *Hitler's Willing Executioners: Ordinary Germans and the Holocaust* (N.Y.: Knopf, 1996); see also J. H. Schoeps, (ed.): *Ein Volk von M Goldhagen-Kontroverse im die Rolle der Deutschen im Holocaust* (Hamburg 1996.)

5. *Spiegel Spezial: Juden und Deutsche* (Hamburg 1992), pp. 61–84.

6. G. Wichert and U. Heinemann, *Zwischen den Zeiten. Geschichts- und Gegenwartsbewusstsein in der Bundesrepublik der achziger Jahre, in: Landeszentrale für politische Bildung,* ed. Nordrhein-Westfalen (Streitfall deutsche Geschichte, Essen 1988); on this topic and its consequences, see R. Boschki and F. M. Konrad (ed.), *Ist die Vergangenheit noch ein Argument? Aspekte einer Erziehung nach Auschwitz* (Tübingen, 1997) and especially J. Manemann, "Wider das Vergessen. Entwurf einer Kritischen Theorie des Eingedenkens aus politisch-theologischer Sicht," in Boschki and Konrad's volume, pp. 89–120.

7. E.g. Klüger 1992, Klemperer 1996, Wiesel, new edition of *Night* 1996.

8. See Aristotle, *Metaphysics* 980b–981a.

9. See Kambartel 1972 for the history of the concept of experience in philosophy.

10. See Danneberg 1996; Avgelis 1996; Burri 1996 for the newer, especially the American discussion about science theory, empiry and empiricism, and the criticism of empiricism by the empiricist W. V. Quine.

11. Kant, "Foundation for the Metaphysics of Morals," Academy edition, vol. 4, pp. 388f.

12. To be sure, pragmaticism attempted to rehabilitate the concept of experience, but it too fell short of the mark. See Wolf 1996.

13. Kierkegaard, *Sickness unto Death,* 1957 Edition, p. 8.

14. Steiner, preface to the German Edition of his book *Martin Heidegger* (1989) pp. 40.

15. Pieper 1996, p. 176.
16. For an overview see Jay 1973; Wiggershaus 1986.
17. See Kraushaar 1988.
18. Benjamin, 1991, vol. II, p. 160.
19. Benjamin, 1991, vol. II, p. 438–65.
20. Bender 1988, p. 126.
21. Adorno 1981, vol. 6, p. 358.
22. See also Rosenberg and Myers 1988; Roth and Berenbaum 1989.
23. Köpf 1982; Track 1982; Herms 1982.
24. Schaeffler 1990, p. 15.
25. Ebeling 1975.
26. E.g. Rahner 1975, especially pp. 387.
27. Schillebeeckx 1980; Mieth 1977.
28. Gutiérrez 1972.
29. The first to openly register the shock of Auschwitz for Christian theology was Johann Baptist Metz, and simultaneously with him Jürgen Moltmann and Dorothee Sölle.
30. While American Christian theologians Alice and Roy Eckardt, Robert Mc Afee Brown, Harry James Cargas, and Darrell J. Fasching connect to the Jewish theology of the Shoah, or as Paul van Buren, John T. Pawlikowski, and Krister Stendahl think theologically in terms of a dialog between Jews and Christians, the philosopher and theologian Johann Baptist Metz draws on the considerations of critical theory and the Jewish concept of memory (see below).
31. Very clearly in Plato, *Meno.*
32. Bormann 1972.
33. Yerushalmi 1982; Manemann 1995; Münz 1995.
34. Metz 1989, 1992.
35. Boschki 1991; Fashing 1992, 1993; Metz 1997.
36. Boschki 1991, 1995.
37. Explicitly, e.g., Wiesel 1997.

REFERENCES

Adorno, Th. W. 1981. *Gesammelte Schriften.* Vol. 6, Negative Dialektik. Frankfurt/M.
Aristotle. *Metaphysik. Schriften zur ersten Philosophie,* trans. and ed. F. F. Schwarz. Stuttgart, 1981.
Avgelis, N. 1996. "Rationale Rekonstruktion und Empirie. Zur gegen-

Reinhold Boschki

wärtigen Problemlage in der Wissenschaftstheorie." In Freudiger et al. (1996), pp. 42–69.

Bender, W. 1988. *Ethische Urteilsbildung.* Stuttgart.

Benjamin, W. 1991. *Gesammelte Schriften,* 14 volumes. Frankfurt/M.

Bormann, C. V. 1972. "Erinnerung." In *Historisches Wörterbuch der Philosophie,* vol. 2, ed. J. Ritter. Darmstadt. Pp. 636–43.

Boschki, R. 1991. "Handeln aus der Kraft der Erinnerung. Das Werk Elie Wiesels als Anstoss für eine „anamnetische Ethik." In *Orientierung. Katholische Blätter für weltanschauliche Information,* no. 12, vol. 55 (1991): 143–47.

———. 1995. *Der Schrei. Gott und Mensch im Werk von Elie Wiesel.* 2nd. ed. Mainz.

Bulthaupt, P. (Ed.) 1975. *Materialien zu Benjamins Thesen 'Über den Begriff der Geschichte.'* Beiträge und Interpretationen, Frankfurt/M.

Burri, A. 1996. "Die Überreste des Empirismus." In Freudiger et al. (1996), pp. 70–92.

Claussen, D. 1988. "Nach Auschwitz. Ein Essay über die Aktualität Adornos." In Diner (1988), pp. 54–68.

Danneberg, L. 1996. "Erfahrung und Theorie als Problem moderner Wissenschaftsphilosophie in historischer Perspektive." In Freudiger et al. (1996), pp. 12–41.

Diner, D. Ed. 1988. *Zivilisationsbruch. Denken nach Auschwitz.* Frankfurt/M.

Ebeling, G. 1975. "Die Klage über das Erfahrungsdefizit in der Theologie als Frage nach ihrer Sache." In G. Ebeling, *Wort und Glaube,* vol. 3. Tübingen. Pp. 3–28.

Fashing, D. J. 1992. *Narrative Theology after Auschwitz. From Alienation to Ethics.* Minneapolis.

———. 1993. *The Ethical Challenge of Auschwitz and Hiroshima—Apocalypse or Utopia?* Albany.

Freudiger, J., A. Graeser, and K. Petrus. Ed. 1996. *Der Begriff der Erfahrung in der Philosophie des 20. Jahrhunderts.* München.

Goldhagen, D. J. 1996. *Hitler's Willing Executioners: Ordinary Germans and the Holocaust.* New York.

Graeser, A. 1996. "Erfahrung und Ethik—Ethik und Erfahrung." In Freudiger et al. (1996), pp. 199–219.

Gutiérrez, G. 1972. *Theologia de la Liberacion.* Salamanca.

Herms, E. 1982. "Erfahrung—philosophisch." In *Theologische Realenzyklopädie* (TRE), vol. 10. Berlin, New York. Pp. 89–109.

Jay, M. 1973. *The Dialectical Imagination; A History of the Frankfurt School and the Institute of Social Research 1923–1950.* Boston, Toronto.

Kambartel, F. 1972. "Erfahrung." In *Historisches Wörterbuch,* ed. J. Ritter. Pp. 609–617.

Kant, I. 1912. *Grundlegung zur Metaphysik der Sitten* (1785). Akademie-ausgabe der Werke Kants. Vol. 4. Berlin.

Kierkegaard, S. 1957. *Die Krankheit zum Tode*. In *Gesammelte Werke*, vol. 24/25, ed. E. Hirsch. Düsseldorf.

Klemperer, V. 1996. *Ich will Zeugnis ablegen bis zum letzten. Tagebücher 1933–45.* 2 volumes.

Klüger, R. 1992. *Weiter Leben. Eine Jugend.* Göttingen.

Köpf, U. 1982. "Erfahrung—theologiegeschichtlich (Mittelalter und Reformationszeit)." In *Theologische Realenzyklopädie* (TRE), vol. 10. Berlin, New York. Pp. 109–116.

Kraushaar, W. 1988. "Auschwitz ante. Walter Benjamins Vernunftkritik als eine Subtheorie der Erfahrung." In Diner (1988), pp. 201–241.

Manemann, J. 1995. *"Weil es nicht nur Geschichte ist"—Die Begründung der Notwendigkeit einer fragmentarischen Historiographie aus politisch-theologischer Sicht.* Hamburg, Münster.

Metz, J. B. 1979. "Ökumene nach Auschwitz. Das Verhältnis von Christen und Juden in Deutschland." In *Gott nach Auschwitz*, ed. E. Kogon and J. B. Metz. Freiburg. Pp. 121–44.

———. 1989. "Anamnetische Vernunft." In *Zwischenbetrachtung im Prozess der Aufklärung* (FS Jürgen Habermas), ed. A. Honneth et al. Frankfurt/M. Pp. 733–38.

———. 1992. "Für eine anamnetische Kultur." In *Holocaust. Die Grenzen des Verstehens*, ed. H. Loewy. Reinbek bei Hamburg. Pp. 35–41.

———. 1997. "Im Eingedenken fremden Leids. Zu einer Brückenkategorie zwischen Theologie und Ethik, zwischen Moral und Religion." In *Katechetische Blätter,* no. 2, vol. 122 (1997): 78–87.

Mieth, D. 1977. *Moral und Erfahrung.* Freiburg (Switzerland).

Münz, Chr. 1995. *Der Welt ein Gedächtnisgeben. Geschichtstheologisches Denken im Judentum nach Auschwitz.* München, Gütersloh.

Pieper, A. 1996. "Erfahrung in der Existenzphilosophie." In Freudiger et al. (1996), pp. 153–77.

Plato *Menon*. In *Sämtliche Werke*, trans. F. Schleiermacher, ed. Otto, Grassi, Plamböck, vol. 2. Reinbek bei Hamburg, 1957.

Rahner, K. 1975. *Theologie aus Erfahrung des Geistes.* Schriften zur Theologie, vol. 12, Einsiedeln.

Rosenberg, A., and G. E. Myers, Eds. 1988. *Echoes from the Holocaust: Philosophical Reflections on a Dark Time.* Philadelphia.

Roth, J. K., and M. Berenbaum. Eds. 1989. *Holocaust: Religious and Philosophical Implications.* New York.

Schaeffler, R. 1990. "Die religiöse Erfahrung und das Zeugnis von ihr. Erkundungen eines Problemfeldes." In *Erfahrung des Absoluten—absolute Erfahrung? Beiträge zum christlichen Offenbarungsverständnis*, ed. B. J. Hilberath. Düsseldorf. Pp. 13–34.

Schillebeeckx, E. 1980. "Erfahrung und Glaube." In *Christlicher Glaube und moderne Gesellschaft,* vol. 25. Freiburg. Pp. 74–116.

Steiner, G. 1989. *Martin Heidegger.* München, Wien. (Including a 1989 preface to the German edition; American edition: New York 1978.)

Track, J. 1982. "Erfahrung—theologiegeschichtlich (Neuzeit)." In *Theologische Realenzyklopädie* (TRE), vol. 10. Berlin, New York. Pp. 116–28.

Wiesel, E. 1996. *Die Nacht* (new edition). Freiburg.

———. 1997. *Ethics and Memory.* Berlin, New York.

Wiggershaus, R. 1986. *Die Frankfurter Schule. Geschichte, theoretische Entwicklung, politische Bedeutung.* München.

Wolf, J.-Cl. 1996. "Pragmatismus mit oder ohne Methode? Rorty versus Dewey." In Freudiger (1996), pp. 231–45.

Yerushalmi, Y. H. 1982. *Zakhor. Jewish History and Jewish Memory.* Seattle, London.

Human and Civil Rights

MARGUERITE S. LEDERBERG, M.D.

Blaming the Victim:
Can We Learn to Stop?
Cancer as the Battleground

THE DANGEROUS VICTIM

Large numbers of traumatized human beings find that their suffering endures long after the end of their ordeal, due to the distancing, rejection, and often blatantly negative moral judgment they experience at the hand of those who should be helping them heal. It may take forty or fifty years not only for them to find the strength to speak, but to find others willing to listen. A prophet of memory like Elie Wiesel is all the more remarkable for his refusal to be silent.

All too many individuals have a stake in keeping victims silent, and worse yet in pronouncing them guilty: the immediate perpetrators with their familiars and neighbors who must hide their guilt by association, and the profiteers eager to retain their lucre and avoid the stain upon it. Even more distant bystanders feel the need to excuse their inaction, sometimes irrationally. Others do not feel personally guilty, but cannot endure their own pain upon hearing the unspeakable spoken. This reaction is innate to every human being with a shred of compassion and is often acted upon with a variety of subterfuges, frequently without any awareness on the part of the individual.

Honoring victims is not only threatening but actually destabilizing to human societies, all of which need to believe that their own society is innately just. Even the benign citizen has a stake

225

in holding victims responsible for their own suffering, because blaming the victim serves as a precondition to feeling that the world is viable, and that he can aspire to remaining safe from harm.

VICTIMHOOD AND CANCER

It is difficult for even well-intentioned human beings to escape the fundamental dynamic of blaming the victim. Hospitals can be the setting for scapegoating under the most civilized and well-meaning guise. Here victims, i.e. patients, are tacitly blamed for their own afflictions as an inadvertent side effect of desperate compassion, when their loved ones cannot tolerate undeserved and incurable suffering.

I was once called to the bedside of a twenty-year-old boy whose parents wanted him evaluated for a psychological eating disorder. I found a moribund young man who felt he was letting his family down by not eating and not having "a better attitude." He even wondered if they were angry at him. Such a thought was so painful that he had become more and more preoccupied with the thought that he was somehow responsible for having become ill. It was easier to blame himself than to think of his parents as arbitrarily deserting him, an example of the all-too-common dynamic of the victim ultimately blaming himself. Maybe he had not lived a healthy enough lifestyle, maybe he had caroused too much in college, maybe he should not have smoked marijuana. Ruminating further, he would wonder about whether he was being punished for having been a jealous, uncooperative sibling . . . then he would pull himself back from such thoughts and become angry, angry at his disease, his treatments, the indignities of patienthood, the callousness of the medical staff, angry at fate, angry at his frightened avoidant friends, his fortunate siblings, and lastly angry at his parents, until he exhausted himself into a state of profound and solitary sadness.

And so it went, during the long hours in his hospital bed, illustrating many of the dynamics seen in victims who, upon enduring blame instead of compassion, come to doubt their reality, begin to blame themselves, to feel shame, followed by rage and despair.

In reality, his parents loved him passionately and were desperate with grief at seeing their child becoming more and more wasted. At some level, they felt they had failed their child in having been unable to protect him against this catastrophe. Racked by their helplessness, they would feel moments of emotional exhaustion and a desire to flee, as well as moments of resentment and rage about their own suffering, all of which led to irrational guilt and anxiety. Yet they were determined to stand by him and function supportively at the hospital bedside even in the face of their looming loss. It was too much to bear without seeking some relief. So, like him, like all of us, they searched for a way out of meaninglessness. The current excitement about the role of the mind in altering the course of cancer provided them with a ready-made framework. It gave meaning and it dictated a course of action. If their son could harness the power of his mind, that, at least, would be a possible intervention in the face of intolerable helplessness. Thus, focusing not on the sick body but on the allegedly underutilized mind, they had made their son responsible for his terminal anorexia rather than confronting and enduring the injustice and tragedy of their situation.

To be sure, the need to seek for explanations that give meaning to toxic events is universal, and self-blame is often preferable to betrayal or random tragedy when the reward is a sense of control, illusory though it is. There are endless variations on this theme. Families badger patients to have a better attitude, to exercise more, complain less, be more upbeat. Such an approach is wearing on the patient under any circumstance, but how much more so when it carries the message that refusal is both a moral failing and an invitation to treatment failure. On the other hand, angry patients accuse family members of having caused their cancer, ensuring long-term suffering in the survivors. Many outpatients request psychiatric support because they believe their inability to surmount their normal feelings of sadness, fear, resentment will be the cause of treatment failure. More resistant ones come asking to be affirmed in their right to have negative feelings. Some keep returning to therapy because they need a safe place in which they can pour out their true feelings without guilt or shame. The most rebellious ones are angry at the demands made upon them and grateful when their anger is accepted without criticism or automatic attempts to get them to have a "more positive attitude."

Cancer is ubiquitous and unpredictable. The treatments are lengthy, difficult to endure, and emblematic of the most frightening aspects of modem science, namely toxic chemicals and radiation. As a result, the stress of undergoing them, added to the fear of failure, drive many patients to try what have been called alternative treatments. Mental disciplines of various sorts that are associated with a sense of empowerment and increased well-being constitute an important category. The best among them are penetrating traditional medicine, a trend that has been well demonstrated by Bill Moyers' television series and the associated book *Healing and the Mind*.[1] Other such disciplines remain in a gray zone. Harnessing the power of the mind and strengthening one's immune defenses by having a positive attitude is one of their most widely touted assets through which a patient is led to believe that he may improve his prognosis, or even be cured.

The use of such methods of treatment is based on a cherished hope that people carry within themselves the seeds of their own salvation. It is a hope deeply entrenched in all of human history, blending together, then as now, traditional goals with life-extending ones. This is indeed old wine in new bottles. In 1903, in *The Varieties of Religious Experience*, William James described both the mood-elevating effects and the possible problems of what he called "mind-cures."[2] Human beings have always wanted to believe they can be the instrument of their own salvation. This strategy may be yet another way of shifting the responsibility for his disease onto the patient, but it is often successful because it plays into patients' own magical wishes, driving many of them to embrace the burden of responsibility because it is the price of hope.

On the plus side of the ledger, there is ample evidence that meditation, relaxation techniques, and various methods of visualization, especially as taught and practiced in a warm, supportive setting, improve patient well-being significantly. It has also been repeatedly observed that patients with good social supports do better than those without. Two small studies, currently under necessary replication, suggest that group interventions increase length of survival in women with advanced breast cancer and prolong relapse-free time in melanoma patients. Lastly, assertive, feisty patients live slightly longer than passive, resigned ones. When one adds this to the fact that psychosocial interventions clearly help patients feel better, tolerate treatment better, maintain their relationships better, and return to previous role functioning faster, there is ample reason to encourage these methods, whether as part of mainstream psychological interventions or as alternative treatments.[3]

COMPASSIONATE COMPROMISES?

How can we work at this level of "mind-body" connection? And how can we do it without betraying and blaming patients as a result of trying to escape from our own pain and anxiety?

In seeking to extract a few general principles from the limited data available, two facts emerge repeatedly: the positive effect of social support for the patient and that of an active stance by the patient him- or herself. We need each other to survive, and we need to remain active on our own behalf.

The group interventions associated with positive outcomes revolved around those two main axes: on the one hand, promotion of relationships, of open communication and sharing of feelings; on the other, the teaching of practical skills such as relaxation techniques and problem-solving methods that empowered patients. Both were associated with a detoxification of painful subjects so these could be freely talked about, and both encouraged patients to be more confident and assertive in their interactions with doctors, family, and friends.

For patients, this means remaining engaged, engaged with people they love, with their medical caregivers, their own treatment, their own hopes and fears. And it must be an engagement which promotes acceptance of those hopes and fears, and of all the feelings generated by their illness. What it does not mean is forced "attitude correction," or demands for mirthless smiles and

Marguerite S. Lederberg, M.D.

vacuous cheer. A good cry with a loving, tolerant person leads to a more constructive sense of emotional release and self-acceptance than empty words and wishful thinking, especially when it is followed by constructive and/or pleasant activities.

And lest family members and bystanders believe they are being asked to devote themselves without any personal benefit, it should be mentioned that in the very active field of research on the families of seriously ill patients, open communication between all members comes up universally as the most important factor in predicting better long-term outcome for the families that practice it.

In the case of the young man described above, having had a chance to share his concerns and hear them normalized, he was given some explanation of what was occurring between him and his parents. The parents were helped to grieve more directly and encouraged to verbalize their sense of helplessness and the contradictory feelings it aroused. Subsequently, they became better able to absorb information about their son's anorexia as an inevitable concomitant of terminal disease. The three of them reaffirmed their feelings and reassured each other, then agreed to follow practical guidelines designed to avoid the focus on food. Incidentally, this helped them to avoid a chronic regression to an adolescent mode of interaction, one of the common and disheartening consequences of severe illness in young adults thrust unwillingly back into their parents' direct care. Food is frequently the vehicle for such a mechanism, just as it is between parents and children at many ages.

But the deeper effect of the intervention was to enable the parents to tolerate pain and injustice, without having to invent an explanation or a reassuring organizing schema that distanced them from their son.

VOLITION AND PSYCHE

Underlying this whole scenario was the belief that *if* the patient's refusal to eat was "psychological" rather than "physical," he could do something to alter it, and that the failure to do so implied some kind of weakness or insufficiency on his part.

We find ourselves face-to-face with another irrepressible human prejudice, namely the conviction that an individual always has more control over "psychological" symptoms than over "physical" ones, over the mind than over the body. The correlate of this conviction is the assumption that physical and psychological symptoms are radically different from one another. This soma-psyche dichotomy is yet another form of the mind-body dichotomy enshrined by Descartes and updated to include a post-Freudian awareness of what can be roughly called, for our purposes, the emotional mind. In the earlier tradition, the mind is the thinking mind, the rational mind, the seat of the will and of self-control. And it is to this sphere that psyche—the realm of the emotions—is too hastily relegated. For, as this tradition claims, if the psyche has no associated "matter," no physicality, then it too belongs to the mind sphere and must partake of volitional attributes.

Hence, according to this schema, the psyche is a domain over which one exercises the same control as is characteristic of the purely cognitive realm. It follows from this definition of psyche as mind and as under the control of the will that psychopathologies are also subject to, and even generated by, the will of those who are afflicted by them. The sufferer is the agent of their own suffering. Once this premise is granted, passing a negative moral judgment on the psychiatric sufferer is inevitable, and we are back full force to blaming the victim.

SCIENCE AND PSYCHE

How can we dismantle the underlying dichotomy that activates the reflex to blame the victim? To many scientists, the mind-body split is a total fabrication. They do not even deem it worth disproving because the evidence for the biological basis of perceptive, cognitive, affective, and behavioral phenomena is so compelling. They can refer to the reproducibility of complex behaviors or cognitive distortions by brain stimulation, to natural experiments with brain-damaged individuals, to powerful animal experiments, to the whole field of neurotransmitter research and the consequent explosion of designer drugs; in brief, the whole world of modern neuroscience.[4]

Marguerite S. Lederberg, M.D.

Unfortunately, some scientists couple this belief with a condescending and reductive attitude to human psychological symptoms, emotional responses, and spiritual needs, dismissing spiritual accompaniment and psychological treatments other than behavioral techniques and the most practical counseling. Not surprisingly, some psychiatrists take the opposite tack, with a nonnegotiable insistence on psychodynamic treatment. This intransigence masks a fear, which in turn betrays an incompletely acknowledged belief that the triumph of the brain will disable their therapeutic armamentarium and make them superfluous. Lastly, some non-scientists feel a visceral terror and revulsion at the possibility that biological interventions might be effective for true emotional suffering, as witnessed by the widespread prejudice against clearly effective treatments for depression and other psychiatric conditions. Though in different camps, scientists, psychiatrists, and lay people all set forth their categorical claims in such a way as to keep the dichotomy intact; the mechanisms for blaming the victim remain unchallenged.

BEYOND THE PSYCHE-SOMA DICHOTOMY

The mind-body dichotomy, the concept or attitude that underlies the practice of blaming the victim, is so deeply ingrained that neither group realizes that both convictions run counter to the evidence. We know so much about the biology of vision, yet the sunset still takes our breath away. All we know and will ever know about the biology of sex does not alter our enslavement to lust or passion. We can map out the architecture of sleep and its alterations under many conditions, but insomnia bedevils us just the same. And all the knowledge in the world will never relieve us of an inescapable wonderment about the mystery and the meaning of existence.

So we need not be afraid of the idea that our thoughts and feelings have a biological underpinning. Will we be any less human, with the implied complement of greatness and abjectness? of willpower and weakness? of valor and cowardice? Are we less unique in the world because our brain is the seat of our emotions and our intellect?

The discontinuity between us and the rest of nature does not depend on these attributes; it rests with our self-consciousness, if indeed we are alone among living creatures in having it. And we willingly (and often casually) relinquish it over and over again, drowning it in alcohol and other drugs, or, in quite different circumstances, consigning ourselves to temporary oblivion under anaesthesia. In these cases, we are not unduly threatened, but rather trust that we will return to ourselves. Indeed, we most often do return—for better or for worse—just as human as we were before.

INTO THE NEW MILLENNIUM

We do not live in a mind-or-body world, a physical-or-psychological world. We do not live in an either-or world at all. Our claim to a sense of self does not lie there, it lies in our awareness, our consciousness of ourselves. Some may call it soul, some invoke a deity, others speak of spirituality. But even the most unbending positivist acknowledges a sense of wonder when he meditates upon human consciousness. He is exercising what Carl Gustav Jung called the psyche's religious function, that universal component of our creature heritage.[5] He was referring to human beings' innate ability to experience awe or ecstatic consciousness. Vercors, in his novel *You Shall Know Them*, made a similar observation when he defined the exercise of any form of symbolic ritualized activity as the defining characteristic of the human species.[6] The ultimate truth lies outside the bounds of verification. But for those who have a crystallized faith, the truth is beyond question. Some of the most confident radiate calm and tolerance. Others demonstrate an ominous insecurity with fanatic intolerance. For the many who do not identify themselves as believers in a defined supernatural agency, the religious function of the psyche still operates, and they do not lack the capacity to experience the "numinous" quality of existence. It does not locate itself so clearly, but it is active nonetheless.

Thus, with or without a leap of faith, we must all work to become more secure in accepting ourselves as part of the earthly biota, understanding that it still leaves our humanity as rich and bewildering as we know it to be, and still leaves the universe as miraculous as we will always find it. But for that to proceed, we must stop forcing ourselves and our experiences into meaningless, Procrustean dichotomies. We must experience our internal reality and our personal iota of life as a seamless whole so we can better experience others as whole as well. We will not disown others if we do not disown any part of ourselves. Then, at last, perhaps, we will be secure enough in our sense of self—and understanding enough of one another—to resist the urge to blame the victim.

NOTES

1. B. Moyers, *Healing and the Mind.* (New York: Doubleday. 1993).

2. W. James, *The Varieties of Religious Experience* (New York: Longmans, Green, 1902).

3. M. S. Lederberg and J. C. Holland, "Psycho-oncology," in *Comprehensive Textbook of Psychiatry VI* ed. H. Kaplan and B. Sadock (Baltimore: William and Wilkins, 1995), pp. 1570–1592.

4. B. S. McEwen and H. M. Schmeck, *The Hostage Brain* (New York: Rockefeller University Press, 1994).

5. C. G. Jung, *Modern Man in Search of a Soul* (New York: Harcourt Brace Jovanovich, 1933).

6. Vercors, *You Shall Know Them* (New York: Popular Library, 1953).

STEVEN T. KATZ

The Aché: A Re-Evaluation

OVER THE LAST SEVERAL decades, Elie Wiesel has traveled the globe in an effort to encourage peace and human harmony in all corners of the world. This effort has found him in the former Yugoslavia, in various parts of the former Soviet Union, in the Middle East, in Cambodia, South Africa, and among the Mosquito Indians in Central America. In addition, he has continuously intervened in world affairs as well as in international trouble spots through written appeals and public statements. These interventions have ranged from his courageous admonition to President Reagan concerning his visit to Bitburg: "That place, Mr. President, is not your place," to his support for the "boat people" of Cambodia and the refugees of Tibet. He has also testified to Congress on behalf of the Genocide Convention and argued in support of the Genocide Implementation Act.

Among these extraordinary personal efforts on behalf of those in need, many of whom have no effective voice of their own, Professor Wiesel, with absolute moral justification, provided Professor Richard Arens with an Epilog for his by now well-known 1976 anthology dealing with the oppression of the Aché Indians of Paraguay, entitled *Genocide in Paraguay*.[1] This book, in turn, made a considerable impact and has been widely cited in the scholarly literature on genocide.

At the time *Genocide in Paraguay* was published, the term

235

'genocide' was still in flux, encouraging a loose application.[2] However, over the past twenty years, the use of the term 'genocide' has greatly proliferated and in response one has had to become increasingly suspicious of its employment. Given the wide abuse of this term, every modern claim regarding a "genocide" must now be closely scrutinized. As part of this critical process one has also to re-examine older claims in order to judge the degree to which the event(s) in question actually conform to the technical meaning of the term. Among these past claims is that of Arens regarding the Aché.

The contemporary treatment of the Aché Indians of Paraguay has been at the center of an intense international controversy over the past two decades.[3] The principle causes of the renewed assault against them and other indigenous peoples are a national program of economic development[4] that involves the acquisition of traditional native lands[5] and a demographic surge in the national population of Paraguay as a whole.[6] In effect, the current mistreatment of the Aché, who today number approximately 1300,[7] and other indigenous groups in Paraguay such as the Mby'a and Ayoreo, is essentially another gruesome example of that economically driven immorality that has defined Indian reality since colonial times.[8] In contemporary Paraguay this rapacious aggrandizement has generally entailed the removal of the indigenous tribal groups, including 700 Toba-Moskay in 1980, from their forest habitats that are repositories of natural and mineral wealth and their subsequent, forced, "integration" into the most disenfranchised classes of the larger national community.[9] This sociocultural transaction, this militant process, has come to be known by scholarly observers of the Paraguayan situation as "sedentarization."[10]

In general terms, for all the tribal and human disruption it has involved and despite all the malevolence that it has embodied, this coercive integrationist policy has worked, and has been constructed so as to work, in a non-genocidal way. The overwhelming majority of Parguay's indigenous population of 50,000 to 100,000 persons[11] in seventeen ethnic groups[12] has been, however disadvantageously and raggedly, acculturated and (marginally) re-absorbed into the national economy.[13] Of course there is much experiential diversity within this larger, incorporative pattern. The Chiripá, for example, have seen much of their traditional lands sold to outsiders, especially foreign corporations and large international investors, who now control Industrial Paraguaya that owns 1.5 million hectares (a hectare is approximately 2.47 acres; it is abbreviated 'ha'). As a consequence they have been forced, and encouraged, to adopt an expanded, if still small, role in the commercial agricultural sector and to serve as itinerant labor, as well as, and most importantly, to continue in the extractive lumber industry that is linked to their historic forest habitats. Creating new settlements in the Jejuí River basin, as well as moving into mestizo society, the Chiripá improved their economic condition and saw their population grow as fecundity increased and medical care improved.[14] At the same time, despite this incipient economic activity, they were able to maintain, at least into the 1970s, a significant degree of independence and ethnic identity. And this because they were relatively successful in their efforts at rejecting Christianity and holding various missionary groups at bay, and also in resisting the deep penetration of their social order by both mestizo society and the capitalist economic order. Unfortunately, more recent development now threatens this relative independence, as their forest habitats are increasingly being drawn into intensive agriculture—between 1975 and 1985, 20 percent of Paraguay's forests were destroyed and replaced by various agricultural projects. This new round of agricultural expansion has, like its predecessors, entailed their transformation into workers within the larger economy.

Alternatively, representing a different model of socio-cultural and economic interaction, many indigenous groups, for example the Mundurucú, have passed almost completely into mestizo society, merging sexually, socially, and economically into this peasant class. But to whatever degree and in whatever form the state programs of sedantarization and incorporation have progressed, i.e., whether modeled on the limited transformation of the Chiripá or the energetic acculturation of the Mundurucú, these national programs have, in the main, carried out their articulated mandate and achieved their goals, however one judges these goals, without mass murder.

Here I also note that the new national constitution of 1992 explicitly recognizes: "the existence of the indigenous peoples which came to be defined as groups before the formation and organization of the Paraguayan state" (Article 62); "the right of the indigenous peoples to preserve their ethnic identity" (Article 63); and "the right [of the indigenous peoples] to the communal property of their land" (Article 64). So far these constitutional guarantees have not meant much but their promulgation is indicative of Paraguayan recognition of the existence of the indigenous community and its right, at least in theory, to be. Thus, for example, one of the important consequences of the 1992 constitution is the recognition of Guaraní, the predominant native language, as an official state language along with Spanish. Moreover, the civilian government that came to power in August 1993—Paraguay's first such government in fifty years—committed itself to "reform, [as] an instrument of rural development . . . aimed at increasing the quality of life of peasants and indigenous peoples."[15] Whether the government will succeed in this ambition remains to be seen.

But what, specifically, of the Aché?

Contact with the Aché in the twentieth century has involved relations with four distinct subgroups and independent populations. The northern Aché, who earlier incorporated several smaller subgroups, lived in the region of the Jejuí River and numbered approximately 550 persons in 1970. The Yvytyruzu group, that lived independently of the larger northern Aché community since the late 1930s, resided south of Caaguazu and east of Villarica and numbered about sixty in the late 1930s and early 1940s. The Ypety group lived in the eastern Yvytyruzu range and near the Monday River and numbered in the thirties in the 1940s and 1950s. And the Ñacunday group lived along the Ñacunday and Yñaro rivers and also numbered between thirty and forty when contact was established in 1976. In 1959 the Ypety and then in 1962 the Yvytyruzu began to settle on or near a ranch operated by a seemingly benevolent patron—though appearances would here be deceptive—Jesus Manuel Pereira.[16] In 1963 the central government created the Arroyo Morotí camp, overseen by Pereira.[17] The Ypety, the Yvytyruzu, and elements of the other Aché groups, misplacing their trust in Pereira, now willingly allowed themselves to be removed to the reservation as well as several other smaller reserves.

The health and nutritional conditions at these camps were very poor and approximately one third to one half of the newly installed population died from disease (primarily respiratory infections) and malnutrition.[18] At the end of 1968, in response to the desperate conditions at Arroyo Morotí as well as to attract more northern Aché to settle, a new larger colony, Cerro Morotí, was established on 2500 hectare of land in the San Joaquin hills to the northwest of the original settlement. But once again conditions were far from acceptable and food and medicine were in short supply. Mark Münzel, whose four reports[19] on the situation of the Aché are primarily responsible for calling their plight to the attention of the world community,[20] has given the following, in important ways inaccurate,[21] accounting of this inhumane resettlement and its punishing consequences:

> We shall never know how many captives have been brought to the reservation, how many Aché have been killed by manhunters proceeding from the reservation, and how many have died or have been sold into slavery. I can, however, establish the minimum figures from the documents at our disposal; I am certain that the real figures are significantly higher. From October 1970 until June 1972 (a period covered by official government statistics and by first-hand statements of reservation inmates), at least 138 Aché have either disappeared from the camp (in all probability dead) or have been killed by manhunters from the reservation.[22] Furthermore, 122 others have been kidnapped and deported to the camp. The minimum estimate of free Aché killed or captured during private raids from September 1968 until November 1973 in Northern Paraguay is 83 according to the existing evidence. However, this is only the visible tip of the iceberg, as most crimes of this kind can never be adequately documented. Summarizing the figures, I can state that

at least 343 persons have either been killed outright or enslaved or induced to die[23] between September 1968 and June 1972.[24]

In response to these very serious, exceedingly disturbing charges of kidnapping, slavery, and murder, the international community rightfully raised the alarm and indicted the Paraguayan government for its crimes against its Aché population. In particular, the government of Paraguay was accused of carrying out a genocidal campaign against the Aché. Indeed, we recall that Arens pointedly entitled the anthology that he edited on the subject (which included Mark Münzel's third report on the Aché), *Genocide in Paraguay*.[25] But what exactly does Arens mean by using this heavily freighted term, and what evidence does he marshall in support of it? I ask these critical methodological questions because what Arens actually substantiates is not the crime of genocide, but rather the different offense that he himself labels "deculturation." Deculturation is, he tells us, to be understood as:

> the disintegration of some or all of the following: political and social institutions, culture, language, national feelings, religion, economic stability, personal security, liberty, health, and dignity. It does not take very much imagination to see death in the destruction of a population's health or economic stability. We need not depend, however, on imagination and empathy alone. Deculturation has been studied for decades, and its lethal effects have been demonstrated beyond reasonable doubt.[26]

Now, while there can be no substantive disagreement with the limited claim that the Aché have been subject to a punishing campaign of deculturation, and that this enacted campaign has entailed the complicity of the state in murder,[27] is this desperate policy and its ruinous consequences the conceptual and legal equivalent of physical genocide?[28]

The actual item by item catalogue of wrongs produced by Arens (and others) in the course of his extended criticism of the Paraguayan authorities substantively documents and supports the phenomenologically distinct charge of ethnocide ("deculturation"), but nowhere does he produce any real evidence of physical genocide. In the absence of authentic evidence Arens mistakenly seeks to make his extreme case, to defend his claims for the occurrence of physical genocide in Paraguay, by associating, actually conflating, the quite separate categories of cultural and physical genocide through an appeal to the notion of "psychic death."[29] According to Arens' tortuous argument in support of this hermeneutical gambit: "the causal relationship between psychological stress and serious psychological disorientation, including psychosomatic symptomology"[30] leads to "a life-threatening despair which is a crime under International law and specifically under the genocide Convention."[31] But this circuitous contention is substantially and conceptually reductionistic and ontologically inexact. To identify the confusion directly: being in despair is not being dead.

Let us stay with Arens' presentation a bit longer. Realizing that his "psychic death" argument is, despite its rhetorical flourish, unpersuasive, he seeks to bolster his tenuous thesis regarding the putative extermination of the Aché by connecting it with the Nazi policy towards Jews. He explicitly suggests that the tragedy of the Aché is a direct consequence of the alleged influence of old-time Nazis upon current day Paraguayan officialdom. "The spirit of Julius Streicher," we are told, "lives in enclaves of Nazi culture maintained in Argentina."[32] And I am sure it does, but its presence is wholly irrelevant to the disputed issue at hand. The unjust war against the indigene was already four centuries old and had done most of its lethal work well before these "enclaves of Nazi culture" ever arrived in South America. Moreover, the morphology of the most recent round of tribal evictions and related violence shows little, if any, novelty or discontinuity relative to the long ugly history of such colonial deportment. Indian hunting, slavery, prostitution, and the exploitation of Indian labor are all traditional forms of injustice, of iniquity, continually represented in the truculent history of Indian–non-Indian relations. The economic and political legitimization of Indian dispossession, of the movement of the Aché to government reserves, was independent of, and required no encouragement from, Aryan bio-metaphysics. This is not to deny that in some contemporary South American circles an effort has been made to justify these duplicitous state policies through racial theories—though this, too, has a considerable pre-Hitler history rooted in the racial theorizing of the nineteenth century. However, even where such theorizing has been present and exerted some post-hoc legitimization to events, such rancid ideological follies are not the primary cause of the unbridled persecution of the indigine. That is to say, the main culprit responsible for the assault that has taken place over the past half-century against the native peoples of Paraguay is not "the pseudo-science of race of Nazi vintage . . . cultivated on South American soil."[33] Arens here badly misuses the "Holocaust Paradigm"[34] for his own purposes and confuses rather than clarifies matters by misinterpreting one historical tragedy in the inappropriate terms of another.[35]

The intent of the Paraguayan government and the extent of its direct involvement in the murder of the Aché is, in the context of the present analysis, of the utmost importance. In his influential essay in the Arens anthology, Mark Münzel suggested that the Paraguayan state was directly, premeditatively, involved in this collective destruction and Arens accepted this non-trivial judgment without reservation. It is important to note, however, that Bartomeu Melia, on whose basic research Münzel drew in fashioning his provocative accusation, explicitly contradicted this particular conclusion. Melia wrote: "the data, then, point toward very frequent but unsystematic killings and kidnappings by Paraguayan farmers, ranchers, and laborers rather than towards organized raids, by say army or police units."[36] Then again, Kim Hill, an anthropologist who has worked among the Aché for many years, directly contradicts Münzel's accusation that the Aché were brought to Cerro Morotí by force: "We shall never know how many captives have been brought to the reservation." Hill stresses in his report of the events of 1968 to 1970 that:

> By the end of 1970 Pereira had developed a successful method of bringing new Aché groups to his reservation. This consisted of sending out friends and relatives of the forest bands, convincing

them to walk out to the nearest road, and then sending a truck to pick them up. *In no case* were armed parties sent out, nor was there any violence or physical coercion involved. Almost as many Aché stayed in the forest as the number that decided to "visit" the reservation. . . . Aché informants emphatically deny previous reports that individuals were forcibly captured and brought to the reservation. There is little doubt, however, that strong social pressure and social coercion were occasionally employed. The bands remaining in the forest throughout this time were led by the most powerful men in the entire northern group, however, and many of those Aché simply refused to leave the forest. They were never "captured," despite common knowledge of their location, and almost all subsequently died without ever leaving the forest.[37]

In evaluating the process whereby the Aché joined the national reservations it must be emphasized that they did this of their own volition and for their own self-interested reasons. The latter included protection, increased food supplies, and personal gain among younger Aché men who often supplanted older Aché men as the dominant males in this new socio-political setting. The evidence on this key issue does not support the charge that the central government has consciously, explicitly, adopted a determinate policy of first kidnapping and then annihilating the Aché.

The Paraguayan leadership has certainly strained the legal and ethical limits of state behavior in regard to the Aché but it has not denied or transcended these limits altogether. It has committed serious crimes of commission and omission against the Aché (and other indigenous peoples), but both the individual and collective nature of these many crimes falls far short of a program of extermination. The national authorities have not protected the Aché as they should—hence my charge above that they have been "complicitous" in the death of many Aché. And others have taken advantage of this indifference—especially local elements intent on dispossessing[38] and exploiting the indigene—but this programmatic unconcern is not simply translatable, and thus indictable, as the equivalent of a well-formed and intentional program of genocidal elimination. Highly relevant to this judgment

243

is the repercussive fact that "no Aché who lived [on the Cerro Morotí reservation] was ever shot by a Paraguayan in the types of skirmishes that had been common throughout the past several hundred years on the Paraguayan forest frontier."[39] At Cerro Morotí neither the camp commandant nor anyone else murdered the Aché for sport[40] nor as a corollary of some ideological mandate. The cultural traditions of the Indian are attacked, even mutilated, and their daily routine reduced, in many ways, to a stylized form of tragic domination and inauthenticity—one thinks here of the proselytizing pressures to which they are regularly subjected—but however desolate their reservation life, they are not murdered; they do not have to become corpses. And assuredly not a nation of corpses. Here I would emphasize, in particular, that Münzel's statistics on alleged manhunts of Aché, the disappearance ("and in all probability death") of Aché, and the murder of Aché, as well as the claims for genocide based on them are, in fact, largely a mythical invention. Contrary to Münzel's claims that approximately 900 Northern Aché were killed or kidnapped by Paraguayans between 1968 and 1972, the actual figures for these categories (killing and kidnapping) are much, much smaller. So much smaller in fact as to implicate a totally different qualitative existential circumstance. For example, Hill and Hurtado estimate that sixty-one Northern Aché have been killed by Paraguayans and sixty-seven Aché children were kidnapped in the entire century. The fantasy aspect of Münzel's numbers is most clearly indicated by the fact that his stated number of deaths and kidnappings—900—is almost twice the number of the entire northern Aché population in 1968.[41]

The basic difficulty that undoes Münzel's work, that reduces it to a series of well-meant but incorrect judgments and statistical errors, lies, as David Maybury-Lewis and James Howe remark, in his deeply flawed methodology:

> Careful readers of his reports will note that Münzel nowhere offers hard evidence—as opposed to inference, surmise, and assertion— to support this conclusion. It will also be noted that the strength

and certainty of his accusations against the Paraguayan government increased over time, after his own first-hand observations had ended. In his first report (1973) Münzel carefully distinguished between the actions of Pereira and the manhunters on the one hand and government officials on the other, suggesting only that the complicity and genocidal intent of the government could be plainly inferred from the chain of events. By the third report (Münzel 1976) published in the volume edited by Arens, these distinctions have disappeared. Actions previously attributed to specific individuals are now described as collective and institutional, as if all Aché deaths had been directly ordered and planned by the government.[42]

Having identified this hermeneutical farrago, this series of conceptual and empirical confusions, Maybury-Lewis and Howe conclude, *contra* Münzel's explicit contention as to the existence of "a deliberate government policy of genocide,"[43] that: "The charges that the Paraguayan government has had an official policy of genocide against the Indians seems . . . unlikely as well as unproven."[44] Likewise, the IACHR, after a year-long investigation of the complaint lodged by the International League for the Rights of Man in 1974 on behalf of the Aché against the government of Paraguay (case no. 1802), concluded in its report of May 1975, "that the Paraguayan government had no policy of physically exterminating its indigenous population; rather, like most other governments of the hemisphere, it adhered to a policy of nationally assimilating or integrating its remaining Amerindian population."[45]

Hill and Hurtado's carefully considered conclusion regarding the accuracy of the charge of genocide vis-à-vis the Aché bears citing in full:

> Observations of Aché deaths from precontact warfare with non-Aché in the 1970s prompted some observers . . . to insist that the Aché were victims of genocide. These old reports have recently resurfaced (Survival International 1993) despite the fact that we have presented a detailed critique of the genocide claim, including concrete demographic data contradicting the basis of that claim. . . .

The data do not suggest that the Aché population was ever in danger of extinction from external warfare before 1970 (in fact the population was growing rapidly during the time they were allegedly being exterminated), nor is there evidence that any group of people (government, corporation, military, etc.) ever intended to exterminate the Aché. On the other hand, many peasants have indicated to us that their intention was to occupy the Aché land and use the Aché as low paid laborers. The Aché contact situation also resulted in extremely high mortality, but this was due to carelessness and incompetence rather than intention, and the contact history is not particularly different from any of hundreds that have taken place in the Amazon over the past few centuries. Since the reports of Aché genocide have been published widely, we feel that it is important to correct erroneous information and to shed some light on the complicated issue of whether the Aché were victims of intentional or de facto genocide. . . . During the latter half of the twentieth century, when the Aché population was alleged to have been nearly exterminated, it was actually growing at a rate of 2.5% per year. . . . All the governments of North and South America have been involved in gross violation of indigenous rights and a long-term trend of displacing native peoples from their traditional lands. All these governments deserve to be condemned equally. Certainly nothing about the Aché situation provides a moral impetus for singling out Paraguay uniquely as being involved in "genocide," nor is there any moral justification for equating the Aché history to that of the Jews during the Second World War. Such loose analogies simply dilute the significance and horror of actual genocide when it is observed.[46]

The historical actuality, the factual circumstance, on the ground in Paraguay in the 1960s and 1970s simply does not conform to Arens and Münzel's misdescription of it. Moreover, we do not lessen the criminality of what did transpire by describing it correctly.

In direct support of this alternative, non-genocidal, reading I cite Kim Hill's first-hand statistics that describe and categorize the fate of a considerable proportion of Aché at the National Colony:

> In the present sample there were 210 such Aché. Of these, 50% are still alive and living with other Aché, 8% are living with Paraguayans, 32% died at contact from illness (more than half died in the forest without ever arriving at the National Colony), 7% have died in the colonies from illnesses contracted some time after the initial contact period, 1% have died in accidents, and 1% died at birth. If we take only those who have died, a full 65% of the Aché deaths in the past 13 years were due to illnesses contracted immediately after contact.[47]

As ever it is bacteriological rather than intentional factors that play the main part in the diminution of the indigenous community. The virgin soil respiratory epidemics that occurred in 1972 and 1973 in particular took their lethal toll of the Aché who had recently arrived at the reservation. Between 1971 and 1977 contact-related illness was the cause of 85 percent of adult deaths and 40 percent of children's deaths.[48] In absolute numbers this translates into 193 of the 544 Northern Aché who were alive in 1970 succumbing to disease in these years. "Of these, 66 died in the forest, 92 at the Cerro Morotí government reservation/Protestant mission, 19 at the Manduvi Catholic mission, and 16 at Paraguayan houses near Curuguaty while waiting for transportation to a mission settlement." In reflecting on this disease-related experience, Hill and Hurtado drew this crucial conclusion relative to categorizing these events as genocide: "Our data do not suggest that missionaries did not want to help the Aché, only that they failed to focus their help effectively during this time period."[49]

This is not to exonerate the government agents and missionaries implicated in this effort from all responsibility for these deaths, for had they provided better medical care, in particular antibiotics to defeat the effects of pneumonia, many of those who died would have been saved. And it is fair, that is, both morally and methodologically required, to argue that the officials and

missionaries involved in the relocations should have been prepared to do this given the centuries-long history of ravaging disease among the indigene after contact. By not being so prepared
they were, in effect, guilty of criminal irresponsibility. Thus one
has, in this context, the re-appearance of an old-new paradoxical
situation: missionaries who have come, in some cases from half-
way around the world, to convert the aboriginal peoples actually,
though indirectly, cause their deaths by their ill-considered actions or lack of them. That such irresponsibility cannot be excused merely as a result of ignorance and must be classed as
criminal after 500 years of massive epidemics, and the introduction of more mundane illnesses, is not debatable. But given the
contrary intentions that energize this context, i.e., the authentic
desire to convert the Indian and improve their lot both materially
and spiritually, one cannot identify this situation, despite the dis-
graceful outcome it entailed, as genocide.

Between 1972 and 1975 the Cerro Morotí reservations were
taken over by the American evangelical New Tribes mission and
further contacts, again initiated by the various Aché forest
groups, took place. In 1974 Catholic missionaries of the Divine
Word order also created an additional mission-reservation near
the Panama River called Chupa Pou. Here again the pattern of
contact, disease, and death repeated itself and up to 50 percent
of those Aché who came into this Catholic center died as a result
of epidemics in 1974 and 1975. A better supervised, medically
superior contact also occurred at this mission-reservation in
1978 resulting in little loss of life due to unfamiliar pathogens.
In effect, between 1972 and 1978 the main administration of the
Aché reserves was in the hands of Protestant and Catholic missionaries from America, South America, and Germany. Even
though considerable depopulation due to disease continued during this period, these missionaries did not come to the Amazon
to kill its native inhabitants.

In 1978 Richard Arens published a second report on the condition of the Aché, this time under the less provocative title *The
Forest Indians in Stroessner's Paraguay: Survival or Extinction.*[50] This
second study, unlike his first, was based on his own first-hand

experience in Paraguay, a trip he undertook to confirm[51] the controversial views he had expressed in his earlier collection. In this second paper Arens is more circumspect about the absolute character of the victimization of the Aché, but in crucial places in his narrative, in remaking and adapting his indictment, he again begins by relying upon the same misanalogy between the SS and Stroessner's regime that he had employed earlier. The first question he takes up is: "Is the Colonia Nacional Guyaki a death camp?" obviously implying comparability, say, to Treblinka. His hedged reply is: "Yes—at least to the limited degree encompassed in death brought on by malnutrition, tuberculosis and neglected malignancies."[52] But given these important qualifications what Arens is actually describing is not a "death camp" à la Himmler's kingdom of night, i.e., a camp created for the primary, if not sole,[53] purpose of killing, but rather a camp in which death occurs (primarily through disease). That is, the defining core of the death camps, of Auschwitz, of Sobibor, of Chelmno, of Treblinka, did not lie—as Arens describes the Aché camps (see next paragraph)—in their appalling sanitation, their foul odor, their poor living conditions, their labor practices, or the malnutrition to be found within them—even assuming that Arens was right in his description of all these issues vis-à-vis the Aché encampments, which he does not appear to be. The defining core of the death camps resided, rather, in their gas chambers and crematoria that were created in order to turn *all* Jews into ashes. This phenomenological disjunction between Death Camps and camps in which people, even many people, die is not introduced in order to minimize the human misery in which the Aché live[54]—and die—but rather to emphasize a basic analytic distinction that must be made in this context if the entire enterprise of scholarly investigation of state crimes, mass death, and genocide is not to collapse completely as a consequence of gross logical errors.[55] Likening the Colonia Nacional Guyaki to Auschwitz by purposely exploiting the hideous connotations that the term "death camp" carries is a basic category mistake. It assumes a phenomenological parallelism that is not justified by the historical actuality represented by the two, unlike, environments. I repeat: at Auschwitz,

Treblinka, Sobibor, all Jews were meant to be killed; these camps came into being to assure that they were killed. At the Colonia Nacional Guyake some Aché may die, and many do die, but no one intentionally murders those who do die, and no one insists that all the Aché be murdered.

Arens' description of the Father Luis Farina Mission of Puerto Casado, in fact, raises more questions than it answers. To begin, he provocatively, if unimaginatively, titles his discussion: "Puerto Cassado—Arbeit Macht Free," an injudicious, consciously manipulative, reference to the notorious motto over the gates of Auschwitz. And in his polemical description of this place he tells his readers about what he identifies as its primitive sanitation, its foul odor—he speaks of "the odor of human excrement" hanging over the camp—its poor living conditions, the prevalence of malnutrition,[56] and the economic exploitation that abounds. However, all of these negative depictions, these repellent characterizations of Aché living conditions, are open to doubt. Kim Hill, for example, questions the veracity of all of these critical claims. Regarding the first two he writes:

> As the Aché are not concerned with the western concept of privacy, their "outhouses" are purely functional. There are numerous "outhouses" at the National Colony. I have never detected [as Arens claims] "the odor of human excrement" lingering over the National Colony.[57]

One suspects that this radical alternation in description and judgment between Arens and Hill is due not only to their differing perceptions of the camp environment but also to their pre-experiential expectations and understanding of what the camp environment was and should be. Arens, a professor of law from Philadelphia, with no extended experience among South American aboriginal peoples employed as a *Gestalt,* used as the basis of his empirical and moral evaluations, qualitative standards and normative absolutes that were inappropriate to the context at hand. In contrast, Hill, a trained anthropological observer of Aché life, perceived, reported, and judged what he "saw" by another, very different, set of criteria.

Secondly, as regards the Aché diet and the central issue of malnutrition Hill argues:

> If Arens had investigated he would have found the diet of the Aché to be equal to and in most cases superior to the diet of the Paraguayan peasant. Recent dietary studies show that reservation Aché spend considerable periods foraging in the forest where they consume a mean of approximately 3700 calories per capita per day. Protein consumption levels are above that consumed by modern Americans. Height and weight measurements also demonstrate that the Aché are not undernourished.[58]

If Hill's (and K. Hawkes'[59]) data on nutrition is correct, if the Aché are consuming 3,700 calories per capita per day, then what we are told in Arens' report regarding the Aché diet represents a radical misunderstanding of what Arens believed he was seeing. That this is, in fact, the case is supported by the mortality figures and statistics on the causes of death for the Aché who have been living on reservations since the 1970s. In contradistinction to being Death Camps, the available statistics indicate that few Aché have died since 1978, i.e., after their having developed a natural resistance to foreign diseases and as a result of improved medical care at the reservation-missions; that 80 percent of those Aché adults that have died have succumbed to illness and 10 percent have been claimed by degenerative diseases; and that only 10 percent of those that died—one in ten—were killed by an accident or an act of violence. (Parenthetically, this breakdown of the causes of death is paralleled by the relevant comparative data on the Kung and the Yanomamo and therefore should not be considered in any way aberrant.) This last statistic is especially striking given that the most common cause of death among the Aché in the forest was conspecific violence, "death at the hands of another human."[60]

The very serious criticism that Arens does not properly understand what he is looking at and therefore continually misdescribes the given situation that he is "observing" is fully supported by Maybury-Lewis and Howes' severe critique of Arens'

Steven T. Katz

unsubstantiated report on the Ayoreo that parallels his work on the Aché.

> Arens' account shows his lack of experience with nomadic Indians and their settlements. He noted the absence of sanitary facilities in a wilderness where people are accustomed to relieving themselves in the bush. . . . He noted the absence of the "normal proportion of adult males" from the village, although he clearly had no way of knowing what the normal proportion of adult males in the village at that time of year . . . or day . . . should be. . . . He describes the houses the Indians lived in as "overcrowded hovels" whereas we found the standard of Ayoreo housing quite good. . . . Arens further claimed that the New Tribe's mission was not providing medical treatment . . . we found that the mission was indeed providing basic medical assistance and vaccinations. . . . Arens reported that the Ayoreo were emaciated and starving. . . . We, on the contrary, found that the Ayoreo were reasonably well-built and healthy looking. . . . We conclude Arens' report on El Faro Moro (the Ayoreo) is as unreliable as his report on the Aché.[61]

Maybury-Lewis and Howes' rebuttal of Arens' assertions point repeatedly to the primary methodological issue: Arens provides no external standard, no measure beyond his own subjective (and misleading) perspective, as to what the reasonably expected norm in a given situation is, and to what degree Ayoreo realia—and by parity of reasoning Aché realia—deviate from that agreed, public norm. In consequence, all of his judgments are, at best, arbitrary opinions, and at worst, serious distortions.

That Arens is an inaccurate and highly biased observer is also indicated by his report on the comparative mortality rates experienced by the Aché in the Protestant and Catholic reservation/missions respectively. According to Arens, the Catholic mission had lower mortality rates than the Protestant New Tribes mission which he identified, as already noted, as a "death camp." However, Hill and Hurtado, in checking this data, conclude that:

> The results [using a discrete-time logistic regression hazards model] contradict Arens and clearly indicate that survivorship was higher

on the Protestant mission than at the Catholic mission during the eleven-year sample. In fact, Protestant missions have about one-fourth the death rate of Catholic missions for children of the mean age in the sample (1.77 years old). This difference is probably due to the better economic status, sanitary conditions, housing, and more frequently available health care at the Protestant mission.[62]

This hard statistical evidence confutes Arens' impressionistic work that is almost wholly free of meaningful statistical data, and completely undermines the credibility of his conclusions. I am not alone in my explicit skepticism regarding the correctness of Arens' contentions. The *Asociation de Parcialidades Indígenas,* the representative Indian group in Paraguay, repudiated Arens' 1978 report and Miguel Chase Sardi and Luis Duarte, secretary of the *Asociation de Parcialidades Indígenas,* replied to Arens' accusations—criticizing them in part and in whole—in an article entitled "API denies the declarations made by Arens," in the February 22, 1978 issue of *HOY.*

This does not mean that the Aché, given the totality of their lived experience, have been treated any way but badly or that the conditions of their daily life are anything but minimal and exceedingly difficult. Nor does my severe criticism of Arens' depiction of the Stroessner regime mean that the Stroessner regime was not a criminal regime.[63] But the crime of which it was guilty was not the crime of genocide.[64] Indeed, the number of Aché has grown 30 percent or more since they were relocated to the national reservations—their present number having risen, as already noted, to approximately 1300.[65] At the same time, the mortality rates on the reservations are much lower than they were in the forest,[66] and all four of the main Aché cultural subgroups are still extant. Moreover, the Aché received legal title to their main reservation in 1988 and this has led to their increased, if still marginal, involvement in horticulture, as well as to their entry, on a limited scale, into the larger wage economy.

In offering this carefully arrived at conclusion I do not want to be misunderstood. The mistreatment of the Aché represents an enormous criminal act, but nothing is gained by misdescribing and misunderstanding it, especially through the use of erroneous analogies, and nothing is lost by respecting its particularity. We owe it not least to the native people whose tragedy we here reflect on, to comprehend their concrete situation as it is and as it has been. That is to say, their determinate tragedy should not, and must not, be treated as just another indistinct instance of man's inhumanity to man, as another ill-defined case in which the actual details and structural configuration do not matter. Instead, any true, and truthful, decipherment of the dark experience of the Aché (and other native American peoples) and any sound comparative judgment about the plight of the Indian relative to the fate of Jews during the *Sho'ah* must rest on the recognition of fundamental systemic contrasts, irreducible structural disjunctions, rather than on overly neat, finally superficial, commensurabilities.

NOTES

1. Richard Arens, ed., *Genocide in Paraguay* (Philadelphia, 1976).

2. According to the U.N. and my own revised definition, the term 'genocide' refers to "the intentional destruction of a people." It is this aspect of the definition, among others, that I will argue the Aché case does not fulfill. The other features of the definition are complex and are subject to intense scholarly debate.

3. For example, in March 1974 the International League for the Rights of Man jointly with the Inter-America Association for Democracy and Freedom formally protested to the United Nations General Secretary that Aché [Guayaki] Indians were being subjected to genocidal actions by the government of Paraguay. The issue was also debated before the United Nations Commission on Human Rights in 1978; see *Human Rights Practice in Countries Receiving U.S. Aid,* U.S. State Department Report to the Joint Committee of the U.S. Congress on Foreign Relations, 8 February 1979 (Washington, D.C., 1979), p. 317.

4. In April 1973, Paraguay and Brazil signed the Treaty of Itaipú to begin constructing the world's largest hydroelectric project on the Paraná River. Eastern Paraguay's good soils, the government's promise of cheap land and credit and the rise in soybean prices after 1973 also contributed to the region's rapid economic growth.

By the late 1970's, an economic boom was taking place in eastern Paraguay. Foreign investors took advantage of the boom, increasing their investment in the eastern border zone from US $1.3 million in 1972 to US $28 million in 1978. Much of this investment was for highly mechanized and capital-intensive agricultural and forestry enterprises.

Before the economic boom, the eastern border zone still contained an estimated 2.5 million ha of dense tropical forest. A 1971 FAO forest inventory, however, warned that "the country's forest reserves will be used up in ten years if the present policy of destruction without afforestation is maintained." The government paid little attention to this warning, and the amount of new lands that were deforested and converted to agricultural uses in the three border zone departments increased by 14 percent between 1971 and 1975. During the following two years, the amount of cultivated lands in this area again increased from 117,000 ha in 1975–1976 to 187,000 ha in 1976–1977—a growth of nearly 60 percent in the area put to agricultural use. (S. H. Davis, *Land Rights and Indigenous Peoples* [Cambridge, Mass., 1988], p. 35)

Additional basic information on this economic development is provided by R. A. Nickson, "Brazilian Colonization of the Eastern Border Area of Paraguay," *Journal of Latin American Studies* 13, no. 1 (1981): 111–31.

5. In 1987, 75 percent of the Chaco, for example, had no land and 50 percent of the indigene in the eastern area of the country had no land title (A. Gray, *The Amerindians in South America* [London, 1987], p. 18).

6. Between 1962 and 1972 non-Indian population growth was considerable, especially in Eastern Paraguay which was the traditional home of the Aché. The departments of Caaguazu, Amambay, and Alta Parana grew at the rates of 67.6, 84.2 and 278.3 percent while the national population grew at 29.2 percent. In the 1970s approximately 300,000 new settlers arrived in the eastern region (Davis, *Land Rights and Indigenous Peoples,* pp. 30 and 35).

7. The number of Aché remaining in Paraguay, divided into four main tribal groups, the Ynaro, the Yvytyruzu, the Nacunday, and the Northern [Aché Gatu], is, according to the most authoritative recent count provided by J. Olson, *The Indians of Central and South America* (New York, 1991), p. 3, approximately 1300. This compares to estimates of a pre-Columbian population of 200,000. See, for example, Frances R. Grant's claims for the size of the pre-contact Aché population in Arens, *Genocide in Paraguay* p. 731. Olson's estimate is, however, far too

high. According to Miguel Chase Sardi, "The present situation of the Indians in Paraguay," in W. Dostal (ed.), *The Situation of the Indians in South America* (Geneva, 1972), p. 193, there were 411 remaining Aché in 1972. This was down from 1000 in 1910, half of whom were lost in the epidemic of 1920. Mark Münzel, writing four years later in Arens, *Genocide in Paraguay,* conjectured that "some 800–1200 [Aché] may still be alive" (p. 39). This aggregate accords with L. Miraglia's count of 1000 Guayaki in his "gli Acce o Guayaki, Pigmoide de Paraguay," *Archivo per L'Anthropologia e La Ethnologiam,* vol. 91 (Florence, 1961), p. 84; and P. Clastre's tallies for the various Aché tribes in the 1960s and early 1970s that together total 775 plus or minus 150 (*Chronique des Indiens Guayaki: ce que savent les Aché, chasseurs, nomades du Paraguay* [Paris, 1972]). Conversely, Sardi's lower aggregate conforms with the researches of J. A. Borgognon who estimated the surviving population by the 1960s at only 350, "Panorama Paraguayo," *SARAP,* nos. 1 and 2 (1968), p. 369. David Maybury-Lewis and James Howe reporting on their trips to Paraguay in November 1978 and January 1979 put the Aché population at no "more than 900 or 1000" (*The Indian Peoples of Paraguay* [Cambridge, Mass., 1980], p. 42).

8. The history of the Aché since contact with Europeans is briefly related by K. Hill and A. M. Magdalena Hurtado, *Aché Life History: The Ecology and Demography of a Foraging People* (New York, 1996), pp. 41–57. They note, in particular, that significant depopulation occurred in the seventeenth and eighteenth centuries as a result of slave raids on Jesuit missions and in consequence of Paraguay's defeat in the War of the Triple Alliance in the late nineteenth century (p. 48). For the larger context of the Aché circumstance see Pierre Clastres, "The Guayakí," in Michael Bicchieri (ed.), *Hunters and Gatherers Today: A Socioeconomic Study of Eleven Such Cultures in the Twentieth Century* (New York, 1972), pp. 138–174. And on the situation of the indigene in Paraguay generally consult *Población y tierras indígenas en la region oriental de Paraguay* (Asunción, 1977); Miguel Chase Sardi et al., *Situación sociocultural, económico, jurídico-politico de las communidades indigenas del Paraguay* (Asunción, 1990); Stephen Kidd, *Las comunidades indígenas lengua, sanapana y angaite* (Asunción, 1992); Esther Prieto, *Algunas consideraciones sobre el Esatuto de las Comunidades Indígenas* (Asunción, 1987); and *Nueva politica indigenista del Paraguay-INDI* (Asunción, 1993).

9. The economic and developmental circumstances in Eastern Paraguay in the 1960s and 1970s are described by R. A. Nickson, "Brazilian Colonization of the Eastern Region of Paraguay." Of prime importance to development in this region were the World Bank–supported projects in the departments of Guairá and Caazapá and sections of Itapúa and Alto Paraná that effected, in particular, many Mby'a groups

and communities. The Caazapá project alone covers some 381,600 ha of land.

10. For more on this process see the sources listed in Olson, *The Indians of Central and South America*, pp. 3 and 462.

11. On some demographic estimates this was also approximately the size of the Indian population at contact in the early sixteenth century. See, for example, J. H. Steward, who estimated this population at 100,000 in 1500 ("The Native Population in South America," in idem. (ed.), *Handbook of South American Indians*, vol. 5 [New York, 1963; reprint of 1949 edition]). Newer estimates are much higher. For full details see my discussion of the situation of New World native peoples in vol. II of my *The Holocaust in Historical Context* (New York, forthcoming).

12. Ramon César Bejarano provides the figure of 50,000; Miguel Chase Sardi and Victor Bonilla both put the number at 46,000. All three estimates are cited in D. Maybury-Lewis and J. Howe, *The Indian Peoples of Paraguay*, p. 18. Esther Prieto, in a more recent essay, put the figure at 100,000 in 1991, "Indigenous Peoples in Paraguay," in D. L. Van Cott (ed.), *Indigenous Peoples and Democracy in Latin America* (New York, 1994), p. 236.

13. This is not surprising given the fact that approximately 75 percent of Paraguay's population is of Guaráni descent and the native dialect is still the dominant language of the country. According to J. Moss and G. Wilson 10,000 Guaráni still live as indigene (*Latin Americans* [Detroit, 1989], p. 124).

14. I am indebted to Richard K. Reed, *Prophets of Agroforestry: Guaraní Communities and Commercial Gathering* (Austin, 1995) for the information on the Chiripá. The data on their increased population and improved birth rate is found on p. 70. On their role in agroforestry see especially pp. 123–65.

15. A more extensive analysis of the 1992 constitution is provided by Esther Prieto, "Indigenous Peoples in Paraguay," pp. 235–258. She describes the 1992 constitution as "yielding . . . traditional [state] hegemony [over Indian lands]" and as indicating a reconsideration of the "traditional understanding of equality, explicitly recognizing Paraguay as a multiethnic and multicultural country. The breadth of rights recognized covers a wide spectrum that embraces several areas of the law" (p. 244). Prieto also notes that the Paraguayan government, "has ratified Convention 169 of the International Labor Organization on Tribal and Semi-Tribal Populations, which guarantees several rights also set forth in the constitution. Paraguay is also a signatory to the International Convention on the Prevention and Sanction of the Crime of Genocide, sponsored by the United Nations."

16. In actuality Pereira, too, exploited the Aché. "His income was almost a direct function of how many Indians he had under his control. He was paid to administer the reservation and was given money and supplies according to the size of the reservation population. Most of these resources were embezzled and used to support Pereira's frequent drinking binges" (K. Hill and A. M. Hurtado, *Aché Life History*, p. 50). The law, however, did eventually catch up with Pereira and he was arrested and found guilty of embezzling government funds intended to be spent on the Indians, and served a short jail sentence for his misdeeds.

17. I here depend on the summary of these events provided by K. Hill and A. M. Hurtado, *Aché Life History*, p. 49.

18. Based on the report of the anthropologist Tomasini cited by M. Chase Sardi in his essay "The Present Situation of the Indians in Paraguay," p. 198.

19. Two of these reports were published in Copenhagen by the *IW-GIA* in 1973 and 1974 under the respective titles, "The Aché Indians: Genocide in Paraguay," and "The Aché: Genocide Continues in Paraguay." Münzel's third paper appeared in B. Melia et al. (eds.), *La Agonia de los Aché-Guayaki: Historia y Cantos* (Asunción, 1973); and his fourth essay, entitled "Manhunt," appeared in R. Arens' edited volume, *Genocide in Paraguay*, pp. 19–45.

20. See, for example, Leo Kuper's dependence on these sources, in his *Genocide: Its Political Use in the 20th Century* (New Haven, 1981), pp. 33–34.

21. Münzel's many errors and inaccuracies will be examined in detail below.

22. Kim Hill, a University of Michigan anthropologist who lived among the Aché in the late 1970s and early 1980s, has argued that: "contrary to Münzel's allegations [1973 report *The Aché Indians: Genocide in Paraguay*, pp. 36, 49, 51] no Aché were killed in these expeditions." I here cite a still unpublished manuscript by Prof. Hill, Chapter 2 of which is entitled "The Aché of Eastern Paraguay: Current Conditions and Recent History," p. 35.

23. Kim Hill argues that, contrary to Münzel's charges, "there were no 'official' hunts. No bands [of Aché] were exterminated," ("The Aché of Eastern Paraguay," p. 36). Moreover, on Hill's evidence, many, if not most, of those who "disappeared" "either voluntarily went to live with Paraguayans, or simply returned to the forest for a while. Others . . . died in epidemics . . . " (ibid., 37). Regarding the 343 Aché that Münzel here lists as "killed outright, enslaved or induced to die" between September 1968 and June 1972, Hill, on the basis of his interviews with the

Aché, offers this alternative accounting: "The Aché recall only 52 who were killed between 1962 and '72, and these were killed by local Paraguayan peasants or Chiripa Indians" (ibid., 37). Hill, as part of his more wide-ranging criticism of Münzel, also questions Münzel's claim to speak Aché fluently (p. 37), and his expertise in deciphering Aché culture (*ibid.*, pp. 37 and 38). Cf. here also R. J. Smith and B. Melia, "Genocide of the Aché-Guayaké?" *Survival International Supplement*, vol. 3 no. 1 (June 1978): 8.

24. M. Münzel, "Manhunt," p. 37.

25. See specifically Arens, *Genocide in Paraguay*, pp. 135–42, where he discusses the controversial issue in a subsection entitled "The Nature of Genocide." Shelton Davis, in this same volume, is explicit about the precise charge of physical genocide. "The Paraguayan government," he writes, "has intentionally planned for the extermination of tribes such as the Aché in its programs for regional development and growth" (p. 145).

26. *Genocide in Paraguay*, p. 137.

27. There is no doubt that the Stroessner military dictatorship in Paraguay in 1955 was a brutal, repressive, authoritarian regime, under which opponents and "enemies" were regularly maimed and murdered. The essential question at hand, however, is whether the form this murder took, even when undertaken on a wide scale, was so constituted as to be correctly, precisely, defined as genocide. The remainder of this analysis is intended to provide a clear and persuasive answer to this question.

28. Again, for more on the philosophical and logical issues concerning the definition of genocide consult my fuller discussion of this issue in chapter four of *The Holocaust in Historical Context* vol. 1 (New York, 1994).

29. Arens, *Genocide in Paraguay*, p. 137. Here Arens appeals for support to the research of Dr. C. Shattan, published under the title "Genocide and Bereavement" in this same volume and to Shattan's earlier, well-known, piece stemming from his work with Vietnam veterans, "Bogus Manhood, Bogus Honor: Surrender and Transfiguration in the United States Marine Corps," *Psychoanalytic Review* (1976). But Shattan is not an expert on the Aché and makes no claim to having ever encountered or interviewed any Aché as he did encounter and interview American soldiers. Therefore, using his research on American veterans of the Vietnam war to explain events among the Aché in contemporary Paraguay is more than a little dubious. Moreover, even were Shattan's research translatable, usable, for shedding light on the Aché tragedy, it would still fall short of supporting allegations of physical genocide. No

Steven T. Katz

amount of evidence on *psychic* phenomena will justify conclusions about collective *physical* annihilation.

30. Arens, *Genocide in Paraguay*, p. 137. In making this argument Arens is dependent on the views of C. Murray Parkes, "Components of the Reaction to Loss of a Limb, Spouse or Home," *Journal of Psychosomatic Research* 16 (1972): 344–48.

31. Arens, *Genocide in Paraguay*, p. 139.

32. Ibid., p. 141.

33. Ibid., p. 139.

34. By which I mean employing the Holocaust as the model used to describe and interpret other events of mass death. For a more extended consideration of this repercussive methodological issue as it applies particularly to the rewriting of medieval history over the past two decades, see my essay, "Misusing the Holocaust Paradigm to Mis-Write History: Examples from Recent Medieval Historiography," in Dina Porat and Shlomo Simonsohn (eds.), *Michael: On the History of the Jews in the Diaspora*, vol. 13 (Tel Aviv, 1993), pp. 103–30.

35. Arens confuses the issue of genocide even further when he likens the situation in Paraguay to "the emulation of the Republic of South Africa in the handling of native population" (p. 140). That is to say, the former apartheid program of South Africa, while morally repulsive, was simply not, as black population figures incontestably demonstrate, genocidal. L. Kuper, *Genocide*, pp. 191–204, also discusses South African policy in relationship to genocide, though he, finally, has the good sense (pp. 203–204) to conclude that the two phenomena are not equivalent.

36. Smith and Melia, "Genocide of the Aché-Guayaki?" p. 11.

37. Hill and Hurtado, *Aché Life History*, p. 51.

38. Thus, I do not question Münzel's allegations, *The Aché Indians: Genocide in Paraguay*, p. 11 about the intrusion of non-Indians onto the Aché reservation. And I do not doubt the information in a letter that he quotes, which reports that: "At present [July 26, 1973], a real invasion of land theoretically ceded to the reservation is taking place. Before the foundation of the reservation, there were some 10 families of settlers on this land. But in recent years around 100 families have come of which about 30 in recent months. As you can see the reservation itself is in danger." However, I am very skeptical of Münzel's reading and manipulation of the contents of this letter. As the basis for my skepticism I call particular attention to the outcome that the anonymous letter writer foresees as being the result of this invasion: "The Guayakí (Aché) will soon seek employment as rural laborers in the [white man's] fields, as they are already beginning to do." This process of dispossession is,

self-evidently, not equivalent to a process of extermination. Dead men do not seek work in other men's fields.

39. Hill and Hurtado, *Aché Life History*, p. 53.

40. I mean to call attention here, by way of comparison, to those commandants of the Nazi death camps who did just this, and to the larger, encompassing regimen of *"sportmachen"* that existed in the Nazi camps. See, for instance, Alexander Donat, ed., *The Death Camp Treblinka* (New York, 1979).

41. Hill and Hurtado, *Aché Life History*, p. 169.

42. Maybury-Lewis and Howe, *The Indian Peoples of Paraguay*, p. 38.

43. Münzel, *The Aché Indians: Genocide in Paraguay*, p. 5.

44. Maybury-Lewis and Howe, *The Indian Peoples of Paraguay*, p. 40. As they point out: "careful readers of his [Münzel's] reports will note that Münzel nowhere offers hard evidence—as opposed to inference, surmise, and assertion—to support his conclusion [as to genocide]" (p. 38).

45. Davis, *Land Rights and Indigenous People*, p. 12. In its subsequent censure of the Paraguayan government for various abuses of the Aché, issued in May 1977, the IACHR still did not include a finding that supported the allegation of genocide. Most recently, in a 1995 publication, anthropologist Richard K. Reed, who worked among the Chiripá Indians of Paraguay, concluded:

> My interest in the Chiripá originated with reports of genocide of indigenous groups in Paraguay (Arens 1976). Although stories of government atrocities were widely disseminated, a study undertaken by Maybury-Lewis and Howe (1979) suggested that the demise of forest societies in Paraguay, as throughout lowland Latin America, was not as simple as a specific policy or program of genocide. My own visit to Paraguay in 1981 reaffirmed the reality of the situation as a complex one (R. K. Reed, *Prophets of Agroforestry*, p. vii).

46. Hill and Hurtado, *Aché Life History*, p. 168.

47. Hill, *The Aché of Eastern Paraguay*, p. 31.

48. Hill and Hurtado, *Aché Life History*, p. 166, and Table 5.4, pp. 175–76.

49. Ibid., p. 167.

50. Richard Arens, *The Forest Indians in Stroessner's Paraguay: Survival or Extinction* [Survival International Document IV] (London, 1978).

51. What actually seems to have occurred on this trip, given the published report of it, was that Arens' *a priori* judgments were "validated"

and contrary evidence to what Arens "knew" must be the case was either rejected or minimized.

52. Arens, *The Forest Indians*. K. Hill comments on this alleged triumvirate of ailments that "Arens did not observe a single case of tuberculosis (extremely rare among the Aché), and malignancies are not neglected" ("The Aché of Eastern Paraguay," p. 51).

53. This qualification is necessary because while all six of Hitler's death camps were created primarily as killing centers some, like Auschwitz, also had slave labor camps, e.g., Buna, attached, while others, like Treblinka and Sobibor, had no purpose other than killing. The literature on the subject is vast. See for instance Yitzchak Arad, *Belzec, Sobibor, Treblinka: The Operation Reinhard Death Camps* (Bloomington, 1987); and Yisrael Gutman and Michael Berenbaum, eds., *Anatomy of the Auschwitz Death Camp* (Bloomington, 1994).

54. Even the extent of this misery is questioned by the Maybury-Lewis and Howe study. They report:

> In strong contrast [to Arens] we found the physical condition of the Aché quite good, and everything we saw and heard suggested that the missionaries genuinely look out for the welfare of their charges . . . the physical circumstances of the mission are, to the western eye at least, quite pleasant . . . the missionaries maintain a medical program at the colony, which though quite rudimentary is fairly typical of the facilities available through most agencies working with Indians and considerably better than the care available to most peasant Paraguayans. . . . All the Indians we saw during our visit appeared quite healthy. (*The Indian Peoples of Paraguay*, pp. 44–45).

Admittedly, this picture appears to exaggerate the positive as Arens' report had exaggerated the negative. But nonetheless, it does have the virtue of warning that Arens is not a credible observer of, or witness to, the everyday realities of Aché existence.

55. Support for a non-genocidal conclusion is provided in part by Arens' own description of the reasonable conditions at the Mission of St. Augustin. "The [Indian] residents," he concludes, "clearly looked upon the staff as friends; nutrition seemed adequate, the atmosphere generally optimistic" (p. 8). But if a truly genocidal national policy existed, directed from the center—the sort of overarching exterminatory program that Arens' interpretation is intent on establishing—would such a carefully guided and determinate effort permit the existence of the sort of benign environment just described? Arens' description, in fact, in contradiction to his larger polemical intention, re-inforces the essential point already made: conditions vary greatly from one camp,

colony, or reserve to another, in large part based on the skill and care of the state personnel who administer them. There is no centrally contrived and imposed plan to annihilate all the Aché.

56. Hill, "The Aché of Eastern Paraguay," p. 48.

57. Ibid., p. 48.

58. Ibid., p. 51.

59. Hill is partially dependent for his data on Aché nutrition on the important study of K. Hawkes, et. al., "Why Hunters Gather: Optional Foraging and the Aché of Eastern Paraguay," *American Ethnologist* 9, no. 2 (May 1982): 379–98.

60. Hill and Hurtado, *Aché Life History*, pp. 167–68.

61. Maybury-Lewis and Howe, *The Indian Peoples of Paraguay*, pp. 65–68. This technical unreliability, this fundamental inability to interpret the apposite raw data, goes to the heart of Arens' credibility as a serious participant in this crucial debate.

62. Hill and Hurtado, *Aché Life History*, p. 191.

63. Arens' credibility gap opens even more widely when he ritualistically invokes the name of Dr. Mengele three times in his summing up of his visit to Paraguay. The first mention of Mengele occurs in the context of Arens' review of the use of torture in Paraguay:

> To those suspected of political opposition to this elite, detention without trial is the rule, and torture a standard operating procedure. . . . Dr. Josef Mengele has, indeed, reason to feel at home in his adopted fatherland and among its leadership. Stroessner has consistently refused to entertain his extradition, and it is alleged and widely believed, has provided the doctor with opportunities to display his talents and experience among Indians as well as political prisoners. (*The Forest Indians*, p. 10)

The second instance comes in the context of a description of Paraguayan racism:

> The *Instituto de Ciencia del Hombre, dedicated to the propagation of the doctrine of Nordic supremacy, is currently moving a branch office to Asunción* from its Argentine headquarters. Needless to say, this move has Paraguayan governmental approval. Yes, indeed, Dr. Josef Mengele has reason to be pleased. (p. 10, emphasis in original)

And finally, Arens seeks to complete the asserted moral and programmatic parallelism between contemporary Paraguay and Nazi Germany through this inventive commentary:

On 26 September 1977, *Time* magazine reported that the Nazi war criminal, Dr. Josef Mengele, was active in the Northern Chaco which was out of bounds to all but a handful of the initi- ated. This information as to a restricted area coincided with in- formation secured by me independently. The evidence, accord- ing to *Time*, strongly suggested that Dr. Josef Mengele had placed his talents (including human experimentation) at the service of a Paraguayan "final solution." (Cf. *Time*, Sept. 26, 1977, p. 36; *The Forest Indians*, p. 12)

Arens uses Mengele's name to shock us. And it does shock us. Beyond that, however, he has not produced a single bit of hard evidence to sup- port these allegations. Hearsay and rumors are not evidence. Charges and innuendoes are not evidence. The introduction of Mengele's name and the casting of his ominous shadow over all sorts of lurid, unsubstan- tiated reports is not evidence. In short, there is no reason to believe that any of this Mengele-hysteria is true. Moreover, the case of [Ariel] Sharon vs. *Time* should make scholars, and everyone else, *extremely* skep- tical about taking *Time*'s reports on anything at face value. For those unfamiliar with the Sharon case, let it simply be said that *Time* was found guilty of false reporting based on speculation and incorrect informa- tion.

64. The final conclusion reached by Maybury-Lewis and Howe on this question of genocide is relevant:

> The problems faced by the Paraguayan Indians are not caused by . . . any government policy to exterminate them. On the contrary, they are the same problems which are faced by Indian peoples in other American countries. . . . They stem from the power of settlers, extractive capitalism, and the expanding national soci- ety. (*The Indian Peoples of Paraguay*, p. 110).

65. This is the demographic estimate by Olson, *The Indians of Central South America*, p. 3. The percentage of growth that this total represents depends on one's estimate of the population in the 1960s, a subject of considerable scholarly debate.

66. Mortality rates during the past fifteen years at reservations have been much lower than those experienced in the forest. In- deed, only twenty Aché between the ages of ten and sixty have died since 1978. Thus, current adult mortality compares favor- ably with that seen in any rural area of Latin America. The Aché are aware that death rates are lower on reservations than prior to contact and emphasize this as a benefit of having given up their forest lifestyle. If mortality during the first two years of life

could be decreased to about 3%, the Aché population would have a life expectancy at birth of around sixty years and a mortality profile that differs little from those of other rural populations in developing countries around the world. (Hill and Hurtado, *Aché Life History,* p. 194)

PER AHLMARK

Is Democracy for Everybody?
A Swedish Perspective

IN THE NINETEENTH CENTURY, several European nations were
convinced of their almost divine mission to forcibly "educate"
underdeveloped peoples. The colonial powers presumed that
they were superior through their achievements, and that it was
for the inferior races to learn from their masters. By elevating
the moral and intellectual standards of the colonized countries,
the latter would gradually be given more say in the governance
of their nations. That vague vision of a future when the colonized
would be enfranchised did not, however, interfere with the often
extreme cruelty of colonial rule.

One idea of imperialists was basically that human rights and
democracy are not for everybody, as everybody is not ready for
them.

* * *

In contrast, judging from the rhetoric of Western nations in
the second half of the twentieth century, we believe that every
nation has a right to govern itself, in freedom, and is capable of
developing democracy. But how deeply rooted is that conviction?

The debate in Sweden on human rights and democracy—a
debate that reached its zenith in the late 1960s and early 1970s—
can help probe the depth of this conviction. Moreover, the ideas
of that period in Sweden reflect similar attitudes in several West-

ern nations. What I found was a surprising tolerance towards dictatorships.

The regime of Mao Tse-tung can serve as an example. Important opinion makers in Sweden were fascinated by and romanticized the Chinese Cultural Revolution. Yet this period in Chinese history was an orgy of violence. Hundreds of thousands of people were murdered, millions deported, tens of millions of families were divided. Intellectuals were particularly assaulted by the Red Guard.

One important Swedish figure who romanticized Mao's China was Olof Lagercrantz, editor-in-chief in the 1960s and early 1970s of the largest and most influential morning newspaper in Sweden, *Dagens Nyheter.* Lagercrantz visited China in 1970, when the terror, deportations, and bloodshed of the Cultural Revolution were already well known. Nevertheless, in sixteen articles in 1970 and 1971, he proclaimed his enthusiasm for the revolution in Chinese society:

> The crucial difference between China and our world is that human beings . . . count for so very much more than with us. . . . In China, human beings come first. . . . People are China's biggest asset, and therefore the value put on human beings is automatically a high one. . . . The role of people is more important in China than elsewhere and realization of this spreads and enlivens millions as they go about their everyday tasks.

This is Lagercrantz's way of describing the role of individuals in a turbulent, totalitarian society.

He goes on to say that "the values on which the [Chinese] Communist regime is founded are the same as ours." Sport in China is chivalrous; people smile readily; the food there is abundant, good and cheap; the system of ideologically motivated "barefoot doctors" with three months' training is a method "both sensible and proper"; the Cultural Revolution has increased the chances of peace; "before long the world will see the present Chinese economy producing astonishing results. . . . " Lagercrantz is of course speaking here of the disastrous Maoist economy.

And the dictator himself, Mao Tse-tung, derives his legitimacy "by virtue of his wisdom": he is both "a great writer and a deter-mined man of action . . . the unrivalled guarantor of China's na-tional independence." The Communists practice democracy at home and direct dictatorship solely against "the enemies of the people." It is a tremendous asset for a country having Mao Tse-tung as its mentor, because "he is practical, experienced and full of living sympathy with the Chinese people."

The articles went on and on like this, day after day, month after month in the most prestigious Swedish daily paper. In the inter-national press we could read reports of what was going on in Communist China. Thus, a liberal paper, where resistance against totalitarian ideas and governments had been a basic belief in pre-vious decades, was totally changed after 1968. Those years trans-formed a large number of the most well-known writers and poli-ticians into followers of dictatorial regimes. Olof Lagercrantz was by no means alone here; thousands of young Swedes as well as important institutions became admirers of the Chinese revolu-tion.

This transformation came on the heels of the unrest of the late 1960s. To be sure, a similar phenomenon could be seen in the 1930s, when famous writers, artists, and other intellectuals assured the Western World that the Soviet Union was building a new and brighter future, which could create a New Man. Fellow travelers of that time also happened to be particularly enthusias-tic about Soviet achievements during exactly those years when the Stalinist regime was especially cruel, deporting, starving, ter-rorizing, and murdering its own citizens. At least in Sweden, the difference between the fellow travelers of the 1930s and late 1960s, then, turned on quantity: in the 1930s, the phenomenon was marginal; in the late 1960s, it became fashionable.

The Swedish attraction to totalitarian regimes was not limited to China and the Soviet Union. Leading Swedish politicians, writ-ers, officials, and journalists have for years been keen on embrac-ing the Castro regime in Cuba, disregarding the fact that thou-sands of people were thrown into prison because of their political views and that no human rights existed (or exist) in Cuba. A similar attitude prevailed in regard to East Germany: we were told that the Honecker regime had modernized its country and brought about steady economic growth. Symptomatic of this trend were the visits of the Swedish Prime Minister, Olof Palme, to Cuba in 1975 and East Germany in 1984. During the visits, there was not one word of criticism heard about oppression in these two nations, but hundreds of words were spoken about common goals, friendship, and mutual struggle for peace and development.

* * *

What explains the attraction of totalitarianism for Western intellectuals? What are the forces that move intellectuals to become fellow travelers and, even more, to become propagandists for totalitarian states? Fellow travelers is a widespread phenomenon. A large number of famous intellectuals in the West belong to the group; they have been fascinated by, wholeheartedly praised, or excused the crimes in Stalin's era, China under Mao, Cuba under Castro, and other Marxist countries. Leftist sympathizers include George Bernard Shaw, Lincoln Steffens, Lion Feuchtwanger, Le Corbusier, Stephen Spender, Romain Rolland, Theodore Dreiser, Arnold Zweig, Heinrich Mann, Louis Aragon, Anatole France, Ilya Ehrenburg, Bertolt Brecht, Ernst Toller, Erwin Piscator, Julian Huxley, Sidney and Beatrice Webb, Harold Laski, Paul Robeson, Isadora Duncan, Edmund Wilson, Upton Sinclair, Jean-Paul Sartre, Simone de Beauvoir, Paul Langevin, Felix Greene, and Noam Chomsky.

And, of course, fellow travelers constitute a community not only by their sympathies for left-wing dictatorships. In the West, when Fascism and Nazism were strong and dominating Europe, hundreds of well-known intellectuals were celebrating Mussolini or Hitler, or at least did express considerable understanding of the goals of these murderous regimes. Sympathizers with these regimes included W. B. Yeats, Ezra Pound, T. S. Eliot, Henry Williamson, James Burnham, Oswald Spengler, Ernst Jünger, Martin Heidegger, Charles Maurras, Louis Celine, Jean Cocteau, Filippo Marinetti, Luigi Pirandello, Gabriele d'Annunzio, and Giovanni Genteles. They gave prestige to the Nazi and/or Fascist regimes of Germany and Italy.

Why did they do it? Paul Hollander has advanced the most brilliant, bold, and controversial explanation of this phenomenon.[1] A large number of intellectuals, says Hollander, feel like strangers in the Western societies, a feeling based partly on ideological conviction, partly on dissatisfaction because they think they receive insufficient recognition and wield minimal influence. Alienated in their home country (the United States or some European democracy), they are easily attracted to political systems and structures which are opposite to their own. Indeed, fellow travelers are often harsh and unforgiving in judgments of their own countries, while at the same time surprisingly generous toward (if uninformed about) other countries. Their coolness towards "their own" is a precondition for their romantization of "the others." Or to put it differently: one cannot idealize totalitarian states unless one stands as an outsider to the Western values which their own country embodies. Fellow travelers display a remarkable ability to commute between moral indignation and absolutism (when describing their own countries) and a strange moral relativism (when they praise dictatorships they have decided to support).[2]

It is one of the great paradoxes of our times that intellectuals, who once were the vanguard of secularism, have later become its victims. They cannot accept the conditions of secular societies, as those offer so little enchantment. They want to embrace "the meaning of life," and capitalism cannot serve as such, argues Hollander. Therefore, fellow travelers feel morally empty in the Western world and instead dream of a big and glorious goal, something truly and absolutely fulfilling.

That explains why they reject the pluralistic and democratic societies. The fellow travelers admire the leaders of totalitarian countries because they want *total* solutions and explanations, while the West often gives them compromises and bargaining. The search for a creed is as important as the need to criticize. It is obvious, Hollander concludes, that we have overestimated rationalism and skepticism among many intellectuals, that we have underestimated their need to *believe.*

Hollander's explanation goes far to explain the position of

271

writers and other outsiders who, because of their alienation, do not feel personally responsible for shortcomings of their own democracy. But it does not explain the phenomenon of the fellow travelers who are actually insiders, who, in other words, exert a huge influence on their societies and who stand at the center of political decision making. From the Swedish scene I refer particularly to Olof Palme, Prime Minister during most of his seventeen years as leader of his party. His position gave him the power to change Swedish politics, and he often did. Given this long career as an insider, it is hard to imagine that Palme did not receive enough recognition or felt alienated by the political structure of the Swedish society. Yet he often embraced certain dictatorial regimes, or kept silent about their worse crimes.

One answer could be that during these years, anti-communism was regarded by many as a reactionary attitude or even as warmongering propaganda. It was dismissed as lack of understanding of "progressive" causes, or as dangerous demagoguery close to McCarthyism. Anti-anti-communism made many people, and not only those of the Left, accept, praise, or close their eyes when Communist atrocities were exposed.

* * *

When discussing the abrogation of human rights that one often found in communist regimes, the fellow travelers claimed that we had to accept these regimes "on their own terms." Several reasons were given: the countries in question had a tradition of harsh rule; or it was said that their cultures were based on values different from our own. Strikingly, this attitude parallels the patronizing ones of colonial philosophies of the nineteenth century. Indeed, colonialists and fellow travelers share some basic premises: Third World people are different and, because they lack education and experience, they are not ready for democracy.

We must not measure others by our own yardsticks was how this notion was formulated by leading Swedish playwright and novelist, P. O. Enquist. In this case, the "others" who should not be measured were the regime of Pol Pot in Cambodia. Enquist was writing just about the time when the Khmer Rouge began exterminating more than a quarter of the Cambodian population; the following apologia epitomizes his position:

> For years, Western imperialism raped an Asian country, killed nearly a million people, transformed a beautiful historic Cambodian city into a ghetto, into a brothel. But the people rose, made themselves free, ejected the intruders, found that this fine city must be restored. They then evacuated the house and began tidying up. They started by scrubbing floors and walls, so that people would live here, not in degradation but in peace and with dignity. Then, in the West, crocodile tears are shed copiously.

> The brothel having been evacuated, cleaning is in progress. This is something which only pimps can regret. All this teaches us, however, that the struggle is not a historic monument, an inanimate memorial; it goes on.[3]

Again, Enquist was proclaiming his support when the press in the free world including Sweden had already told horrifying stories about the deportations of hundreds of thousands of people out of Cambodian cities; the genocide had in fact already begun.

What Enquist implicitly meant, however, was that the mass murder of Cambodians was not deplorable in the same sense as mass murder of Europeans. We have to be tolerant of their ideological creeds. When Chinese, Cambodian, Cuban, Arab, or other leaders are killing thousands of their own citizens, one is called on to judge them on their terms and not on ours. Yet here toleration has become neighbor to disastrous prejudice. Enquist again outlined this stance when he defended Pol Pot in June of that same year:

> There is a kind of implacable moralism which is only a manifestation of cultural imperialism; we translate our values directly onto other cultures and find that the others are inferior if they have not been willing pupils and adjusted to our way of seeing.[4]

I would call Enquist's objection to this translation of values in relation to non-Western peoples *an inverted racism,* meaning that one pretends to respect other peoples when, in fact, one despises them. By being an advocate for their cause, one leads people to believe that one has deep sympathy for values other than one's own while, in reality, one actually dismisses the fundamental rights of Third World peoples.

Ironically, this dismissal echoes certain aspects of colonial ideology. To be sure, this tolerant attitude towards terror in the 1960s and 1970s was founded on different ideas from those of colonialism. But the two are related insofar as they both accept dictatorial rule in faraway countries. (It is true that the European imperialists assumed that the rulers would belong to their own continent or culture. The Marxists usually took it for granted that the oppressors would belong to the people they oppressed.) Moreover, both fellow travelers and colonialists refer to undemocratic traditions when excusing dictatorial regimes, rejecting certain universal goals: rule of law, respect for human life, and the ambition of extending free elections and free speech to others.

A double standard characterizes both positions. It is typical that those who praised Mao, Castro, or Honecker seldom wanted to import their terror; it is crucial that the social experiments for which these leaders were responsible be conducted at a distance. Even more moderate undemocratic reforms are subject to this double standard: any attempt, for instance, to introduce the slightest limitation of free speech in a Western country would face a storm of protest from those who have seldom championed free speech in Third World nations. Thus the curtailment of rights is an acceptable measure for others, for those living in faraway lands, but not for the citizens of one's own country.[5]

* * *

Tyrannies are intolerance incarnated; and tolerance toward intolerance can engender its own lethal consequences. Accordingly, research shows that support for non-democratic government threatens the stability of world order and imperils human rights. There are at least three major ways democracies contribute to the well-being of the world.

First: democracies virtually never wage war against each other. There is today a consensus among experts that free nations have established "a separate peace," a kind of tacit peace treaty among democratic nations. Quincy Wright analyzes 116 major wars between the French Revolution and 1941. Not one of them involved democracies on opposite sides.[6] More recently, Bruce Russett comes to a similar conclusion. He studies all the wars since 1815 between independent countries, where more than a thousand people have died on the battlefields. He contends: "It is impossible to identify . . . any wars between democratic states in the period since 1815."[7] Even the devastating conflicts of the twentieth century do not vary the pattern. According to Dean Babst, thirty-three independent nations took part in World War I; of the ten democracies, no one fought each other. Again, fifty-two independent countries participated in World War II; none of the fifteen democracies ever shot at the other.[8] Generally, then, the absence of war between democracies, writes Jack Levy, "comes as close as anything we have to an empirical law in international relations."[9] Two centuries after the German philosopher Immanuel Kant presented a similar theory, a wave of research confirms it.[10] The more democracies we have on earth, the higher the probability that wars could be avoided.

Second: democracies rarely commit mass murder of civilian population; totalitarian and authoritarian regimes often do.[11] Regrettably, an extraordinary number of civilians have been killed in genocide and mass murder in our century for political and ideological reasons. R. J. Rummel has presented statistics which indicate that about 170 million people have been murdered because rulers in certain nations wanted to wipe them out. (170 million is about four times more than all the battle-dead of all the wars in our century). Except for two million people, all this killing was committed by totalitarian and authoritarian regimes.

The three most murderous empires are the Soviet Union with about 62 million killed in non-war situations, Communist China with 35 million, and Nazi Germany with 21 million murdered. These figures are incredible and unimaginable. Could we really understand what they tell us? 170 million men, women, and children have been gassed, "shot, beaten, tortured, knifed, burned, hung, bombed or killed in any other of the myriad ways governments have inflicted death on unarmed, helpless citizens or foreigners" (Rummel).

The reason why democracies usually do not mass murder civilians is the openness of a free society, the checks and balances, the free press and opposition, leaders accountable to their people, and limited government. The totalitarian states are their opposites.

Third: democracies prevent famines. Remarkably, there has apparently been no instance of famine—serious starvation causing mass death—in any parliamentary democracy, anywhere. The economist Amartya Sen sketches the essential relation between a country's ability to feed its citizens and democracy:

> One of the remarkable facts in the terrible history of famine is that no substantial famine has ever occurred in a country with a democratic form of government and relatively free press. They have occurred in ancient kingdoms and in contemporary authoritarian societies, in primitive tribal communities and in modern technocratic dictatorships, in colonial economies governed by imperialists from the north and in newly independent countries of the south run by despotic leaders or by intolerant single parties. But famines have never afflicted any country that is independent, that goes to elections regularly, that has opposition parties to voice criticism, that permits newspapers to report freely and to question the wisdom of government policies without extensive censorship.[12]

Thus Sen indicates how crucial democracy is not only for developed but for developing countries, providing a means to ward off famine.

* * *

Initially, in the case of the nineteenth-century colonialists, the explicit double standard toward colonized peoples victimized the Third World nations. In the case of twentieth-century fellow travelers, the double standard they implicitly invoked had a similar victim, dismissing or weakening the rights of foreign peoples while protecting those at home. In each case the injustice committed against the Third World nation was profound, justifying and thus enabling authoritarian rule over peoples and nations and disabling the essential development of democratic institutions (free speech, free press, free elections). While we see the disasterous legacy such double standards bequeathed to individual nations, we see that the implications of the struggle for democracy are also transnational, reverberating in developed as well as developing countries. Hence, democracy is for everybody means on the one hand that every nation is similarly and absolutely entitled to the peace and plenty that democratic institutions usually nurture. On the other hand, democracy is for everybody means that the fate of the world rests on a progressive increase in the number and stability of democracies the globe sustains.

NOTES

I have made most of the above remarks at international conferences chaired by Elie Wiesel. The themes have been more amply developed in my two latest books, *Vänstern och tyranniet* [Tyranny and the Left] (Stockholm: Timbro, 1994) and *Det öppna såret* [An Open Sore] (Stockholm: Timbro, 1997).

1. Paul Hollander, *Political Pilgrims: Travels of Western Intellectuals to the Soviet Union, China and Cuba, 1928–1978* (New York: Oxford University Press, 1981). See also Hollander's *The Survival of the Adversary Culture: Social Criticism and Political Escapism in American Society* (New Brunswick: Transaction, 1988) and *Anti-Americanism: Critiques at Home and Abroad, 1965–90* (New York: Oxford University Press, 1990). See also David Caute, *The Fellow Travelers: Intellectual Friends of Communism*, rev. ed. (New Haven: Yale University Press, 1988).

2. When, in the 1930s, the West was struck by mass unemployment, the Soviet Union seemed to them to represent economic stability and development, rationalism and social justice. When the West was demoralized during the Vietnam war the attraction of Communist China, Cuba, North Vietnam, and sometimes North Korea, Albania, and Eastern Germany, was at its height. Some fellow travelers have searched for a Utopia in the Communist world. Others have longed for concrete progress of economic structure and administration. Additionally, romanticization of Marxist countries in the Third World indicates another phenomenon: underdevelopment was given the attraction of the innocent, the virgin.

3. *Expressen*, Stockholm, then the largest daily in Scandinavia, May 15, 1975.

4. *Expressen*, June 9, 1975.

5. Of course there are countries where tragic political circumstances have made the practice of democracy almost impossible. But their failure and intolerance must never become an ideology or apology for others. Dictatorships always invite disaster.

6. Quincy Wright, *A Study of War, with a Commentary on War since 1942*. 2nd ed. (Chicago: University of Chicago Press, 1965).

7. Bruce Russett, *Grasping the Democratic Peace: Principles for a Post-Cold War World* (Princeton: Princeton University Press, 1993).

8. Dean Babst, "Elective Governments—A Force for Peace," *The Wisconsin Sociologist* 32 (1964).

9. Jack Levy, "Domestic Politics and War," *Journal of Interdisciplinary History* 18 (1988).

10. Of course, this rule does not govern the relations between democracies and non-democracies.

11. See R. J. Rummel, *Death by Government* (New Brunswick: Transaction, 1994); *Democide: Nazi Genocide and Mass Murder* (New Brunswick: Transaction, 1992); and *Lethal Politics: Soviet Genocide and Mass Murder since 1917* (New Brunswick: Transaction, 1990).

12. Amartaya Sen, "Freedom and Needs," *The New Republic* (Jan. 10 and 17, 1994). See also Amartaya Sen, *Poverty and Famines: An Essay on Entitlement and Deprivation* (Oxford: Clarendon, 1982); and recently, *The Political Economy of Hunger: Selected Essays*, ed. Jean Dreze, Amartaya Sen, and Arthar Hussain (Oxford: Clarendon, 1995).

IRWIN COTLER

The Holocaust, Nuremberg, and Human Rights: Elie Wiesel and the Struggle against Injustice in Our Time

I

This essay is being written at a historic moment of remembrance, witness, and reaffirmation. For 1998 marks the fiftieth anniversary both of the *Universal Declaration of Human Rights*—regarded as the *magna carta* of humankind—and the *Genocide Convention*—the testament of man's inhumanity to man. The year 1998 also commemorates the fiftieth anniversary of the State of Israel, the establishment of which, in the aftermath of the Holocaust, served as a testament to humanity.

I write also at the time of the fiftieth anniversary of the Nuremberg Trials and of the Nuremberg Principles which emerged out of these trials. These Principles gave substance to international humanitarian law and provided the inspiration for international human rights law, including the *Genocide Convention* and the *Universal Declaration*.[1] The Nuremberg Principles determined that not just abstract entities like states but that individuals are personally responsible for criminal violations of human rights including, in particular, the Nuremberg offenses of "Crimes against the Peace," "War Crimes," and "Crimes against Humanity." The Principles also mandated that individuals could no longer plead "acts of state" or "superior orders" as exculpatory grounds for their criminality. For these Nuremberg offenses were crimes against humankind itself; the individuals who committed them were *hostis humani generis*, the enemies of humankind, for the reason that the rights they violated included every protected right enshrined in the *Universal Declaration of Human Rights*.

Reference to the crimes perpetrated by those tried at Nuremberg also calls forth the memory of another Nuremberg. For during the Nazi era Nuremberg was associated with two pernicious features of Nazi rule: 1) the massive rallies that took place in the city of Nuremberg; and 2) the racial edicts of 1935 known as the Nuremberg laws, legislation that went a long way toward legally justifying virtually wholesale discrimination against Jews. Nuremberg thus reverberates with a dual connotation: the Nuremberg of jackboots and racial edicts as opposed to the Nuremberg of judgment, of racism as opposed to law (or of racism institutionalized as law). Indeed, my own remembrance as a child of the Nuremberg of jackboots came full circle recently when my ten-year-old son, reading from Carol Matas' children's book on the Holocaust entitled *Daniel's Story*, pointed to the first reference in the book to Nuremberg: "Look Daddy," he said, "It mentions Nuremberg."[2]

This dual connotation of Nuremberg (of race laws, on the one hand; of principles, on the other) finds related expression in two post-war world developments: a) the dialectic of the human rights revolution and counter-revolution, that is, in the entrenchment of international human rights law, on the one hand, and the criminal violation of human rights, on the other. And b) a parallel revolution and counter-revolution in the specific arena of human rights and the Jewish condition (particularly the aspect of the Jewish condition that relates to the State of Israel), a revolution that has also moved dialectically between a Dickensian best of times and worst of times.

On the one hand, human rights has emerged as the organizing idiom of our political culture; indeed, it functions as the new secular religion of our time and serves as the common language of humanity. Moreover, human rights victories thought impossible at the beginning of the 1980s (the withering away of the Soviet Union, the dismantling of Apartheid, the march of democracy from Central Asia to Central America, the reunification of Germany) have not only happened, but have already been forgotten, or are in danger of being forgotten.

Moreover, this revolution of human rights has itself been anchored in, and inspired by, the Nuremberg legacy: the worldwide recognition of human rights law and the humanization of international law. This legacy includes the following developments:

- the increasing reference to, and invocation of, the sources of international human rights law (custom, treaty, general principles of law recognized by the community of nations, judicial decisions, and *opinio juris*), not only as authoritative juridical principle and precedent, but as the discourse of diplomacy and democracy;
- the dramatic increase in international human rights treaties combatting torture, prohibiting racial discrimination, defining the rights of women, or protecting the rights of the most vulnerable and powerless: children, workers, prisoners, refugees, indigenous people, and minorities;
- the emergence of an *International Bill of Rights* (the *UN Charter,* the *Universal Declaration on Human Rights,* the *International Covenant on Civil and Political Rights,* and the *International Protocol*), some of whose provisions have even secured the status of authoritative norms of customary international law binding on all nations;
- the protection of human rights in armed conflict both international and internal (the protection referred to here bespeaks not just a right—*un droit d'ingérence*—but a duty to intervene in situations which exhibit "a consistent pattern of gross violations of human rights");
- the establishment of Ad Hoc International Criminal Tribunals respecting serious violations of International Humanitarian Law in the former Yugoslavia and in Rwanda;
- the affirmation in 1995 by the Appeal Chamber of these tribu-

nals of the distinguishable Nuremberg offense of "Crimes against Humanity";

- the decision of the International Court of Justice in the matter of the illegality of the use of nuclear weapons;
- the increasing invocation of international human rights law by domestic and regional courts as a "relevant and persuasive authority," in the words of the Supreme Court of Canada. For example, in the 1990s alone the Supreme Court of Canada invoked the Nuremberg legacy in upholding the constitutionality of Canada's anti-hate laws as well as its recently enacted War Crimes law (the "made in Canada 'Nuremberg' legislation," as it has come to be called).

In summary, then, the Nuremberg legacy lives through, *inter alia,* the constitutionalization and universalization of human rights; the internationalization of human rights and the humanization of international law; the emergence of the individual as subject and not just object of international law; and the responsibility not just of states but of state *officials* for criminal violations of human rights. As Father Robert Drinan has stated, "the elevation of human rights into an international juridical norm is the most dramatic development in the history of contemporary jurisprudence."

Strikingly, the developments in world history have their parallel in Jewish history; the revolution in human rights generally has its correlate in the sphere of human rights and the Jewish/Israel situation, where:

- Soviet totalitarianism, as Gorbachev himself said, has "withered away," and Zionism, the scapegoated victim of that totalitarianism, has prevailed;
- "Closed borders"—the metaphor of the post-war Jewish condition in the former Soviet Union, East Europe, Ethiopia, and Syria—has been turned on its head, and the exodus of Soviet, Ethiopian, and Syrian Jews resonates not only as a humanitarian metaphor but as a human miracle;
- The United Nations has repealed the Zionism is Racism Resolution, returning, as it were, Israel to diplomatic history, and

enabling Israel to enjoy diplomatic relations with over 150 states in the international community;

- Israel and the Palestinians have agreed on a joint Declaration of Principles followed by the *Oslo Accords,* both of which provide a framework for peace. Israel also has entered into a historic peace treaty with Jordan and has developed diplomatic exchanges with much of the Arab world.

I I

Yet we witness not only a human rights revolution but also a counter-revolution, a betrayal, as it were, of the legacy of Nuremberg, wherein the criminal violations of human rights not only continue unabated but have intensified. Indeed, the refugees of humanity, the hungry of Africa, the imprisoned of Asia and the Middle East, the women victims of a "gender Apartheid" can be forgiven if they think that the human rights revolution has passed them by. The silent tragedy of the Kurds, the ethnic cleansing of the Balkans, the agony of Rwanda are cruel signs of the assault upon, and abandonment of, the Nuremberg Principles. As David Rieff eloquently teaches, the unspeakable crime, genocide, has emerged as the paradigmatic form of armed conflict in the 1990s.[3]

In other words, the echoes of the other Nuremberg—the racist anti-semitic Nuremberg—have become only too manifest, lending credence to the notion of anti-semitism as an endemic and enduring hatred. And so it is, then, that the counter-revolution in human rights worldwide is also paralleled by the counter-revolution in the predicament of the Jews and Israel in relation to human rights:

- the dialectics of Glasnost and democracy in the former Soviet Union have unleashed the repressed demons of racism and anti-semitism;
- the new extremist Russian Right blames the Jews for bringing about Communism, and the old extremist Communist Left blames the Jews for the downfall of Communism;
- in unified Germany Neo-Nazis walk the street in search of

l'étranger—the foreigner—and a new xenophobia stalks across Europe, for which the *"Le Pennization"* of France has become message and metaphor;

- the United Nations, founded as an alliance against racism and anti-semitism, becomes a forum for the dissemination of hatred against Israel and the Jewish people;
- Iran decrees an international "fatwa" against Israel, and Israel emerges not only as the "Jew among the Nations," but as the "Salmon Rushdie" of the nations for radical Islamic fundamentalism;
- Holocaust denial emerges as the cutting edge of anti-semitism, old and new;
- the State of Israel, founded as a metaphor for human rights, emerges as a metaphor for a human rights violator.

It is not surprising, then, that the rhetoric of the human rights revolution may invite the not uncynical rejoinder that human rights is so much rights without writs, rhetoric without remedy, semantics without sanctions; that Nuremberg Justice has given way to Nuremberg Crimes; that, in the double connotation of Nuremberg, it is not the Nuremberg Principles but the legacy of racial laws that holds sway.

Nor is it surprising that the rhetoric of the "Jewish revolution" may also invite the rejoinder that this, too, is nonsense; that for Jews, the United Nations has emerged not as aid but as adversary; that those who speak the language of human rights are well-meaning but naive people who do not realize that there are things in Jewish history too terrible to be believed, but not too terrible to have happened; that Israel remains the outcast, the collective Jew among the Nations.

III

It is the underlying theme of my remarks, however, that we court disaster if we take a cynical view of the human rights revolution; that it is not the Nuremberg Principles that has betrayed us, but we that betrayed Nuremberg. Indeed, the list of accomplishments of the revolution is staggering:

- that all people everywhere are entitled to the protection of their fundamental rights to life, liberty, and security of the person;
- that these rights are as indivisible as they are universal; that all states have an obligation to protect the rights of their people, and NGOs and individuals a right—indeed, a responsibility—to protest the violations of these rights;
- that there are certain universal norms which oblige us all—that neither murder, nor rape, nor racism, nor ethnic cleansing, can be respected by any faith, culture, or people that respects humanity—that respects Nuremberg justice;
- that individuals—and not just states—are accountable for "Nuremberg Crimes"; and that under the "principle of universal jurisprudence," every state has a duty to bring these war criminals to justice.

These bedrock principles must underlie the human rights agenda—the struggle against injustice in our time—fifty years after Nuremberg. Indeed, we ignore not only the human rights revolution—the Nuremberg Principles—at our peril, but also the "Jewish Recollection" of Israel as antidote to Nuremberg Racism, not only as the targeted victim of the "Collective Jew among Nations" but Israel as the guarantor of human rights of this "collective" Jew.

The State of Israel, then, is not only the juridical embodiment of Jewish sovereignty, but the juridical instrument of Jewish self-determination. As such, it is the ultimate guarantor of the human rights of the Jewish people. A few examples might suffice.

Israel provides refuge for the Jewish oppressed, for those who, during the period of the Holocaust, were denied refuge. The *Law of Return*, providing immediate citizenship and protection for oppressed Jews, is a Charter of Rights for Jews fearing persecution and discrimination, thereby providing juridical support for, and implementation of, the dictum of "we are each the guarantor of the other" and more. It is a standing invitation to world Jewry to participate in Jewish self-determination—in the self-determination of Jews as a people exercising sovereignty and not just as individuals or diaspora committees.

Israel as a sovereign Jewish state can engage, per state, in humanitarian intervention on behalf of the Jewish people, be it securing the release of Jewish hostages in Entebbe, or negotiating the airlift of Ethiopian Jews, thereby providing, once again, juridical support for, and implementation of, the dictum, "the release of the imprisoned."

Israel alone, pursuant to its *Nazi War Criminal and Collaborating Law,* can prosecute Nazi war criminals not only for Crimes against Humanity (according to the principle of universal jurisdiction for war criminals) but also for Crimes against the Jewish People. It alone can bring Nazi war criminals to justice (as in the *Eichmann* case) in the name of the Jewish People as well as in the name of humanity. Israel's special status gives juridical meaning to the dictum, "You shall not stand idly by while your neighbor's blood is being shed."

The State of Israel, then, is the best evidence of the notion of sovereignty not just as an abstraction of political theory but as the guarantor of human rights, of Jewish self-determination in the individual and collective sense. This "bedrock principle" must also underline the human rights agenda—the Jewish agenda—fifty years after Nuremberg. As set forth at the outset of this essay, it is being written not only fifty years after Nuremberg, but on the eve of the fiftieth anniversary of the *Universal Declaration of Human Rights,* the *Genocide Convention,* and, additionally, the fiftieth anniversary of the State of Israel—the collective expression of the human rights revolution and the Jewish revolution. What, then, have we learned? What is it that we must do?

IV

I would like to summarize the existential lessons of Nuremberg and of Holocaust remembrance: of the agony and hope of Nuremberg in relation to human history and Jewish history. For as Aldous Huxley said, "life must be lived forwards, but it can only be understood backwards"; or in the poignant words of Rabbi Yisroel Bal Shem Tov, "forgetfulness is exile; remembrance is redemption." In this closing meditation, the lessons to be learned and the action to be taken are guided by the words and example of Elie Wiesel himself.

1: Unmasking Evil

The first lesson, as Wiesel has instructed us, is "the need to discern evil . . . in times of stress we must at least know the difference between evil and what is not evil. We cannot allow evil to take on the mask of good."[4] Indeed, what Nuremberg teaches is that crimes against humanity can be anchored in, and sanctioned by, the face of law itself, as in the Nuremberg race laws. "Why," Wiesel continues, "was the Nazi era so horrifying? Because the law itself was immoral . . . the killers were convinced that they were obeying the law, and indeed it was the law to kill children, parents, old men and women, all those who needed protection. It was the law to be inhuman."[5]

In order to protect against using the law as a cover for evil ends, the Nuremberg legacy found expression in the development of international human rights law (with the *Universal Declaration* as metaphor and message of this rights legacy) and with the United Nations as repository of the developing human rights revolution. Yet here too, as Wiesel reminds us, we cannot allow what was intended to be the antidote to evil—the United Nations—to become the mask for evil itself. For when the United Nations declares that Zionism is Racism or systematically singles out Israel for differential and discriminatory treatment, then evil is being allowed to take on the mask of good. "Law," once again, is immoral; and it is our responsibility to unmask the evil, to anchor law in justice.

2: Confronting Evil

Nuremberg teaches us that wherever we discover evil, we must confront it, lest our acquiescence to evil make us an accomplice to evil. As Wiesel teaches, we must resist it, even if such resistance is hopeless. Even if we have no chance of winning, we must fight. For in resisting evil, we save something in our own self. We save a certain image of ourself. We save a certain sense of dignity which may be seen as a source of strength by those who live with us and who will live after us.

3: Vulnerability of the Powerless

Evil preys on the powerlessness of the victim. Nazism almost succeeded, not only because of the pathology of hatred and technology of violence, but because of the powerlessness of the victim and the vulnerability of the powerless. It is not surprising, then, that the *triage* of Nazi racial hygiene—the Sterilization Laws, the *Nuremberg Race Laws*, the Euthanasia Program—targeted those whose "lives were not worth living." It is revealing, as Henry Friedlander points out in his recent book on *The Origins of Nazi Genocide*, that the first group targeted for killing were the Jewish handicapped—the most vulnerable of the powerless.[6]

4: Israel as an Antidote to Jewish Powerlessness

Nazism almost succeeded, again not only because of the pathology of hatred and technology of violence, but because of the powerlessness of the Jew, and hence because of the vulnerability of the Jew. Israel, then, is an antidote to Jewish powerlessness, the *raison d'être* in the most profound existential sense, for Jewish self-determination. In the words of Uriel Simon—an Israeli dove—"Jewish morality has only been respected when it has had an army behind it."

In a word, it is not the case, as we are sometimes told, that if there had not been a Holocaust, there would not have been an Israel. The sense of "compensatory justice" here is neither just nor compensatory. For six million Jews—1.5 million of whom were children—cannot have their lives recompensed for by a State. If, as the Talmud teaches us, a person who saves the life of a single human being saves an entire world, surely the opposite is no less true: that the murder of a human being is the destruction of an entire universe. The murder of six million, the destruction of six million universes—"One, by One, by One," as Judith Miller phrased it.[7] It is, therefore, the other way around—and we should never forget it—if there had been an Israel, there might well not have been a Holocaust, or the horrors of Jewish history. Certainly, many lives, many universes would have been saved, if nothing else but by the existence of one refuge while the gates of "humanity" remained closed. Israel, then, at its core, is the expression and embodiment of Jewish self-determination.

This is not to say, and I would not wish to have it inferred from any of these remarks, that Israel should be above the law, or that Israel should not be accountable for any violations of human rights law. On the contrary. Israel, like any other state, is responsible for any violations of international law, and the Jewish people are not entitled to any privilege or preference because of the Holocaust or the sufferings of Jewish history. But the problem, I suggest to you, is not that Israel seeks, or that any of us should seek on Israel's behalf, that it be above the law, but that Israel has been systematically denied equality before the law in the intentional arena; not that Israel should respect human rights—which she must—but that the human rights of Israel are also deserving of respect; not that human rights standards should be applied to Israel—which they must be—but that they must be applied equally to everyone else. It is our responsibility, then, to seek equality before the law—international due process for Israel or any other state—in the international arena.

*5: The Integrity of Words: The Nuremberg Code and
the Misappropriation of the Holocaust*

One must guard against the appropriation, or misappropriation, of Holocaust metaphors to contemporary issues in human rights and medical ethics. As Arthur Caplan states, "the invocation of analogies to the conduct of the Nazis requires an understanding and caution that are notably absent in many of those who glibly make the claim of moral equivalence."[8] In a word, blanket invocations such as "abortion is today's Holocaust" or "legalized euthanasia is the Nazification of medicine," or the characterization of feminists as "femi-Nazis" not only bespeak a callous ignorance of the Nazi Holocaust, but a misrepresentation of issues in human rights and ethical conduct today. (As Caplan indicated, "to use the Nazi analogy with abandon is to abandon history.") This does not mean, for example, that Nazi abuse of medical experimentation cannot be a point of reference or that the Nuremberg Code is not source and substance of contemporary international human rights law respecting medical experimentation on human beings. On the contrary, the Nuremberg Code is, in effect, the Nuremberg Principles on medical ethics; as Jay Katz set forth, the Nuremberg Code serves as an international covenant for the inviolability of the human person, for the inherent worth of every human being.[9]

6: Nuremberg, Racism, and the Holocaust

Nazism almost succeeded not only because of the ideology of hate and the industry of death, but because of the internalized legacy of racism, that is, an ingrained culture of racism and anti-semitism. Indeed, it is this culture of racism, this eliminationist anti-semitism anchored in the theory and practice of racial hygiene (in the use of medical metaphors in the sanitizing of racism) that transformed "ordinary Germans," in Daniel Goldhagen's phrase, into "Hitler's willing executioners".[10]

Why single out the Germans? To be sure, anti-semitism was not only German but European. Ordinary men also became willing executioners in Lithuania or Occupied Europe; even Norway enacted Nuremberg Race Laws and deported its Jewish population to Aushwitz. But only in Nazi Germany did you have the convergence of a critical mass of ideology of hate, industry of death, technology of terror, elite complicity and legitimization, cultural legacy, bureaucracy of death, indifference of the bystander, neutrality of the friend, and, of course, the medicalization of genocide.

7: Against Racism—The Universality of the Human Rights Struggle

As history has taught us only too well, while it may begin with Blacks, Asians, or Jews as victims of the violations of human rights, it does not end with them. The struggle against racism and anti-semitism must therefore not be seen simply as a Black issue, or an Asian issue, or a Jewish issue, but as a justice issue of the first import. The familiar words of the German Protestant theologian, Martin Niemüller, bear not only recall, but action.

> They first came for the Catholics, but I wasn't a Catholic so I did nothing. Then they came for the Communists, but I wasn't a Communist so I did nothing. Then they came for the trade unionists, but I wasn't a trade unionist so I did nothing. Then they came for the Jews, but I wasn't a Jew so I did nothing. Then they came for me, and there was nobody left.

8: Nuremberg, Assaultive Speech, and Genocide

Testimony and documentary evidence of the Nuremberg trials— of the trial of Julius Streicher, for example—demonstrated that the Holocaust began with defining a group of people as racially other, as, in other words, being no longer entitled to basic human and civil rights. More recently, in upholding the constitutionality of anti-hate law, the Supreme Court of Canada wrote: "The Holocaust did not begin in the gas chambers; it began with words."[11] Racist language assails human dignity. We must begin by combating the kind of speech that leads to the teaching of contempt. For words can wound, assault, maim, and can even, as in Rwanda, Bosnia, and Burundi, lead down the road to genocide.

9: Holocaust Denial: From Assaultive Speech to Criminal Conspiracy

The Holocaust denial movement—the cutting edge of anti-semitism old and new—is not just an assault on Jewish memory and human dignity in its accusation that the Holocaust is a hoax; rather, it constitutes an international criminal conspiracy to cover up the worst crimes in history. Here is the historiography of the Holocaust in its ultimate Orwellian inversion. First, we move from the genocide of the Jewish people to a denial that the genocide ever took place; then in a classic Orwellian coverup of an international conspiracy, the Holocaust denial movement whitewashes the crimes of the Nazis even while it excoriates the so-called "crimes" of the Jews. It not only holds that the Holocaust was a hoax, but maligns the Jews for fabricating the hoax. It is therefore our responsibility to unmask the bearers of false witness and to expose the criminality of the deniers as we protect the dignity of their victims.

10: Bringing Nazi War Criminals to Justice— The Nuremberg Lessons

The question of bringing Nazi war criminals to justice is inextricably bound up with the struggle against Holocaust denial. As Holocaust denier Ernst Zundel claimed, "As we all know, the so-called Holocaust is nothing else but a hoax, a gigantic fraud . . . and if there were no crimes, that must mean that there are no criminals—there are no so-called Nazi war criminals to be brought to justice." Accordingly, if we do not bring Nazi war criminals to justice there may be those who will say ten or twenty years from now, "you see, there were no criminals, therefore it must be that there were no crimes." Hence, every time we bring a Nazi war criminal to justice, we strike a blow against the Holocaust denial movement.

Moreover, the presence of Nazi war criminals amongst us fifty years after the Nuremberg trials is a moral and juridical obscenity. Indeed, the word "war criminal" is itself a misnomer. For we are talking not only, or mainly, about the killing of combatants in the course of the prosecution of a war, but the murder of civilians in the course of the persecution of a race.

11: The "Trahison des clercs"

Nazism almost succeeded not only because of the "bureaucratization of genocide," as Robert Lifton formulated it, but because, as Eli Wiesel has described it, of the *trahison des clercs*—the complicity of the elites—physicians, church leaders, judges, engineers, architects, educators, and the like. Indeed, one only has to read Ingo Muller's study of Hitler's courts to appreciate the complicity and criminality of judges;[12] to read Deborah Dwork and

Robert Jan Van Pelt on the architecture of Auschwitz, to be appalled by the minute involvement of engineers and architects in the design of death camps, and so on.[13] Nuremberg crimes, then, were also the crimes of the Nuremberg elites.

And in this "science" of death and destruction, doctors bear a special responsibility; for physicians sworn to uphold the Hippocratic Oath of never harming the patient became the architects of racial hygiene; the high priests of Aryanization; the legislators/theorists of demonization; the practitioners of torture; the executioners of genocide.[14]

12: Minorities and Human Rights

A world which will not be safe for democracy and human rights will not be safe for women, for minorities, for the disabled and disadvantaged, whoever they may be—and so we have a responsibility for the promotion of democracy and the protection of human rights. But a world which will not be safe for minorities, women, disabled, or the disadvantaged will not be safe for democracy and human rights—and so we have a responsibility for the promotion and protection of their rights. The test of any civilization is the way it treats its minorities; and, as Wiesel observed—and so cited by the late Premier of Quebec René Levesque—the test of civilization has been the way it treats its Jews.

13: The Crime of Indifference

Nazism almost succeeded, not only because of the ideology of hate and the technology of terror, but because of the crime of indifference, the conspiracy of silence. Indeed, we have witnessed an appalling indifference in our day to the unthinkable—ethnic cleansing—to the unspeakable—genocide—and worst of all—the preventable genocide in Rwanda. It is our responsibility, then, to break the walls of indifference, to shatter the silence wherever it may be. As Wiesel expresses it, "neutrality always means coming down on the side of the victimizer, never on the side of the victim"—coming down on the side of the torturer, never on the side of the tortured. And so it is our responsibility always to stand with the victim, even if, again following Wiesel, we both lose, lest the victim stand alone and abandoned. Let there be no mistake about it: to avert one's eye from evil—to be indifferent—is to be an accomplice to evil. For indifference begets acquiescence, and acquiescence becomes complicity.

14: Raoul Wallenberg and the Courage to Resist

Some, however, refuse to be indifferent. As Raoul Wallenberg demonstrated, it was possible to resist, to confront evil, and to prevail.[15] The problem was that there were too few Wallenbergs; indeed, as Wiesel reminds us, the world hid the story of the true Wallenberg, lest it embarrass us all by showing what could have been done.

And so each one has an indispensable role to play in the indivisible struggle for human rights and human dignity. Each one can and does make a difference. And if we ever get tired or fatigued—burnt out to use the popular metaphor—then let us remember that one Swedish non-Jew named Raoul Wallenberg saved more Jews in the Second World War than any government; that one Andrei Sakhorov stood up against the whole Soviet system and prevailed; that one individual, Nelson Mandela, twenty-eight years in a South African prison, nurtured the dream and came out to bring about the dismantling of apartheid.

And so, we can each be responsible for helping to unmask evil, for repudiating false witness, combating assaultive speech, for helping to bring war criminals to justice, for combating racial incitement, for sounding the alarm against genocide, for helping to reform the United Nations, for coming down on the side of the victim, the vulnerable, the powerless. This, then, must be our task: to speak on behalf of those who cannot be heard; to bear witness on behalf of those who cannot testify; to act on behalf of those who put not only their livelihood, but their lives on the line. And so may the Nuremberg legacy—and the fiftieth anniversary of the *Universal Declaration,* the *Genocide Convention,* and creation of the State of Israel—be not only an important act of remembrance, which it is, but may it also be a remembrance to act, which it must be.

NOTES

1. Robert Drinan succinctly characterizes the Principles: "The 'Nuremberg Principles' consist of the London Charter (the agreement for the prosecution and punishment of major war criminals of the European Axis, dated August 8, 1945), the War Crimes Trial indictment, and the judgment rendered by the Nuremberg Tribunal in the War Crimes Trial. In 1946, the General Assembly of the United Nations unanimously adopted the 'Principles of International Law Recognized by the Charter of the Nuremberg Tribunal.'" The War Crimes Trial was the first of the Nuremberg Trials. See Robert F. Drinan, "The Nuremberg Principles in International Law," in *The Nazi Doctors and the Nuremberg Code: Human Rights in Human Experimentation,* ed. George Annas and Michael Grodin (New York and Oxford: Oxford University Press, 1992) 175.

Article Six of the Charter of the International Military Tribunal (IMT) at Nuremberg set forth crimes within the Tribunal's jurisdiction for which there was to be individual responsibility—crimes against peace, war crimes, and crimes against humanity. In the words of the Charter of the IMT:

> The following acts, or any of them, are crimes coming within the jurisdiction of the Tribunal for which there shall be individual responsibility:
>
> a) Crimes against peace: namely, planning, preparation, initiation or waging of a war of aggression, or a war in violation of international treaties, agreements or assurances, or participation in a common plan or conspiracy for the accomplishment of any of the foregoing.
>
> b) War Crimes: namely, violations of the laws or customs of war. Such violations include, but are not limited to, murder, ill-treatment or deportation to slave labour or for any other purpose of civilian population of or in occupied territory, murder or ill-treatment of prisoners of war or persons on the seas, killing of hostages, plunder of public or private property, wanton destruction of cities, towns or villages, or devastation not justified by military necessity;
>
> c) Crimes against humanity: namely, murder, extermination, enslavement, deportation, and other inhumane acts committed against any civilian population, before or during the war, or persecutions on political, racial or religious grounds in execution of or in connection with any crime within the jurisdiction of the Tribunal, whether or not in violation of the domestic law of the country where perpetrated.

2. Carol Matas, *Daniel's Story* (New York: Scholastic, 1993).

3. David Rieff, *Slaughterhouse: Bosnia and the Failure of the West* (New York: Simon and Schuster, 1995).

4. Elie Wiesel, "Witness," in *Nuremberg Forty Years Later: The Struggle against Injustice in Our Time,* ed. Irwin Cotler (Montreal: McGill-Queen's University Press, 1995), p. 20.

5. Ibid.

6. Henry Friedlander, *The Origins of Nazi Genocide: From Euthanasia to the Final Solution* (Chapel Hill, N.C.: University of North Carolina Press, 1995).

7. Judith Miller, *One, by One, by One: Facing the Holocaust* (New York: Simon and Schuster, 1990).

8. Arthur Caplan, "The Doctors' Trial and Analogies to the Holocaust in Contemporary Bioethical Debates," in *The Nazi Doctors and the Nuremberg Code: Human Rights in Human Experimentation,* ed. George Annas and Michael Grodin (New York and Oxford: Oxford University Press, 1992), p. 270.

9. Jay Katz, "The Consent Principle of the Nuremberg Code: Its Significance Then and Now," in *The Nazi Doctors and the Nuremberg Code,* pp. 227–39.

10. Daniel Goldhagen, *Hitler's Willing Executioners: Ordinary Germans and the Holocaust* (New York: Knopf, 1997).

11. Statement of Justice Peter Cory, Ontario Court of Appeal, in *R. v. Andrews and Smith* (1988) 43 C.C.C. (3rd) 193 (Ont. C.A.O. 211), cited by the Supreme Court of Canada in *R v. Keegstra* (1990) 3 S.C.R. 697.

12. Ingo Muller, *Hitler's Justice: The Courts of the Third Reich,* trans. Deborah Lucas Schneider (Cambridge: Harvard University Press, 1991).

13. Deborah Dwork and Robert Jan Van Pelt, *Auschwitz: 1270 to the Present* (New York: W. W. Norton, 1996).

14. See Benno Müller-Hill, *Murderous Science: Elimination by Scientific Selection of Jews, Gypsies, and Others, Germany 1933–1945* (Oxford: Oxford University Press, 1988); Robert Proctor, *Racial Hygiene: Medicine under the Nazis* (Cambridge, Mass.: Harvard University Press, 1988); Michael Kater, *Doctors under Hitler* (Chapel Hill: University of North Carolina Press, 1989); Robert Jay Lifton, *Nazi Doctors: Medical Killing and the Psychology of Genocide* (New York: Basic, 1986); Annas and Grodin, ed., *The Nazi Doctors and the Nuremberg Code.*

15. Recent accounts of Wallenberg's extraordinary intervention and subsequent tragic disappearance include John Bierman, *Righteous Gentile: The Story of Raoul Wallenberg, Missing Hero of the Holocaust* (London: Penguin, 1995); and Sharon Linnen, *Raoul Wallenberg: The Man Who Stopped Death* (Philadelphia: Jewish Publication Society, 1993).

PNINA LAHAV

"Who Is a Jew":
A Tale of Fathers and Daughters

Two JEWISH MEN fathered daughters and wished them to be raised as "Jews." I have put "Jews" in quotation marks because, as we will come to see, these men, born and raised in different countries, also differed quite radically in their conception of Jewishness. Yet the men also had several important, and related, things in common—first, they were both married to non-Jewish women; second, they were committed to their own Jewish identity; third, their notion of who is a Jew was not based on a Halachic definition of who is a Jew. The two fathers had yet another important thing in common: for different reasons, they both enlisted the help of the legal system in their crusade to define and raise their daughters as Jews. One father, Benjamin Shalit, went to the High Court of Justice in 1968 in Israel. The other father, Maury Klein, went to a family court in 1996 in North Carolina, U.S.A. In the essay that follows, I explore the response of the Israeli and American legal systems to the fathers' insistence on the Jewish identity of their daughters; I then draw on the contrast between the two approaches in order to offer some thoughts about the present controversy of "who is a Jew."[1]

I

Benjamin Shalit, born and raised in Israel, was an army officer. His wife, Anne, was not Jewish, but when they were married (by

Pnina Lahav

civil marriage, outside of Israel), she decided to follow Benjamin to his native land and agreed to raise their children as Jews. In several ways, the Shalits were typical of modern secular Israelis of the 1960s. They were atheists who felt that religion should have no place in their private lives; they were also committed Zionists, who believed that in the state of Israel Jews no longer needed religion in order to foster a sense of authentic national and ethnic identity. In Israel, they believed, the "old" religion had been replaced by Zionism, by the revived Hebrew language, by the study of Hebrew literature, Jewish music, and Jewish history, and by the communal celebration of national (and Jewish) holidays (from Rosh Hashanah to Hanukkah to Passover)—in short, by the developing Israeli culture, imbued by the themes of the sovereign Jewish people who had been restored to its own land. For Shalit, then, being Jewish meant being an Israeli Zionist, and modern national identity replaced the premodern religious one in determining who is a Jew.

Yet in the state of Israel, the official criteria for determining Jewish identity is a complex mix of citizenship, religion, and nationality. So when daughter Galya was born, and Shalit came to the Population Registrar to register her as an Israeli citizen, he was introduced into a system that divided identity into two categories: nationality and religion. Every Israeli citizen, he learned, was classified twice, once on the basis of his or her religious affiliation and the second time on the basis of his or her nationality. The clerk at the Registrar observed that since the baby was not born of a Jewish mother, she was not halachically Jewish, but Shalit did not object to writing "no religion" in the blank space provided for that category. When the clerk, however, next observed that because the religious affiliation of the child was not Jewish, she could not be considered a member of the Jewish people, and that therefore the blank space for nationality would have to remain empty, Shalit was enraged. He insisted that the nationality of his daughter was Jewish. If need be, he was prepared to compromise, and write "Hebrew" or "Israeli," but he would not hear of leaving the space empty. He meant for his daughter's national identity to be Jewish, in the sense of being an Israeli

Zionist, and he experienced any official denial of his daughter's Jewishness as an affront to his dignity. He felt that the state was robbing her of the identity that was hers by right. This is why he petitioned the High Court of Justice, thereby precipitating one of the most blistering episodes in Israeli legal history.

Israel's High Court of Justice was not very happy about the need to decide "who is a Jew." For that reason Chief Justice Simon Agranat offered the government a compromise solution whereby the Court would not have to address the issue. He suggested to the Attorney General (Meir Shamgar, who later joined the Court and was promoted to the Chief Justiceship) that the Knesset amend the Population Registry Law and drop the category of "nationality," thereby leaving only the category of religion. Those applying for citizenship would have to indicate their religion, but not their nationality. This change of procedure might spare people in Shalit's situation (or at least some of them) the indignity that Shalit himself had been made to suffer.

But Agranat's proposal faced formidable opposition. For the religious parties (at that time represented in the Knesset by the National Religious Party and Agudat Yisrael), attaching the term 'Jewish' to one who does not meet the Halachic criteria was unacceptable. Nor was this group prepared to entertain the thought of creating a new category for nationality in the Jewish state, such as "Israeli" or "Hebrew" ("Torah and Israel," went the slogan, "are one and the same"). Moreover, the religious parties found an ally in the nationalist camp, whose spokesperson, Menachem Begin, objected to any split between religion and nationality. Since in 1968 members of both the religious and the nationalist parties were included within the government coalition, these members threatened a coalition crisis if the Agranat proposal were to be accepted. Unwilling to face such a crisis, the cabinet rejected the proposal, forcing the High Court of Justice to adjudicate the case and reach a decision.[2]

After deliberating for over a year, the Court held in favor of Shalit. It ruled that the Population Registrar, being merely a clerk employed by the state to obtain information, had no business inquiring into the question of the daughter's identity. The Registrar, the majority held, should have accepted the father's claim that his daughter was Jewish. However, the Court was bitterly divided: Shalit won by a margin of five to four. Moreover, each of the nine justices had written his own individual opinion, a response that thereby signaled the depth of Israeli disagreement about the question of "who is a Jew."

In the justices' written opinions, some responded to Shalit's arguments, while others were content to hide behind a technical and formalistic interpretation of the Registrar's bureaucratic duties. The justices of the majority tended to adopt a more formalistic stance, claiming that " 'who is a Jew' is not the question" and insisting that the only question was whether the law allowed the Registrar to inquire into Galya Shalit's Jewishness. These justices also acted with political savvy, striving to reach a result that would be modern and secular, while at the same time seemingly neutral and unobtrusive. For this reason, only the opinions of the dissenting justices contain more elaborate inquiries into the question of "who is a Jew."

These opinions can best be set forth by reviewing three of Shalit's arguments. The first argument was historical and invoked the evil of Nazism and the lessons Israel should learn from the most traumatic event in twentieth-century Jewish history— the Holocaust. Nazism exposed the ugly face of racism. In their zeal to purify the Aryan race of Jewish blood, the Nazis resorted to a biological criterion by which to determine who was a Jew. Their infamous Nuremberg Laws declared the Third Reich to be "thoroughly convinced by the knowledge that the purity of German blood is essential for the further existence of the German people" and provided an intricate system by which a person who has had two Jewish grandparents would be classified as Jewish. Shalit argued that the Halachic rule of "who is a Jew," which classifies persons as Jewish if their mother was Jewish, was similar to the Nazi laws. Israel, he argued, should eschew any law which even faintly resembles a racist notion that people's identity can be predetermined on the basis of biological descent.

Shalit's second argument also invoked history, but focused on one of the most exhilarating events of twentieth-century Jewish history—the establishment of the state of Israel. The founding of a Jewish state and the triumph of Zionism meant the return of the Jewish people to history. From now on, Jews were to be like any other nation—a people with a state to call their own. Just like the English have England and the French have France, so the Israelis have Israel. And just like in modern England or France an English or French atheist is still English or French, so in the modern Jewish state is Shalit's daughter Jewish (in the national, not the religious sense), regardless of her mother's religious affiliation. Shalit argued that the fact that in Israel one term designates both nationality and religion is merely the result of the passage of the Jewish people from exile to statehood, from tradition to modernity. Israel should either coin another term for nationality (Hebrew, Israeli) or learn to live with a term (Jewish) which allows for multiple interpretations.

Shalit's third argument was psychological and rested on notions of equality. An adherence to the Halachic rule, he claimed, would deny him, as both a man and a father, the dignity of transmitting his identity to his daughter. Furthermore, such a rejection of the father's identity would also nurture feelings of inferiority in the child. She would grow up among Jewish children, speaking their language and sharing their culture, but would be marked as different, would not be as "fully Jewish" as the others.

How did the dissenting justices counter Shalit's arguments? The first argument, that the Halachic rule was painfully similar to the Nuremberg laws, met with two responses. Chief Justice Agranat conceded that indeed there was an unhappy similarity between the two, as both relied on a biological or ethnic component. But the fact that two relied on a similar biological criterion, said Agranat, did not necessarily mean that condemning the one should lead to discarding the other. The Nuremberg Laws were based on a depraved, discriminatory policy designed to solidify a hierarchy of superior and inferior races. Not so the Halacha; its choice of a biological criterion (a Jewish mother) was meant to prevent the extinction of the Jewish people. Justice Silberg strengthened this position. The Halacha, he said, has no room for racism: "Judaism knows not the conception of racial inferiority and is not concerned with racial purity. All Judaism requires of the non-Jew is conversion. "A convert becomes a son of the Jewish people . . . even if he is a descendant of Blacks or Native Indians."

Both Agranat and Silberg's arguments persuasively reject the notion of the kinship between the Nuremberg Laws and the Halacha. However, what remained unarticulated was a related issue: the fingerprints of the Holocaust on the present understanding of who is Jewish. This aspect was most forcefully recognized in one of the first statutes passed by the state of Israel, the Law of Return. The law, which until the aftermath of the Shalit case did not contain a definition of who is Jewish, did open the gates of Israel to all Jews, including those who did not meet Halachic criteria. The state thus implicitly recognized that after the Holocaust, the definition of "who is a Jew" does lend itself to multiple interpretations, and that justice required the broadening of the definition beyond the Halachic one.

The psychological argument, that both father and daughter would suffer indignities and discrimination as a result of the denial of a paternally transmitted line of Jewish identity, proved a much more difficult problem to resolve. Chief Justice Agranat simply conceded that denial of Shalit's petition would indeed result in psychological harm to the child(ren): "The refusal to register . . . as Jewish . . . the child of the Jewish father may breed feelings of unjust discrimination vis-à-vis the child of the Jewish mother and . . . create feelings of inferiority in relation to his status in the Jewish-Israeli society, where he has integrated from the secular-social-political perspectives."

Justice Silberg, however, decided that the best defense was an offense, and pointed a blaming finger at the parents: "The children of the petitioner . . . are poor, lovely non-Jewish children, who did not get an entry ticket to the Jewish nation because of the stubborn opposition of their parents." It is interesting that retired Prime Minister David Ben Gurion, Israel's founding father, agreed with Chief Justice Agranat's assessment, and in a newspaper article opined that a child born of an Israeli-Jewish father should be entitled to inherit his identity. However, Prime

Minister Golda Meir joined Justice Silberg in blaming the mother: had she converted to Judaism, the entire problem would have never arisen.

There remained the Secular-Zionist argument. To the notion that there could be two separate systems for determining Jewish identity—one nationalistic, the other religious—adherents to the Halachic religious definition responded by asserting that such a division would carry enormous social cost. It might split the Jewish people and create two camps: on the one hand, orthodox men and women who remain loyal to tradition, and on the other hand the non-orthodox who prefer modernity. This argument, the threat to the unity of the Jewish people, has been the quintessential argument used against any deviation from the Orthodox way. It has served both to warn against secularization (for example, the introduction of civil marriages or civil divorce) and against the recognition of pluralism within Judaism (for example, the recognition of the conservative and reform religious movements).

Indeed, the Justices of the dissent seized this argument and tried to turn it into a powerful weapon against father and daughter. Chief Justice Agranat went as far as saying that the split would have far-reaching consequences on Diaspora Jewry, and that the American Jewish Community would certainly see any such split as counterproductive and harmful to the interests of Jewish solidarity and unity. Yet, ironically, in the name of unity the dissenting justices accepted a split in the family (father Jewish, daughter non-Jewish) in order to avoid the potential split of the Jewish people at large.[3]

When the decision in the Shalit case was announced, instructing the Registrar to register Galya Shalit as Jewish, Israeli public opinion, which was decidedly secular at the time, was buoyed. The decision was seen by secularists as a victory for Zionism's enlightened and pluralistic spirit and as a defeat to clericalism. But the majority Justices did not have much time to bask in their newfound glory. Within weeks the Knesset amended the law, which has since read: "A Jew is a person who was born of a Jewish woman or who has converted."[4] It is clear that in Israel a Jewish father cannot officially transmit his identity to his daughter if her mother is not, or does not become, Jewish.

II

The case of Maury Klein, the second father, took place in a cultural system guided by different criteria for determining Jewish identity. Importantly, the United States differs from Israel in construing the alignment between citizenship, religion, and nationality. First, since religious affiliation falls within the province of personal autonomy, citizens make no official indication of their affiliation. Hence religion in no way determines nationality. Second, citizenship is equated with nationality: all American citizens are considered to possess American nationality. Emphasizing personal autonomy rather than the claims of the collective, the American court used different criteria to ascertain the Jewish identity of the daughter than did its Israeli predecessor.

The background of the case has the following elements. Klein, an American Jew from North Carolina, fathered a daughter from a non-Jewish mother. The couple (who were not married) agreed in advance that their child would be raised as a Jew. Here is a major difference between the Israeli Shalit and the American Klein. In one case, Shalit did not care for religion. For him "Jewish" was a matter of nationality. In the other case, it is likely that Klein did not see Jewishness as a matter of nationality but rather as a matter of religion. He wanted his daughter to grow up Jewish religiously: to go to Jewish Sunday schools, to be active in the life of the local Jewish community, to attend services in the synagogue, and to observe the Jewish holidays—in short, to grow up as an American Jew. While Shalit chose to interpret Jewish as pertaining to nation, Klein chose to interpret Jewish as pertaining to religion—yet religion as defined by the religiously liberal Reform Jewish movement. So despite their differences, Shalit and Klein had in common that they were both children of modernity; both rejected the orthodox definition of being Jewish. Thus both of their chosen forms of identity, however different from each other, shared the common denominator of rejecting, and being rejected by, Jewish Orthodoxy.

Klein's insistence on the Jewish identity of his daughter came before an American court of law in the following way. After his daughter was born, his relations with her mother took a turn for the worse and the two separated. The mother then refused to abide by the original agreement to raise the daughter exclusively as a Jew. She, a Christian, now wished her daughter to be raised as both Jew *and* Christian. As a result, the daughter who had thus far been raised as Jewish became bewildered and confused. Klein decided to go to court to ask for a re-evaluation of the custody agreement and to have the original agreement as to the child's religious identity enforced. Here then is another feature Klein shared with Shalit: he felt strongly enough about his daughter's Jewish identity that he was ready to go to court to fight for his— and her—rights. These two fathers did not conform to the general stereotype of the Jewish man who compromises his religious identity by associating with non-Jewish women. The prediction that the (Jewish) father will abandon his tradition and assimilate into the culture of his (non-Jewish) companion did not prove true in either of these cases. Both men continued to place a high premium on their Jewish identity and, according to their conviction of what it meant to be Jewish, they were determined to transmit this identity to their daughters.

The court, applying the doctrine of the "best interests of the child," heard testimony concerning the daughter's sense of identity. It concluded that the child's sense of Jewish identity had been solid, meaningful, and beneficial and that, given the original agreement and given the positive role that Judaism had played in the child's life, she should continue to be raised as Jewish. Here is what the Court found:

> [t]hat Ashley has had substantial involvement with the Judea Reform Synagogue . . . and the Jewish community since birth, and the self-concept she derives from this association is vital to her mental well-being . . . [and] that Ashley has had a positive sense of identity as a Jew . . . and interference with her worship as a Jew and fellowship with other Jews will adversely impact her emotional well-being. . . .[5]

What is interesting about this opinion in relation to the Israeli court's approach to the question of "who is a Jew" is the total absence of the orthodox point of view. The question of Jewish identity, which in this case was much more substantive than in Shalit, because it dealt with actual practice rather than with official labels, was resolved without any reference to the Halachic rule. It did not occur to Klein or to the Court to base their assessment of his daughter's Jewish identity on the fact that her mother was a non-Jew. What interested them, and what they considered to be dispositive under the circumstances, was the child's sense of identity. If she felt Jewish, and was accepted as such by her Reform Jewish community, she was Jewish.

Herein lies the fundamental difference between the two legal cultures. In Israel, the Jewish state, the definition of who is a Jew is imposed from above and is crystallized in a legal definition that is at variance with that subscribed to by the majority of the Jewish people in the world today. It is this variance which made the Knesset formulate the Law of Return in such a way that men and women who consider themselves as Jews, or are considered as such by others (the Nuremberg Laws again come to mind), but who might fail to meet the criteria set by the Halachic definition, will still be granted the right of return—i.e., to immigrate to Israel and be eligible for Israeli citizenship. In so doing, the Knesset implicitly conceded that, in the wake of the Holocaust, one is required to supplement the Halachic definition of "who is a Jew." Moreover, the Knesset decision also signaled that if Israel wishes to provide a haven for persecuted Jews, it must turn not to the Halachic but, ironically, to the Gentile perception of who is a Jew. The litigation about "who is a Jew," the sense of crisis that any decision by the Israeli courts brings about, and the political maneuvering which accompanies the public debate, are all due to the fact that in Israel the government makes it its business to ask people about their national and religious affiliations.

In contrast, in the United States the legal definition of "who is a Jew" does not come from the top down but rather issues out of how an individual (or, in this case, the father of a child) wishes to define him or herself as a Jew. American courts defer to the principle of personal autonomy. It is for this reason that from the perspective of an American family court, a father is free to transmit his religious identity to his child, unless that identity undermines the best interests of that child. Larger issues, such as what is good "for the people" or "for the state," do not enter the fray as valid considerations.

Contrary to the claims of many, this approach to defining "who is a Jew," at least in cases of this sort, strengthens rather than weakens the individual Jew's commitment to the Jewish community. Maury Klein has remained a loyal member of the Jewish people. He has proven so by fighting for his right to transmit his identity to his daughter. Presumably, she will honor that commitment because she experiences his deep commitment. Most importantly, at this stage in her life, his daughter is not told by the state that she is "other," that she is not as truly Jewish as her father. The state thus has allowed her to nurture the parental bond rather than question its validity, and by doing so has promoted a situation that will likely go a long way toward solidifying a positive sense of religious self.

Of the three arguments presented in the Shalit case—the impact of the Holocaust, the sense of discrimination and inferiority that would stigmatize father and daughter, and the reconstituted Jewish (Israeli) nationhood—only the last two appeared to have been implicitly echoed in the Klein opinion. Equality between father and mother in the right to transmit identity to the child and the best interests of the child as trumping age-old formulae (modernity overriding tradition) are certainly a part of the Klein opinion. To be sure, the mother's right to transmit her Christian identity to her daughter was rejected on the basis of the original agreement plus the psychological confusion that an introduction of a new identity at this stage caused; it is not unlikely that in other circumstances the Court would have recognized a bireligious identity as compatible with the best interests of the child.

The question of the meaning of the reconstituted Jewish nation is slightly more tricky. In one sense, the North Carolina Court could not have been interested in the question of the meaning of Jewish nationhood after the creation of the state of

Israel. And yet, in another sense, Jewish pluralism since emancipation has been implicitly recognized by the Court, along with one's right to define oneself as Jewish without meeting orthodox criteria. More specifically, by assuming that the Reform movement belonged under the Jewish umbrella, the Court implicitly recognized it as a member of the Jewish family. The North Carolina Court thus endorsed the notion that there are a plurality of ways of defining who is a Jew.

There is a lesson to be learned from these two cases for the current controversy raging in both Israel and the Diaspora Jewish communities about the question of "who is a Jew." The American experience shows that Jewish pluralism in the United States in no way harms the strong sense of belonging and co-existence.[6] The threatened split has not materialized. It may well be a straw threat, designed to preserve the monopoly of one faction, rather than to maintain the cohesion of the people. In any case, one possible solution to the "who is a Jew" controversy would be a revival of the Agranat proposal, this time in a more expansive form. Amending both the Law of the Population Registrar and the Law of Return so as to omit the categories of nationality and religion would render the entire conflict largely irrelevant. Thereby, the energies that are presently invested in this issue could be freed to focus on the more urgent question of the transmission of Jewish heritage to the next generation.

Yet the question is really not new. Questions of inclusion and exclusion, where and how to draw the boundaries, have always accompanied the Jewish quest for identity. In his book *Sages and Dreamers*, Elie Wiesel deals with the question of exclusion and inclusion in terms of the "stranger," the "Other." He makes a strong case for allowing the individual—for him, the stranger; in the context of this essay, the non-Halachic Jew—the autonomy to define who and what they are. Moreover, one infringes on this autonomy at considerable ethical cost:

> In general, Jewish tradition insists on every person's right to be different. Having been a stranger in Pharaoh's Egypt, one is therefore compelled to respect all strangers for what they are. One must

not seek to change their ways or views: One must not try to make them resemble oneself. Every human being reflects the image of God, who has no image: mine is neither purer nor holier than yours. Truth is one but the paths leading to it are many. In the eyes of the Father, all His children are worthy of His love. In my eyes, the Other is the center of the universe, just as any Other ought to be in his or her eyes. Only in totalitarian regimes do all citizens look and speak and act alike.[7]

NOTES

1. A clarification of the title: does it make a difference that it is *daughters* whose identity is at issue in these cases? Does a son's situation differ in any crucial way? Indeed, the *Halacha* (Jewish law) treats daughters and sons equally: neither is considered Jewish if the mother was not Jewish by birth or conversion.

Yet several reasons lead me to highlight the situation of fathers and daughters. First, the non-Jewish son of a Jewish father has a recourse if he wishes to transmit to his children his Jewish identity: he can marry a Jewish woman and his children will be Jewish, in keeping with his and his father's heritage. This solution is not available to his sister. Even if she marries a Jewish man, their children will still be non-Jews according to the Halacha. The daughter thus finds herself doubly excluded by the Halachic rule: she is different from her father in the eyes of the Halacha, because he had a Jewish mother and she did not, and she is different from her brother because he can marry a Jewish woman and can thereby have a role in fostering Jewish identity, whereas if she were to marry a Jewish man she would still be denied that role. By comparison to her (Jewish) grandmother and her (Jewish) sister-in-law she is "the other," the non-Jew. She can only amend this situation by conversion, thereby raising a fence between herself and her mother. The difference between the non-Jewish daughter and her (Jewish) grandmother and sister-in-law stems not from a difference in the practice of Judaism, which they presumably all share, but rather from the immutable characteristic rooted in biological descent. Fathers and daughters thus face a mountain much taller than that of fathers and sons.

2. My discussion of the Shalit case relies on my previous analysis that appeared in Pnina Lahav, *Judgment in Jerusalem: Chief Justice Simon Agranat and the Zionist Century* (Berkeley: University of California Press, 1997). Additionally, my review of the case relies primarily on the arguments by the dissenting justices, who were more willing to confront the substantive question of "who is a Jew."

3. The split in the family did indeed come to pass after the Knesset had overruled the Shalit Court by amending the law. Whereas both Galya and her brother Oren as the result of the Court order were registered as possessing Jewish nationality, their younger brother Tomer, born after the amendment had come into effect, was registered as without nationality.

4. See A. Rubinstein, *Who is a non-Jew? Haaretz,* Aug. 12, 1997. It is this provision that the Netanyahu government wishes presently to amend so as to deny reform and conservative conversions a legal validity.

5. MacLagan *v.* Klein, 123 N.C.App. 557, 564 (1996).

6. For an exploration of the differences between the American and Israeli Jewish communities, see C. L. Liebman and S. M. Cohen, *Two Worlds of Judaism* (New Haven, Conn.: Yale University Press, 1990).

7. Elie Wiesel, *Sages and Dreamers* (New York: Summit, 1991).

JOSHUA LEDERBERG

Literacy, the Internet, and the Global Village

ELECTRONIC COMMUNICATION HAS properly been compared with the invention of the printing press as a quantum leap in the reticulation of the human community. We cannot exclude the telephone, telegraph, and telefax as elements in that evolution, but they related to interpersonal correspondence, point-to-point exchanges among identified individuals. The broadcast media—radio and television—have dominated dissemination of information, advertising, and propaganda, but these have lent themselves to exploitation as natural monopolies in the use of the electromagnetic spectrum and have remained mainly in the hands of governments and foci of wealth and power.

The exponential growth of the internet, and particularly of the World Wide Web, has given us new media in the hands of the many: an extraordinary democratization of access to the minds of any who care to look. Beyond e-mail, there are now thousands if not millions of sites where data files of information are posted, and are accessed electronically at the push of a button. Everyman can be his own publisher, his own librarian, his own critic, his own browser. We can just begin to foresee the implications of this liberty for political and economic life, and in popular culture. For a time, I had hoped that e-mail would supplant the telephone, and encourage the return of literacy in personal discourse.[1] I had not counted on the rapidity of the development of the electronic chips that have brought super-computers (we call them PCs) into every home—and with that the use of the internet for graphics, movies, and voice, so that unadorned text is once again rare. Nevertheless, the bulk of intellectual content remains literary: we properly speak of literature as our legacy.

Electronic storage has come just in time, as our libraries have become overstuffed with tons of paper, much of it crumbling, and journals have escalated to unaffordable prices. Online bibliographic services for citations and abstracts give us a taste of the convenience and thoroughness of what might be available to us as full texts of all contemporary scholarly production, and eventually of what has accumulated in the archives. This move toward extraordinary individual access is already under way, as a do-it-yourself program: pick any topic and you will find many postings of texts, pictures, and movies—often overlapping what has appeared in more traditional formats.

One search engine on my laptop, for example, returned a list of 1,056 documents mentioning Elie Wiesel (and 24,915 for "holocaust"). Most of these documents are not likely his own books, but any manner of news, book reviews, biography, and critical commentary about Wiesel. Much of his personality will be revealed in innumerable interviews, and many a photograph.[2] But the web is an open forum containing unfiltered raw material and consequently includes under this listing a slanderous denunciation from Islamic Radio (Stockholm). On scientific and medical topics, the information available runs the gamut from the latest pictures of Mars, courtesy of NASA, and the abstracts of current medical literature on MEDLINE, to the peddling of snake oil remedies and UFOs.

On the technological front, therefore, we have ample proof of the means to displace the world's libraries and bring its content into every office, classroom, study, kitchen, and bedroom. We are a long way from structuring the economic, legal, and sociological framework to enable this to be an advance of civilization. Some of the root conflicts that question the internet's civilizing worth are exhibited in the ongoing controversy over traffic in pornography. We do not doubt why autocratic regimes have much to fear from liberating media of communication; at the same time we will argue about the limits of free speech in the dissemination of hate propaganda and of recipes for terrorism. It is next to impossible to contain any of that exuberance or excess within national boundaries, boundaries which are hardly recognized either by the "electromagnetic ether" or by a globalized economy. Burn all the books in one country, and they can be supplanted by a few minutes of electronic data retransmission across the border.

Most creative works—fiction, poetry, drama, music, arts—are financed by royalties from the audiences and enjoyers of the products, sometimes supplemented by subventions from the state and private philanthropies. Scholarly communications have a different base. Their authors are affiliated with institutions for teaching and research, and sales of intellectual products, some textbooks aside, play a small part in the academic economy. The currency of reward is recognition, and this is convertible into preferment for jobs, grants, and status. Far from demanding royalties, the authors are sometimes willing to pay page charges for the privilege of publication. They, and their institutions, already bear their own expenses in mounting their material on the web. This could already be described as a worldwide vanity press.

In this essay, then, I focus on scholarly communications: science and letters, what have been the grist of journals and books, of academic publication. The new media now pose severe challenges to what has passed for earned and attributed authority in the worlds of learning.

On the one hand, scholars will not forego the universal library; on the other, there are mounting frictions and burden-passing. For example, Virginia Polytechnic University recently announced a program of web-mounting all of its masters theses and doctoral dissertations.[3] This provoked a storm of complaint from publishers, and instant anxiety for the authors. The existing print journals would not accept such texts as original publications, rejecting them as candidates for their print versions. The battle is joined concerning which party holds the keys to authenticity, regard, dignity, and the keys to acceptance for academic reward.

This is not just a battle of the pundits: it touches on the legiti-

Joshua Lederberg

macy of expertise in every sphere, including the courts. The battle embraces the due process of peer review, the procedure by which personal skills and expertise are subject to the organized skepticism of the academic community. (My entire discourse is plainly rooted in experimental science—and has a strongly pre-postmodern flavor.) The task of the academic community is to plan the succession to the editorial boards and critical discourse of conventional academic literature, and adapt these review procedures to the electronic marketplace.

In principle, this task might entail a simple transposition of standard procedures; and some commercial and university presses are starting to float electronic journals with just those features. But we need a critical apparatus not only for the first offerings of these media, but for all the rest that appears on the web as well. It remains to be seen whether the publishers can find pricing schedules that will appear more reasonable than the thousand-dollar and up subscriptions that pertained to some of the specialty journals put on the market in recent years. Now there is the potential for effective competition from the academically motivated learned societies and from the source institutions—like Virginia Tech—who could in principle convert their own postings to a peer-reviewed roster to match any external overseers, if not to use them.

Meanwhile, the commercial publishers hold copyrights to all the historic material, and many legal and policy battles are in the offing over definitions and practice of "fair use" exceptions. Given the high level of public investment in the conduct of the research whose outcome is embedded in the copyrighted reports, there will be growing resentment over the conversion of the invaluable research results to the exclusive private interest of the publisher. Of course some balance must be struck here, and incentives must not be summarily withdrawn for the value provided by those publishers. The authors, the scientists, have not yet found the means to organize behind their own interests in maximizing the dissemination of their wares, in fact at the lowest feasible price. This is particularly poignant for scholars in poorer countries.

An abundance of further problems remain: notably, who takes responsibility for the accountability of published claims and the authenticity of the texts and authorship? The technical means exist, the equivalent of watermarks and signatures, by which to assure that neither a text nor its authorship has been tampered with. But this presupposes a durable archive, a locus of responsibility for preserving the heritage of material which it is no longer feasible to store as marks on paper, if only for the impossibility of efficient search and retrieval. The technical problems are formidable—less the durability of the physical item like a CD platter than the unlikelihood that the machines and software to read the incunabula will remain available over the decades and centuries. To avert great losses will require institutions for the maintenance of obsolete machines: try to find a vacuum tube for a 1930 radio today! This problem of maintenance becomes ever more difficult to envisage with the rapidly increasing density and sophistication of the storage systems. An alternative or backup will be the refreshment of storage every decade or two, whilst media are in transition. (Now is a good time to be sure all of your 5-inch floppy disks have been converted to the 3.5-inch format, and perhaps to the latest CDs as well. Ten years from now, you will have to resort to the antique shops; in twenty, the specialty museums.) Some students in computer science recently asked me to exhume some old "IBM" punch cards—they had never seen them. And I would be hard put now to find a machine that could read them.

We have to think hard about who pays for this preservation and restoration; and how to organize the triage that will define what is left of our heritage. There will be great expectations that someone else is doing it.

As we observe the expansion of the global electronic library, we can foresee that it becomes our principal resource for information and lies. Many people have spoken how electronic media could lend greater efficiency to educational processes, but that just scratches the surface. For one matter, vocabulary in language learning should become largely superfluous: programs exist today that could furnish an instantaneous word-for-word transliteration of texts. With that facility, a very different kind of learning becomes important for students, for everyone, interested in partaking of different literate cultures. Automatic translations of unpredictable quality and the subject matter for many jokes are not far behind. But such translations are dangerous in the hands of the illiterate, or wrongly lettered user. The well-educated will be those who have experienced many such translations and learned what to take seriously, where are the meaningful ambiguities, where the ludicrous errors.

The same applies to the overall abundance of purported knowledge on the net. "Reading the web," developing critical judgment about assessing the claims made, learning how to access critical sources and further opinions, should become the central goal of modern education. This is *explication de texte* in a new form, probably the most relevant preparation for the new age.

The task of teachers is to participate in the critical discourse that can enlarge the meaning, exemplify the process, and enhance the dignity of the rich palette before us. Not every generation will use the same primary medium, but the message for humanity may echo timelessly round this planet and beyond.[4] Computer maven or not, with 1,056 (probably many more) references on the web, Elie Wiesel is already a pioneer in that process. And his festschrift is rewritten day-by-day.

NOTES

1. J. Lederberg, "Digital Communications and the Conduct of Science: The New Literacy." *Proceedings of the IEEE* 66, no. 11 (1978): 1314–19.

2. Try URL=: http://www.achievement.org

3. http://www.ndltd.org

4. J. Lederberg, "Options for the Future: Symposium on Electronic Publishing, ICSU/UNESCO, February 22, 1996, Paris," *D-Lib Magazine,* May 1996, ISSN 1082–9873. URL=: http://www.dlib.org

Concluding Meditations

SHLOMO BREZNITZ

The Holocaust Experience as
a State of Mind

WHAT IS A STATE OF MIND?

A state of mind (SOM) can be defined as *the thoughts, images, and feelings produced by a particular situation.* While some aspects of a SOM are determined by prior experiences in similar circumstances, others are the direct outcome of the nature of the situation itself. It is this second determinant of a SOM that ensures a certain amount of universality in the way different people experience similar situations.

This is related to Levi-Strauss' notion that there is a "repertory of ideas," pointing towards a certain form of intellectual determinism common to societies and individuals.[1] In the case of a SOM, however, the commonality is seen as the outcome of the properties of the life situations themselves.

It thus should not come as a surprise that many situations provide the basis for shared symbols and metaphors. As such they represent a prototypical SOM. Research in comparative symbolism indicates that often similar symbols represent similar things in many different cultures that did not come into contact with each other. While Jung[2] saw this as a proof of his notions of "collective unconscious" and "archetypes," I wish to argue that situation-based shared SOMs lead to the same result without the need to postulate such mystical concepts.

Consider, for instance, the SOM produced by watching a sunrise. Independent of a person's background, sophistication, or personality, the situation evokes thoughts and images of a new beginning and optimism. Consequently, the chances that sunrise will symbolize rebirth are high in any culture, irrespective of its degree of isolation from other cultures. The point is that *while watching a sunrise it is almost impossible not to think of a fresh start.*

The capacity of the human mind for mental representation in the absence of external stimuli makes it possible for us to experience such a SOM, although perhaps in a weaker form,[3] by looking at a picture of a sunrise or just by reading about it. Such vicarious situations significantly enlarge the relevant domain and frequency of experience of any SOM.

In addition, we should take into consideration that many other situations have the capacity to evoke essentially the same SOM, namely, that of a fresh start. The list is a long one: New Year's Eve, birthdays, starting a school year, moving to a new house or a new job, buying a new dress, changing a hair style, beginning a new relationship, or even ending an unsatisfactory old one are just a few possibilities. These situations are very different, and yet they share some common elements powerful enough to potentially produce a similar SOM.

The capacity of different situations to evoke the same or very similar SOMs provides the basis for *empathy.* Through it we can appreciate the other's ordeal without the need of having experienced his or her situation directly. *It is sufficient to have experience with other situations that produce the same SOM in order to empathize with the other's feelings.*

For the same reason, namely, that different situations lead to similar SOMs, they have a large potential to enrich our lives, since they seriously reduce the difference between the extreme and the ordinary. It is, in fact, possible to some extent to experience the first within the second. But there is also a question whether the empathy that allows one to experience the same SOM has limits, whether there are some experiences that *can be comprehended solely by those who have lived through them?* Specifically, *can people who are not survivors of the Holocaust comprehend the SOM of those who are?*

Within the context of our present analysis, this issue can be rephrased in the following form: What SOM does the Holocaust consist of? Are there other situations or experiences that evoke the same, or a highly similar, SOM? If yes, what are they? And if not, what are the psychological implications of such an entirely unique and isolated experience?

For the survivors, the Holocaust as a SOM clearly defies any attempts at explication, but feelings of a *total and irretrievable loss* certainly constitute one of its most basic elements: loss of loved ones, of home and family, of freedom, of personal dignity, and of the sense of what is normal. The victims' personal and social world, as well as their cultural world, all vanished forever.

Another salient element was the sense of *helplessness in the face of total terror*. All of continental Europe, that seemingly friendly and civilized part of the globe, suddenly became one large killing field. In it, the powerful armies of evil were engaged in mercilessly hunting the helpless Jew. *Being singled out as the prey* was thus yet another core feature of this SOM. So were feelings of *loneliness*. The world became a perennial threat, and friends of yesterday often turned to enemies or to uncaring spectators. With dear ones gone, we were virtually alone.

For those who did not experience the Holocaust directly, i.e., for the overwhelming majority of people, the SOM that reference to the Holocaust evokes is, of course, dramatically different. While to some extent the non-survivor SOM obviously includes the elements described above, they are not embedded within a personal context. Instead, *abstract knowledge* occupies a much more prominent position. While this SOM may sometimes include stories told by survivors, most of it consists of information from the public domain.

It is in this setting that terms such as "Holocaust," "six million," "final solution," "Zyklon B," "transport," "selection," "crematorium," the names of the "concentration camps" (Auschwitz-Birkenau, Bergen-Belsen, Dachau, Majdanek, and others) circulate and acquire their emotional potency. So do the images of the "Muselman," of the little boy with the sad dark eyes behind the barbed wire, and of course the heaps of shoes and human bones.

The list of salient terms and images is not a long one. This should not come as a surprise in view of the constant leveling and sharpening processes[4] taking place within the domain of collective memory. Consequently, by virtue of its limited size and variation, the content of this SOM is shared by many people.

The difference between the SOMs of those who experienced the Holocaust directly and those whose experience is indirect[5] parallels the psychological distinction between *episodic memory* and *semantic memory*.[6] The first denotes facts that are encoded in respect to the person, with specific time and place of occurrence, whereas semantic knowledge is encoded primarily in relation to other knowledge, with few or no individual markers. The two types of memories are apparently stored in the brain separately, as witnessed by studies of amnesic patients who lost most or all of their episodic memory while their semantic memory remained intact. The importance of this distinction to our analysis is directly related to the role of retrieval cues in evoking a SOM.

The question whether non-survivors can empathize with the SOM of Holocaust survivors can be answered affirmatively only if one of the following two conditions is fulfilled: a) if the relevant SOMs of the two groups are sufficiently similar; or b) if other, unrelated situations can evoke SOMs that are sufficiently similar to promote empathy with the Holocaust experience.

Starting with the first condition, even a superficial analysis leans overwhelmingly against similarity. The discrepancy between personal, episodic memory and semantically stored facts is too big to negotiate. For the survivor, the events and the emotions associated with them have clear stimulus properties, such as location, sounds, smells, none of which are even remotely related to common knowledge about the Holocaust. On the other hand, the abstract information about the Holocaust is by necessity of only secondary interest to the survivor. It was *his* concentration camp that mattered, *his* tattooed number, and *his* daily fears during selection. Moreover, the relatives lost were *his* relatives, and no national or historical perspective can ever change that.

The second condition is more complex, for there is no shortage of major personal loss experienced by humans everywhere.

Loss of loved ones, of freedom and of dignity, while generally experienced on an incomparably smaller scale, are frequent encounters for most of us; the slings and arrows of outrageous fortune and the natural shocks that flesh is heir to know few exceptions. Neither are we protected from feelings of helplessness and loneliness. To some extent, then, others can empathize with the ordeal of survivors. It is the second condition that is clearly crucial: abstract knowledge contributes little, but the stuff of life itself—the losses suffered and accumulated even during normal experience—can go some distance toward bridging the gap between the SOM of survivors and non-survivors.

This may explain the surprisingly powerful impact of more recent Holocaust memoirs. Why should these memoirs, published after so many others have already appeared, be read so avidly? The answer may lie in the difference in focus between the early and late memoirs. The earlier memoirs often chronicled extreme situations of all kinds. While clearly powerful, these situations— for example, the devastating dilemma of a mother forced to decide which child to try to save—were also overwhelming and were out of the reach of the experience and even the imagination of most readers. Recent memoirs often have a different focus and hence a different effect, chronicling what one might call more mundane situations of trauma: a child whose parents have disappeared, for instance. Recent memoirs thus focus on situations of loss and loneliness that are more likely within the orbit of a reader's experience and empathy. In today's world of frequent divorce, for instance, the loss of contact with a parent is not an unusual phenomenon.

And yet there is a problem. Can one disregard the difference of scale between the SOM of a survivor, on the one hand, and someone whose losses are the stuff of normal experience, on the other? While for a person bereaved of a child who died in an accident or from illness, the personal loss and sadness equals that suffered by victims of any cataclysmic event, not all losses are of such magnitude. If scale matters, and if the depth and intensity of the loss is one of a SOM's defining properties, then we can suggest that only individuals *who experienced major personal suffering are in the position to empathize with Holocaust survivors.* There are, it appears, limits to empathy; some SOMs are accessible almost solely to certain restricted experiences. Let us attempt to explicate some of the implications of a SOM with such limited access.

Put in an extreme form: What if the SOM of the Holocaust survivor could not be evoked by any person or situation ever? This will effectively mean an entirely *isolated domain* with no contact with anything else in life. To be sure, in this form the SOM of the survivor will be protected from attenuation and retain its purity. Such protection, however, is not without its costs—costs both personal and social. Not unlike what Jung termed a psychological "complex," the survivor SOM exists as an entity governed by internal rules of its own. The social costs are also great: by virtue of staying out of everyday life, the SOM loses its potential to impact human affairs. Once closed behind such an impenetrable curtain, the chances that the terrible lessons of the Holocaust will affect the general patterns of behavior are irretrievably lost.

ENTRIES AND EXITS

The modus operandi of any SOM consists of stimuli (situations) that evoke it and raise it to consciousness, and stimuli (situations) that serve as exit points. Unless the SOM is entirely isolated, the entries and the exits are its dynamic aspect, connecting the SOM to the rest of a person's experience. Moreover, *the various parameters of entry and exit have the capacity to shape a SOM over time.*

Stated differently, a particular SOM is significantly affected by the one that precedes as well as the one that follows it. In the ebb and flow of the stream of consciousness, elements from the immediate neighbors leak from both sides. In the case of the preceding SOM the leakage is due to persistence, whereas in the following SOM leakage occurs through anticipation. How does the notion of entries and exits bear on, or resist, the isolated SOM of the survivor?

THE HOLOCAUST SOM AS ABSORBING STATE

The lives of many of those who have been through the Holocaust are still dominated by their experience and will remain so for the rest of their days. For them the Holocaust is not something to dwell on to commemorate a specific day of remembrance, but rather a SOM that occupies a significant part of their days and nights. They do not wish it, but cannot avoid it. The specific SOM is so salient in their minds, and has so many entries, that almost any situation can eventually lead to it.

At this point it is necessary to make yet another distinction between types of human memory, namely *explicit* versus *implicit* memory. Explicit memory is memory of which we are aware; we know that we have learned something, and we can talk about what we have learned to others. (For this reason, some psychologists prefer to use the term "declarative memory.") Implicit memory is unconscious; we cannot talk directly about its contents. However, the contents of implicit memory can affect our behavior, as illustrated by memory of skills. Implicit memory appears to operate automatically and does not require deliberate attempts on the part of the person to memorize something.[7]

It is primarily through this automatic process that a person for whom a particular domain is highly salient finds him- or herself helpless vis-à-vis the frequent entries without awareness. By the time he or she realizes what has happened, it is too late. A smell, a melody, even perhaps just a movement of the hand, and one is again in Auschwitz. This is the stuff that obsessions are made of. This too is the texture of a post-traumatic stress disorder, so frequent among Holocaust survivors.

Entries to and exits from this SOM can happen to us several times a day without our awareness. Its emotional traces, however, may linger for a while. Thus, we may suddenly feel anxious or sad without understanding why. Or at night we may have a sudden urge to check whether all our family members, but particularly the children or the grandchildren, are safe in bed. These memories, residing beneath awareness, are omnipresent companions that will stay with us forever.

Certain streams of consciousness predictably and invariably lead to the same SOM, the end point of which is an absorbing state. In a milder, but more prevalent form, this type of process is well illustrated in the case of worrying.[8] When something weighs heavily on our mind we find ourselves returning to it again and again, often in spite of trying to forget it. There is no simple way to control our thoughts, and deliberate attempts to distract our mind from something which bothers us are often doomed to failure.

Is there a way to deliberately stop thinking about something? Can conscious effort effectively control unconscious automatic processes? These questions, usually the focus of psychotherapeutic theory, are of much wider relevance to all of us. Their analysis brings us to the issue of *exits.*

SOM EXITS

Whereas entries contaminate the Holocaust SOM by overusage, exits do so by promoting contact with unrelated mundane events. How should a visit to a Holocaust Museum end? Should the exit lead to the parking lot? If yes, what could be the psychological implications of the switch from Auschwitz to the search for the car? How about rushing to the next museum, or to the National Art Gallery? Or grabbing a sandwich?

Once again, like in the case of irrelevant entries, it appears that some exits are by necessity mixing the holy with the profane. Such mixtures, through anticipation, leak into the SOM itself, with the potential of polluting it beyond recognition. Some SOMs produce such a powerful emotional experience that one cannot switch them off in an arbitrary and abrupt manner.[9] When that happens for external reasons, one is often left with a stale taste of dissatisfaction. Since the Holocaust SOM does not offer any natural and smooth exits and transitions to the next SOM—in that sense it is clearly an absorbing state—the danger of irrelevant and abrupt ones is particularly great.

SOCIAL IMPLICATIONS: LANGUAGE DYNAMICS

Let us consider the word "Holocaust" itself. Its overriding relevance to the Holocaust makes it an obvious point of entry. It is sufficient for someone to be exposed to this word in order to evoke the SOM. For some time after it was coined, the word denoted the destruction of European Jewry, and nothing else. However, over the years, its usage became less exclusive. Thus, one could hear the word used for other major disasters and sufferings. Once that happened the word was cleared for a gradual but persistent downgrading.

The most extreme form of this devaluation of the word Holocaust that I encountered was when a sports commentator referred to one of the soccer teams as experiencing a "holocaust" on the field. The commentator was probably too naive to realize the importance of his utterance. By his unfortunate choice of a word he contributed to the *dilution and cheapening of the Holocaust experience,* and thus did a harmless game of soccer attain a foothold in the innermost sanctum of human evil.

The way we think and feel about some issues is to a great extent determined by the network of associations of key words in that domain. In such circumstances our disappointments and outrage are matched only by the naiveté of the hope to retain the purity of language. The process is invariably the same: *through overuse, and abuse, a word is eventually used up.* When that stage is reached, denotation becomes a prisoner of connotation. In other words, the meaning of the word is now determined primarily by the variety of contexts in which it is being used.

In some cases, there could have never been a realistic presumption that this would not happen. Take for instance the concept of "six million." Even just calling it a concept is misleading already. After all, the Holocaust experience could not expect to monopolize the language for its exclusive usage, although the purists among us might have wished just that: let nobody ever dare use the combination of "six million" in any other context! Nor, for that matter, words like "selection" or "final solution."

Although for some of us these words still have the potential for being an entry point to the Holocaust SOM, the awkward feeling they evoke when confronted outside that context is weakening, and it is only a matter of time when it will disappear altogether. Most people never even think about it anymore and cannot see the point. The chief source of difficulty resides in the usefulness of the words themselves. Unlike "Holocaust," which by its very essence prescribes low-frequency usage, the other words are simply needed too often, and adequate replacements are not easily available.

Words are building blocks that can be used in a variety of contexts. By contrast, some images are evoked exclusively in the setting in which they were first constructed. This property of selectivity depends primarily on the specificity of the image itself. When available, it may to some extent protect a SOM from the deleterious effects of unwarranted entries. Let me illustrate by creating a highly specific image of the number six million.

Imagine a great multitude of people forming a line, each given just one meter of space. The line starts in Jerusalem, leading from among the olive trees of the Judean hills down to the citrus groves of the Sharon, reaching the Mediterranean, entering the sea, passing by the islands of Cyprus and Crete, reaching the Peloponnesus, crossing all of ancient Greece, reentering the sea westward, emerging out near ancient Rome, this endless line of Jews, young and old, standing there, given just one meter each, turning now north to cross the Alps and reaching what was the German Reich, still compact, still packed, the line finally finding its way to Auschwitz, and there, impossible to believe, turns around and winds its way through bloody Europe all the way back to Jerusalem. The line has not formed a closed circle of people. Their number—six million.

Such an image communicates the enormity of that figure much more effectively than the abstract number itself. In addition, by virtue of being highly artificial, its exclusive usage is practically ensured. The above example also provides yet another major distinction between survivors and non-survivors. The minds of the survivors are filled with countless specific images taken directly from their episodic memory. The power of these images often rests in details that are beyond the reach of language.

SOCIAL IMPLICATIONS: COMMUNAL DYNAMICS

If many individuals share major elements of a particular SOM, communal dynamics set in. This is clearly the situation in respect to the Holocaust SOM in Israel. The mutuality of powerful emotions that can be triggered by similar entries ensures that the Holocaust experience occupies a prominent position on the national agenda. It was thus not surprising that the entire country was virtually spellbound by the long proceedings of the Eichman trial. The annual Holocaust Memorial Day casts a long shadow on the mood of the populace, and the publication of a new book or the airing of a new film bearing on the subject becomes the centerpiece of common interest.

This centrality of the Holocaust SOM makes it a tempting political instrument, and Holocaust-related imagery and language enter the political discourse. The protagonists on both sides of the national debate often use the so-called lessons learned by the Holocaust experience to advance their arguments. Given the intensity of the political schism in Israel—an intensity no doubt exacerbated by dwelling in the shadow of continuous civilian terror and security threats—such deliberate manipulation of the SOM further enhances its relevance to everyday life.

The enemies of Israel are well aware of this exceptional vulnerability and sometimes try exploiting it deliberately. This was carried to its extreme during the Gulf War. The following passage written at that time illustrates this vulnerability:

> Here is my problem: As I dwell on the fate of my family during those darkest days of Europe, Baghdad radio is boasting that Iraqi Scud missiles have turned Tel-Aviv into a "crematorium." That was their exact word, aired today, January 19, 1991. They could have phrased it differently, using any of a number of alternatives: devastation, misery, defeat, desert, wasteland, destruction, ruin, fall, havoc, or even fire or hell. But the word they chose, taken from the unholy vocabulary that dominated my childhood, was targeted to hit the most vulnerable part of their victims' souls, with a precision exceeding by far that of the missiles themselves.[10]

The threat of turning our cities into "crematoria" by bombing them with "gas" aims at the absolute core of the Holocaust SOM. Combined with the sense of helplessness and passivity, waiting for the missiles to hit, the Gulf War brought to the surface that which was barely skin deep. It is still there, urging us never to forget.

NOTES

1. R. A. Champagne, *Claude Levi-Strauss* (Boston: Twayne, 1987).

2. C. G. Jung, *Collected Works* (New York: Pantheon, 1957).

3. It is an open question whether external stimuli have invariably stronger impact than imagined ones. This is a critical issue particularly within the context of trauma, a major concern of this paper.

4. *Leveling* implies the simplification of complex memories, the introduction of uniformity where diversity ruled before. It is the art of condensation at the expense of the true richness of a phenomenon. *Sharpening* refers to selecting a few items from a large memory store and upgrading them to a quasi-symbolic level.

5. The case of watching a non-documentary film is more ambiguous, because of the visual media's power to elicit identification with the story.

6. E. Tulving, "How Many Memory Systems Are There?" *American Psychologist* 40 (1985): 385–98. See also L. R. Squire et al., "Memory: Organization of Brain Systems and Cognition," in *Symposium on Quantitative Biology: The Brain*, vol. 55 (Cold Spring Harbor, N.Y.: 1990).

7. H. L. Roediger, "Implicit Memory: Retention without Remembering," *American Psychologist* 45 (1990): 1043–56.

8. S. Breznitz, "A Study of Worrying," *British Journal of Social and Clinical Psychology* 10 (1971): 271–279.

9. The thirty-second commercial break that intrudes into a moving film inevitably alters its impact. Moreover, the anticipation of such intrusions may flatten the emotion throughout the entire experience.

10. Shlomo Breznitz, *Memory Fields* (New York: Knopf, 1993).

VÁCLAV HAVEL

In Memory of Our Holocaust Victims

WHENEVER I AM faced with documents about the Holocaust—the racial laws, the concentration camps, the mass extermination of Jews by Hitler, and the endless suffering of the Jewish people during World War II—I feel strangely paralyzed. I know I should say something, do something, draw conclusions. Yet I feel that any words that I could say would be false, inadequate, inept, or deficient. I can only stand in silence and incomprehension. I know that one must not remain silent, yet I find myself desperately speechless.

That state of paralysis proceeds from a deep—perhaps even a metaphysical—feeling of shame. I am ashamed, if I may put it this way, of the human race. I feel that what happened to the Jews is humanity's crime and humanity's disgrace, and therefore it is my crime and disgrace as well. That paralysis suddenly allows me to perceive the depths of human guilt, to recognize my own co-responsibility for human actions and for the condition of our world. As a human being, then, I feel suddenly responsible for humanity as such and, staring uncomprehendingly at this cruelty, I cease to understand myself, for I, too, am human.

I have been thinking about what it means when it is said that the Jews are the Chosen People. One of the things this phrase may be interpreted to mean is that humanity, so to speak, "chose" them, regrettably and horribly, as its scapegoat, as a substitute

Václav Havel

sacrifice. Aware of its own narrow-mindedness, mediocrity, and inadequacy, tormented by a desperate lack of self-affirmation, permanently disappointed by the world and by itself, haunted by the demon of its complexes and unable to cope with its existential grief, humanity at large looked for someone to blame for its own misfortune, wretchedness, and failure.

Such ignoble feelings were likely the breeding ground for antisemitism, and subsequently for the Holocaust itself. And such feelings, paradoxically, were also a breeding ground for something that compels us to perceive the true weight of our responsibility for this world. And, through that dual role, we are led to see that the Jews were evidently chosen in another sense of the word as well. The Jews were chosen by fate for the horrible task of confronting modern man, through their suffering, with his global responsibility, and thereby to cast him down to the depths of true metaphysical self-awareness. To look at the documents of the Holocaust, to look at the atrocities humanity is capable of committing, awakens one to a profound feeling of shame, and by means of shame to an increased sense of responsibility for the conduct of the whole human community. The senseless suffering of the Jews in the Holocaust thus acquires a tragic meaning and becomes a lasting challenge to each and every member of the human race to awaken to his humanity.

It was the hand of a Czech official of the Nazi Protectorate that once penned an order, in Czech, that contained the following sentence: "Seats may be occupied by Jews only when they are not required for Aryans." And it was the hand of a Slovak journalist that once committed to paper, in Slovak, this vaunting headline: "The strictest racial laws concerning Jews are Slovak laws."

I believe that orders and newspaper headlines of this kind, written by non-homicidal murderers, should be forever recorded, as a warning, in all Czech and Slovak history textbooks. I believe that the challenge to our sense of responsibility for this world that addresses us from the Holocaust era, when thousands of anonymous, non-homicidal antisemites helped send their fellow citizens to the gas chambers, must never be silenced, suppressed, or pushed out of sight. Indeed, the challenge must be heard by all future generations.

When I was a little boy, I envied the yellow, six-pointed stars that some other children wore on their breasts. I thought they were some kind of badge of honor. If children are never again to be compelled to wear a brand on their clothes—a brand designed to indicate that they are inferior and to warn others against the threat they allegedly pose—we need to remind ourselves over and over again of the horrors that befell the Jews during the Holocaust, that befell the people regrettably chosen to arouse the conscience of humanity.

People tend instinctively to avoid what shocks them. Yet we all need to be repeatedly exposed, in our own interest, to a certain kind of shock, one that tells us we cannot evade the universal nature of our responsibility. We need to face the documents about the Holocaust, even though—or especially because—it is so difficult, and yet so necessary, to do so.

CYNTHIA OZICK

Afterword

ELIE WIESEL IS THE sublime moral hero of our profoundly flawed, unredeemed, and now rapidly vanishing century. His character, his influence, his variegated achievements, and his humane inspirations have already been clarified for us by the words of the grand Nobel: "Wiesel is a messenger to mankind. His message is one of peace and atonement and human dignity."

All this has long been understood. Inscribed in American history is that mammoth and blazing moment when Elie Wiesel stood before a president of the United States and said of Bitburg, "That place, Mr. President, is not your place." The man who sent forth these simple, clear, cleansing words has by now been awarded the Nobel Peace Prize, the Presidential Medal of Freedom, the United States Congressional Gold Medal, and membership in the French Legion of Honor; but the voice that spoke so plainly owned an authority that did not derive from worldly acclaim: it was the still, small voice that teaches us the distinction between the holy and the unholy.

Elie Wiesel's very first work, the singular *Night*, has entered the conscience of humankind, side by side with Anne Frank's testimony—and, it must be added, even more powerfully, because the *Diary* describes the passage while *Night* records the destination. And the passage fails of its meaning without the destination. Consequently, this orphaned son and this lost daughter are read

335

everywhere and permanently by the children of the world and by everyone who has ever been father or mother to a child.

If we have learned to equate Elie Wiesel with a prophetic vision of civilization, it is important to note that he has never sought that mantle. What he has sought, as man and as poet, is the delineation, the illumination, not of any inaccessible nobility, but of an indispensable sense of obligation—in a word: *menshlichkayt*. And if for us he has come, in a way, to symbolize prophecy, let us be reminded that this is all our doing, not his. Unlike Shelley, he has not looked to become humanity's legislator. What he has looked to, as the poet he is, are stories, hope, history, the dailiness of responsibility that some call holiness and also, though one must utter this syllable quietly, God.

Above all, he has given his passion to the sustenance of peoplehood. To say it bluntly, he stands up for Israel in the clear knowledge that to stand up for Israel now is the defining act of Jewish valor for our generation.

He has published forty books. The most recent are the two volumes of his memoirs, the first of which, *All Rivers Run to the Sea*, is soaked in memory and innocence, in faithfulness and bravery and love and richness of incident, and, inevitably, in tears. In what amounts to a midrash on his own work, he writes:

> Commenting on a verse of the Prophet Jeremiah according to which God says, "I shall weep in secret," the Midrash remarks that there is a place called "secret" and that when God is sad, He takes refuge there to weep.
>
> For us this secret place lies in memory, which possesses its own secret.

In volume after incandescent volume, he has portrayed the lives and legends of the Hasidic masters; he has offered us an electrifying play for the stage; and he has told us story upon story. It was he who first gave tongue to the buried-alive Jews of the Soviet Union; long ago I listened to him speak, in Yiddish, on the radio, of the anguish of Soviet Jews at a time when these forgotten Jews of Silence were met by our own silence. I know that silence firsthand: my own father, separated from his Moscow sisters and brothers for fifty years, died without ever hearing their voices. But Elie Wiesel had not forgotten them, and it is through the power of his early inspiration that my Russian cousins are today grateful citizens of Israel.

The Forgotten is, aptly, the name of one of his novels. It is a remarkable and tragic story of the necessity, the urgency, the inescapable humanity of Jewish remembering. What makes us Jews? A pair of choosings. We have chosen the One God of *Shema;* and we have chosen historical memory. We inscribe, we do not erase. We do not forget, we strive to remember.

And it is for this reason exactly that Elie Wiesel earns his extraordinary place among us. He is our generation's great Memory Teacher. He helps us remember not only what has happened, but who we are and what we are intended to *mean.*

At the close of *The Forgotten,* a father speaks to his son in words that may be called, without embarrassment, politically incorrect, since they argue unashamedly for Jews loving Jews, for Jews daring, for the sake of humanity, to put Jews first:

> Don't tell your son and don't tell your father, that we must belong to the world at large, that we must transcend ourselves by supporting all causes and fighting for the victims of every injustice. If I am a Jew, I am a man . . . If I am not, I am nothing. A man like you can love his people without hating others. I'll even say that it is because I love the Jewish people that I can summon the strength and the faith to love those who follow other traditions and invoke other beliefs.

Which is just what the Nobel Prize committee understood. And what matters even more is that *we* understand.

CONTRIBUTORS

PER AHLMARK is a writer, human rights activist, and former politician living in Stockholm. He served as Deputy Prime Minister and Minister of Labor in Sweden from 1976–78, and also led the Swedish Liberal Party. His most recent publications include two books, *Vänstern och tyranniet* (Tyranny and the Left) and *Det öppna såret* (An Open Sore).

AARON APPELFELD was born in Czernowitz, Bukovina in 1932 and spent the war years in a camp in Transnistria. He came to Israel in 1946, served in the army, and studied Yiddish and Hebrew literature at Hebrew University. He has authored some thirty books of fiction and essay, for which he has been awarded many important literary prizes. His novel, *Iron Tracks*, was published in 1998.

REINHOLD BOSCHKI teaches in high schools in Germany, lectures at the Ludwigsburg College for Education, and is a researcher at Tübingen University. He writes on theology, ethics, and education after the Holocaust and specifically on the work of Elie Wiesel. His publications include *Der Schrei: Gott und Mensch im Werke von Elie Wiesel* (The Cry: God and Humankind in the Work of Elie Wiesel) and the edited *Ist die Vergangenheit noch ein Argument? Aspekte einer Erziehung nach Auschwitz* (Is History Still an Argument? Aspects of Experience after Auschwitz).

SHLOMO BREZNITZ was born in Czechoslovakia and came to Israel in 1949. After serving in the army, he studied psychology at the Hebrew University in Jerusalem, where, after receiving his doctoral degree in 1965, he became a member of the faculty. He currently divides his time between the New School for Social Research and the University of Haifa, where he is the Lady Davis Professor of Psychology. He has published seven books and numerous articles mainly dealing with stress and coping and their effects on health. *Memory Fields,* the account of his childhood during the Holocaust, was published in 1993.

Irwin Colter is Professor of Law at McGill University and an international human rights lawyer. He has served as legal counsel to political prisoners in the former Soviet Union, South Africa, Latin America, and Asia. A constitutional and comparative law scholar, he has written extensively on Nuremberg-related issues, including war crimes, crimes against humanity, and genocide. His recent books include the edited *Nuremberg Forty-Five Years Later: The Struggle against Injustice in Our Time.*

Alan Dershowitz is the Felix Frankfurter Professor of Law at Harvard Law School. While as a trial lawyer he is known for defending clients such as Anatoly Scharansky, Claus Von Bulow, O. J. Simpson, Michael Milken, and Mike Tyson, he continues to represent numerous indigent defendants as well. His latest book, *The Vanishing American Jew,* was published in 1997 and joins other non-fiction works such as *The Abuse Excuse* and *Chutzpah.* His novels include *The Advocate, Devil* and forthcoming *Just Revenge.*

Ariel Dorfman is a Chilean expatriate who lives with his family in Durham, North Carolina, where he is Distinguished Research Professor of Literature and Latin American Studies at Duke University. He went into exile with the overthrow of Salvador Allende in 1973, and since that time has actively promoted human rights in his native continent and around the world. He is the author of *Konfidenz, Mascara,* and *Death and the Maiden,* as well as many other works that have been translated into some thirty languages and received numerous awards. His most recent book is *Heading South, Looking North: A Bilingual Journey.*

Contributors

MAURICE FRIEDMAN is Professor Emeritus of Religious Studies, Philosophy, and Comparative Literature at San Diego State University. He is the author of many books, including *Martin Buber's Life and Work* (3 volumes), *Abraham Joshua Heschel and Elie Wiesel: "You Are My Witnesses,"* and *The Affirming Flame: A Poetics of Meaning.*

NANCY HARROWITZ is Associate Professor of Italian at Boston University. She is currently writing a book on Primo Levi and science and is editing another book on Levi. She has previously written on the topics of antisemitism and misogyny and their intersection in the nineteenth century.

VÁCLAV HAVEL was born in Prague in 1936. A writer of fiction, drama, and essays, he was imprisoned several times for his efforts on behalf of Czechoslovakian democracy and human rights. He was one of the first spokesmen for Charter 77 and a leader of the Velvet Revolution in 1989. He served as the last President of Czechoslovakia and serves currently as the President of the Czech Republic. His recent books include *The Power of the Powerless, Open Letters,* and *The Art of the Impossible.*

STEVEN T. KATZ is Professor of Religion and Director of the Center for Judaic Studies at Boston University. He is the author of, among other works, *The Holocaust in Historical Context* (1994), *Historicism, the Holocaust, and Zionism* (1992), and *Post-Holocaust Dialogues* (1983). He is the editor of four collections of essays on comparative mysticism and also edits the journal *Modern Judaism.*

PNINA LAHAV is Professor of Law at Boston University where she teaches constitutional law, political and civil liberties, and comparative law. She has written extensively on the constitutional law of Israel and other related subjects. Her most recent book, *Judgment in Jerusalem: Chief Justice Simon Agranat and the Zionist Century* (1997) won the Seltner Award in 1998. Professor Lahav is also the President of the Association for Israel Studies.

Contributors

JOSHUA LEDERBERG is President Emeritus and Professor Emeritus of Molecular Genetics and Informatics of the Rockefeller University. He received the Nobel Prize for his work in genetic structure and function in microorganisms. He also researches in artificial intelligence and has served the United States government and international community as a consultant in health-related matters. He has authored and edited many books including *Science and Man, Human Values in a Technological Society,* and *Emerging Infections: Microbial Threats to Health in the United States.*

DOCTOR MARGUERITE S. LEDERBERG is a Psychiatrist Attending at Memorial Sloan-Kettering Cancer Center and a Clinical Professor of Psychiatry at Cornell University Medical Center in New York. She was trained in pediatrics and psychiatry at Stanford Medical Center and received her M.D. degree from Yale Medical School. She has lectured and published about the psychological and psychiatric aspects of cancer in patients, families, and medical staff, about the interface of ethics and psychiatry especially in relation to terminal care issues, and about the relationship of spiritual beliefs to health behaviors.

HILLEL LEVINE is Professor of Sociology and Religion at Boston University. A student of Jewish intellectual and social history, social theory, and ethics, Levine's recent books include *Death of an American Jewish Community: The Tragedy of Good Intentions* on ethnic conflict and changing neighborhoods, *Economic Origins of Antisemitism* on early modern East European Jewry, and *In Search of Sugihara* on a Japanese rescuer of Jews during the Holocaust.

JEFFREY MEHLMAN is University Professor and Professor of French Literature at Boston University. His books include *A Structural Study of Autobiography, Revolution and Repetition, Cataract: A Study in Diderot, Legacies of Anti-Semitism in France, Walter Benjamin for Children: An Essay on His Radio Years,* and *Genealogies of the Text.* Among the works he has translated are Bredin's *The Affair: The*

Case of Alfred Dreyfus and Vidal-Naquet's *Assassins of Memory*. Professor Mehlman is currently writing a study of émigré French intellectuals in New York during World War II.

CYNTHIA OZICK is the author of novels, short stories, essays, and a play. She has won numerous prizes and awards, including the PEN Award for the Art of the Essay and Rea Award for Distinction in the Short Story, and has most recently served as editor of *Best American Essays 1998*. Her latest novel is *The Puttermesser Papers*, a National Book Award finalist.

JOSEPH A. POLAK is the Hillel Rabbi to the Jewish community at Boston University, where he is also an Assistant Professor of Public Health (Health Law). In addition, he serves as the chair of the law committee of the Rabbinical Court of Boston, Massachusetts. Rabbi Polak writes about the human experience in the aftermath of the Holocaust, of which he is a survivor.

NEHEMIA POLEN is Associate Professor of Jewish Thought and Associate Dean of Students at Boston's Hebrew College. He is author of *The Holy Fire: The Teachings of Rabbi Kalonymus Shapira, The Rebbe of the Warsaw Ghetto* (1994) as well as many academic and popular articles on Hasidism and Jewish Spirituality. He received his doctorate from Boston University, where he studied with and served as teaching fellow for Elie Wiesel. He is currently working on a new book, tentatively titled, *From Judgment to Mercy*, based on the memoirs of Malkah Shapiro, daughter of the Kozienitzer Rebbe.

ALAN ROSEN teaches English and Holocaust literature at Bar-Ilan University in Israel. He received his doctoral degree from Boston University, completing his work under the direction of Elie Wiesel. His book on catastrophe, tentatively titled *(Dis)Locating the End: Climax, Closure, and Invention of Genre*, is soon to be published. He is currently writing a book on representing the Holocaust in English.

Contributors

JOHN K. ROTH is the Russell K. Pitzer Professor of Philosophy at Claremont McKenna College where he has taught since 1966. The author, coauthor, or editor of more than twenty books, his works include *A Consuming Fire: Encounters with the Holocaust and Elie Wiesel, Approaches to Auschwitz: The Holocaust and Its Legacy,* and *Private Needs, Public Selves: Talk about Religion in America.* Roth, a member of the United States Holocaust Memorial Council, was named the 1988 U.S. National Professor of the Year by the Council for Advancement and Support of Education (CASE).

JOHN SILBER is currently Chancellor of Boston University, where from 1971 to 1996 he held the position of president. In January 1996, Governor William Weld appointed Silber Chairman of the Massachusetts Board of Education. Silber has written widely on philosophy, education, and social and foreign policy. His work has appeared in philosophical journals as well as in the *Atlantic, Harper's, The New Republic,* the *New York Times,* and the *Wall Street Journal.* His book, *Straight Shooting,* was published in 1989.

DOROTHEE SÖLLE was born in Cologne, Germany in 1929. From 1975 to 1987 she served as Professor of Theology at Union Theological Seminary in New York. She currently resides in Hamburg, where she continues to write on theology, religion, and ethics. Her books include *Suffering, Great Women of the Bible in Art and Literature,* and most recently, *Mystik und Widerstand* (Mysticism and Resistance).